A RESIDENT'S GUIDE TO THE BEST OF THE CITY AND THE SUBURBS

By the Staff of Peachtree Publishers, Ltd.

PEACHTREE

ATLANTA

PUBLISHED BY
Peachtree Publishers, Ltd.
494 Armour Circle, N.E.
Atlanta, Georgia 30324

Text © 1995 Peachtree Publishers, Ltd.
Maps© 1992, 1995 The Cartography Research
                  Laboratory, Department of Geography,
                  Georgia State University

Book design by Kathryn D. Mothershed
Cartography by Cartography Research Laboratory

10 9 8 7 6 5 4 3 2 1

Manufactured in the United States of America

ISBN 1-56145-088-X

Library of Congress Cataloging–in–Publication Data

Peachtree Publishers, Ltd.
         Across Atlanta: A resident's guide to the best of the city and suburbs
    Peachtree Publishers, Ltd.
                  p.   cm.
         ISBN 1-56145-088-X (trade paper) :
         1. Atlanta (Ga.)—Guidebooks.   2. Atlanta Region (Ga.)-Guidebooks.
         I. Titlle.
         F294.A83M38
         917.58'2310443—dc20

CONTENTS

About This Book

Whether you are a longtime resident or a newcomer to Atlanta, and whether you call Virginia-Highland or Vinings home, you have chosen the perfect guide to make the most of the capital of the New South. You can find just the right place for inexpensive sushi, schedule your calendar around the city's special events, and research the area's garden clubs all within these pages. This is not a tourist's overview of the city, but a resident's resource that encompasses the greater metropolitan area. So get out your highlighter and learn more about Atlanta's almost infinite offerings.

In compiling our information, one of the chief concerns was making the entries as user-friendly as possible. Every listing includes a brief description, any special recommendations, an address, and a phone number. *Across Atlanta* often leans toward up-and-coming organizations rather than the larger, more famous Atlanta establishments. Space is limited, so our lists are always *selections* from many fine organizations. We have also tried to select entries from every corner of the metro area to give you the flavor of many different locales. No person or establishment has paid to be included in this residential guide; all of these entries are based on uniqueness of service, outstanding quality, or personal recommendation.

In order to orient you in terms of location, each address is accompanied by a neighborhood designation. We have included a map in the back of this book for quick reference of these areas, but some discussion of boundaries will be helpful before you jump in the car.

Buckhead's center is easily located—just look for the triangle created by Peachtree and Roswell roads—but where does it actually begin and end? The "Buckhead Community" sign stands at Lindbergh Plaza, so we have used this landmark as our southern boundary. The Chattahoochee River serves as the western border, with Roswell Road in Sandy Springs the northern line. "Brookwood" falls between Buckhead and Midtown, extends south from Colonial Homes Drive and stretches to the Brookwood railway station. "Brookhaven" falls just north of Buckhead, from the intersection of Peachtree and Peachtree-Dunwoody roads to Ashford-Dunwoody Road in DeKalb County. Sandy Springs begins at the intersection of Roswell and Wieuca roads.

But most baffling of all, how to distinguish Midtown and Downtown? We have designated the area between North Avenue and Pershing Point as Midtown, and south of North Avenue to Interstate 20 as Downtown.

As you read through these entries, you will notice the phrase "Mail only." These locations are private homes; please contact these organization by telephone or mail to arrange appointments.

We here at Peachtree Publishers do not intend this listing of information to stay the same; in fact, we know it won't. We are planning to update *Across Atlanta* about every two years, and we want your help. If you have a suggestion for a business we missed, want us to consider a new section, or have had a bad experience with one of the organizations listed here, let us know. We will check out your information and try to improve our guide each time it is revised. To make your input easier, we have included a reader form in the back of this book. Please help us to make *Across Atlanta* the best resource it can be by giving us your input.

So dive right in and make Atlanta yours! We hope *Across Atlanta* will help enrich every part of your life.

CHAPTER 1

Dining Out

While traditional Southern restaurants—with their crispy fried chicken, spicy barbecue, and fresh, flaky biscuits—haven't lost any popularity in Atlanta, dining out in our city can also be an international adventure.

We've listed the restaurants in this section with a focus on ethnicity, so whether you're in the mood for an Indian curry or a Russian pirozhki, you'll find it easily. Vegetarian restaurants have their own section, while the "Steaks" subsection was created with meat-lovers in mind. "Light Dining" includes a listing of the newly popular coffeehouses, as well as lunch spots and dessert bars. We close with a listing of specialty takeout locations.

Each entry is coded according to its average dinner entreé price:

$—Inexpensive: under $15 per person;

$$—Moderate: $15–$25 per person;

$$$—Expensive: over $25 per person.

Serving hours are not listed, as they change frequently.

AMERICAN

Our regional and traditional cooking, especially the various Southern cuisines, and our willingness to adapt the culinary traditions of other cultures, make American cooking especially enticing. Atlanta presents a fine selection of restaurants that make the most of it all, including the delicatessen and the diner, both American institutions.

Atkins Park. Atkins Park serves burgers and casual fare until the wee, wee hours. Prime rib, assorted pastas, and seafood make dining special in a setting that's superior for people-watching. This is one of Atlanta's oldest restaurant sites. 794 N. Highland Ave., Virginia-Highland. 876-7249. $

Café Gamay. This contemporary, casual café serves salads, sandwiches, and pastas. Pizza toppings may include wild mushrooms and goat cheese; the grilled salmon salad with applewood-smoked bacon is marvelous; and the assorted fruit sorbets are great desserts. The handy location is perfect for a serene lunch after hectic shopping. 3391 Peachtree Rd., Swissôtel, Buckhead. 365-0065. $

Café Tu Tu Tango. This multi-ethnic eatery features fifty moderately priced menu items and a number of daily specials. The appetizer-sized selections are designed to be ordered in multiples and shared with friends; reorder a different selection of items when the first sampling has been gobbled up. Spontaneous entertainment occurs while local artists paint, display, and sell their work at stations throughout the restaurant. No reservations except large groups, open seven days a week for lunch and dinner. 220 Pharr Rd, Buckhead. 841-6222. $$

Chefs' Café. The California-style cooking at this unusual café features inventive pasta dishes, grilled entrees, and fabulous crab cakes. Wines offered by the glass include excellent selections. Brunch is super, with such unusual dishes as "killer" crab cakes Benedict. 2115 Piedmont Rd., Comfort Inn, Northeast. 872-2284. $$

Chefs' Grill. This Chefs' Café affiliate *(see above)* serves tasty pizzas, sandwiches, and salads to the crowds that pack the Woodruff Arts Center before and after performances. At press time, it was closed for renovation, but expected to reopen soon. 1280 Peachtree St., Woodruff Arts Center, Midtown. 881-0652. $$

City Grill. A handsome, "private club" interior makes this Peasant Corporation restaurant perfect for business entertaining. The menu changes daily and focuses on contemporary American–style fare with light sauces. With an emphasis on fish and seafood, the dishes are inventively prepared and presented. The corn lobster chowder is a City Grill favorite. The good wine list offers many selections by the glass. 50 Hurt Plaza, Hurt Bldg., Suite 200, Downtown. 524-2489. $$$

The Coach & Six. A landmark among Atlanta restaurants, the Coach is famous for its black bean soup, breads, prime steaks, stone crab claws, and relish bowls. This establishment has been celebrated for the last who-knows-how-many years. 1776 Peachtree Rd., Brookwood. 872-6666. $$

The Downwind Restaurant and Lounge. OK, be sure to wear your aviator sunshades so you can fit right in, because you'll be dining in the administration building of DeKalb-Peachtree Airport. Sandwiches and salads are the best choices at lunch. The boss is from Greece, so expect a few Greek touches on the dinner menu. 3915 Clairmont Rd., DeKalb-Peachtree Airport, Chamblee. 452-0973. $

The Flying Biscuit Café. You can get breakfast all day at this funky yet homey restaurant, but you can also order lunch and dinner items throughout the day. Regulars love the mismatched decor— none of the dishes, tablecloths, or silver match—and swear by the food. The organic oatmeal pancakes topped with fruit salsa and warm maple syrup are a favorite, as are the homemade biscuits. Don't miss the homemade apple butters—the fruit combinations change with the seasons. This is comfort food! Dinner specials start at 5 P.M. 1655 McClendon Ave., Candler Park. 687-8888. $

Georgia Grille. Despite the name, Southwestern-style cooking is the game. Corn sauce and black beans accompany the chicken Monterey; terrific Texas barbecue beef fills the fajitas; and the chicken and cheese quesadillas are really worth mentioning. 2290 Peachtree Rd., Brookwood. 352-3517. $

Houston's. Satisfying salads, prime rib, sandwiches, and some unexpected touches such as couscous and the Thai-inspired grilled chicken salad hit the spot. Have some cobbler for dessert. Arrive extra early or extra late because the lines get very long. Four locations: 3321 Lenox Rd., Buckhead. 237-7534; 2166 Peachtree Rd., Brookwood. 351-2442; 3539 Northside Pkwy., at W. Paces Ferry Rd., Buckhead. 262-7130. 1905 Powers Ferry Rd., Marietta. 563-1180 or 365-3394. $$

Mick's. Great burgers, pasta, chicken, seafood, salads, and calorie-bashing desserts such as chocolate cream pie keep all the restaurants crowded. The atmosphere is casual and high-energy. Eleven locations around town; the original is at 557 Peachtree St., at Linden Ave., Downtown. 875-MICK (6425). $

MillAround. Neil and Kay Davis painstakingly restored an 1837 gristmill that continued to grind corn until the 1950s. They turned it into a white tablecloth operation serving steaks, prime rib, grilled chicken, and seafood. The space is broken into several smaller, more intimate dining areas, many of which overlook White Water Creek. The dress code calls for casual but nice attire. The limited wine list, mostly American, is reasonably priced, and some selections are offered by the glass. 1095 W. Hwy. 54, Fayetteville. 460-MILL (6455). $

Murphy's. Long established and very popular, this casual spot is famous for tasty breakfasts, sandwiches, salads, pasta dishes, vegetarian chili, and desserts. The crème caramel is super. Continuous service; catering, takeout, and business lunch delivery. 997 Virginia Ave., Virginia-Highland. 872-0904. $

Oxford Espresso Café. It's dynamite for an inexpensive lunch, with good, healthful sandwiches, stalwart double espresso, and heavenly brownies and other sinful treats. This neat little haven is tucked away from all of the bustle and noise of Buckhead. 360 Pharr Rd., Oxford at Buckhead. 266-8350. $

The Peasant Restaurant and Bar.
The Peasant Corporation's Trio became The Peasant and reverted to the classic Peasant chalkboard menu presentation. Dishes range from pasta to steamed fish to catfish in a Thai-style preparation. 3402 Peachtree Rd., Buckhead. 231-8740. $

Peasant Uptown. A quiet, garden-like interior provides a pleasant respite from hectic shopping. Enjoy nice pastas, salads, and light meals at lunch, and more substantial fare at dinner. Peasant desserts are legendary and calorie-loaded. 3500 Peachtree Rd., Phipps Plaza, Buckhead. 261-6341. $$

The Pleasant Peasant. The bistro that launched the Peasant Corporation was an instant hit in a building that everyone said would never house a successful restaurant. Sorta reminds you of the scout who was certain Yogi Berra would never make it in baseball. Soups, salads, light dishes, and apple walnut pie keep the place popular. 555 Peachtree St., at Linden Ave., Downtown. 874-3223. $$

The Public House. This pre–Civil War building on Roswell's main square was originally a general store. Soups, salads, and sandwiches make it easy to restore your energies after a stint of shopping in Roswell. The upstairs loft holds a piano lounge. 605 S. Atlanta St., Roswell. 992-4646. $$

R. Thomas Deluxe Grill. This place never closes, and only quiets down about 5 A.M.! R. Thomas serves light dishes, salads, and grilled meats. 1812 Peachtree Rd., Brookwood. 872-2942. $

Van Gogh's. Roswell revels in its bistro-like ambience, its menu of continental and American fare, and its assortment of adventurous desserts. Inventive and well-executed appetizers, along with lots of veal dishes, enhance the menu. 70 W. Crossville Rd., next to Crabapple Sq., Roswell. 993-1156. $$

Vickery's Crescent Avenue Bar and Grill. An ethnic twist that yields exciting, imaginative dishes. Vickery's describes their cuisine as "Southern Continental with a Cuban theme." The vegetarian Black Bean Cakes and the Backwater Bayou Seafood Sauté are two of the most popular selections. The atmosphere is casual but hip, and no reservations are accepted. 1106 Crescent Ave., Northeast. 881-1106. $$

DELICATESSENS

Boychik's. Borscht, knishes, fish platters, and matzoh ball and chicken noodle soups are Boychik's stock-in-trade. French toast is made from challah bread—yum! 4520-A Chamblee-Dunwoody Rd., at I-285, Georgetown Shopping Center, Dunwoody. 452-0516. $

Harry Baron's. This classic Atlanta deli has all the flavors of its New York counterpart. Harry Baron's is noted for its blintzes and bagels, and its chopped liver, soups, and sandwiches. 1230 Peachtree St., near Woodruff Arts Center, Midtown. 607-6888. $

Stage Deli of New York. Meat is trucked in from New York for the corned beef and pastrami sandwiches—the same truck brings the weekly load of mustard, pickles, and kraut. Close your eyes, and the aromas will transport you to the Big Apple. 3850 Roswell Rd., Buckhead Ct., Buckhead. 233-DELI (3354). $

DINERS

Buckhead Diner. The diner that other diners want to be when they grow up—this elegant diner, designed by Patrick Koleta, serves wonderful veal meatloaf, homemade potato chips with Maytag blue cheese, huge calzones, upscale pizzas, and lots of wine by the glass. Continuous service. This is a good spot for after-performance nibbles and celebrity-watching, as it's open until midnight every evening except Sunday, when it closes at 10 P.M. Did we mention Elton John likes to come here? 3073 Piedmont Rd., Buckhead. 262-3336. $

Gorin's Diner. It started with ice cream in lots of inviting flavors, like cinnamon and Oreo cookie. Now, in addition to myriad north metro locations that serve sandwiches, salads, and the ice cream of note, there's also a diner. Breakfast and hearty entrees—meatloaf, burgers, and grilled chicken sandwiches—are served until the wee hours on weekends. 1170 Peachtree St., at 14th St., Midtown. 892-2500. $

Johnny Rockets. Delicious, handmade burgers, really thick malteds, and great fries are the standards in this classic diner. Locations include: 6510 Roswell Rd., near Abernathy Rd., Sandy Springs. 257-0677; 5 W. Paces Ferry Rd., Buckhead. 231-5555. 3500 Peachtree Rd., Phipps Plaza. 233-9867. $

Majestic Food Shop. For people-watching, nothing beats this Atlanta institution. Now owned by Greeks, this diner, established in 1929, serves Southern food with the occasional moussaka special. 1031 Ponce de Leon Ave., Poncey-Highland. 875-0276. $

OK Café. Some good interpretations of Southern cooking are served by waitresses whose outfits make us think of 'fifties diners. Service is 'round-the-clock, and breakfast is especially good. 1284 W. Paces Ferry Rd., West Paces Ferry Shopping Center, Buckhead. 233-2888. $

The Varsity. A visit to the Varsity is a must stop for everyone, from ordinary out-of-towners to campaigning politicians. "Walk a dog," as they say in Varsity patter. The onion rings are greasy, and the hot dogs are nothing like Barker's famous dogs, but they are the way generations of Varsity patrons want them. Join 'em if you agree. Three locations in Atlanta: the original—61 North Ave., at Spring St., Downtown. 881-1706; **Varsity Jr.**, offering a "light" menu—1085 Lindbergh Dr., at Cheshire Bridge Rd., Northeast. 261-8843; **Varsity Gwinnett**—6045 Dawson Blvd., I-85 Access Rd., Norcross. 840-8519. $

Zesto Drive-In. This classic diner serves shakes, burgers, onion rings, and fries. There are many metro locations, and more are being planned, but so far this is the best: 544 Ponce de Leon Ave., Virginia-Highland. 607-1118. $

SOUTHERN

Aunt Fanny's Cabin. This has been an Atlanta institution for half a century. Busloads of tourists usually occupy the premises at lunch, but at dinner it's open to the public. Everybody should sample the fried chicken and squash casserole. 2155 Campbell Rd., Smyrna. 436-5218. $

Baby Dumpling Family Restaurant. Very local and very Southern, this old-fashioned family restaurant dishes up the traditional entree of a meat and two vegetables. Very inexpensive. 227 Griffin St., McDonough. 957-9855. $

Burrell House. A Southern lunch buffet is served seven days a week in this antebellum house. At dinner, served Thursdays through Saturdays, prime rib and seafood are the main contenders; on Friday and Saturday nights, the seafood buffet features Alaskan crab legs, fried catfish, broiled perch, popcorn shrimp, and broiled scallops. 2689 Summers St., Kennesaw. 421-9170. $$

The Captain's Roost. A landmark in East Point, this is the source for Southern-style seafood—breaded, deep-fried, bad for you, and wonderful (but you can also get it broiled if you must). 2873 Main St., East Point. 761-9468. $

The Colonnade. An Atlanta institution, the Colonnade laces its service with lots of "honey and sugar to butter up" the patrons. Our favorites are the sautéed mountain trout and the baked ham. 1879 Cheshire Bridge Rd., Northeast. 874-5642. $

Deacon Burton's Soul Food. Extraordinary, classic Southern fried chicken, pound cake, and vegetables at prices that make you wonder if this is a mission rather than a business. An eclectic group of diners forms the hungry crowd. Breakfast and lunch only. 1029 Edgewood Ave., Inman Park. 525-3415. $

Lickskillet Farm. Classic Southern cooking, from fried chicken to surf and turf, remain the favorites in this Atlanta dining landmark. Patrons who want wine with dinner make their selections in the adjoining wine room. 1380 Old Roswell Rd., Alpharetta. 475-6484. $$

Mama's Home Cooking. True "Southern" is both cooked and spoken at Mama's, housed in a homey old building. The main dining room seats only 48. Owner Joe Upchurch uses his mother's recipes for such Southern favorites as fried chicken, meatloaf, pot roast, and veggies. No alcohol. 5749 N. Henry Blvd., Stockbridge. 474-8076. $

Mary Mac's Tea Room. Margaret Lupo has been dishing up the staples of Southern cooking to the famous and the nameless for a long time. This is a "meat-and-three" institution. 224 Ponce de Leon Ave., Midtown. 876-1800. $

1904 House. Built in 1904, this charming house now is home to a family-style restaurant. Somehow, it dishes up prime rib and filet mignon for less than $14. Steak and gravy, fried catfish, and grilled trout make good impressions. No alcohol is served, but you may bring your own. 115 N. Main St., Woodstock. 926-1904. $

In 1907, when president-elect William Howard Taft visited Atlanta, the Chamber of Commerce threw a banquet that featured, among numerous other dishes, barbecued Georgia opossum. Sophisticated tastes may have preferred the quail course, which was accompanied by G.H. Mumm's Extra Dry Champagne.

Paschal's. This meeting place for Atlanta's leadership offers a good breakfast—and a firm foundation for understanding Southern cooking. The pork chops and chicken liver omelets get high marks. 830 Martin Luther King, Jr., Dr., Northwest. 577-3150. $

Pine Crest Restaurant. An established, rustic restaurant with a splendid view of the North Georgia mountains, Pine Crest serves a buffet that features fried green tomatoes—available long before there was a movie by that name. The Southern fare also includes chicken and dumplings, country fried steak, fried chicken, and traditional veggies. The banana pudding and blackberry-peach cobbler have been made by the same person for years. The reception area is arranged to resemble an old-fashioned country store. Take Exit 7 off 575. 4088 Holly Springs Pkwy., Holly Springs. 345-5424. $

Stringers Fish Camp & Restaurant. It's about as elegant as anything called a "fish camp" could be. Specialties include superb fried catfish and shrimp, softshell crab hoagies, fresh frogs' legs, and really good gumbo. Many entrees may be broiled. The owner's from Queens! But his wife is a good ole gal from South Georgia. 3384 Shallowford Rd., Chamblee. 458-7145. $

Thelma's Kitchen. Go for the okra pancakes, but check in advance to see if they're on the menu, which changes daily. Everything is fresh, and the crowd includes a large number of business people. Plan to lunch here on your next trip to CNN Center. 190 Luckie St., Downtown. 688-5855. $

Barbecue

Aleck's Barbecue Heaven. Founded in 1942, Aleck's is far from elegant, but the barbecue sauce has a lively tang of vinegar and spices, and it comes on beef, pork, and chicken. The Brunswick stew is also good. Catering. 783 Martin Luther King, Jr., Dr., Southwest. 525-2062. $

Auburn Avenue Rib Shack. Tender ribs and chicken are sparked with a distinctive barbecue sauce. Catering. 302 Auburn Ave., Downtown. 523-8315. $

Down East Bar-B-Que. This is genuine North Carolina-style 'que, which is tangier and more vinegar-y than Georgia-style. But we Atlantans must appreciate it—their pork barbeque sandwich was voted "best in Atlanta" by *Atlanta* magazine. Whole pigs, chickens and ribs are cooked over a hickory and charcoal pit, and side dishes are fresh and good. Takeout available. 2289 S. Cobb Dr., Smyrna. 4343-8887. $

The Georgia Pig. The cabin was built with 150-year-old boards taken from tenant houses in Brunswick, Georgia, and the tables are also made of the old wood. Boston butts are smoked over a brick hearth, and the roasted corn is a favorite. Ask about full-service catering (including pâté if you wish!). 1072 Green St., Roswell. 642-6668. $

Johnny Brown's Country Fixins. Traditional dishes, featuring pork barbecue, are made from fresh ham. The tender, hand-chopped meat is dressed in a tangy sauce spiked with vinegar (also sold by the jar). Open Thursday through Saturday. 1430 Johnson Rd., Hogansville, near Newnan. 706-637-8808. $

Lowcountry Barbecue. This sit-down outpost of Bennett Brown's catering operation offers the same wonderful barbecue previously available only to Brown's catering clients. Downtowners are very fortunate! 14 Park Place South, Downtown. 522-1546. $

Melear's. After nearly a half-century, Melear's has got it down pat. The same family has always owned this area barbecue institution, which is as famous for its Brunswick stew as for its barbecued pork and beef. Catering. 6701 Roosevelt Hwy., Union City. 964-9933. $

Sconyers Bar-B-Que. Old-fashioned, pit-cooked barbecue is the specialty, and it wins lots of local attention for its quality. Catering is available. 4518 N. Henry Blvd., Stockbridge. 474-1165. $

Spiced Right Barbeque. Voted "Best Barbecue in the 'Burbs" by *Atlanta* magazine, Spiced Right has also taken firsts at the Stone Mountain Barbecue Cook-off in the Brunswick stew and barbecue sauce categories. Hickory-smoked, hand-pulled pork barbecue, sliced barbecued beef, baby back ribs, and what some friends call the "best boneless, skinless chicken you'll ever taste" make it famous. Catering is available. 5364 Hwy. 29, Lilburn. 564-0355. $

Cajun and Creole

French Quarter Food Shop. The enthusiastic young staff came to Atlanta direct from Lafayette, Louisiana. They cook straightforward Cajun food, which you order at the counter. This is the classiest bread pudding we've ever seen, and it's great savored with the dark, rich coffee. 923 Peachtree St., at 8th St., Midtown. 875-2489. $

Huey's. The sweetness of Creole cuisine comes to Atlanta in the form of Huey's beignets. These sugar-decked, puffy fritters similar to doughnuts are great with Huey's fortifying, chickory-laced coffee. The sandwiches are also good, and the patio allows diners to watch the parade on Peachtree. Takeout. 1816 Peachtree Rd., Brookwood. 873-2037. $

Main Street Café. This establishment, located in a small, restored building, is relatively new—but the Schaeffer family has more than fifteen years' experience in the restaurant business. Originally from New Orleans, the Schaeffers specialize in Creole cooking. Dishes include traditional seafood entrees (shrimp Creole), red beans and rice, *muffuletta*, and their own bread custard soufflé—topped with meringue and served with a warm rum sauce. The wine list and beer selections are very basic. 190 E. Main St., Canton. 479-3911. $

McKinnon's Louisiane/The Grill Room. All dishes are prepared in either Creole or spicy Cajun style, and the seafood is excellent. The casual Grill Room, which does not accept reservations, features, of course, grilled meats and seafood. 3209 Maple Dr., Buckhead. 237-1313. $$

A Taste of New Orleans. The Cajun and Creole fare served in this casual little restaurant seems not only to endure but to get even better. Patrons fill the place—even on weeknights—to savor the traditional dishes (red beans and rice) and special fare (seafood cakes with jalapeño tartare sauce). A good selection of wines by the glass makes solo dining easy. Takeout and catering available. 889 W. Peachtree St., Midtown. 874-5535. $$

STEAKS

Bones. The very clubby, "male sanctum" decor primarily attracts businessmen. Spectacular steaks and chops are the fare. 3130 Piedmont Rd., Buckhead. 237-2663. $$$

Chops. Not just steaks, but fine seafood and interesting salads (at lunch) make Chops a cut above the average steak house. The atmosphere caters to business dining. A good wine list features excellent by-the-glass options. 70 W. Paces Ferry Rd., Buckhead. 262-2675. $$$

Coasters Supper Club. Southsiders come here to enjoy the numerous varieties of steak—Coaster's main claim to fame. The 22-ounce T-bone is a humdinger. Coaster's also serves mesquite-broiled chicken with a special sauce, as well as shrimp, grilled or fried. Beer, wine, and full liquor service. This is a family-oriented place with a dance floor *(See chapter 2)*. 125 Quarry Rd., Stockbridge. 474-5929. $$

CowTippers. The eight-ounce filet is the best-seller at this always busy steakhouse, but don't miss the margaritas or the "armadillo eggs"— jalapeño peppers stuffed with cream cheese and lightly breaded. The eclectic casual atmosphere leans definitely toward country-western. Be prepared for a wait on the weekends, including Sunday. 1600 Piedmont Ave., Midtown. 874-3469. $

Ernie's Steakhouse. Notwithstanding the emphasis on steak, the kitchen also knows how to prepare fish. Succulent salmon, a frequent "catch of the day," comes perfectly grilled. The regular clientele make each of the ten or so locations—most in Marietta— feel friendly. Original: 2940 Johnson Ferry Rd., Marietta. 642-4518. $

Joey D's Oak Room. Good steaks, hamburgers, seafood, and soups, as well as excellent deli fare make up the popular menu. Monster sandwiches, piled high with meat brought in straight from New York's Carnegie Deli, were an instant hit with all Atlantans. Business people convene there for lunch, and families love the quality and price of the dinners. 1015 Crown Pointe Pkwy., Dunwoody. 512-7063. $

Longhorn Steaks. The popularity of this local chain cuts across a lot of lines. The Texas roadhouse style relaxes even the stiffest of patrons, and the steaks are everything steaks are supposed to be. And their salmon is fabulous. Thirteen locations around the city.

Original: 2151 Peachtree Rd., Buckhead. 351-6086. $$

Morton's of Chicago. Morton's signature steak is the 24-ounce Porterhouse, but the twenty-ounce New York strip and prime rib are not far behind. Morton's is probably the ultimate place for meat lovers—the rolling menu cart allows diners to choose their own cuts of meat. Live Maine lobsters satisfy the non–meat eaters. 245 Peachtree Center Ave., Downtown. 577-4366. $$$

Outback Steak House. Founded in Tampa and popular all over South Florida, Outback came to Marietta and Lilburn in 1991. There are currently seven Atlanta area locations. Steaks, prime rib, chicken, fish, and pasta are served in a casual, somewhat Australian ambience. Very good Australian wines are listed and available by the glass. Locations include: 2400 Delk Rd., at Powers Ferry Rd., Delk Spectrum, Marietta. 850-9182; 4800 Lawrenceville Hwy., Ashley Sq., Lilburn. 381-7744. $$

Pilgreen's. Many locations dot the metro area, but the original and the one in Morrow are our favorites. At the East Point location since the mid-1940s, Pilgreen's started business in 1932. Known for fine steaks—some folks think these are Atlanta's best—and baked potatoes, Pilgreen's also serves fried chicken, fried shrimp, and onion rings. Full liquor service. Original: 1081 Lee St., East Point. 758-4669; 6335 Jonesboro Rd., Morrow. 961-1666. $$

Sun Dial. Offering a spectacular view of Atlanta, the Sun Dial sits at the top of the Westin Peachtree Plaza Hotel. The steaks are an excellent choice. Stroll-

ing musicians accompany dinner
Wednesday through Saturday. 210

Peachtree St., Downtown. 589-7506.
$$$

CONTINENTAL

This term used to designate nondescript, French–style European cooking with heavy sauces and much boredom *à la crème*. Today's continental dishes recall French cooking methods but incorporate flavors from other traditions, so Middle Eastern dishes may come prepared with a French or Italian touch. After all, you can eat some terrific couscous in Paris—though it's not like what you'll find in Morocco.

The Abbey. Long one of Atlanta's landmark restaurants, it is owned and managed by the same team that operates **The Mansion**, across the street from The Abbey in the late-nineteenth-century Peters' house. The Abbey is housed in a 1915 church, which retains its original stained glass windows. Rack of lamb and mixed grill are two of the constants on the menu. Waiters are robed as monks, and a harpist adds to the heavenly air. The wine list holds some excellent values. 163 Ponce de Leon Ave., Midtown. 876-8532. $$$

Atlanta Fish Market. Fish and seafood are given serious, *haute cuisine* treatment. The wharf-inspired decor is wonderfully airy, with mosaic floors and an open kitchen complete with fresh fish on display. The pan-seared cod with celery mashed potatoes is simply spectacular. Our favorites are the crab cakes and the calamari. The kitchen is happy to grill fish and leave the sauces on the side, if you wish. 265 Pharr Rd., Buckhead. 262-3165. $$

Azalea. Chef Thomas Catherall calls it "fusion" cuisine, but why bother with labels? Just relish deep-fried catfish flavored with bits of ginger and lemon, unique pasta dishes, and killer desserts. Azalea has a sleek, upscale interior and accepts no reservations, so get there early (6 P.M. or so) or be prepared for a long wait. 3167 Peachtree Rd., Buckhead. 237-9939. $$

Basil's Mediterranean Café. A soothing atmosphere and a deck overlooking a mellow Atlanta street give Basil's a distinctive neighborhood flavor. The menu features dishes from Middle Eastern, Greek, Italian, and French cuisines. The lamb medallions stuffed with mushrooms, pine nuts, black olives, tahini and mint, topped with Barolo sauce, are a house favorite. Basil's is owned by a Lebanese family, and Mother makes many of the dishes, especially the appetizers. All scrumptious desserts are made in-house. 2985 Grandview Ave., Buckhead. 233-9755. $

Carbo's Café. Carbo's is special to Atlantans and has been for more than a decade. Owners Carmen and Bob Mazurek renovated much of the interior themselves. The establishment is elegant, filled with antiques for special allure. Menu standards include fresh dover sole, steak *au poivre*, and—inspired by a Mazurek visit to Italy—a veal T-bone steak with garlic and olive oil. Check out the soufflés for dessert, then move on over to the bar to enjoy the music *(see chapter 2)*. The upstairs ballroom is available for special events. 3717 Roswell Rd., Buckhead. 231-4433. $$$

The Dining Room, Ritz-Carlton, Buckhead.
Consistently rated one of the best restaurants in the country; Chef Guenther Seeger ranks among the nation's most inventive chefs. In an elegant yet comfortable setting, Seeger prepares beautiful dishes of rare squab and fresh fish, as well as unusual desserts. The four-course menu, with appropriate wines (optional), ranges through Seeger's current thinking. The service is superior, but don't rush this chef. Reservations are essential. 3434 Peachtree Rd., at Lenox Rd., Ritz-Carlton, Buckhead. 237-2700. $$$

The Green Manor.
This restored Greek Revival–style house was built in the early twentieth century by the founder of Union City; it's now the site of a continental restaurant where the menu ranges from seafood fajitas and quesadillas to chateaubriand. Open Tuesday through Friday for lunch. 6400 Westbrook St., Union City. 964-4343. $$

Hedgerose Heights Inn.
The restaurant's milieu is a Buckhead neighborhood that was once called Hedgerose Heights. Located in a former residence, the inn is a longtime favorite for elegant dinners. The buffalo steak, a wintertime standout, as well as seafood and pheasant dishes, are splendid. The wine list is extensive. 490 E. Paces Ferry Rd., Buckhead. 233-7673. $$$

Kurt's.
Kurt Eisele bought the old River Manor Restaurant and moved his original operation out from Peachtree Corners. A slight German touch accents the dishes—for example, spätzle, Black Forest ham, schnitzel—because owner Kurt Eisele is German and his wife, Verena, is German-Swiss. Eisele has a gift for preparing seafood, as demonstrated in a curry-sauced veal and shrimp dish. Eisele makes the terrific desserts as well. 4225 River Green Pkwy., Duluth. 623-4128. $$

LaTour.
Opulence rules in this frankly formal restaurant known for lavishly prepared food: rack of lamb, chicken breast with champagne sauce, Muscovy duck, Dover sole meunière—a mingling of the classics of French cooking with an international touch. 3209 Paces Ferry Pl., Buckhead. 233-8833. $$$

Nikolai's Roof.
Waiters dressed in Cossak-inspired outfits recite a menu that changes seasonally, but pirozhki and borscht are constants. Start with a flavored vodka and savor the extraordinary view. If game is available, and it often is, give that option some serious reflection. The wondrous wine list requires perusal. 255 Courtland St., Atlanta Hilton and Towers, Downtown. 659-3282. $$$

103 West.
A lavish interior, inventive French cooking, impeccable service, and a fine wine list make 103 West extra-special. Food is prepared in the classic French manner but often with

American ingredients. The downstairs facilities for banquets are elegant yet intimate. 103 W. Paces Ferry Rd., Buckhead. 233-5993. $$$

Opus. Initially, Martin Gagne established the culinary quality in this coolly elegant, quiet dining room. Gagne has gone to City Grill, but the kitchen still has great direction in the hands of young Ken Vedrinski from the Four Seasons in Chicago. The tasting menu lets patrons sample the chef's current ideas. Great breads are made in-house *(see chapter 6)*. 3391 Peachtree Rd., Swissôtel, Buckhead. 365-0065. $$

Pacific Bar & Grill. Another establishment from the Catherall & Kane duo that opened Azalea, Pacific Bar & Grill replicates some of the dishes of its Buckhead parent (the deep-fried whole catfish, for instance). The menu explores flavors of the Pacific Rim, Italy (pizzas and pastas), and the American Southwest (ribs, pulled pork sandwiches, nachos, and quesadillas). 3525 Mall Blvd., Gwinnett Esplanade Shopping Center, Duluth. 623-9111. $$

> *The Trout House Exchange opened in 1860 and featured "Bonescure, Norfolk, and Savannah oysters," as well as wild game and a well-stocked bar.*

Pano's and Paul's. One of Atlanta's all-time favorite restaurants, Pano's and Paul's has a blatantly lush interior, but it's the food that keeps patrons coming back. Favorite selections include the fried lobster tails, pheasant any way Paul Albrecht cares to prepare it, sweetbreads, soft-shell crab, foie gras, and grilled tuna. The wine list is hefty. A great value, even though

expensive. 1232 W. Paces Ferry Rd., West Paces Ferry Shopping Center, Buckhead. 261-3662. $$$

The Restaurant, Ritz-Carlton, Atlanta. Formal, yet as comfortable as a familiar club, the Ritz-Carlton, Atlanta's flagship dining room hasn't the fame of its Buckhead sister, the Dining Room *(see p. 12)*. Still, many dishes achieve a standard other establishments wish they could muster. It's popular with the business crowd that gathers for lunch to enjoy the inventive light fare. The extravagant Sunday brunch is a delight. 181 Peachtree St., Ritz-Carlton, Atlanta, Downtown. 659-0400. $$$

Victorian House. The formerly private Victorian residence houses some great culinary secrets. Maria and Antonio DaSilva, both Portuguese, offer a continental menu with lots of lamb, chicken, and beef. But once in a while some Portuguese goodies slip in among the specials. The classic *caldo verde* goes over well, and other Portuguese specialties can be ordered. The wine list features American, French, and, naturally, Portuguese wines. 1973 Rockdale Industrial Blvd., Conyers. 922-5621. $$

Village Café. Friends in Fayetteville rate the café "number one" for consistency and excellence in continental cuisine. This charming restaurant, small and intimate, is tucked into a modern shopping center. Frenchman Patrick Boutier, owner and chef, and his wife Susi attract local praise with such dishes as seafood fettucini and pecan-grilled chicken breast with a honey mustard glaze. The wine list offers American wines and a few French selections. Some wines are available by the glass. 119 Banks Station, Banks Station Shopping Center, Fayetteville. 460-9449. $$

INTERNATIONAL

Covering everything from sturdy British fare to the ultra-exotic, this section includes the rapidly growing contingent of Asian restaurants, many of which present some of the best dining Atlanta offers. This list shows one of the reasons why Atlanta is becoming a truly international city.

ASIAN

Chinese

Ho-Ho. We'd give a lot for the oyster pancake recipe. Some fussy folks find the place less tidy than they might wish, but it's gotten better lately, and the food remains some of the best Chinese fare in Atlanta. The menu includes everything from *moo goo gai pan* to jelly fish. 3683 Clairmont Rd., Chamblee. 451-7240. $

Hong Kong Delight. The mix of cuisines that characterizes the cooking of this island city is evident in such delights as Hong Kong stuffed chicken and Hong Kong steak with black pepper sauce. 5920 Roswell Rd., Ste. B-111, Parkside Shopping Center, Sandy Springs. 255-3388. $

Hong Kong Harbour. The mostly Chinese clientele—families, couples, business people—create a boisterous atmosphere that makes occidentals feel as though they're actually in Hong Kong. The food reflects a dedication to authenticity, with good noodle dishes, silken tofu graced with savory sauces, and the wonderful salt-and-pepper fried squid. 2184 Cheshire Bridge Rd., Northeast. 325-7630. $

Honto. Adventuresome palates seeking out the real thing should ask for translations of the dishes listed on the wall. Don't come for the decor; do come for the authentic Chinese cooking. Such dishes as salt-and-pepper squid get raves from all cultures. 3295 Chamblee-Dunwoody Rd., Chamblee. 458-8088. $

Jade of China. A subtle Oriental garden serves as the entrance to a quiet, elegant restaurant. Cross a bridge and nod at the large, golden *koi* that swim beneath it. Entrees include Hunan lamb and Peking duck. The staff is helpful and takes pains to explain the dishes. 8560 Holcomb Bridge Rd., Alpharetta. 641-8980. $$

Little Szechwan. Savor the spicy delights of Szechwan cooking: piquant green beans, chicken with hot sauce, zingy tender eggplant. None of the same old thing here—and this is fast food! Pick up your order and grab a table in the middle of one of Atlanta's most unusual fast food courts. 5389 New Peachtree Rd., Chinatown Mall, Chamblee. 457-0702; 5091 Buford Hwy., Doraville. 451-0192. $

Japanese

Hashiguchi. This reliable restaurant offers lovely sashimi and good traditional dishes. The staff loves the little people and takes care of them, and their grown-ups, with affection. 3000 Windy Hill Rd., Marietta. 955-2337. $$

Kamogawa. Among the most elegant and expensive of Atlanta's Japanese restaurants, Kamogawa is the jewel of the Hotel Nikko in Buckhead. The *kaiseki* dinner is a major fixture in the restaurant's offerings. To dine here is to be transported. 3300 Peachtree Rd., Hotel Nikko, Buckhead. 365-8100. $$$

Kamon. A sleek, comfortable, and casual interior suggests modern Japan. At lunch, Japanese businessmen and their Norcross associates dine on fine lunchtime specials (scallops and pork cutlet are two favorites). The dinner menu offers more unusual dishes, such as pickled octopus. Good sushi and sashimi. 6050 Peachtree Pkwy., Norcross. 449-0033. $$

Nakato. One of Atlanta's oldest Japanese restaurants, Nakato is now ensconced in an elegant new building that combines features of both Japanese and Western architecture. Our favorites include the dependably good sukiyaki, sushi, and teriyaki. One young native of Tokyo says Nakato hits closer to home than any other Japanese restaurant in Atlanta. 1776 Cheshire Bridge Rd., Northeast. 873-6582. $$

Nickiemoto's. This restaurant specializes in Japanese–style dishes prepared with a deliberate American accent, specifically Californian. The sushi is fine, but then move on to grilled tuna and other Japanese-inspired American dishes. 247 Buckhead Ave., Buckhead. 842-0334. $$

Sa Tsu Ki. This simply decorated establishment is one of the few Japanese restaurants in Atlanta to offer the traditional salt-grilled method of cooking fish: salt-grilled mackerel, yellow tail, and salmon stand out—but other traditional Japanese dishes are also on the menu. 3043 Buford Hwy., Northeast. 325-5285. $$

Suntory. Cooking foods in boiling liquid sounds a bit like fondue, and *shabu shabu* gets close to that concept. But the boiling liquid is not oil but broth, which acquires the flavors of the foods cooked in it. At Suntory, *shabu shabu* is a major experience, and must be ordered for two. *Teppan yaki* is a multi-course affair, as is the formal *kaiseki*

ACROSS ATLANTA

dinner. The special Japanese menu is for the adventuresome. 3847 Roswell Rd., Buckhead. 261-3737. $$$

Umezono. This unpretentious establishment, when on target, serves up some of the best Japanese food in Atlanta—some say *the* best. Specialties include *agadashi-dofu* and *udon*. The cooking at dinner seems to be better than at lunch. 2086-B Cobb Pkwy., Smyrna. 933-8808. $$

Korean

Garam. This place is the hands-down favorite of folks who've lived in Korea. They come for the Korean barbecue, *bolgogi*, and wonderful vegetables, which vary daily. The environment is comfortable and sparkling. 5881 Buford Hwy., Doraville. 454-9198. $

Go Hyang House. Family-style Korean fare, including very good barbecue and green bean–oyster pancakes, is served in a casual atmosphere. 5728 Buford Hwy., Pinetree Plaza, Doraville. 457-8510. $

Kang Suh. Seafood, traditional Korean barbecues (both beef and pork), intriguing side dishes of traditional pickled and spiced vegetables (the radish-like daikon is especially good), and delicate soups make choices difficult. Takeout, delivery, catering. 5181 Buford Hwy., Pinetree Plaza, Doraville. 451-8989. $

Mirror of Korea. Your basic mom-and-pop kind of place, Mirror serves what some folks who've lived in Korea think is among the best Korean fare in town. 1047 Ponce de Leon Ave., Poncey-Highland. 874-6243. $

Thai

Hot Pepper. A favorite of Peachtree Publishers' staff at lunchtime, this friendly Thai restaurant serves generous portions in next to no time. The Pad-Thai is seasoned just right, and the chicken-coconut soup served with the entrees shouldn't be missed. Also open for dinner. 2257 Lenox Rd. Northeast 320-1532. $

Phuket. The contemporary interior makes Phuket a good choice for business lunches and dinners. Named for Thailand's island city, it produces all the good, traditional standards of Thai cooking. The satay (pork threaded on bamboo skewers, then grilled) seems especially good here. 2839 Buford Hwy., Clock Tower Shopping Center, between N. Druid Hills Rd. and Cheshire Bridge Rd., Northeast. 325-4199. $$

Sukothai. Named for an ancient city in Thailand, this is Cobb County's first Thai restaurant—and it's an elegant one. Make sure to sample the seafood, easily done by ordering a succulent seafood platter. Good soups, noodle dishes, and red curry dishes. 1995 Windy Hill Rd., Smyrna. 434-9276. $$

Surin of Thailand. Some connoisseurs of authentic Thai food think this one hits the mark. The appetizers and the *yum yai* salad with traditional peanut dressing are enticing, but don't miss the noodle dishes and distinctive curries. 810 N. Highland Ave., Virginia-Highland. 892-7789. $$

Taste of Thai. The extensive menu includes traditional dishes prepared with good attention to detail, as well as more unusual fare. For example, the salads include the inevitable, and wonderful, *yum yai,* but be sure to try the spicy shrimp and lemon grass salad or the crispy catfish salad, as well. 5775 Jimmy Carter Blvd., Suite B-2, Norcross, behind Pier 1. 662-8575. $$

Thai Restaurant of Norcross. An early success in Atlanta's budding Thai restaurant industry, this place has maintained its consistency despite having changed hands. The soups seem especially good here, as do the Thai omelets and the curries. 6065 S. Norcross-Tucker Rd., Norcross. 938-3883. $

Zab-E-Lee. One of Atlanta's best Thai restaurants occupies an off-the-beaten-path location in College Park, south of the city. Never mind that it sits in a strip mall with a nationally known discount store—it serves excellent soups, salads, and unusual dishes. 4835 Old National Hwy., College Park. 768-2705. $

Vietnamese

Bien Thuy. The flavors of Vietnamese cooking—strong cilantro, ample ginger—permeate soups, spring rolls, vermicelli dishes, salt-braised entrees, and other standards. Bien Thuy is a tucked-away neighborhood restaurant where both Vietnamese and American patrons respond with smiles to the enticing smells coming from the kitchen—but you gotta like the real thing to enjoy this one. 5095-F Buford Hwy., Northwoods Plaza, Doraville. 454-9046. $

Song Huong. The inventive menu offers both Vietnamese and Chinese dishes, but the tastes to experience come from the Vietnamese cuisine. The adventurous list of dishes even includes eel, but the sugar cane shrimp cake will appeal to everyone. 4795 Buford Hwy., Chamblee. 451-2944. $

BRITISH

Reggie's. Reggie's has been holding forth on behalf of "the thin red line" for a long time, with such items as bangers and mash, fish and chips, Cornish pasties, and lots of ale to wash them down with. Atmosphere contains RAF photos and Reggie-cum-mustache himself, if you're lucky. 317 CNN Center, Downtown. 525-1437. $$

Ugly Mug Pub. Savor a very nice shepherd's pie or good fish and chips, and drink a Woodpecker Cider. The atmosphere is very American, but lots of British and Scottish memorabilia—flags and such—hang on the walls. Cheerio! 3585 Peachtree Industrial Blvd., Howell Center, near Pleasant Hill Rd., Duluth. 497-1459. $$

CARIBBEAN

Caribbean Deli. Huge sandwiches such as the *medianoche* and the Cuban are delicious, and one order could easily feed two people. Don't miss the good black bean soup, silky cheese flans made dense with cream cheese, and Cuban coffee. 1622 Woodcliff Dr., Briarcliff Rd., Briarcliff Shopping Center, Northeast. 320-0256. $

Coco Loco. Cuban food, Miami-style, is the specialty. Black bean dishes, yucca, plantain, and similar Caribbean delights dominate the menu. But Coco Loco's versions of classic Spanish dishes, such as *bacalao a la Vizcaina* (salted cod with tomatoes, peppers, and olives) and *lechón asado*

(roast pork) are splendid, and portions are huge. Great Cuban coffee! 2625 Piedmont Rd., Ste. G-40, Buckhead Crossing Mall (on the Sidney Marcus Blvd. side), Buckhead. 364-0212; 6301 Roswell Rd., Sandy Springs Plaza, Sandy Springs. 364-0212. $.

Indigo Coastal Grill. This casual restaurant is a busy place on most nights, so come early (around 6 P.M.) or be prepared to wait. The menu's emphasis is on fresh fish prepared with the flavors of the Caribbean. Vegetarian dishes are prepared with style and zest. The Key lime pie is a knockout. Indigo offers lots of wines by the glass. 1397 N. Highland Ave., Virginia-Highland. 876-0676. $$

EASTERN EUROPEAN / RUSSIAN

Papa Pirozki's. This intimate restaurant presents food inspired by the fare of Czarist Russia. Start with flavored vodka and progress to borscht or *hkarcho* (lamb soup). The pirozhkis—stuffed turnovers—are among the best in town. Grilled rack of lamb marinated in herbs and honey mustard may not seem Russian, but who cares? It's terrific. 4953 Roswell Rd., Sandy Springs. 252-1118. $$$

Romanian Restaurant. Oxtail soup, stuffed cabbage, lamb shank, and homemade sausages are served in an airy and friendly space. This fare will definitely put a smile on your face. 3081 E. Shadowlawn Ave., Buckhead. 365-8220. $

FRENCH

Anne Marie's. Traditional rustic French cooking has made this restaurant a favorite for many years. Special dinners include cassoulet and bouillabaise. One Frenchman was overheard to exclaim that this was the only

French restaurant, in this country, that he could tell was owned by a Frenchman (actually a woman, in this case). 3340 Peachtree Rd., Tower Place Courtyard, Buckhead. 237-8686. $$$

Cassis. Emphasis is on the flavors of southern France. The menu varies seasonally, but the food is always light and balanced. High notes are the duck and seafood dishes, and the wine list includes some Provençal selections. 3300 Peachtree Rd., at Piedmont Rd., Hotel Nikko, Buckhead. 365-8100. $$$

Ciboulette. In 1992, Thomas Coohill left City Grill and joined forces with his former mentor, Jean Banchet, who used to operate Le Français in Wheeling, IL, outside of Chicago, widely esteemed as the best French restaurant in this country. The two created Ciboulette, where traditional French dishes are attractively prepared. We'll be back for more of the lentil salad, the pâtés, the lamb, and the delicious coq au vin. The wine list presents French and American selections, with many offered by the glass. 1529 Piedmont Ave., at Monroe Dr., Clear Creek Shopping Center, Midtown. 874-7600. $$

Le Café Crêpe. The charming bistro sits alongside a railroad track, making dining an intimate, fun experience. Lunch is served Monday through Friday, but dinner is served only on Thursday, Friday, and Saturday, when a special four-course menu is offered for **Gourmet Nights**. Special parties may make reservations for dinner on Monday through Wednesday. 90 Marietta Station Walk, Marietta Square, Marietta. 426-8003. $

Patio by the River. French-inspired cooking—on the banks of the Chattahoochee—has been the mainstay of this Atlanta favorite for many years. Salad of grilled quail, wonderful oysters, and in-house-cured salmon are among the dishes that have kept a steady stream of folks coming to dine. The outdoor facilities are great for private parties, especially weddings. 4199 Paces Ferry Rd., Northwest. 432-2808. $$

South of France. Tonino Spinucci, an Italian whose wife, Ginette, is of French descent, has accomplished an about-face in the quality of the food. The bistro-inspired French fare is now on target and is served in generous portions. The rabbit hunter-style is terrific, as are duck à l'orange, French-style pepper steak, stuffed quail, and, of course, French onion soup. Charming, Provençal-style ambience. 2345 Cheshire Bridge Rd., Cheshire Square, Northeast. 325-6963. $$

Violette. The bistro comes to town, takes over the location of a former bank, and oo-là-là! The classics of bistro fare—chicken tarragon, terrine, and pork in creamy peppercorn sauce—are prepared with skill. Many dinner entrees cost about $8, while fish dishes are higher (about $13)—good sized portions, too. This place is getting popular: neighbors recently found it booked solid on a Friday night, so make reservations. 3098 Briarcliff Rd., Northeast. 633-3323. $

GREEK

Evelyn's Café. The specials focus on Greek fare, including *pastitsio*, lamb, grape leaves, and Greek-style hamburgers laden with *tzatziki* sauce. Savor the Greek pastries of all kinds. 3853 Lawrenceville Hwy., Ste. F, Brockett Sq., Tucker. 496-0561. $

Jimmy's on the Square. This family-owned Greek restaurant has loyal patrons who swear that this is the best Greek food this side of the Old Country. And many will further swear that the Greek salad is the best anywhere, *including* the Old Country. 164 Roswell St., near the Square, Marietta. 428-5627. $$

INDIAN/PAKISTANI

Chat Patti. A self-service line and a modern, utilitarian interior keep 'em coming for lunch and dinner. The assertively seasoned food, much of it vegetarian, appeals to folks who like spicy dishes. The chickpeas, for instance, are wonderful, but to define the seasoning as "mild," as one staffer does, understates the intensity. 1594 F Woodcliff Dr., Briarcliff Shopping Center, Northeast. 633-5595. $

Haveli. Cobb County's favorite Indian restaurant serves a popular lunchtime buffet of Indian dishes that's also available on Saturday. Keep that in mind next time you're shopping at Cumberland Mall or Galleria because the restaurant is right up the road. All the classics of Indian cooking are nicely prepared. 2706 Cobb Pkwy., Smyrna. 955-4525. $

Heera of India. Said by some to be the best Indian restaurant in Atlanta, Heera offers lamb in a number of unusual preparations as well as numerous vegetable dishes. The chickpeas *channa massala* are super. 595 Piedmont Ave., RIO Shopping Center, Downtown. 876-4408. $

Himalayas. Now a fixture among Atlanta's Indian restaurants, Himalayas serves wonderful lamb and chicken dishes and out-of-the-ordinary vegetable dishes. 5520 Peachtree Industrial Blvd., Chamblee Plaza, Chamblee. 458-6557 or 455-9686. $

Indian Delights. Stuck in a nondescript shopping center, this vegetarian restaurant could convert hard-line carnivores. In its simple interior, the hot-table contains savory samosas, bhajee (onion/vegetable fritters), and lentil dishes. 1707 Church St., Scott Blvd., Scott Village, Decatur. 296-2965. $

Poona. An elegant interior with a small stage for weekend sitar music—jam sessions Indian style—showcases a fair buffet at lunch and on the weekends. But it's best to order from the menu—samosas, onion bhajee, chicken tikka, lamb roghan, and lassi, a wonderful mango-flavored yogurt drink. 1630 Pleasant Hill Rd., Wal-Mart Shopping Center, Duluth. 717-1053. $$

ITALIAN

For years only Italian-American cooking was available in Atlanta. Starting with La Grotta, however, a spate of new restaurants has brought the culinary treasures of the homeland to our table, so to speak. We've divided this section into three parts: "Classic," denoting authentic Italian cooking; comforting, familiar "Italian-American;" and "Pizza & Pasta." Some restaurants offer a combination of styles, so we've had to make a judgment call in those instances.

Classic

Abruzzi. The elegant, cool New York–style ambience is the setting for traditional northern Italian food. Regulars will just specify "veal" or "fish," and let the kitchen do its will with the material. Italians, including Italian-Americans, report especially warm receptions. 2355 Peachtree Rd., Peachtree Battle Shopping Center, Buckhead. 261-8186. $$$

Capri. We love to challenge the chef to invent intriguing new sauces for the fresh pasta, such as vegetables on linguine or capellini. Entrees include many well-prepared standards of the Italian repertoire (veal francese and piccata, for instance). Quiet; good business atmosphere. 5785 Roswell Rd., Sandy Springs. 255-7222. $$

LaGrotta Ristorante. Good veal and pasta dishes are served in an elegant setting that attracts a lot of Atlanta glitterati. Reservations are essential. Two locations, one in town and one in Dunwoody. 2637 Peachtree Rd., Peachtree House Condominium, Buckhead. 231-1368; 4355 Ashford-Dunwoody Rd., Dunwoody. 395-9925. $$$

La Strada. This casual, neighborhood trattoria proves that northern Italian food need not be fiercely expensive. Good pasta with imaginative sauces, a warm welcome for children, and a good wine list made La Strada an instant hit. No reservations, but sometimes there's a fair wait for a table. 2930 Johnson Ferry Rd., Marietta. 640-7008; 8550 Roswell Rd., Dunwoody. 552-1300. $

Michaelangelo's. Piero Gusberti takes pride in the restaurant's Italian specialties, such as *zuppa di pesci,* a soup of fresh fish and shellfish. Patrons praise the Rollatine Michaelangelo—veal rolled with prosciutto and mozarella cheese, and sautéed with fresh sage and mushrooms. Gusberti also bakes homemade breads and desserts on site. Cast members from the films and television shows produced in nearby Covington often dine here. 951 Railroad St., Conyers. 929-0828. $$

Pricci. Buckhead Life Restaurant Group—corporate owner of five distinctive Buckhead restaurants—recently opened this casual, northern Italian establishment. Formerly called

Capriccio, Pricci turns out excellent food in its restyled modern interior. On one occasion, the risotto of the day came with sweet, barely cooked scallops and fresh spinach—a huge portion for reasonable money. The excellent, well-priced wine list is all Italian. Pasta, pizza, and unusual appetizers—such as shrimp with white beans—get high marks. Pricci's grilled quail is perhaps the best we've ever had. Family-style service on Sundays. 500 Pharr Rd., Buckhead. 237-2941. $$

Raffaelo. Rimini native Cesare Tini, of Donatello restaurant in Tampa, came to Atlanta a few years ago. He brought with him his charming son, Paolo, to manage his new establishment. Specialties include fine pasta dishes with light sauces, good veal, and superb fish dishes. The creamy tiramisù is sheer seduction. Italian wines of good lineage form the wine list. 3102 Piedmont Rd., south of Peachtree Rd., Buckhead. 233-8123. $$$

Veni Vidi Vici. A handsome, warmly modern interior and a high-energy atmosphere is the setting for classic home-style Italian food: arugula salad with shavings of ricotta salata cheese, fettuccine with lemon-cream sauce, chicken braised with onions, extraordinary carrot cake. The wine list is almost all Italian, and many good selections are offered by the glass. Patio dining and a bocci court. 41 14th St., Midtown. 875-VICI (8424). $$$

Italian-American

Altobeli's. A popular neighborhood restaurant that fairly hums with happy suburban patrons, Altobeli's does a fine job with seafood dishes. The *lumache* (snails) and homemade rice pudding also reap heavy praise. The well-priced wine list contains Italian, French, and California selections. 3000 Old Alabama Rd., Haynes Market Shopping Center, Alpharetta. 664-8055; 5370 Hwy. 78, Stone Mountain Square, Stone Mountain. 413-1111. $

Azio. This casual Italian restaurant dishes up good pasta and pizza. The large, comfortable deck on this second-story establishment is a treat in nice weather. Prices make a night out with the kids and grandma possible, but it's filled with business types at lunch. 220 Pharr Rd., Buckhead. 233-7626. $

Camille's. Brooklyn-born Camille Sotis understands Italian-American cooking—maybe even better than "Mamma." Dip deep-fried rice balls into thick, chunky tomato sauce, and be sure to try the squid Fra Diavolo at this comfortable neighborhood hangout. 1186 N. Highland Ave., Virginia-Highland. 872-7203. $$

Ippolito. The pillow-sized calzone are stuffed with lotsa cheese and good salamis. Huge *panini* (sandwiches, loosely translated) are actually wedges of dough stuffed with anything—such as aromatic eggplant Parmesan. Ippolito is your basic neighborhood Italian restaurant—American style—and the crowds love it. 1375 Holcomb Bridge Rd., King's Market Shopping Center, Roswell. 998-5683. I

Mario's. This long-standing neighborhood favorite serves standard Italian-American dishes, and they really hit the comfort zone when they're on target. Mario's stays filled with loyal patrons who enjoy Italian-American–style red sauce. The veal or sausage with peppers is especially good. 3644 Shallowford Rd., Doraville. 451-0979. $

San Gennaro. Camille Sotis serves up her magnificent tomato sauce on all kinds of homegrown dishes. Eggplant Parmesan, meatballs, and calamari with chunky marinara sauce for dipping are classics of Italian-American cooking. A casual, family place. 2196 Cheshire Bridge Rd., Northeast. 636-9447. $

Pizza & Pasta

California Pizza Kitchen. Wood-fire pizzas are almost cliché nowadays, but this outfit still draws a crowd. The pasta and salads are also good, and, except for being mobbed, this is a handy spot for lunch when shopping at Lenox. 3393 Peachtree Rd., upper level, Food Court, Lenox Square, Buckhead. 262-9221. 181 14th St., Midtown. 892-4343. 4600 Ashford-Dunwoody Rd., Dunwoody. 393-0390. $

Everybody's. Popular with the student crowd. The unique cheese crisps have wafer-thin crusts with light toppings, such as onion and cheese (fewer calories that way). Beer is on tap. 1593 N. Decatur Rd., Northeast. 377-7766; 1040 N. Highland Ave., Virginia-Highland. 873-4545. $

Fellini's. The superior, thin-crust pizzas with fresh toppings attract appreciative patrons who also value the very good prices. Fellini's is especially fun if you like very funky surroundings. Five locations: Little Five Points, Midtown, Poncey-Highland, and the original: 2813 Peachtree Rd., Buckhead. 266-0082. $

Mellow Mushroom Pizza Bakers. Mention this Atlanta-based pizzeria, and the first thing you'll hear is "spectacular crust!" They pile on the pizza toppings, so it can be a little sloppy but it's worth it. The soft pretzels are made out of the famous pizza dough and are another favorite. Calzones, sandwiches, and assorted salads round out the menu. Although Mellow Mushroom has expanded to several locations, you never get that "chain restaurant" feeling; each location has its own distinct neighborhood feel. The fourteen locations across town include 3902 Highway 78, Snellville. 978-3800; 30 Pharr Rd., Buckhead. 233-3443; $

Mo's Pizza. At this student hangout, lots of beer (much of it imported) comes in bottles or from the tap. The pizza has not diminished in quality as the years have passed. Whole wheat pizza is available, as are good sandwiches and salads. Mo's delivers within a three-mile radius for a small fee. 3109 Briarcliff Rd., Northeast. 320-1258. $

Olympia Pizza House. Billy Mabros serves a Greek-style pizza that Southsiders adore. The Olympia Special, topped with hamburger, pepperoni, peppers, onions, feta, and olives, is especially popular. 5537 N. Henry Blvd., Stockbridge. 474-6744. $

Partner's. One of Atlanta's original pasta bistros, Partner's makes fresh pasta daily. Jade Shrimp is a dish of fresh red pepper pasta topped with sautéed shrimp and Asian herbs, fermented black beans, and garlic. Other entrees include seafood and poultry, and the beef tenderloin is very popular. All red wines are available by the glass, as are several whites. 1399 N. Highland Ave., Virginia-Highland. 876-8104. $$

Rocky's Brick Oven Pizza. This is contemporary pizza for the gourmet. Favorite toppings include fresh pesto and homemade mozzarella, prosciutto, and sweet onions. We like the thin crust rather than the thicker Sicilian (but that's just our opinion). Good desserts. 1770 Peachtree St., at 26th St., Brookwood. 876-1111; Takeout and delivery: 3210 Roswell Rd., Buckhead. 262-7625. $

Rocky's Pizza & Subs. No relation to the intown Rocky's, this establishment is owned by Paul Cappozzoli, who uses his grandmother's Sicilian dough recipe for his pizza. Southsiders appreciate the homemade Italian sausage used as a topping, along with other fresh ingredients and low-fat mozzarella cheese. Submarines are also popular. 8113 Tara Blvd., Jonesboro. 478-2620. $

MEXICAN/SOUTHWESTERN

Azteca Grill. Posole is one of the mainstays of the peasant cooking savored in parts of Mexico and the American Southwest. Rich with hominy and pork, and spiked with piquant ancho chilis, posole is not usually seen on Atlanta menus. It's worth the trip. Carne guisada, literally translated as "cooked meat," and green chili are other rarities available at Azteca Grill. 1140 Morrow Industrial Blvd., Southlake Mall, Morrow. 968-0907. $

Caramba Café. The usual Mexican-American dishes are prepared with unusual care, resulting in well-flavored enchiladas, tamales and chiles rellenos. Out-of-the-ordinary Mexican stew and a dense flan are special. 1409 N. Highland Ave., Virginia-Highland. 874-1343. $

El Charro Taquería. Two locations, one (Buford Highway) rather raucous, bring some fine, rustic Mexican food to Atlanta. Order a sampler of good tacos with unusual fillings (tongue, for instance). 2581 Piedmont Rd. (actually on Sidney Marcus Blvd.), Buckhead. 264-0613; 5000 Buford Hwy., Chamblee. 457-9039. $

El Eradero. At first look, the menu seems ho-hum. All the Texas two-step music in the air confirms the Tex-Mex character of the place, from the food to the all-American clientele. But the food is freshly made, and the plump quesadilla is crisp and satisfying. Very fine flan. 2479 N. Cobb Pkwy., Kennesaw. 423-1213. $

El Azteca. Numerous locations from Stone Mountain to Sandy Springs and downtown make the restaurant's name synonymous with Mexican-American food all over town. Some traditional dishes, such as carne asada, are available, but most offerings are the combination dinners Americans enjoy. The atmosphere, while not upscale, is attractive and inviting. Each location has a patio, which is the best spot for enjoying the margaritas. Original location: 6078 Roswell Rd., Sandy Springs. 255-9807. $

La Cazuela. Fine ceviche, tacos *al carbón, carnitas,* and stuffed chile *poblano* lift this Atlanta-based quartet of restaurants above the run-of-the-mill chains. Its four locations include Snellville, Duluth, Lilburn, and the original, which has superior mariachi music on Sunday evenings: 4606 Jimmy Carter Blvd., Smoketree Shopping Center, at Britt Rd., Norcross. 493-8341. $

La Fonda Latina. The Spanish dishes include giveaway-priced paella and sangría, and Latin American touches are everywhere in the popular black beans, quesadillas, and blue corn chips. Leave room for flan. 1150-B Euclid Ave., Little Five Points. 577-8317; 2813 Peachtree Rd. 816-8311. $

La Quebrada. Sunday morning is the time for genuine Mexican treats, such as *caldo de camarón,* a wickedly spicy broth with huge shrimp. Thus braced, go on to savor as wide a variety of authentic Mexican dishes as one will find in Atlanta. On the regular menu are the usual dishes, but the potato-filled burritos are not to be missed. Two locations, but only Shallowford Road offers the authentic Sunday morning specials: 2580 Shallowford Rd., Shallowford Plaza, Northeast. 982-0631. $

Mambo Restaurante Cubano. Dive into huge portions of Cuban specialties such as paella (both regular and black) and excellent *ropa vieja.* The Argentine wines (Humberto Canales Cabernet Sauvignon, for instance) are unusual finds. 1402 N. Highland Ave., Virginia-Highland. 876-2626. $$

Rio Bravo Cantina. Besides the margaritas and Corona beer sipped with lime, the young business crowd likes the chili con queso and fajitas. Six locations. Original: 3172 Roswell Rd., Buckhead. 262-7431. $

Sundown Café. From the same folks who gave Morrow the fine Azteca Grill comes a restaurant serving outstanding Mexican and Southwestern food. In a sleek, modern interior of Spanish Colonial influence, savor turnip greens and *poblano* corn chowder, two of the establishment's signature dishes. Don't miss the trout—dipped in blue cornmeal batter and deep-fried—and Eddie's Pork, grilled pork tenderloin with roasted jalapeño peppers. Plan to have some sweet potato cheesecake for dessert. 2165 Cheshire Bridge Rd., Northeast. 321-1118. $

Tortillas. This delightful hole-in-the-wall spot serves California-style Mexican fare, such as a smashing quesadilla that's wonderful with the jalapeño-spiked salsa verde. 774 Ponce de Leon Ave., Poncey-Highland. 892-3493. $

U.S. Bar y Grill. In Atlanta, the classics of Mexican cooking don't get any better than the grill's red snapper, Veracruz–style (with the traditional green olives), and *cabrito* (roast baby goat). Three locations—Sandy Springs, Brookhaven, and the original: 2002 Howell Mill Rd., at Collier Rd., Northwest. 352-0033. $$.

MIDDLE EASTERN

Lawrence's Café & Restaurant. A mainstay of the ethnic scene, this casual restaurant has gotten better and better. Excellent hummus, baba ganoush, and kibbeh are served. Catch the traditional dancing—that's the belly kind—for evening entertainment. Takeout available. 2888 Buford Hwy., Northeast. 320-7756. $$

Nicola's. Good Middle Eastern cooking—hummus, baba ganoush, tabbouleh, kibbeh—is served in spare, unpretentious surroundings. Open evenings only. 1602 Lavista Rd., at Briarcliff Rd., Northeast. 325-2524. $$

MOROCCAN

The Imperial Fez. Atlanta's one and only Moroccan restaurant has opened the town's eyes to the splendor of fine North African cooking. Remove your shoes at the door, settle down on some cushions, and wash your hands in a ceremonial silver font, as all dining is done with the fingers. Thus readied, break some whole wheat bread, savor *harrira* (a cumin-scented lentil soup), salads, and *b'stella* (cinnamon-flavored Cornish hen in light pastry). Vegetarian dishes and the succulent stews called *tagines*, as well as couscous and lamb are among the choices in a five-course menu. Cornish hen replaces the more traditional pigeon. 2285 Peachtree Rd., Peachtree Battle Condominium, Buckhead. 351-0870. $$

LIGHT DINING

Snacks, tea, and after-performance nourishment are serious matters in our view. So, too, is lunch, which Americans all too often give short shrift. And coffeehouses, the caffeine trend exported from Seattle, have hit Atlanta full-force. Chains such as Caribou Coffee and Starbuck's are opening up new locations around the city; we've listed some smaller establishments that offer Atlantans all the caffeine and pastry they could want.

COFFEE & DESSERT

Aurora Coffee. One of the first espresso bars to come to Atlanta, Aurora now has four metro locations. Pastries are baked fresh everyday, and beans are available for wholesale. 992-A N. Highland Ave., Virginia-Highland. 892-7158; 468 Moreland Ave., Little Five Points. 523-6856; 230 Peachtree St., Buckhead. 524-1515; 1752 Piedmont Rd., Midtown. 607-9994.

Café Intermezzo. Multilayered cakes with seductive icings and glazes, bracing espresso, and cappuccino attract crowds to this European–style coffee house. Both locations are usually packed after performances. Sandwiches and cold plates are available, but the desserts are the primary lure. 1845 Peachtree Rd., Brookwood. 355-0411; 4505 Ashford-Dunwoody Rd., Park Place, Dunwoody. 396-1344. $

Café Mythology. A restored 1920s home with four fireplaces and patio and balcony seating is the site of this popular after-theater café that offers light fare, a full bar, and an almost limitless array of continental coffees. The busiest time is 10 to 11 P.M. , but they're open until 2 A.M. 1140 Crescent Ave. Midtown. 873-0794.

Cappuccino Joe's. Located in the old Emory train depot (and the former location of the Depot), this coffeehouse features pastries, sandwiches, and desserts along with its cappuccino and assorted coffees. 662 Asbury Cir., at Clifton Rd., Emory University, Northeast. 633-5599.

The Dessert Place. Just as it says, that's what you get—along with good, strong coffee. The cakes, cookies, pies, and out-of-this-world brownies are all homemade. 279 E. Paces Ferry Rd., Buckhead. 233-2331; 1000 Virginia Ave., Virginia-Highland. 892-8921. $

Sweet Stuff. Nibble extravagant, delicious desserts and pastries, and sip good espresso and cappuccino. The pastries come from Sweet Stuff's companion, the Finishing Touch Bakery (*see chapter 6*). 3102 Roswell Rd., Buckhead Shops, Buckhead. 841-6612. $$

LUNCH

The Cedar Tree. Scrumptious falafel topped with tahini sauce, simply superb *fattoush* (greens, mint, olives, and feta cheese with an herb dressing), and good pita bread make this spot a hit with the student crowd. Takeout, gourmet items, and deli service are also available. 1565 N. Decatur Rd., Emory Village Shopping Center, Decatur. 373-2118. $

The Copenhill Café. A short self-service line offers food prepared by Proof of the Pudding, the official caterer for the Jimmy Carter Library and Museum. Salad highlights include chicken salad with huge chunks of chicken, orzo salad sparked with tiny capers, and a fresh fruit medley. Some hot selections are

also served, as are tempting desserts. An outside patio is ideal for alfresco lunches. Tours can arrange special lunches. 1 Copenhill Ave., near Little Five Points. 420-5136. $

Culinary Expressions. Wonderful, light salads (such as dilled potato or chicken Veronique) and yummy desserts (such as white chocolate brownies) make quick lunches interesting. Catering, takeout, and office delivery. 6135 Peachtree Pkwy., at Hwy. 141, Marketplace Shopping Center, Norcross. 446-5515. $

The Cupboard. A Victorian house is the setting for lovely lunches. The main attraction is the homemade pie—the coconut cream, for instance, is just like the kind grandma used to make. 645 Whitlock Ave., west Marietta. 424-8994. $

Delectables. This place gives the term "cafeteria" a whole new spin with such delectables as tarragon chicken salad, gazpacho, and heavenly desserts. Lunch is served in a bright, cheerful space. Good catering. 1 Margaret Mitchell Square., lower level, Atlanta–Fulton County Library, Downtown. 681-2909. $

Expresso's. A quiet, refined spot for breakfast or lunch, Expresso's is away from the Buckhead bustle. Breakfast on yogurt or grits and eggs, and savor muffuletta or salad for lunch. Lots of pasta salads. 3434 Peach-tree Rd., Ritz-Carlton, Buckhead. 266-8028. $

Joan's. The hot lunch specials vary daily, and the friendly staff prepares fine sandwiches (we favor the vegetable sandwich). Many dishes encourage healthy eating, but you'd never know it to taste them. Catering. 563 Plasamour Dr., Northeast. 873-5803. $

Maison Robert. At the front, a splendid bakery and confectionery tempt patrons. A tearoom and lunch service in the rear feature quiches, sandwiches, and desserts from the house bakery. Boxed lunches are available and there's free delivery for orders of ten or more (within five miles of the shop). Offering classic French "cuisine bourgeoise," Maison Robert is a good spot for after-shopping tea and a slice of the bakery's fine fare. Open from the early morning to late afternoon. 3867 Peachtree Rd., Cherokee Plaza, Brookhaven. 237-3675. $

Magnolia Tea Room. This charming tearoom in the antebellum village of Stone Mountain offers Southern lunches and afternoon tea. Dinner is served Tuesday through Saturday. 5459 E. Mountain St., Stone Mountain. 498-6304. $

Peachtree Grill. This elegant self-service café offers a baked-potato bar, sandwiches, salads, and a couple of hot dishes. Corn muffins are a plus. Breakfast and lunch. 1355 Peachtree St., Barnett Bank Bldg., Midtown. 874-9448. $

Rainbow. Tucked in the back of the city's niftiest natural grocery, this small, mostly vegetarian café prepares excellent salads, soups, and sandwiches that get no meatier than tuna fish. Service is continuous through the dinner hour, but it's most popular for lunch. Takeout is available in both the restaurant and the grocery store. 2118 N. Decatur Rd., at Clairmont Rd., Decatur. 633-3538. $

Swan Coach House. Reconnect with your lost cotton gloves before lunching at this charming spot near the Atlanta History Center. Men are welcome, but the ladies always have the majority. Light fare, featuring soups, salads, and sandwiches, is served by a friendly staff. Don't miss the adjacent gallery and gift shop. 3130 Slaton Dr., Buckhead. 261-0636. $

Taste of Europe. Lunch on hot or cold delights, including tasty rotisserie chicken, superb hot dogs, singular salads, and excellent sandwiches. Catering and takeout. 6631 Roswell Rd., Abernathy Square, Sandy Springs. 255-7363. $

VEGETARIAN

Whether you're concerned about animal rights or your waistline, Atlanta's vegetarian restaurants can help you ease your hunger guilt-free. Don't forget about the great Indian restaurants listed above, too.

Eat Your Vegetables Café. While predominately vegetarian, this casual, full service restaurant does offer some poultry and seafood dishes. The menu focuses on ethnic dishes adapted to accommodate vegetarians; one such favorite is the tofu manicotti. The Eat Your Vegetables salad is a lunch and dinner favorite, with a combination of tabbouleh, leaf lettuce, red and green cabbages, sunflower and sesame seeds, and more. All sorts of sandwiches round out the menu, along with daily pasta specials. 438. Moreland Ave. Little Five Points. 523-2671. $

Delights of the Garden. This vegetarians' delight combines a casual atmosphere with your choice of raw fruits and vegetables: tabbouleh fruit pies and kush (cracked bulgur wheat in spring water) are just a few of the Garden samples. The Moroccan plate, with cucumber, tomatoes, tabbouleh and hummus, is their specialty. Nut meat and nori rolls, seaweed sheets wrapped with kush, veggie tuna, etc., are also favorites. Hours are 11 A.M. to 11 P.M. weekdays, noon to midnight Friday and Saturday, and noon to 11 P.M. Sunday. Reservations are accepted. 1081 Juniper Street NE. 876-4307. $

Homage. Situated in the heart of Little Five Points, this vegetarian coffee house provides a pub-style veggie menu and live music every night. Besides traditional veggie favorites, Homage offers a daily pasta special and some of their own alternative creations like the Basil Lettuce Tomato and Tempeh (BLTT) sandwich. Or drop by on Wednesday evening to create your own fish-free sushi for **Suave Sushi Night.** 1174 Euclid Ave., Little Five Points. 522-7471. $

Lettuce Souprise You. This Atlanta-based soup 'n salad spot draws a crowd for build-your-own salads, good soups, and yummy muffins. Seniors receive a dollar off their tab. The seven locations are Sandy Springs; Alpharetta; Roswell; Duluth; Cumberland Mall, Northwest; Pharr Rd., Buckhead; and the original: 2470 Briarcliff Rd., Loehmann's Plaza, Northeast. 636-8549. $

Veggie Delight. Stir fries galore, pasta, and all kinds of veggie dishes can be found at this casual restaurant. Pecan pie and baklava are two of our favorite desserts. Open every day but Sunday from 11 A.M. to 9 P.M. 1051 Ponce De Leon Ave., NE., Poncey Highland. 872-4539. $

Veggieland. This fast-food vegetarian establishment takes special pride in its veggie burgers and tofu cheesecake. The wide variety of salads is also impressive. Absolutely no animal by-products are used, and all desserts are

sugar-free. 211 Pharr Rd NE, Buckhead. 231-3111. 209 Sandy Springs
Circle NW, Sandy Springs. 252-1165. $

TAKEOUT

These listings will help you when a few people are coming to dinner
and you've had no time to cook...or when too many people are
coming to dinner and you can't face cooking for all of them...or when
you're dining with that special significant other—and don't trust your
own cooking. Our choices among Atlanta's many distinguished caterers
are listed in Chapter 7(Services & Resources). Also, many of the
restaurants listed in this chapter will prepare takeout, even for formal
dinners, and check the markets listed in Chapter 6 (Shopping Around).
The following establishments offer takeout only, or emphasize that
aspect of their culinary repertoire.

Easy Way Out. Tucked into a misbe-
gotten space beside a convenience
store, this is a must for those who don't
want to cook for summer picnic-con-
certs. Pâtés of all sorts, including wonderful Mississippi catfish pâté, salads,
and assorted cold dishes are perfect
for Chastain or Galleria. 2449 Peach-
tree Rd., Buckhead. 262-9944. $$

Happy Herman's. Outdoor tables are
the only dining accommodations at
both large locations, so most folks
pick up sandwiches and cold salads
to go. Freshly prepared entrees are
also available, and we suggest you
pick up dessert and a bottle of wine
from the fabulous offerings. (Takeout is
not available at the mall locations.)
2299 Cheshire Bridge Rd., Northeast.
321-3012; 204 Johnson Ferry Rd., at
Sandy Springs Cir., Sandy Springs. 256-
3354. $

Harry's Farmers Market. The pre-
pared foods case stocks lots of won-

derful entrees. Rich lasagne, meatloaf,
herb chicken, Swedish meatballs, beef
burritos, eggplant Parmesan, tortellini
and other pastas, incredible pizzas and
calzone, and various vegetables are
all found in the "Harry's in a Hurry"
section. Dishes are prepared daily—
not frozen—and are designed to be
warmed in the microwave. Pick up
rotisserie chicken and ribs in the deli.
Platters can be ordered for pickup,
and the fruit and gift baskets are avail-
able at all three locations (see chap-
ter 6). 1180 Upper Hembree Rd.,
Alpharetta. 664-6300; 2025 Satellite
Pointe, Duluth. 416-6900; 70 Powers
Ferry Rd., Marietta. 578-4400 $

Harry's in a Hurry. These are smaller
versions of the huge Harry's Farmers
Markets, above. Whether you need to
pick up a few vegetables to round out
your dinner, or a package of home-
made ready-to-heat lasagne for six,
this is the place to stop. All sorts of
prepared foods are here for the choos-

ing—from "briefcase" salads to specialty pizzas to steamed shrimp. Fresh
breads, desserts, and flowers round
out the offerings. 1875 Peachtree Rd.,
Brookwood. 352-7800; 3804 Roswell Rd.,
266-0800.

Morrison's Takeout. Operated by the
same folks who purvey home cooking
in these metro area cafeterias, the
takeout spots are highly regarded for
their vegetable dishes and desserts,
especially the pies. There are several
locations throughout the city, including: 1544 Piedmont Ave., Ansley Mall,
Midtown. 872-8091; 1025 Virginia Ave.,
Hapeville. 761-8066; 1397 Roswell Rd.,
Marietta. 509-1003. $

Indigo Out-to-Go. Wicked brownies
and vegetable sandwiches on thickly
sliced bread are specialties of this
establishment, which abuts Partner's
and, like Partner's and Indigo Grill, is
also owned by Alix Kenagy and Dan
Carson. 1399 N. Highland Ave., Virginia-
Highland. 873-5899. $

Preferred To-Go. This is the takeout
spot owned by Preferred Caterers. Unusual appetizers and entrees make
assembling a rather fancy meal a...
piece of cake. The dishes ramble
among cuisines, from Italian to old-
fashioned rotisserie-roasted chicken.
2221 Peachtree Rd., Shops of Buckhead, Brookwood. 352-8099. $

Tanner's Chicken Rotisserie. Now
you know the specialty. But, while the
rotisserie chicken is moist and nicely
seasoned, you can also get your
chicken barbecued. A three-pound
bird goes for about $7. Table service is
offered, but the big deal is takeout.
Every item on the menu is available
for takeout, including the honey mustard and barbecue sauces. Ask about
catering, business lunch delivery, and
picnic baskets. Eight locations include
the original: 350 Northridge Rd., Dunwoody. 642-7777. $

Tastebuds. The hot and cold entrees
change daily, but the offerings always
include something vegetarian, something low in fat and cholesterol, and
other good-for-you things that taste
sinful, but aren't. The sweet onion pie
is a treat to get when it's available.
Catering available. 3145 Peachtree
Rd., Buckhead Commons Shopping
Center, Buckhead. 240-0423. $

CHAPTER 2

Night Life

Want to make the most of your after-hours time? Take a look at the following pages for a selection of night spots around the metropolitan area. Feel like an evening of country-western music and dancing? We've got a section just for you. Darts with the gang? "Taverns and Pubs" can help you find the perfect spot.

Different areas of Atlanta have very different atmospheres. Buckhead offers a dazzling array of restaurants and bars for your entertainment; don't be discouraged by the weekend crowds. Virginia-Highland and Little Five Points cater to a funky, eclectic crowd, with lots of eateries, bars, and evening shopping. Downtown is home to many of the city's best dance clubs as well as the entertainment emporiums of Underground Atlanta. But you don't have to come into the city to have a great evening—our listings include night spots all around the metro area. Add all this to the fine performances listed in Chapter 3 (All About the Arts), and you can make plans for every night of the year!

BILLIARDS & SPORTS BARS

Billiards is still a gentleman's game, but many billiards establishments around town make a special effort to accommodate women players, and some are family oriented. Billiards parlors and sports bars often occupy the same space, as many of the former offer TVs tuned in to sports events, so you can choose your activity.

American Pie. An inland beach bar and grill, "the Pie" has been in Atlanta for five years and gathers a loyal crowd. Billiard tables, dart boards, shuffleboard, and golfing games keep the patrons entertained, and at night a DJ plays favorite dancing tunes. The menu offers hamburgers and similar fare at dinner. Casual and friendly, it also has a popular deck that overlooks Roswell Road. 5840 Roswell Rd., Sandy Springs. 255-7571.

Barley's Billiards. Soon after opening, this establishment was called the classiest billiards room in the nation. With 23 tables, Barley's offers league play and free lessons. Light fare includes such items as Philly cheese steaks and turkey Reubens. 6259 Peachtree Industrial Blvd., Doraville. 455-1124.

Buckhead Billiards. In the heart of Atlanta's throbbing nightlife scene, this spot has a pleasant atmosphere with ten tables and a few TVs usually tuned in to sports events. Lessons are available but not on any special schedule. The patrons reflect every age group. Light fare is served, and the bar is open daily. 200 Pharr Rd., Buckhead. 237-3705.

Champions. Located in the Marriott Marquis Hotel, this is the king of sports bars. Big TVs, pool tables, a putting green, and football and basketball games are among the attractions. Also displayed are George Foreman's gloves and assorted baseball cards to pump up the sporting atmosphere. In the hotel lobby, you'll often see your favorite professional players, who frequently lodge at this super, sports-minded hotel. You might get an autograph or two! 265 Peachtree Center Ave., Atlanta Marriott Marquis, Downtown. 586-6017.

Chicago Pizza & Sports Arena. With 65 TVs, five large-projection screens, and five satellites, there's not a "sportier" place in the world. The Buford Highway location is the only bar in the Southeast with a **QB-1**, a sports trivia game that pits bar patrons from all over the country against each other. Rounding out the game scene are two billiard tables, pinball machines, and a putting game. Guest blues and rock bands play on Fridays and Saturdays. The Sandy Springs location has 35 TVs and three satellites. A cover is charged when live music entertains. The menu consists of brick-oven baked pizza—thin, pan, and stuffed. 8610 Roswell Rd., Dunwoody. 522-1717; 2715 Buford Hwy., near Lenox/Cheshire Bridge Rd., Northeast. 634-8630.

Dirty Al's. Noise, fun, and lots of activity center around several pool tables, sports games, and too many TVs to count. The ubiquitous tube is tuned in to sports events taking place all across the globe. Sit back and enjoy the casual, friendly crowd along with your favorite sport. 6600 Roswell Rd., Sandy Springs. 843-1260; 1402 Northside Dr., Northwest. 351-9504.

Famous Pub and Sports Palace. This sports bar for all seasons has four satellite dishes, almost 30 TVs, eight billiards tables, dart boards, and oodles of video games. Dancing and a DJ also spice things up. Full menu and no cover. 2947 N. Druid Hills Rd., Northeast. 633-3555.

Frankie's Food, Sports, & Spirits. One of Atlanta's most popular sports bars, Frankie's even attracts professional players from Atlanta's pro teams as well as their visiting competitors. Some 80 TVs and two big-projection screens broadcast sports from around the world. Live music is offered every night except Monday, and there is never a cover. The music varies from jazz to classic rock, and the menu offers mostly American fare, with a touch of Mexican and Italian. 5600 Roswell Rd., The Prado, Sandy Springs. 843-9444.

Grandstand's Food & Spirits. This sports bar is a hit with the yuppie crowd. Billiards, pinball, video games, and darts amuse the patrons, and several TVs are tuned in to sports events from around the nation. Casual attire is the order of the day and night. 3069 Peachtree Rd., Buckhead. 262-7908.

The Green Room. A quiet, refined atmosphere, with only a few small TVs, marks the Green Room as a serious billiards parlor. The menu offers sandwiches and light fare, and a complimentary buffet is served on Tuesdays and Fridays. Business people enjoy the 30 minutes of free pool included with lunch on weekdays. Busch League, handicapped Straight Pool League, and United States Pool Players Association tournaments are on the agenda. The unique Green Room also doubles as an art gallery, with rotating art shows and occasional receptions. Catering and corporate facilities are available. 4073 LaVista Rd., Northlake Tower Festival, Northeast. 934-3981.

Jocks & Jills. Co-owners include former Hawks players Doc Rivers, John Battle, Scott Hastings, and Randy Wittman. A true sports bar with 23 TVs and four satellite dishes, the place also offers an all-American menu (hamburgers and the like). Odds are that you'll run into some of Atlanta's favorite sports stars, writers, and broadcasters here. Sports mementos decorate the place, including a pair of Evander Holyfield's boxing gloves and a ball from a Braves no-hitter. A framed *Sports Illustrated* article about this bar hangs proudly in full view. Casual, fun, and friendly, the crowd mixes every age group. The Norcross location boasts the sports pennants of various teams from the last 50 years. 112 10th St., Midtown. 873-5405; 1 CNN Center, Downtown. 688-4225; 771 Britt Rd., Norcross. 491-1535; 2569 Cobb Pkwy., Marietta. 952-8401.

KB's Sports Bar. KB's "Cheers"-like atmosphere attracts many regulars, including women who say they feel comfortable here. Decidedly a neighborhood place, it serves up reasonably priced dinners and Sunday brunch, so patrons can dine while watching nine TVs. The nibble fare, including good nachos, is another draw. 2775 Clairmont Rd., at Briarcliff Rd., Williamsburg Shopping Center, Northeast. 321-0303.

Pew & Brew Restaurant and Gathering Place.
This place boasts of being Atlanta's oldest sports bar. At present, it has three satellite dishes and about a dozen TVs, several of which are big-screen. One room is dedicated to minor league baseball, and patrons travel to games in faraway locations just so they can return to the Pew & Brew with a pennant for the bar. The menu offers basic bar fare, with burgers, salads, and chicken grills. 80 Powers Ferry Rd., Marietta. 565-7397.

Sandy Springs Billiards.
Competition awaits both the expert and the novice at this popular 5,000-square-foot northside parlor. Fifteen tables, one snooker table, two big-screen satellite TVs, and one smaller set keep the crowds happy. Play free pool with lunch Monday through Friday. Full bar service is available, and lunch and dinner, including half-pound burgers done anyway you want are served. Open daily to the wee hours.

In Atlanta's earliest days, Whitehall Street was the site of the White Hall Tavern, where soldiers from the 530th Militia District gathered for drill on "muster" day. The area was frequently the scene of rowdy behavior, but especially when the militia showed up. After the drill, a cow was awarded to the soldier who was the best shot, but no matter who won it, the beast was slaughtered, cooked, and consumed, together with much whiskey.

Ladies' night, on Monday after 6 P.M., offers half-price pool. On Tuesday nights, members of the Anheuser Busch League for nationally sanctioned handicapped tournament pool take over. 5920 Roswell Rd., Parkside Shopping Center (on the back side, which is actually Sandy Springs Cir.), Sandy Springs. 257-0888.

Sports Oasis.
This sports bar boasts a giant ten-foot projection TV screen plus four smaller TVs and video games. On weekends, the live band plays a variety of tunes, and a jukebox spins at other times. The full menu includes prime rib, baby back ribs, big shrimp, and steaks. Beer and wine only. 1792 Panola Rd., at Flakes Mill Rd., in the Ingles shopping center, Ellenwood, Southeast. 593-9505.

Stooges Sports Bar & Restaurant.
The original owners of this casual sports bar say *this* was Atlanta's first sports bar (established 1980). Who knows? The atmosphere invites patrons to relax, enjoy their favorite sporting events, and possibly rub elbows with a sports celebrity or two. Steaks, burgers, munchies, and potato skins are on the menu. Lunch specials offer down-home cooking, Monday through Friday. 2020 Howell Mill Rd., Howell Mill Village Shopping Center, Northwest. 355-5445.

Three Dollar Cafe. The cafe's very casual atmosphere comes with a giant TV screen that's always tuned in to sports. The wings are the specialty on the good, inexpensive menu. The Buckhead location has an appealing atmosphere that attracts singles and young couples. The Marietta and Dunwoody locations are more family oriented; they serve no liquor but a variety of beers, including lots of non-alcoholic brews, and some wines are offered. They also have several TVs for sports fans. 3002 Peachtree Rd., at Pharr Rd., Buckhead. 266-8667; 8595 Roswell Rd., Dunwoody. 992-5011; 2580 Windy Hill Rd., at I-75, Marietta. 850-0868; 2166 Highpoint Rd., Snellville. 736-1000.

BLUES

The South, as is well known, is the home of the Blues—and one of the best places to listen to this music is right here in the capital of the New South.

Blind Willie's. Long a favorite night spot of Atlanians who like blues and don't mind cramming into a narrow, brick-walled space, Blind Willie's hosts some of the best blues anywhere. Visiting musical groups and headliners appear nightly, often drawing large crowds that spill out onto the sidewalk. Cajun and zydeco are also featured *(see below).* 828 N. Highland Ave., Virginia-Highland. 873-2583.

Blues Harbor. When nationally famous Blues Harbor moved from Buckhead to its new location in refurbished Underground Atlanta, a New Orleans–style band slid down Peachtree Street to the slow rhythm of a jazz funeral dirge. Certainly, the old place deserved such an adieu—but the new one, which features a blues pianist, swings with very high energy. Chicago–style blues is the draw these days. Visitors and locals of every age mix here, drawn by the inexpensive and often surprisingly good food. 2293 Peachtree Rd., Buckhead. 605-0661.

CAJUN & ZYDECO

Finally getting the recognition it so richly deserves, the traditional music of Louisiana is a unique Southern sound.

Blind Willie's. Down-home Cajun music fills the air from time to time, played by bands that are often brought directly from Louisiana. Recent examples include Chubby Carrier, John Delafose and the Eunice Playboys (all zydeco), and Filé (Cajun). *Laissez les bons temps roulez!* See p. 37. 828 N. Highland Ave., Virginia-Highland. 873-2583.

COMEDY

Atlanta's comedy scene gets real respect from many nationally famous funny folks. From time to time, they show up just to check out the local chuckle factor. Who knows who you'll see!

A Comic Cafe. Choose your dinner from a full-service prime rib–type menu, then sit back and savor top comedic talent. Open Monday through Saturday. Cover charge. 1215 Powers Ferry Rd., Marietta. 350-6990.

The Punch Line. A major fixture on the Atlanta comedy club scene, The Punch Line brings fine local talents and national comedy stars to its stage. Eddie Murphy has been known to fly in from Los Angeles—unannounced of course—to try out new material on lucky Punch Line audiences. 280 Hilderbrand Dr., Balconies Shopping Center, Sandy Springs. 252-5233.

COUNTRY & WESTERN

Authentic American music—that's what "CW" really is. Atlanta offers some fine opportunities to take in the best.

Austin Avenue Buffet. Definitely a good ole boy (and gal) place, it offers impromptu jam sessions from time to time. A fellow named "Slim Chance," a well-known regular at this fifty-year-old pub, leads the old-fashioned, down-home hootenannies. (By day, Slim is a behavioral specialist who treats mentally handicapped children.) Hamburgers, hot dogs, and beef stew make up the fare. 918 Austin Ave., Inman Park. 524-9274.

Buckboard Country Music Showcase. Country music by the house band, with special performances by outstanding spotlight entertainers, has made the Buckboard a thumpin' place for more than a decade. Call for information on star attractions (Garth Brooks appeared here in 1990!). The cover charge depends on the entertainer. For two hours on Mondays and Wednesdays beginning around 7 P.M., free dance lessons help patrons to untangle their feet. Generally open until 3 A.M. six days a week. 2080 Cobb Pkwy., Windy Hill Plaza, Smyrna. 955-7340.

Copper Dollar Saloon. Live country music and dancing really get this crowd going to the country sounds of the Ron Kimble Band. Wings, sandwiches, and light fare sustain the crowds, and the pool tables and dart boards augment the entertainment. Open daily. Cover charge Thursday through Saturday only. 2272

Lawrenceville Hwy., Decatur. 325-5342;
5938 Buford Hwy., Doraville. 457-1448.

Crystal Chandelier. Seating 3700, the
Crystal Chandelier is the largest Country-Western club this side of the Mississippi. Besides sponsoring well-known
national acts, the Crystal Chandelier
offers dance lessons Wednesdays, Fridays, and Saturdays. Ladies Night on
Wednesdays features the Balloon
Drop, where thousands of balloons are
released from the ceiling stuffed with
cash and other prizes. Family Day on
Sunday is alcohol free and the $5
cover charge includes dance lessons
and a free buffet. The eleven member
house band, Hired Guns, opens for
every in-house concert in addition to
playing Wednesdays through Saturdays. Special arrangements for group
functions are available. 1750 North
Roberts Rd., Kennesaw. 426-5006.

Miss Kitty's Saloon & Dance Hall.
Miss Kitty's in Marietta is a study in local
culture. With live music from Tuesday
to Saturday and a nightly full-service
menu at the Texas Cafe inside the
saloon, this is the place for low-down
country music and dancing to the
good ole Texas two-step. Travis Tritt
performed here before moving on to
win the prestigious County Music Horizon award. Classes in the two-step,
swing, and line dances are offered on
Mondays and Tuesdays from 8 P.M. to
11 P.M. 1038 Franklin Rd., Marietta. 426-
9077.

Dodge City Saloon & Dance Hall.
Dancing, live country music, pool
tables, and a full menu make this a
popular place in Norcross. 5525 Jimmy
Carter Blvd., at I-85, Norcross. 263-6097.

DANCING

If you've got two left feet, check out some of the learning opportunities
in Chapter 9 (Expanding Your Mind), then hit the places listed below
to show off your newly acquired skills.

Another World. Atop the Atlanta Hilton
Hotel, Another World has long been a
favorite of both visitors and locals. A DJ
plays music from the '50s, usually until
2 A.M. 225 Courtland St., Atlanta Hilton
and Towers, Downtown. 659-2000.

Backstreet Atlanta. For an alternative
experience, head to Backstreet, a 24-
hour gay nightclub featuring drag
shows and adult dancers. Voted the
best place for men to meet men,
Backstreet is a wildly eccentric club
dedicating its entire bottom level to

dancing. Every weekend night is the
tantalizing **Charlie Brown's Cabaret**.
Backstreet offers special discounts for
members. 845 Peachtree St., Midtown.
873-1986.

Bentley's Lounge. A popular hotel
bar, Bentley's boasts a regular, local
clientele that dances to top-40 tunes
spun on a CD jukebox (Fridays and
Saturdays) until 2 A.M. Bentley's is also a
sports bar with eight TVs. Both appe-
tizer and full meal (prime rib–type)
menus are available. On Tuesday and

Wednesday nights, karaoke begins at 9 P.M. Vince, the singing bartender, usually starts the show, and then the patrons break into song. Their performances are recorded on laser disc, and a cassette tape copy goes to the singing patrons, some of whom are very good. No cover. Casual to dressy. 4711 Best Rd., Atlanta Airport Marriott, College Park. 766-7900 (ext. 6663).

Candide. Dance Wednesdays through Fridays until 4 A.M., Saturdays until 3 A.M., and Sundays until 4 A.M., with a DJ making the music spin. Most patrons are on the younger side of forty, but older folks often check it out. Regularly changing art exhibits are part of the scene, which is marked by a pleasant ambience and good fun. 3055 Peachtree Rd., at Bolling Way, Buckhead. 231-1574.

> One of Atlanta's most colorful society figures was Lucy Peel, wife of Colonel William Lawson Peel and a significant contributor to Atlanta's long-term relationship with the Metropolitan Opera. Referring to this dowager society queen, another matron was heard to exclaim: "Atlanta people love a romp. Always have. Surely you've heard of Lucy Peel?" Mrs. Peel was indeed known for "loving a romp."

Chicagos. Monday through Friday, it's Chicagos Restaurant and Nightclub, offering business lunches and an after-work buffet from 5 P.M. to 8 P.M. A keyboard vocalist entertains during the buffet, which is themed differently each night. After 9 P.M., Monday through Thursday, it becomes a nightclub. On Friday and Saturday nights, the place restyles itself as Chicagos Latin Dance Club and comes alive to the throb of *salsa* and other Latin rhythms played by live groups. Open until 2 or 3 A.M. No food after 8 P.M. or on the weekends, but full bar service is available. Cover charge. 4401 Shallowford Rd., Roswell. 993-7464.

Houlihan's. A northside happy hour and dance spot with a DJ playing the top 40 for an audience ranging from ages 25 to 55, Houlihan's is a jammed and thumpin' place. The dining room serves a full menu. Three locations, but only Dunwoody has a dance floor: 4505 Ashford-Dunwoody Rd., Park Place, Dunwoody. 394-8921.

Johnny's Hideaway. This is a popular place with all age groups, but the forty-plus crowd has made it their special spot. Dancing to 'forties and 'fifties music, with some newer tunes thrown in for universal appeal, means Johnny's is no longer a hideaway. A large bar and lots of conversation and fun are supplemented by the varied, reasonably priced menu. Lunch is served daily, and food service continues until 4 A.M. 3771 Roswell Rd., Buckhead. 233-8026.

The Masquerade. A multilevel nightclub warehouse located in the old Excelsior Mill, Masquerade houses **Heaven, Hell** and **Purgatory**. Heaven features a concert hall continually hosting big name bands. Smaller local acoustic bands play in the Purgatory bar. The Masquerade's dance club Hell is available for rentals, clubbing out, and private parties Sunday through Tuesday nights. 695 North Ave., Downtown. 577-8178.

The Ritz-Carlton, Buckhead. The **Café Bar** fairly hums with live music and dancing on Friday and Saturday nights. 3434 Peachtree Rd., Buckhead. 237-2700.

Rupert's. An alive and electric setting matches the music from large ensembles and vocalists. Open Tuesday, Thursday, Friday, and Saturday. Be sure to call ahead to see who's playing. Check out the complimentary buffet served at 5:30 P.M. (except on Saturdays). Cover after 8 P.M. 3330 Piedmont Rd., Buckhead. 266-9834.

Sherwood's Southside's Finest. A DJ plays music from the '50s through the '90s for dancing. A great people-watching place, it serves hamburgers and offers a happy hour buffet. 4736 Best Rd., Renaissance Hotel, College Park. 762-7676.

Stouffer Waverly Hotel. The big band sound and dancing start at 7 P.M. on Friday evenings. Until 10 P.M., when the dancing ends, the music fairly reverberates off the marble atrium walls in this elegant hotel. There is an admission charge—and, for another moderate charge, you can enjoy a buffet and the dancing at one price. The dance is free to registered hotel guests. 2450 Galleria Pkwy., Northwest. 953-4500.

Studebaker's. A DJ plays music from the '50s through the '90s for dancing. Its two locations are great people-watching places. Marietta offers a happy hour buffet. 2359 Windy Hill Rd., Marietta. 984-2315; 4736 Best Rd., Renaissance Hotel, College Park. 559-7329.

T-Birds. Oldies rock 'n' roll reigns here with a DJ who spins the best dance music from the '50s, '60s, and '70s. A live band sometimes takes over the same eras on Thursdays—though a few new tunes are thrown in now and again. That's why T-Birds attracts a crowd aged 25 to fifty. Pizza and subs are the fare, and the dress is casual. Cover, but on Wednesday nights ladies are admitted free. 5831 Memorial Dr., Stone Mountain. 292-2838.

Velvet. Featured in *Newsweek* as one of the hottest nightclubs in the nation, this high-energy place presents progressive dance music and an occasional live club act for entertainment. Generally open until 3 A.M. No food. Cover. 89 Park Pl., Downtown. 681-9936.

FILM

From art film cinemas to suds-and-celluloid establishments, Atlanta offers a variety of choices when it comes to going to the movies. For art film cinemas, see Chapter 3 (All About the Arts).

Cinema N' Drafthouse/Cinema Grill. North Springs shows films on their second run for a fraction of what it cost to see them as first-run films. Beer, wine, and a dinner menu are available. Comfortable tables and chairs make for a very relaxing night at the movies. This is the only such place in the metro area at the time of this writing. 7270 Roswell Rd., North Springs Shopping Center, Sandy Springs. 395-0724.

JAZZ

Like blues, jazz is closely identified with the South and is a uniquely American musical form. Check out the following for some fine sounds.

Cafe 290. Live jazz seven nights a week makes this neighborhood cafe a lively spot. Regulars love the place. An American menu is available for light dinners. Open until 4 A.M. Call for the performance schedule. 290 Hilderbrand Dr., Balconies Shopping Center, Sandy Springs. 256-3942.

Dante's Down the Hatch. Popular for more than twenty years—and for good reason—Dante's, Buckhead, has been home to one of the best jazz groups in the country, the Paul Mitchell Trio. Folk singers hold forth on the wharf, and sometimes there's classical guitar. And, yes, at both locations, you actually board ship! The music starts around 5 P.M., depending on the day of the week and the location. As to food, it's been fondue forever at Dante's. The long-popular chocolate fondue is reserved for weekdays (no holidays), and must be ordered two days in advance for a minimum of six persons (Buckhead only). Ask to have Dante Stephenson serve it personally, if possible. Cover. 3380 Peachtree Rd., Buckhead. 266-1600; 60 Upper Alabama St., Underground Atlanta, Downtown. 577-1800.

Just Jazz. Guest artists start the music around 9 P.M. and play until the late...later...latest hours. Complimentary buffet on Friday evenings. Cover. 2101 Tula St., Bennett Street, Brookwood. 355-5423.

La Carrousel Lounge. One of Atlanta's best black jazz clubs and a favorite of the entire Atlanta community for more than thirty years, this lounge features local and national jazz ensembles of major significance. Free buffet at Friday's happy hour. 830 Martin Luther King, Jr., Dr., Northwest. 577-3150.

Peachtree Cafe. Jazz played until about midnight infuses one of Buckhead's most popular spots with some fine sounds. A new chef from one of Atlanta's poshest restaurants has revived a tired menu with light, appetizing dishes (pasta, seafood, chicken). An upwardly mobile crowd dresses in tastefully casual style. 268 E. Paces Ferry Rd., Buckhead. 233-4402.

Ray's on the River. Overlooking the Chattahoochee, this large yet intimate restaurant is the scene of some spunky, live jazz until about 1 A.M. The casual menu offers sustenance for the evening. 6700 Powers Ferry Rd., Northwest. 955-1187.

Ritz-Carlton Hotels. Both hotels, one in Downtown and the other in Buckhead, feature jazz groups in their bars. Elegant in decor and with clientele to match, The Bar at each hotel is an excellent place to relax and enjoy friends along with the music. The music plays each night until about midnight, sometimes later on Saturdays. At the Ritz-Carlton, Buckhead, The Bar is often the scene of performances by jazz musicians of national importance. No cover and no reservations are required (except for selected performers). 181 Peachtree St., Downtown. 659-0400; 3434 Peachtree Rd., Buckhead. 237-2700.

PIANO BARS

Easy listening and the fun of a sing-along make piano bars permanently popular. These are among Atlanta's best.

590 West. Finish an evening Downtown and enjoy one of Atlanta's most breathtaking skyline views. Piano entertainment every day but Sunday begins at 5 P.M. and continues until midnight during the week and until 1 A.M. Friday and Saturday nights. A light bar menu of fruits and cheese is available. 590 W. Peachtree St., Penta Hotel, Midtown. 881-6000.

Jellyrolls Dueling Pianos & Sing-a-Long. Guaranteed to keep your night rockin' and rollin' with dueling pianos, Jellyrolls is a perfect place for a lively night on the town. Two pianists on stage at a time take requests from the audience and play anything from the '50s to the present. Popular for birthday and bachelorette parties, Jellyrolls is

known for its unabashed audience interaction. 295 East Paces Ferry Rd., Buckhead. 261-6866.

Killeen's Restaurant & Piano Bar. The piano bar plays the standards as well as top-40, and in the early evenings, music from the '30s through the '90s fills the air. The dance floor is tucked away in a living room setting on a mezzanine level, perfect for after 10 P.M. The atmosphere is posh and sophisticated as well as warm, intimate, and casual. Part of the warmth comes from the original stone and brick walls that formed the 1838 Roswell mill. In the dining room, an American-Continental menu features good steaks, seafood, oversized salads, and pasta dishes. The value-conscious wine list contains lots of California wines. This is a one-stop entertainment place, offering everything from cocktails to after-dinner dancing. 85 Mill St., at Hwy. 120 and Roswell Rd., Roswell Mill, Roswell. 518-0835.

Ottley's Lounge. Jazz and show tunes warm up an elegant setting that invites lots of after-work and before-dinner conversation. This is simply one of Atlanta's most inviting spots, especially for those who disdain a raucous, electrifying ambience. 3300 Lenox Rd., J.W. Marriott Hotel, Lenox Square, Buckhead. 262-3344.

Otto's. This sophisticated piano bar has an ambience that attracts the well-heeled and cosmopolitan. Once a jazz club, it has been enlarged without loss of its intimacy. This popular spot is the place to see and be seen, yet the atmosphere is friendly. A limited pizza menu is the only fare. 265 E. Paces Ferry Rd., Buckhead. 233-1133.

Park Place Cafe. Entertainment begins at 6 P.M., Monday through Friday, in this popular after-business gathering spot. The versatile pianist also sings and plays the sax. Lots of regulars enjoy both the music and the buffet. 4505 Ashford-Dunwoody Rd., Park Place, Dunwoody. 399-5990.

Winfield's. Ginny Cole has been the regular here for several years. She plays a wide variety of selections, ranging from classical to jazz, Broadway to oldies, and pop to Gershwin. It's a good after-work spot, and the music continues until late in the evening on weekends. The restaurant, a Peasant establishment, serves good contemporary American fare. 1 Galleria Pkwy., Galleria Specialty Mall, Northwest. 955-5300.

ROCK

Blending the best of American folk music—especially gospel and blues—rock today is as universal as air. These Atlanta establishments are on the cutting edge.

Chameleon Club. Rock, alternative/progressive music, and blues (on Wednesdays), keep the club open every night until 4 A.M., and there's a big dance floor. Dress is very casual, and very light snack food (popcorn and pretzels) is available. This community-oriented club does frequent benefits. Cover. The adjacent pub, **Heights**, has pool tables, a big-screen TV, and the same munchies. No cover. 3179 Peachtree Rd., next to Sound Warehouse, Buckhead. 261-8004.

Charley Magruder's Bar & Deli. If you can find room on the dance floor, rock out with the DJ and swing to hit tunes from the '70s, '80s, and '90s. The good menu presents full meals. Cover. 6300 Powers Ferry Rd., Powers Ferry Village Shopping Center, Northwest. 955-1157.

Cotton Club. The shows begin at 10 P.M., but the club is open only when entertainment is booked. If you're a rock fan, watch for the schedule in the weekend paper, as the club brings in some top talent. Known to support good causes, the Cotton Club sometimes charges a special entrance fee of canned food. 1021 Peachtree St., Midtown. 874-9524.

Dark Horse Tavern. Live entertainment, from rock to reggae, is presented every night downstairs. Casual dress is appropriate for the tavern atmosphere. Upstairs is a full-service restaurant and bar. Cover. 816 N. Highland Ave., Virginia-Highland. 873-3607.

Good Ol' Days. A longtime favorite of the young crowd, this is a good place to meet old friends and make new ones. It's casual and presents live rock music. The menu is simple but satisfying. No cover. Three locations: 3013 Peachtree Rd., Buckhead. 266-2597; 5841 Roswell Rd., Sandy Springs. 257-9183; 401 Moreland Ave., Little Five Points. 688-1006.

Oxford Espresso Acoustic Cafe. The Oxford bookstores have never been content to be merely outstanding book stores, but have always wanted to be more. The largest, Oxford Buckhead, has a coffee shop that becomes a superior "hangin' out" place three days a week. On Sundays, Mondays, and Tuesdays, beginning at 8:30 P.M., acoustic performances are held in the Oxford Espresso Cafe. No alcohol, just great espresso. Now we understand what keeps that parking lot packed on Sunday evenings. 360 Pharr Rd., Buckhead. 266-8350.

The Point. Every night a different group entertains with updated, upbeat rock and reggae. Shows usually start at 10 P.M. Nationally famous, The Point often works for good causes, so sometimes the cover is several cans of food. Cover. 420 Moreland Ave., Little Five Points. 659-3522.

Scrap Bar. The Scrap Bar is hard to overlook with its intriguing scrap metal decor. Catering to a business lunch crowd by day, the pace at the Scrap Bar picks up at night until 3 A.M. This unusual watering hole has a full bar and an inexpensive menu serving pizzas, salad, and sandwiches. Each night live bands vibrate the walls with music ranging from heavy metal to blues and ska. 1080 Peachtree St., Buckhead. 724-0009.

Trackside Tavern. This downtown Decatur establishment entertains the neighborhood crowd, so there's no cover. Acoustic music, all original, is performed by such talents as Indigo Girls (appearing occasionally), Michelle Malone, Kristen Hall, and Kodac Harrison. 313 E. College Ave., Decatur. 373-9170.

Wreck Room. It caters to all ages, but since a special reduced cover is reserved for Georgia Tech students with ID, lots of the college crowd shows up. A one-dollar general admission cover is charged on Mondays and Thursdays. Music—mostly assorted styles of heavy metal and rock—plays until 4 A.M. Monday through Saturday. 800 Marietta St., Downtown. 874-8544.

TAVERNS & PUBS

Southerners aren't accustomed to the idea of the "neighborhood" tavern that's a fixture in the North. But these spots capture the atmosphere that made them—and their British and Irish counterpart, the pub—quickly popular in Atlanta.

Aunt Charley's. This is an authentic neighborhood bar with a congenial atmosphere and lots of local patrons. The darts are a major source of fun competition. Billiards and backgammon are also popular. Lunch and dinner offer a simple but well-prepared menu, and the burgers are great. Charley's patio overlooks Buckhead Park. 3107 Peachtree Rd., Buckhead. 231-8503.

Churchill Arms. Regulars hang their own mugs in this very "pubby," very British neighborhood spot. Darts, chess, backgammon, and Trivial Pursuit are the favorite "sports." Friday and Saturday nights rock to piano sing-along entertainment. The Peachtree Chorus Barbershoppers sing on Mondays, and darts competition usually gets underway on Monday for any interested patrons and on Wednesday evenings for league players. Not much in the way of food, but plenty in the way of conviviality. 3223 Cains Hill Pl., Buckhead. 233-5633.

County Cork. County Cork has been doing rollicking business for a half-dozen years or so. The bill of fare includes Irish stew, sausage, meat pie, and, as a special, really good fried oysters—that sort of Irish pub grub. The lilt of Irish tunes wafts through the air, and the second Sunday afternoon of each month brings authentic Irish music into the place. Performances are live. A real fiddler, with companions on drums and other traditional instruments, performed one Sunday afternoon. 56 E. Andrews Dr., Andrews Square, Buckhead. 262-2227; 5600 Roswell Rd., Sandy Springs. 303-1976.

Dudley's Food & Spirits. Two satellite dishes and many TVs sometimes make this a southside sports connection. Dance to top-40 tunes as a DJ spins your favorites while laser karaoke flashes images and lyrics on a screen. The menu features south-of-the-border fare, burgers, seafood, and sandwiches. 2565 Wesley Chapel Rd., Decatur. 289-8783.

Dugan's. The collection of beers would dazzle any champion suds slugger. The number of brands inventoried has been reduced to make room for more patron space, but they'll still stock about sixty internationally popular beers, plus numerous beers on tap. Unusual liqueurs and after-dinner potables round out the bar service. The fare consists of chicken wings—which the establishment claims originated at Dugan's—nachos, salads, and sandwiches. A pleasant patio and ten or so TVs contribute to the atmosphere. 777 Ponce de Leon Ave., Poncey-Highland. 885-1217.

Dugan's Tavern. Little brother to the Ponce de Leon operation, Patrick Dugan's other establishment is a bit more refined (the food is served on china rather than paper plates, for instance). The same menu and beers galore are offered. The outside patio is nifty. 5922 Memorial Dr., Stone Mountain. 297-8545.

Limerick Junction. Join singers from the auld sod and come prepared to make requests and to perform your own version of "The Unicorn." Irish eats such as Irish stew, Irish brew and whiskey, and a warm, neighborhood pub atmosphere attract the families who live nearby in Atkins Park and Virginia-Highland—though it's surprising how many patrons on any given night hail from the outer reaches of the metro area. 822 N. Highland Ave., Virginia-Highland. 874-7147.

Manuel's Tavern. In the original location, established in 1956, the college crowd, politicos, and business people gather after work to bend elbows and munch hot dogs. A former U.S. president and his wife, whose offices are nearby, have been known to drop in for just such refreshment. Not a quiche type of place. There are several Manuel's around town, but none equals the original's great tavern atmosphere: 602 N. Highland Ave., Poncey-Highland. 525-3447; other locations: 3330 Peachtree Corners Cir., Norcross. 446-8250; 4877 Memorial Dr., Stone Mountain (a sports bar loaded with TVs). 296-6919.

McNeeley's. After a dozen years, the atmosphere remains relaxed in this neighborhood tavern, where co-owners John McNeeley and Susan Lindley

are usually on site. Known primarily for its food, McNeeley's has a 38-item menu featuring salmon fingers, grilled chicken, and mushroom quesadillas. Cajun fried shrimp and baby back ribs are also popular. Sports by satellite and live entertainment, Thursday through Saturday, appeal to a large audience. The deck overlooking Peachtree Street is usually thronged with hungry folks. Takeout available. 1900 Peachtree Rd., at Collier Rd., Brookwood. 351-1957.

Prince of Wales. An English pub overlooking Midtown's Piedmont Park. Mahogany bar and oak benches create a cozy atmosphere to enjoy traditional "pub grub" such as steak and ale pie. The bar features twelve draft beers and a wide selection of single malt whiskies. Ask about their yards of ale. 1144 Piedmont Ave., Midtown. 876-0227.

Rocco's Pub. A neighborhood bar and restaurant, Rocco's mixes an eclectic group of patrons, from attorneys and physicians to construction workers. Owner Danny Ciorrocco is a six-time winner of the Georgia Chili Cook-Off, so don't miss this Texas treat—the kind without beans. Danny and wife Mindy are usually on site to add the personal touch. 1393 Roswell Rd., Town and Country Shopping Center (1/2 mile east of the "Big Chicken"), Marietta. 971-8806.

Rose and Crown. Located in downtown Buckhead, this authentic English pub features specialties such as fish n' chips, chicken and Guinness pie, and bangers and mash. The massive stone hearth fireplace creates an Old World atmosphere where patrons can enjoy real draft ales, billiards, and darts. 288 East Paces Ferry Rd., Buckhead. 233-8168.

The Stein Club.

Midtown simply wouldn't be Midtown without the Stein Club. For more than thirty years, it's been famous for its entertaining mix of characters and its jukebox—probably the largest in the area, with over 3,000 titles. Regular patrons bring in their favorite 45s to play on it. The annual spelling bee, held the last Saturday in January, brings out some of Atlanta's finest orthographic talents. 929 Peachtree St., Midtown. 876-3707.

Taco Mac.

How long would it take to drink your way through all these imported beers? Taco Mac stocks about 100 different brands in each location, so nibble the buffalo wings while you sample the brews (several nonalcoholic brands are also always available). All locations present a casual, neighborhood bar atmosphere, and seven of them dot the metro area. Some are sports bars. Call the original to find the location nearest you: 1006 N. Highland Ave., Virginia-Highland. 873-6529.

VARIETY

Many fine Atlanta night spots offer assorted entertainments, ranging from excellent vocalists to instrumental performances to virtual reality games.

Banks & Shane.

Sometimes crazy, sometimes wild, always funny and always fun, Banks & Shane is a popular local spot. Guest stars appear frequently with Banks Burgess and Paul Shane, who play music while injecting a good bit of humor into the performance. The well-known dinner menu has a terrific steak, and now lunch is served by popular Atlanta restaurateurs, the Cashins. 315 Watercress Dr., Roswell. 642-2041.

Carbo's Cafe.

Sophisticated music and conversation are this bar's offerings. On Monday nights, a guitarist takes over. Appetizers and desserts from the regular menu are available every weeknight until 10:30 P.M. and later on weekends. 3717 Roswell Rd., Buckhead. 231-4433.

Dave and Buster's.

Add a little mystery to your evening by enjoying a three part Murder Mystery Dinner that invites you to solve the mystery at the end of the show! Complete with a showroom, shuffleboard, black jack, billiards, video games, and the new "virtual reality world," Dave and Buster's promises a night of unique entertainment. Private shows may be arranged for parties of sixty or more. 2215 D & B Dr., Marietta. 951-5554.

The Freight Room.

This popular spot has been in the old Decatur railway depot for more than a decade. Wednesday night is musical showcase night for local artists, and Sunday is open mike night, usually featuring an acoustic music jam. Bluegrass, featured on Thursday nights, is also popular. The menu offers a variety of sand-wiches and salads. No cover unless there's a special performance. 301 E. Howard Ave., Decatur. 378-5365.

Homage Coffee House. From Thurs-day through Sunday live bands play a variety of music to an eclectic audi-ence. Food items range from sand-wiches to salads, stirfries to soups *(see chapter 1)*. Free jazz plays throughout Sunday brunch, but a cover is charged at most other times. Open Monday through Friday for lunch. Homage is also an art gallery that features con-temporary work by local and area art-ists. Available for private parties. 255 Trinity Ave., Downtown. 681-2662; 1174 Euclid Ave., Little Five Points. 522-7471.

Joyful Noise. This long-established Chris-tian supper club presents a variety of family entertainment and a buffet supper. One ticket includes both the show and the supper. 2669 Church St., East Point. 768-5100.

CHAPTER 3

All About the Arts

Atlanta audiences wholeheartedly support the arts in their hometown, flocking to take in theatrical, dance, and symphonic performances, to enjoy the jazz and the arts festivals, and to hear the opera and assorted fine choirs.

The Woodruff Arts Center serves as one of Atlanta's most vital cultural hubs as home to the Atlanta Symphony Orchestra and the Alliance Theater. The ASO is recognized as a major force in the international music scene, with fourteen Grammy Awards, while the Alliance Theater was chosen as one of only four theaters in the United States to host the touring production of the Tony-award-winning *Angels in America*.

Many other professional, college and community theaters flourish here as well, from Theatre Gael, the only Celtic theater in the Southeast, to the highly acclaimed Center for Puppetry Arts. Film is also gaining a foothold in Atlanta, from international film festivals to actual filmmaking. The trend started with *Gone with the Wind*, but more recent projects have included *Driving Miss Daisy*, filmed in the Druid Hills area, and Terry Kay's *To Dance with the White Dog*, a Hallmark Hall of Fame television movie.

DANCE

Each holiday season, relive the enchantment of *The Nutcracker*, performed annually by many resident Atlanta dance groups. Enjoy the performances of visiting dance troupes, such as Mexico's vibrant Ballet Folklórico Nacional or the Dance Theater of Harlem. Explore the city's rich variety of concert dance experiences and assortment of dance expressions.

Atlanta Ballet. Founded more than 60 years ago by the late Dorothy Moses Alexander, the Atlanta Ballet is the nation's oldest continuously performing regional ballet company. The company performs a range of works, from the classics like the annual presentation of The Nutcracker, to new works by emerging choreographers. The Atlanta Ballet and its orchestra, under the direction of Thomas Ludwig, perform at the Civic Center. 477 Peachtree St., Downtown. 873-5811 (office); 892-3303 (tickets).

Atlanta Dance Unlimited. The performance company for the Dancer's Studio/Backstage, Atlanta Dance Unlimited presents ballet, jazz, and tap. More than a decade old, ADU enlists top choreographers from across the country and performs throughout the year. An annual spring concert and the "Jazz on Tap" festival are highlights. Performances are at the 14th Street Playhouse, and other venues around the city *(see chapter 9)*. 8560 Holcomb Bridge Rd., Ste. 118, Alpharetta. 993-2623.

Ballet Rotaru. Dancer Pavel Rotaru spent a year with the Atlanta Ballet before forming his own company. International Ballet Rotaru focuses on the classics; its *Carmen* is just one ex-

ample of this professional company's exciting productions. Rotaru's full-length productions of many ballets never before performed in their entirety by an Atlanta company, such as *Don Quixote*, are major events in the city's arts calendar. Rotaru says that this is the only company in the United States that trains dancers in the Kirov tradition. The company is composed of approximately 25 full-time professional dancers and fifteen full-time apprentice dancers on scholarship *(see chapter 9)*. All performances are at the Fox Theatre. Studio: 6000 Peachtree Industrial Blvd., Norcross. 662-0993; Office: 3162 Maple Dr., Buckhead. 395-5322.

Ballethnic Dance Company. Former members of the Dance Theater of Harlem and the Atlanta Ballet, Nena Gilreath and Waverly Lucas formed this new Atlanta company in 1990. A professional company, Ballethnic presents classical and ethnic dance with an emphasis on dramatic expression. Besides performances, the company offers workshops, classes, demonstrations, and residencies *(see chapter 9)*. P.O. Box 7749, Atlanta, 30357-0749. 762-1416.

Beacon Dance Company. Begun as the Decatur-DeKalb Ballet more than thirty years ago, Beacon Dance Company has evolved into a 38-member organization serving professionals, apprentices, and juniors. Affiliated with the Decatur School of Ballet *(see chapter 9)*, Beacon is a contemporary dance company that performs a diverse repertoire under the direction of D. Patton White. The company commissions ballets from local, regional, and national sources. Many of its professional dancers and choreographers come from the Atlanta area, providing needed work opportunities in dance. Often collaborating with artists in other media, Beacon performs three to four times per year. The company strives to bring dance programs to seniors and children who do not experience much artistic enrichment. Performances are at various locations in the metro area. Studio and office: 410 W. Trinity Pl., Beacon Hill Arts Center, Decatur. 377-6927.

Dancer's Collective of Atlanta, Inc.

This nonprofit, grant-supported group is an umbrella organization that supports local dancers through such activities as fund raising and marketing. It is especially noted for contemporary dance presentations and performance art. Events on the agenda include symposiums, workshops, classes, lectures, and demonstrations by visiting and local artists. Performances are at various locations around town. Mail only: 4279 Roswell Rd., Ste. 604-335, Atlanta, 30342. 233-7600.

Emory Dance Company. Students

taking dance courses at Emory often perform, choreograph, and produce their work with guest artists. The company regularly commissions works by local and national guest artists. Discounts are available for seniors, students, and artists. Performances are at Dobbs University Center, 605 Asbury Cir., Emory University, Northeast. 727-6187 (box office).

Georgia Ballet. A jewel in Atlanta's

suburban fine arts crown, this Marietta-based company was founded over thirty years ago. Directed by Iris Hensley, it brings internationally acclaimed artists to Cobb County to perform classic and original works. Known for its outreach programs, which bring ballet to area schools, it annually performs *The Nutcracker*. Ticket prices are extremely reasonable, making this one of Atlanta's performing arts values. All performances are at the Cobb Civic Center. Studio: 999 Whitlock Ave., Marietta. 425-0258.

Lee Harper & Dancers. One of At-

lanta's seasoned troupes, this company performs a variety of styles, from classical to contemporary. Lee Harper has extensive credentials, having attended Julliard and graduated from the North Carolina School of the Arts. She has performed with many well-known groups, including the Alvin Ailey American Dance Theatre. Partner Jan Duffy, a former member of the company, studied at East Carolina University, where she performed with the East Carolina Playhouse Dancers. Seven Stages is among the company's favorite performance venues. Harper and Duffy are also well known for their teaching *(see chapter 9)*. Studio: 721 Miami Cir., Ste. 106, Buckhead. 261-7416.

Room to Move. Established in New York

City in 1981, this contemporary dance company found its way to Atlanta in

1984. Directed by Amy Gately, it produces two major performances a year at the 14th Street Theater, showcasing the work of Gately, guest choreographers, and participating artists from other media. The "Seniors in Motion" program is a unique series of movement workshops for older adults. As a result of this program, RTM's focus has changed from children to seniors. It plans to take this program to several senior citizen centers throughout Atlanta and to Fulton County libraries (see chapter 9). P.O. Box 8555, Atlanta, 30306. 847-0453.

Ruth Mitchell Dance Theatre. For three decades, Ruth Mitchell has cultivated a contemporary repertoire of jazz and ballet. Her professional company also presents new works by Mitchell as well as other local and regional choreographers. Mitchell is well known as a teacher of dance (see chapter

9). Performances, including the company's interpretation of Nutcracker, are staged in a variety of local venues. 3509 Northside Pkwy., at W. Paces Ferry Rd., Buckhead. 237-8829; 81 Church St., Marietta. 426-0007.

Total Dance Theatre. In 1980, Princeton and Rutgers graduate Terrie Axam-Austin pioneered her troupe in Macon, Georgia, as part of an innovative black arts center. Since it arrived in Atlanta in 1985, the Total Dance Theatre Company, a professional ensemble, has presented contemporary dance in its tours throughout the South. Its youth-oriented activities include performance programs, classes, outreach, summer camps, and after-school programs (see chapter 9). Performances are staged at various locations around town. Studio: 595 Piedmont Ave. 892-8486.

FILM

Ever since Gone With the Wind, Atlanta has been hot, so to speak, on movies. Native son Alfred Uhry took both a Pulitzer and an Oscar for his play and film, Driving Miss Daisy. Atlanta is hometown to current film favorites Julia and Eric Roberts, Holly Hunter, and Bill Nunn. Director Spike Lee attended Morehouse College before making his celluloid mark, and the town is becoming a popular place in which to make films.

Cinefest. This operation replaces the Lyceum Theater at Georgia State University. A commercial operation that leases the former Lyceum space at the University, Cinefest shows films that would not ordinarily be seen in Atlanta, including documentary, experimental and off-beat films, pure entertainment, and the classics. The black-

and-white classics are not colorized because Cinefest's directors, Eric O'Neill and Michael Williams, are determined to present the films as their creators intended. Open to the public, Cinefest charges a nominal admission, but discounts are available for films presented before 6 P.M., and on occasion second-run films are shown all day at a discount. 66 Collins St., at Decatur St., Ste. 218, Downtown. The theater itself is in Ste. 211. 651-CINE (2463).

Emory Film. As part of its undergraduate program in film studies, Emory presents film festivals that usually focus on specific themes. For information on academic programs in film, check the Department of Theater and Film Studies, Emory University, 727-6463. Emory's Harland Cinema charges the student body and the public a nominal admission to view foreign, educational, and first-run films. Dobbs University Center, Emory University, Northeast. 727-ARTS (2787).

Goethe-Institut Atlanta. Contemporary and classic German films are shown, as well as films on German topics. Films may be in English or in German with English subtitles. Free. For the Institut's other programs, see chapters 9 and 10. 400 Colony Sq., Midtown. 892-2388.

High Museum Film Series. The classics, foreign language films, works by independent studios—all varieties of films, except those in current distribution—are shown year-round in the Rich and Hill auditoriums. Gable, Garbo, and Truffaut are the stuff of this series. Museum patrons are admitted free, and seniors and children enjoy reduced rates. 1280 Peachtree St., Woodruff Arts Center, Midtown. 733-4570.

IMAGE Film/Video Center. A nonprofit media arts center founded in 1977, IMAGE strives to "assist, encourage, and promote independent, noncommercial film and video makers and to cultivate and strengthen the audi-

ences for their work." Toward that end, IMAGE presents public screenings of films and videos not available in commercial venues. Among other activities, the center sponsors the Atlanta Film and Video Festival (see chapter 4) and publishes a quarterly newsletter. Memberships are welcomed. 75 Bennett St., Ste. M-1, Brookwood. 352-4225.

Lefont Garden Hills Cinema. First-run and classic fine films, both American and foreign, have made Garden Hills a mecca for film buffs. 2835 Peachtree Rd., Buckhead. 266-2202.

Lefont Screening Room. Showing both foreign and American art films and classics, the Screening Room is itself considered a classic by Atlanta's film enthusiasts. The Screening Room also sponsors several annual film festivals, including gay/lesbian and ethnic series. 2581 Lindbergh Plaza, Buckhead. 231-1924 or 231-2009.

Cinema N' Drafthouse / Cinema Grill. See chapter 2. 7270 Roswell Rd., Atlanta. 395-0724.

Silent Film Society. The best of silent films is what interests this group: Wings, Dr. Jekyll and Mr. Hyde, and The Son of the Sheik are typical viewing. Screenings are on Friday evenings in Building 77 in the Piedmont Hospital complex, near the parking deck. 1968 Peachtree Rd., Buckhead. P.O. Box 95481, Atlanta, 30347. 633-5131.

MUSIC

Atlanta is home to a number of fine musicians, many of them internationally renowned, and the city is becoming a "must" stop for the world's excellent classical performers as well as visiting symphony orchestras and directors. Keep in mind that academic institutions and many of the groups listed below offer free and low-cost musical presentations, making access to fine performances available to all.

BANDS & ORCHESTRAS

Army Ground Forces Band. Organized in 1845 in Texas, this organization has been the band for Headquarters Forces Command, Fort McPherson, since 1973. It is the only U.S. Army band that boasts a presidential combat distinction—the right to wear red piping in commemoration of its service during the 1846 Battle of Monterey, Mexico. The band performs throughout the year. Specialized groups within the band include the Concert Band, the Dixieland Band, and the Jazz Ensemble. Ft. McPherson, Southwest. 752-2717.

Atlanta Balalaika Orchestra. Twenty-three volunteer members constitute one of the city's most unusual musical groups. Organized in 1981 and directed by David C. Cooper, the group performs throughout the year in academic and public venues, and gives a major concert every spring. Some members are available for private events. To offer volunteer assistance, see chapter 10. P.O. Box 33811, Decatur, 30033. 288-9512.

Atlanta Pops Orchestra. Offering many free concerts throughout the year, the Pops brings music to young audiences and gives young musicians a chance to perform. Directed for more than forty years by Paris-born Albert Coleman, the Pops plays local venues from Chastain to Galleria. Coleman is often invited to conduct other orchestras around the country. Favorites include the score from *Gone With the Wind*, jazz, and "classic country." P.O. Box 723172, Atlanta, 30339. 435-1222.

Callanwolde Concert Band. About fifty volunteer musicians are directed by Raymond Handfield, a graduate of the Eastman School of Music of Boston University. Most concerts are free, but the group accepts donations to defray expenses. Accomplished musicians are welcome to audition for this all-wind-instrument band. Callanwolde Fine Arts Center. 980 Briarcliff Rd., Druid Hills. 872-5338.

DeKalb Wind Symphony. Organized in 1974 at DeKalb College, this concert band consists of about 45 volunteer and professional musicians chosen by audition. Director John Mitchum invites guest soloists to perform at the three formal concerts per year, held at the college. Informal concerts (lawn, mall, picnic, holiday) are presented around town, chiefly in DeKalb County. Selections vary from classical music to pops and marches. Free and open to the public. 555 N. Indian Creek Dr., Music Department, DeKalb College, Clarkston. 299-4136.

Emory Wind Ensemble. Directed by Steven Everett, the fifty-member student group performs contemporary works written for the ensemble as well as traditional wind chamber literature. Performances are usually held at Glenn Memorial Church Auditorium. 1652 N. Decatur Rd., south of Clifton Rd., Emory University, Northeast. 727-6445; 727-6187 (box office).

Kennesaw State College Community Band. Michael Walters directs a sixty-member student and community concert band that performs classical concert literature. Free and open to the public. Kennesaw State College, 3455 Frey Lake Rd., Kennesaw. 423-6151.

Founded in 1945, the Atlanta Symphony Orchestra was originally composed of former high school musicians. By 1954, it had grown in size and stature, and celebrated its 10th anniversary with an NBC nationwide broadcast (February 6, 1966).

Morehouse College Concert Band and Jazz Ensemble. Blake Gaines directs a 65-member student concert band and a thirty-member student jazz ensemble that perform both on and off campus. 830 Westview Dr., Northwest. 215-2601.

North Fulton Community Band. Providing a musical outlet for adult musicians for more than a decade,

the North Fulton Community Band consists of former professionals, amateurs, and military-trained band members. The all-volunteer exhibition band presents free concerts on the square in Roswell, at Wills Park in Alpharetta, and in other venues throughout the Atlanta area. The director is Ellis Cannon. This band records for Kender Music's demo records, which are then circulated to 50,000 stores and schools around the world. P.O. Box 566521, Atlanta, 30356. 475-7030.

The Ritz-Carlton Orchestra. Under the direction of William Noll, this recently established group has enjoyed success after success. Individual members form the jazz and chamber sections, which play at the Ritz-Carlton, Buckhead, for hotel-sponsored events and for private parties held at the hotel and off property. The orchestra's 1990 debut album, *Swing Ye Noel!* for Newport Classics Premier, was followed by a Time-Life special Christmas recording in 1991. The Ritz-Carlton Orchestra makes annual broadcasts for PBS television. 3434 Peachtree St., Ritz-Carlton, Buckhead. 237-2700.

Sentimental Journey. This seventeen-member big-band-sound group has been a hit around Atlanta for almost twenty years. The members include business leaders, doctors, lawyers, and a dentist, among others, who have kept up their musical skills over the years. A male and a female vocalist accompany the group. Available for private functions. P.O. Box 54101, Atlanta, 30308. 875-5923.

South Metro Concert Band. This all-volunteer, 75-member band performs four concerts annually at the Clayton County Performing Arts Center and at about thirty other community events. During its "Lollipop Concert," a child conducts the famous Mickey Mouse song. Some events are free. The band's director is Dr. Edward Bridges, a former U.S. Army band conductor and former head of Georgia Tech's Department of Music. P.O. Box 111, Morrow, 30260. 946-9362.

Spelman Jazz Ensemble. This all-women student group often performs in major metropolitan areas throughout the country. Although generally not music majors, the students include instrumentalists, vocalists, and percussionists, all of whom bring depth and professionalism to their work. They often give an annual spring concert at the campus. In 1992 they opened for a Wynton Marsalis concert in Atlanta. Joseph Jennings, a well-known area musician who also serves on the faculty, directs the group. Department of Music, Spelman College, 350 Spelman Lane, Northwest. 223-7673.

CHAMBER

Agnes Scott College Flute Ensemble. The ensemble, consisting of ten students, is directed by Carol Lyn Butcher, a member of the music faculty. Free and open to the public, many performances are off campus. Mail only: 1698 Noble Dr., Atlanta, 30306. 876-3219.

Apollo's Musicke. Under the direction of Martha Bishop, this group is devoted to early music performed on reproduction period instruments—German Baroque, for instance—and performs in churches and selected facilities around town. Mail only: 1859 Westminster Way, Atlanta, 30307. 325-4735 or 320-7130.

Atlanta Camerata. Trinity United Methodist Church is usually the scene of the group's performances, which present medieval and Renaissance works. 265 Washington St., Downtown. 378-0595.

Atlanta Chamber Players. The 1995-96 season will mark this group's twentieth anniversary as Atlanta's oldest professional chamber music ensemble. The players' busy schedule permits about 100 performances each year in the Atlanta area and throughout the country. Now associated with Georgia State University's School of Music as its chamber group in residence, the players perform, teach, and conduct workshops and open rehearsals in an outreach program aimed at the growing audience for chamber music. 68 GSU, Georgia State University, P.O. Box 4038, Atlanta, 30302. 651-1228.

Atlanta Contemporary Chamber Ensemble. The ensemble is composed of professional musicians devoted to presenting work by local, national, and international composers who write for a variety of instrumental, vocal, and electroacoustic com-

binations. Organized in 1980, the group is gaining a national reputation for its performances around Atlanta and the Southeast. 570 Sheringham Court, Roswell, 30076. 998-7286.

Atlanta Musica Antiqua. Teresa Texeira, artistic director, keeps these chamber performers busy with the Concerts by Candlelight series. The group plays on Baroque and Renaissance instruments and performs in period costumes. Most recitals are held at the Rock Spring Presbyterian Church. 1824 Piedmont Ave., Northeast. 476-1725.

Atlanta Virtuosi. Headed by violinist Juan Ramirez, member of the Atlanta Symphony Orchestra and Georgia State University music teacher, this award-winning group was founded in 1977. Its active performance schedule includes appearances in Europe and Mexico, local churches, and even shopping malls. It has also commissioned chamber music from American composers. P.O. Box 77047, Atlanta, 30357. 938-8611.

Atlanta Youth Wind Symphony. Steven Everett and Leo Saguiguit conduct a fifty-member high school group that performs contemporary wind ensemble literature. Free and open to the public. Glenn Memorial United Methodist Church Auditorium, 1652 N. Decatur Rd., south of Clifton Rd., Emory University, Northeast. 727-6445; 727-6187 (box office).

Emory Chamber Ensembles. Various instrumental chamber groups composed of student members and directed by the faculty perform regularly at Emory University. These groups include saxophone, percussion, flute, and trumpet ensembles, as well as brass and woodwind choirs. Free and open to the public. 208 White Hall, Emory University, Northeast. 727-6445; 727-6187 (box office).

Emory Ensembles. **The Early Music Consort**, directed by John McDonald, performs Renaissance and Baroque works on early instruments. About ten students and faculty members make up the group. Free concerts are held both on and off campus. 208 White Hall, Emory University. **The Emory Brass Ensemble**, conducted by Michael Moore, a member of the Atlanta Symphony Orchestra, consists of about fifteen community and university members. The students' twenty-member **Emory Jazz Ensemble** is directed by Steven Everett, Emory's director of instrumental music. Most performances are held at Glenn Memorial Church Auditorium, 1652 N. Decatur Rd., south of Clifton Rd., Emory University, Northeast. 727-6445; 727-6187 (box office).

Georgian Chamber Players. Principals are members of the Atlanta Symphony Orchestra, but the group is artistically and financially independent of the symphony. Guest artists join the players for three performances a year at the Georgia-Pacific Center auditorium. 133 Peachtree St., Downtown. P.O. Box 77013B, Atlanta, 30357-1013. 352-2584.

Kennesaw State College Ensembles. Directed by Bill Hill, the twenty-member **College Community Brass Ensemble** is composed of student and community performers. It performs classical brass literature, and each year premieres at least one new work by local composer Charles Knox. With eighteen student and community performers, the **Jazz Ensemble**, directed by Wayne Everett Goins, often premieres original works and also performs traditional and modern jazz compositions. Free and open to the public. Kennesaw State College, 3455 Frey Lake Rd., Kennesaw. 423-6151.

Lanier Trio. Dorothy and Cary Lewis (cello and piano) formed the Lanier Trio in 1979. Since then it has performed and recorded classics of chamber literature. The trio has recorded the works of contemporary American composers Samuel Adler and Arnold Schoenberg for Gasparo Records, and Portuguese chamber music for Educo Records, both with violinist William Steck. Currently, William Preucil is the violinist with the Lanier Trio. Mail only: 1284 Vista Leaf Dr., Decatur, 30033. 636-6265.

Musica da Camera. Founded in 1980, this diverse group of professional musicians performs several times a year at various locations around town. The classical composers get most of the attention—Beethoven, Rachmaninoff, Mozart, Debussy, and their peers. 636-6265.

Pandean Players. This chamber music ensemble is directed by Barbera Secrist. Now in its second decade, the acclaimed group performs around the Southeast, in various venues. Mail only: 30 Trammell St., Marietta, 30064. 427-8196.

Thamyris. Peggy Benkeser and Laura Gordy, artistic directors, founded Thamyris (TAM-er-is) in 1988 to present twentieth-century chamber compositions in a variety of locations around town. Consisting of five professional performers, Thamyris commissions new works, holds residencies, and conducts outreach programs, lectures, and demonstrations. Last year, Thamyris was named resident chamber group at Spivey Hall. P.O. Box 1282, Decatur, 30031. 634-9560 or 373-6129.

CHORAL

A Cappella Singers of Atlanta. This ensemble of the DeKalb Choral Guild is a sixteen-voice group selected from the larger chorus. Formed in 1982, the A Cappella Singers focus on sacred and secular works composed through the ages for small choral groups. Selections range from Renaissance to popular madrigal programs performed in costume. P.O. Box 1931, Decatur, 30031. 264-6101.

Agnes Scott College Choral Music Groups. Rowena Renn directs a thirty-member student glee club that is almost 100 years old. Pops, traditional holiday programs, and serious choral works are performed in concerts that are free and open to the public. Devoted to gospel music, **Joyful Noise** is directed by Nathan Grigsby, an artist affiliated with the college. Ron Burnside directs **London Fog**, an ensemble specializing in swing and big band tunes. Most, but not all, programs by these two groups are free and open to the public. Gaines Auditorium, Presser Hall, Agnes Scott College, Decatur. 371-6263.

Atlanta Bach Choir. Porter Remington says she founded this volunteer group in 1980 because she wanted to hear all the Bach cantatas. The choir is especially well-known for its annual celebration of Bach's birthday: **Bach Around the Clock**, a series of concerts held on a single day or weekend in March. The choir's approach to Bach is joyous and enthusiastic, but the all-volunteer group is dedicated to its art. Performances are at various locations around town, but the choir is based at the Druid Hills Presbyterian Church, where Remington serves as director of music. P.O. Box 15543, Atlanta, 30333. 872-BACH (2224).

Atlanta Boy Choir. One of Atlanta's most renowned choral groups, the Boy Choir was founded by Fletcher Wolfe in 1955 to develop and promote choral singing and to train future generations. It tours Europe and Mexico annually, and has performed with the Atlanta Symphony Orchestra. Periodic auditions are held and are usually advertised via public service announcements. 1215 S. Ponce de Leon Ave., Druid Hills. 378-0064.

Atlanta Master Chorale. Founded in 1978, this volunteer group has appeared in Atlanta, the Southeast, and Europe, performing the great classical and contemporary choral works as well as shorter pieces. Walter Coffey directs. P.O. Box 450902, Atlanta, 30345. 451-8809; 469-0423.

Choral Guild of Atlanta. William Noll, who also directs the Ritz-Carlton Or-

chestra serves as music director and conductor of Atlanta's oldest independent chorus. Founded more than a half-century ago, the guild emphasizes unusual material not available from other sources. It also commissions new works. Performances are given throughout the city, region, nation, and world. P.O. Box 7872, Atlanta, 30357. 435-6563.

Cobb Community Chorus. Founded in 1978, the volunteer chorus is a sixty-to-eighty-voice group that presents music ranging from Baroque and classical works to musicals, pop, and patriotic pieces. Performances are given at the Cobb Civic Center and elsewhere throughout Cobb County and the metro area. Members are chosen by audition, and some minimal costs are involved for dues and purchase of music. For information, contact either Linda Carter, director, or Guy Cummings, assistant director. Mail only: 688 Grove Pkwy., Marietta, 30067. 953-3259 (Carter); 952-3781 (Cummings).

Decatur Civic Chorus. Mary Anne Sharp directs this nonprofit community organization. Founded in 1948 and composed of volunteer members, it is one of the oldest continually performing groups in the Southeast. The choir's repertoire covers all kinds of choral literature, and it has performed in Belgium, Austria, Mexico, Germany, and Great Britain. P.O. Box 1361, Decatur, 30031. 469-7610.

DeKalb Choral Guild. This fifty-voice choir performs *a cappella* works as well as major concert pieces with orchestra. Its selections range from Handel to Stravinsky to Vaughn Williams. Founded in 1978, it is a community organization whose members come from many professions and are selected by audition. Lenora Holloway co-directs with founder William O. Baker. P.O. Box 1931, Decatur, 30031. 264-6101.

Emory University Chorus / Concert Choir / Britten Choir. The **Emory University Chorus**, featuring 140 to 150 student voices, has a varied repertoire, including major works from the choral-orchestral repertoire. The forty to fifty students who make up the **Concert Choir** perform works from the Renaissance through the twentieth century. The recently formed **Britten Choir** is a professional group in residence consisting of sixteen to twenty singers who specialize in early music and music of the twentieth century. The choir presents three to four concerts per year in and around the metro Atlanta area. All three groups are conducted by Alfred Calabrese, and all performances are free. Glenn Memorial United Methodist Church. 1625 N. Decatur Rd., south of Clifton Rd., Emory University, Northeast. 727-6445; 727-6187 (box office).

Festival Singers of Atlanta. Founded in 1981, this ensemble consists of approximately 24 community musicians chosen by audition. The group sings with a straight tone in the Anglican tradition of choral music. The repertoire emphasizes the music of the Renaissance with its a cappella ideals, but also includes works of the twentieth century. Its director is N. Lee Orr, a member of the faculty of the School of Music at Georgia State University. Mail only: 2855 Royal Path Ct., Decatur, 30030.

Georgia Harmony Chorus. A chapter of Sweet Adelines International, this group of women has been presenting barbershop harmony in the Atlanta area for over a dozen years. Director Elaine Miller and a 51-member chorus entertain at private and public functions. Performances are at various locations and events; meetings are at Cross of Life Lutheran Church, 1000 Hembree Rd., Roswell. 992-2017.

> Enrico Caruso first sang with the Metropolitan Opera in Atlanta in 1910, when he performed Ramades in Aida and Canio in Pagliacci. Total attendance was about 27,000. During his 1917 appearance with the Met in Atlanta, Caruso and a quartet interrupted the final performance of Rigoletto by singing the national anthem and waving flags. The United States had just entered World War I.

Kennesaw State College Chorale. Stephen Ten Eyck began the chorale program at the college in 1991. Its forty student members perform at the college. Howard Logan Stillwell Theater, Kennesaw State College. P.O. Box 444, Marietta, 30061. 423-6151.

Marietta Chorale. Jeannette Sheeler directs this nearly thirty-year-old choral group in a variety of programs throughout the year, with special pre-

sentations at Christmas and Easter. Performances take place in area churches and retirement homes, and at local conventions. One or two light operas are scheduled annually. Mail only: 144 Whitlock Ave., Marietta, 30064. 422-1892.

Michael O'Neal Singers. Much praise by local critics has been heaped on this 115-voice community chorus and its sixteen-voice professional chamber ensemble, founded in 1989. The group has toured Europe, performing at Canterbury Cathedral, Notre Dame, and the Haydn Festival in Austria. Performances, ranging from the work of Andrew Lloyd Webber to classical literature and popular tunes, are at the Roswell United Methodist Church and Pearce Auditorium, Brenau College, Gainesville. P.O. Box 2431, Decatur, 30031. 594-7974.

Morehouse Chorus and Glee Club. This is one of Atlanta's best-known choral groups. Its repertoire includes classical literature as well as folk and spiritual. Now directed by Morehouse alumnus David Morrow, who also directs the Morehouse College Quartet, the glee club's student members represent myriad majors and perform locally as well as nationally and internationally. The group performed at the Kennedy Center Honors to celebrate Robert Shaw's contributions to the choral arts. Local performances are on campus—especially at the Martin Luther King, Jr., International Chapel—and elsewhere throughout the city. 830 Westview Dr., Northwest. 681-2800.

Morris Brown Concert Choir. Director Lloyd Douglas Brockington leads a group that has performed at national events, on tour, and with local professional organizations, such as the Atlanta Symphony Orchestra and the Atlanta Ballet. Its versatility leads from the classics to Renaissance religious music, traditional gospel, and spiritual works. 643 Martin Luther King, Jr., Dr., Morris Brown College, Northwest. 220-0320.

Oglethorpe University Singers and Chorale. Dr. W. Irwin Ray is Director of Musical Activities at this liberal arts college in north Atlanta. Regular concerts are presented with the chamber orchestra—which he also directs—throughout the year. Guest artists and local performance groups often join those affiliated with the university. Concerts are open to the public; most are free. 4484 Peachtree Rd., Lupton Auditorium, Oglethorpe University, Brookhaven. 364-8429.

Society for the Preservation and Encouragement of Barber Shop Quartet Singing in America, Inc. Also known as the **Big Chicken Chorus** (after the famous icon to American culinary culture that sits prominently in Marietta on U.S. 41), this 127-voice organization is part of a national group that's dedicated to barber shop harmony. The Big Chicken Chorus is one of four Atlanta area chapters of SPEBSQSA, and has won many national awards. Proceeds benefit the National Organization of Logopedics, which helps people suffering from the inability to talk. For information on joining a chapter, contact Jack Bolton. Mail only: 1325 Belmore Way, Atlanta, 30350. 393-1173.

University Choral Society. About 100 voices selected from Georgia State

University students, faculty, and the community form this society, which grew out of a Christmas program for Underground Atlanta a few years ago. Most concerts are free and open to the public and are presented in the Georgia State University Concert Hall. School of Music, Georgia State University, University Plaza, Downtown. 651-3676.

The Young Singers of Callanwolde.

For twenty years, young voices under the direction of founder Steve Ortlip have enchanted Atlanta audiences. The 175 member youth choir annually performs a classic concert series during the months of December, March, and May in various churches around the city. In addition, The Young Singers provide concerts for weddings and other special events upon request. Aside from various recordings for television and radio, this youth choir made its film debut in the opening scene of Steve Martin's "Twist of Fate." 980 Briarcliff Rd., Atlanta. 873-3365.

OPERA

The Atlanta Opera.

Regional opera in Atlanta is up and running—full speed. Performing three classical operas a year, the Atlanta Opera has enjoyed substantial growth since its founding in 1979. Now under the artistic direction of William Fred Scott, the Atlanta Opera is getting rave reviews and playing to sold-out audiences. Sets are lavish, the orchestra and chorus are brilliant, and the audiences grow annually in number as well as in knowledge and appreciation. As an aid to growing audience enjoyment, a screen placed high above the stage displays a running translation of the original language. The opera's season runs from spring to fall. Performances are in Symphony Hall at Woodruff Arts Center. Office: 1800 Peachtree St., Ste. 620, Midtown. 355-3311.

Onyx Opera Atlanta.

Established in 1988 to give voice to the musical talents of African-American composers and performers (although other performers often share the stage), Onyx celebrates all forms of operatic expression, from Joplin to Verdi. P.O. Box 90486, Atlanta, 30364. 762-1194.

Savoyards Light Opera.

The spirits of Gilbert and Sullivan govern this dynamic company, whose name is derived from the 1881 Savoy Theater, built especially for the famous pair's productions. Light operetta, which often includes work by Sigmund Romberg, is its stock in trade. The season runs October through May, with three plays staged three times each. Georgia Tech Theater for the Arts, 349 Ferst Drive, Midtown. 233-0750

SYMPHONY ORCHESTRA

African-American Philharmonic Orchestra and Chorale. John Peek and Thomas W. Stewart direct this equal-opportunity organization, which presented its first concert to a sold-out audience at the Civic Center. Since then, it has been busy performing on behalf of the city's Bureau of Cultural Affairs and the Fulton County Arts Council; it has also performed in Peru. Its goals are to perform works by African-American composers, to expand performance opportunities for musicians, and to reach the youth who, says Peek, "know nothing about the history of black music." The group performs classical, contemporary, jazz, and gospel music. Mail only: 2563 Woodhaven Cir., East Point, 30344. 346-3417.

Agnes Scott College Community Orchestra. Philip Rice directs this fifty-member group, two-thirds of whom are community members; the remainder are Agnes Scott students and faculty members. Regular performances of classical works are free and open to the public. Gaines Auditorium, Presser Hall, Agnes Scott College, Decatur. 638-6263.

Atlanta Community Orchestra. Founded in 1958 as part of the Atlanta Music Club, ACO performs six free concerts a year. Local soloists often join the orchestra, which frequently plays for local events and organizations. ACO also presents concerts throughout the state and provides young performers an opportunity to solo. 1900 The Exchange, Ste. 160, Northwest. 872-9670.

Atlanta-Emory Orchestra. Conducted by Jere Flint, a cellist with the Atlanta Symphony Orchestra and the Atlanta Symphony Youth Orchestra, this student-, faculty-, and community-based orchestra performs a standard orchestral repertoire. Concerts are free and open to the public. Glenn Memorial United Methodist Church Auditorium. 1652 N. Decatur Rd., south of Clifton Rd., Emory University, Northeast. 727-6445; 727-6187 (box office).

Atlanta Symphony Orchestra. Music Director Yoël Levi and Music Director Emeritus Robert Shaw present many innovative programs in addition to the regular **Master Season**, with its brilliant performances and celebrity guest conductors and soloists. The orchestra has won many awards and critical accolades for its recordings and performances. The **Meet the Artist Series** features guest musicians for brown bag conversations. The **Family Concert Series**, the **Champagne** and **Coffee Concerts**, the **Open Rehearsal Series**, and the **Atlanta Symphony Youth Orchestra** all attract wide audiences. **Summerfest** (free summer concerts in area parks), pre-concert lectures, and the **Summer Pops Series** at Chastain Park Amphitheatre also summon big crowds. Regular season performances are at Symphony Hall, Woodruff Arts Center. *(For additional programs, see chapter 10.)* Office: 1293 Peachtree St., Ste. 300, Midtown. 892-2414 (box office); 733-4900 (administrative offices); 733-4800 (subscription information).

Cobb Symphony Orchestra. Professional musicians and community volunteers make up this fifty-member orchestra. Its season runs from October through April, with occasional summer concerts. The CSO now boasts a professional music director, Steven Byess, now in his fourth season. 548 Clay St., Anderson Theater, Cobb Civic Center, Downtown Marietta. 424-5541.

DeKalb Symphony Orchestra. Conductor Thomas Anderson, a professor at DeKalb College, brings outstanding guest performers to this symphony's season. Performances are usually held at the college, but some special programs go off-campus. Children's concerts, pops programs, and the **Blue Sky** brown bag lunch series on the piazza over the MARTA station in Decatur are highlights. 555 North Indian Creek Dr., DeKalb College Central Campus, Fine Arts Auditorium, Clarkston. 299-4341; 299-4136.

Orchestra Atlanta. Tom Hallam, a Delta pilot and violinist, joined the chamber orchestra at Mercer University; when it disbanded, Hallam formed a chamber orchestra of his own. Delta Airlines became a sponsor of the new group, now Orchestra Atlanta. From October through May, this 55-member volunteer orchestra brings nationally recognized artists to one of Atlanta's northern suburbs. Musical Director Philip Rice leads the performances at the Roswell Municipal Auditorium, 38 Hill St., Roswell. Office: 89 Grove Way, Roswell 30075. 992-2559.

University Symphony. Directed by William Fred Scott and based in the Georgia State University School of Music, this orchestra combines the talents of several Atlanta area colleges, including GSU, Georgia Tech, and Clark Atlanta University. Free and open to the public, the performances are held at the University Concert Hall. School of Music, Georgia State University, University Plaza, Downtown. 651-3676.

THEATER

Atlanta's theatrical heritage is a long one, stretching from the Atheneum, built before the Civil War, to today's experimental theater, and even puppetry. Academic centers also have well-developed theatrical groups, and many fine community troupes complement the professional ones. For more information about the theater arts in Atlanta, call the Atlanta Theater Coalition at 873-1185.

The Academy Theatre. After a difficult period, Georgia's oldest professional resident company is back. Founder and director Frank Wittow has good reason to be proud of this extraordinary troupe and its youth programs. The **Human Service** program, which the theater deems to be "a voice for the disenfranchised," and the **New Play** program further the academy's aim of bringing theater to all people. P.O. Box 191306, Atlanta, 31119. 525-4111.

Actor's Express. Artistic director Chris Coleman leads Actor's Express in the production of a wildly eclectic mix of classic and contemporary plays in the King Plow Arts Center. 887 W. Marietta St., King Plow Arts Center, Midtown. 607-7469.

Agatha's A Taste of Mystery Dinner Theater. At this unique dinner theater, everyone dines together to participate in the mystery. Savor a five-course dinner with wine, and murder for dessert. Shows are original productions that each run for ten weeks. 693 Peachtree St., Downtown. 875-1610.

Alley Stage. An experimental theater producing original plays as a part of Theatre in the Square. 11 Whitlock Ave., Downtown Marietta, behind Theatre in the Square. 422-8369.

Alliance Theatre Company. Artistic Director Kenny Leon runs an established theater that presents classics of the American and English stage as well as contemporary American plays. The **Alliance Children's Theatre**, founded in 1928, adapts classics and creates new works for children. Established in 1979, the **Alliance Theatre School** teaches acting to both adults and children, and its "Drama in Education" program trains teachers to use acting and the dramatic arts in the classroom. 1280 Peachtree St., Woodruff Arts Center, Midtown. 733-4600 (subscriptions); 733-5000 (box office); 733-4650 (information).

Atlanta Shakespeare Company. Although it first performed in Atlanta's famous Manuel's Tavern, the company now has its own 175-seat facility where it stages the Bard's plays in authentic Elizabethan style, often with audience involvement. Shakespearean plays alternate with period pieces and other classics of English and Western theater. Box suppers featuring British pub-style food are prepared by Chef for a Night *(see chapter 7)*. Wine and beer service is also available. 499 Peachtree St., Downtown. 874-5299 (box office).

Center for Puppetry Arts. A unique institution, the center presents both classics and new material for the puppet theater. This outstanding theater not only specializes in works for children but also mounts puppet productions for adult audiences. A fascinating gift shop sells splendid puppets and accessories for puppetry. The center's collateral museum *(see chapter 5)* exhibits a permanent collection of puppets. 1404 Spring St., at 18th St., Midtown. 873-3391.

Centerstage. A community theater, Centerstage gets raves for its mainstage performances of classic American theater. Auditions for the mainstage season are open to all interested actors, whether Centerstage members or not. The company also accepts bookings for privately held mystery parties. The Art Place—Mountain View, 3330 Sandy Plains Rd., Marietta. 565-8286.

DeKalb College Theatres. Two theatrical companies are based at DeKalb College—the **DeKalb Music Theatre** and the **DeKalb Theatre Company**. The music theater offers two musicals a year with full orchestra. The theater company presents three plays during the year, ranging from Shakespeare to contemporary comedy. Fine Arts Auditorium, DeKalb College, Central Campus, North Indian Creek Dr. and Memorial College Dr., Clarkston. 299-4270.

DramaTech. Founded in 1947 by the Department of English at the Georgia Institute of Technology, DramaTech introduces art into an otherwise non-artistic educational environment. Funded by the school's student government, it offers students both an academic opportunity and an extracurricular activity, but some participants are drawn from the community. Its director is Greg Abbott, a part-time faculty member, but all productions are student driven. Shakespeare, sci-fi, classics, and summertime studio shows focusing on original material by local authors are within DramaTech's purview. A winter "International Festival" features plays from around the world. Nominal general admission is charged to the public, and discounted admission is available to students. Performances are held at the Georgia Institute of Technology Theater for the Arts., Downtown. 894-2745.

Dunwoody Stage Door Players. American classics and new plays drive this suburban theater, founded twenty years ago as a project of the Dunwoody Women's Club. No longer performing upstairs in a local bank, the players offer a strong season of six plays and a "Summer Stage" program. Its reputation for fine, professionally accomplished performances continues to grow. 5339 Chamblee-Dunwoody Rd., North Dekalb Cultural Center, Dunwoody. 396-1726.

Georgia Ensemble Theatre and Conservatory. After a successful premiere season in 1993-94, Robert Farley's Georgia Ensemble Theatre and Conservatory continues to provide professional theater entertainment to audiences throughout North Georgia. In addition to exciting performance, the Conservatory offers performing arts educational experiences for adults and Saturday workshops and a summer conservatory camp for children. Performances at Roswell City Auditorium, Roswell. Mail: P.O. Box 607, Roswell, GA 30077-0607. 641-1260.

Georgia Shakespeare Festival. The festival presents summertime under-the-tent Shakespeare on a university campus. Bring supper to dine before the play, or, on selected dates, feast on a traditional Elizabethan dinner—all while savoring pre-performance entertainment. Arrive early to get one of the few tables or prepare to picnic on a blanket. **Camp Shakespeare** draws youngsters ages 5–12, and the conservatory teaches drama to high school students. 4484 Peachtree Rd., Oglethorpe University, Brookhaven. 688-8008.

Georgia State University Players. The players perform at least three shows per year, depending on the funding received from the student government. Original work by faculty and students, as well as classics of the theater, are part of the company's repertoire. A one-act festival produced and directed entirely by students is planned as an annual event. Performances are free to GSU students and a guest; discounted admission is available for senior citizens and students from other campuses; and the general public is charged a nominal admission. Alumni Hall, Georgia State University, Courtland St. at Gilmer St., Downtown. 651-2225.

Horizon Theatre Company.

A professional theater, Horizon has been part of Atlanta's theatrical world since 1983. Committed to contemporary theater, Horizon solicits new works from both established and emerging dramatists, and it develops original pieces about the South and by or about women. In Horizon's **Teen Ensemble** and **Young Playwrights** programs, young people experience professional theater. 1083 Austin Ave., Inman Park. 584-7450.

Jomandi Productions.

This spirited, innovative company is the state's oldest and largest black professional theater company. Focusing on works by and about African-American artists, Jomandi productions run the gamut, from drama to musicals to comedy. The majority of performances are at the 14th Street Playhouse. 1444 Mayson St., Midtown. 876-6346.

Just Us.

Local and national press rave about Just Us, a theater company whose principals, poet and writer Pearl Cleage and novelist Zaron Burnett, Jr., offer performance art that reflects their view of African-American social reality. The Just Us speak-easy-style **Live at Club Zebra** is a presentation series that distills aspects and images of African-American culture. Witty with a purpose, artful, outrageous, and provoking, the monologues that Cleage and Burnett deliver have been hits at the National Black Arts Festival. Performances feature live music and original video. Just Us performs at the Civic Center and other local venues. P.O. Box 42271, Atlanta, 30311-0271, 753-2399.

Neighborhood Playhouse.

Since 1980, this volunteer-supported theater has been producing popular, classic, and contemporary comedy, drama, and musicals throughout the year. Seating about 170, the Neighborhood Playhouse boasts one of the largest season ticket memberships in Atlanta. The Playhouse draws actors and technicians from the community. Sondra Nelson serves as executive artistic director. 430 W. Trinity Pl., Decatur. 373-5311 (tickets); 373-3904 (information).

The Playmakers.

Oglethorpe University's drama company performs several times each academic year. It focuses on the classics of European and American theater. 4484 Peachtree Rd., Brookhaven. 364-8343.

Seven Stages.

The Seven Stages Arts Center is the nucleus of a vital environment devoted to contemporary art performances. The resident theatrical company keeps busy presenting avant-garde theater, from dramas to musicals. Other companies perform here as well. Seven Stages Arts Center, 1105 Euclid Ave., Little Five Points. 523-7647.

Southside Theatre.

Founded in 1972, this volunteer group, with about 70 active members, claims to be Atlanta's oldest community theater. The theater's 192-seat facility has been sold out for presentations of such popular productions as *Steel Magnolias*. Southside presents four to six shows each year, choosing from musical, dramatic, comedic, or youth production literature. Auditions are open to the interested public. Admission is nominal, with discounts for seniors and students. Opening night always offers two tickets for the price of one. 20 W. Campbellton St. (Hwy. 92), I-85 south to Hwy. 78 (Exit 13), Fairburn. 969-0956.

Telltale Theatre. John Schmedes, founder and artistic director, brings extensive professional theatrical experience into the lives of children. Presenting original dramatic material for young audiences, Schmedes' troupe of twenty actors and designers presents plays and workshops for schools, churches, and special events. Summer acting classes are for children of all ages. 30 Trammel St., Marietta. 427-8206.

Theater Emory. The producing organization for Emory University's Department of Theater and Film Studies, Theater Emory presents classics from Western theater as well as contemporary professional and student work. As a research and teaching facility, it brings theater professionals from around the country and abroad to work as instructors for the students. Performances are in the Mary Gray Munroe Theater, Dobbs University Center. 605 Asbury Cir., Emory University, Northeast. 727-6187 (box office).

Theatre Gael. Now an established Atlanta theater, Theatre Gael is the only Celtic theater in the Southeast. Plays for both adult and youth audiences, and special events featuring Celtic music and dance, are presented at the 14th Street Playhouse. The youth productions, designated as the **Worldsong Children's Theatre**, tour area schools and draw on diverse stories and myths from around the world. P.O. Box 77156, Atlanta, 30357. 876-1138.

Theatre in the Square. Called "one of the Southeast's most charming per-forming spaces," this popular professional theater boasts an extensive outreach program and a **Theatre for Young Audiences** program. With nine world premieres to its credit, including Maxwell Anderson's *The Masque of Queens*, Theatre in the Square has won numerous awards. The facility's 165 seats came from Atlanta's historic Fox Theatre. Located on historic Marietta Square. 11 Whitlock Ave., Marietta. 422-8369.

Theatrical Outfit. This sparkling company offers lively productions of classics, comedies, and new plays presented in an intimate theater. Founded in 1976 as an experimental theater collective, it has gained stature and a national reputation. Hits from previous seasons include *Appalachian Christmas, Beowulf,* and *Children of Jazz* . Attesting to its popularity, the Outfit attracts about 20,000 theater-goers annually, making it one of Atlanta's most popular theaters. Artistic director is Phillip DePoy. 14th Street Playhouse, 173 14th St., Midtown. 872-0665.

Tri-Cities Community Theater. This volunteer, nonprofit theater is the only local theater, professional or community, to stage the award-winning play *One Flew over the Cuckoo's Nest.* Founded in 1985 by a handful of folks who sought funding from three south Fulton County towns, Tri-Cities serves College Park, East Point, and Hapeville. These municipalities still contribute funding support to the theater. Today, half the membership of about thirty active volunteers comes from East Point, and the remainder hail from all over the metro area. Tri-Cities also incorporates a **Children's Theater Production Company**. The facility seats only 65 and is housed in a former Firestone Tire Store. Admission is nominal. 2750 East Point St., off Main St., East Point. 681-6091.

Village Center Playhouse. With two theaters (265 seats and 200 seats), both crafted out of movie theaters, this facil-

ity is home to a community company that specializes in romantic, family-oriented comedy. Performances by the local professional and volunteer actors are scheduled year-round. 617 Holcomb Bridge Rd., at Alpharetta Hwy., Roswell Village Shopping Center, Roswell. 998-3526.

SPECIAL PROGRAMS

Special programs, readings, and series are part of Atlanta's distinctive and rich performing arts life. Look for special presentations and lectures that take place around the lunch hour as well as immediately after work, making it a simple matter to enjoy performance art in Atlanta.

Art & Ideas at Oglethorpe. Lectures, concerts, special performances, and theatrical productions are presented at the university throughout the year. High points include the concert presented by the year's winner of the **Gina Bachauer International Piano Competition** as well as the annual **Boar's Head Ceremony and Holiday Concert** in December. 4484 Peachtree Rd., Brookhaven. 364-8423.

Atlanta Symphony Orchestra. Throughout the season, the orchestra offers a wide variety of special series designed to enhance and enlarge its audience. **Family Concerts**, conducted by George Hanson on selected Sunday afternoons, blend music with other arts in lively presentations designed to attract the young listener. **Champagne and Coffee concerts**, conducted by William Fred Scott, are presented on selected Friday and Saturday evenings and on the same Saturday mornings. Complimentary champagne is served after the evening

concerts, and on Saturday mornings complimentary coffee is served at 10 A.M., followed by a pre-concert discussion at 10:30 A.M. The concert itself is held at 11 A.M. During the **Open Rehearsal Series,** on selected Thursday mornings, the audience watches the symphony prepare for the weekend's Master Season performance. 1280 Peachtree St., Woodruff Arts Center, Midtown. 892-2414 (box office); 733-4900 (information).

Callanwolde Performance Series. An extensive performance series for both adults and children is presented quarterly. Dance, drama, concerts, poetry readings, and storytelling are among the offerings. The **Poetry Series** meets monthly for poetry readings, usually original works by guest poets. A summer poets' and writers' conference convenes annually. 980 Briarcliff Rd., Druid Hills. 872-5338.

Coca-Cola International Series. Anything from ballet troupes to Chinese acrobats will show up in this annual series. All performances are held at the Fox Theatre, 660 Peachtree St., Midtown. 881-2100; 249-6400 (tickets).

Composers' Resources. Established in 1980, this is a nationally known composer advocacy organization, presenting premiere performances of new music from local, national, and international sources. Howard Wershil, its founder, has long been involved in advancing the cause of new music, both instrumental and electro-acoustic. Composers' Resources is frequently supported by the Fulton County Arts Council and the Georgia Council for the Arts. 570 Sheringham Court, Roswell, 30076. 998-7286.

Decatur Concerts on the Square. Arrive early to pick your favorite picnic spot at the Old Courthouse in Decatur every Saturday evening during the months of May and September. This free concert series provides a variety of musical entertainment and gives you a chance to relax, put up your feet, and enjoy the community spirit of Decatur outside under the stars. Also during the months of May and September is the **Blue Sky** concert series, occurring weekly on Wednesdays at noon. Old Courthouse Square, Decatur. 371-8262.

Garden Concerts on the Great Lawn. At the Atlanta Botanical Gardens, a three-part summer series features various kinds of concerts, including big band, opera, and pops. Bring a picnic, relax on a blanket, and enjoy (see *chapter 5*). Piedmont Park, 1345 Piedmont Ave., Midtown. 876-5859.

Georgia State University School of Music Series. In addition to the Terrace Concerts listed below, the School of Music at GSU presents **Conducted Ensembles**, the **Faculty Artists Series**, and a **Guest Artist Series**—all free and open to the public. Georgia State University Concert Hall, Gilmer St. and Peachtree Center Ave., Downtown. 651-3676.

Glover Park on the Square. Historic Marietta Square is the setting for every kind of music: country to jazz, classical to swing. Picnics are welcome, and beer and wine are permitted. These free concerts take place on the last Friday of the month from April through August. Marietta Parks & Recreation Department, Marietta. 528-0616.

Jubilee Summer Concert Series. Presented by the Jubilee Cultural Alliance, this free series brings to summertime audiences several Sunday evenings of light classical, patriotic, and popular music. Picnics are everywhere, and early arrivals get the best spots. The Galleria, I-285 and Hwy. 41, Northwest. 988-9641.

Piano Gallery Series. From September through May, Barbara Kirby's Piano Gallery of Atlanta presents concerts and events at the gallery. Artists include local music personalities as well as Steinway artists who are making special appearances in the city. Get on the mailing list for announcements and the gallery's newsletter. 2140 Peachtree Rd., Ste. 125, Brookwood Square, Brookwood. 351-0550.

Roswell Concerts on the Square. The City of Roswell and the Historic Preservation Commission present old-fashioned "Concerts on the Square" the first Saturday evening of each month from May through October at 7:30 P.M., weather permitting. Informality and conviviality govern, so bring a blanket and a picnic supper. In front of the gazebo, Roswell City Square, Roswell. 594-6444.

Southern Keyboard Concert Series.

At Southern Keyboard's Marietta location, a recital hall accommodating 120 people is the site for semimonthly concerts performed by local musicians January through May. Additionally, local teachers may use the facility to present recitals. A nominal admission is charged for the semimonthly concerts, but teacher-sponsored recitals are free. Contact Tom Love, general manager, for information. *See chapter 6.* 1898 Leland Dr., Marietta. 953-0938.

Terrace Concerts at Georgia State University.

Top-level international artists present chamber music in conjunction with the John F. Kennedy Center for the Performing Arts in Washington, DC. Eight concerts are performed throughout the season. The quartets, soloists, and ensembles presented in this series reflect the highest caliber of musical achievement. The series is one of the most reasonably priced classical performance values in town, and special prices are available for seniors and full-time students. Georgia State University Concert Hall, Gilmer St. at Peachtree Center Ave., Downtown. 651-3676. Also TicketMaster Southeast, 249-6400.

Theater of the Stars.

This civic, nonprofit production company was founded in 1953 to unite private and public efforts devoted to developing theater in Atlanta. Since that year, some 600 productions of all kinds, including musicals, plays, ballets, and operas, have reached millions. Now the resident company at the Fox Theatre, Stars produces dramatic works locally and presents others on tour throughout the country. Christopher B. Manos, producer; Louise Hudson, executive producer. P.O. Box 11748, Atlanta, 30355. 252-8960.

Windstorm Productions.

Anything from Cajun to Nouveau Flamenco to folk is apt to emerge from Windstorm's work. The summer series unfolds at the Variety Playhouse. P.O. Box 8711, Atlanta, 30306. 874-2232.

LUNCHTIME ARTS

Alliance Lunchtime Theatre.

The **Acting Intern Company** performs four shows during the year on the main stage or in the studio, from 12 to 1 P.M. A small fee is charged. Bring your own sandwich and savor short takes of the theater. For dates check the newspaper or call 733-4650. 1280 Peachtree St., Woodruff Arts Center, Midtown.

Art at the Heart.

Cosponsored by Georgia-Pacific and the Fulton County Arts Council, "Art at the Heart" is presented in the fall and spring. Programs encompass all the performing arts and are held on the mezzanine of the Georgia-Pacific building. "Art at the Heart" starts with a thirty-minute performance at 12:15 P.M., followed by a break and another half hour performance. There is no seating, as listeners stand around and observe in an informal manner. Contact Robin Wrinn in Corporate Communications. 133 Peachtree St., Downtown. 652-4896.

Atlanta Symphony Orchestra "Lunch and Learn" Concerts. This informal brown bag lunch series features guest artists performing and participating in informal discussions. Meets on Fridays at 12:30 P.M. in the Woodruff Circle Room, third floor of the Woodruff Arts Center. 1280 Peachtree St., Midtown. 733-4900.

Blue Sky Concerts. The DeKalb Symphony Orchestra presents weekly **Out to Lunch** concerts on the square in downtown Decatur. 299-4341.

PERFORMING VENUES

In addition to theaters built as performance facilities, many fine auditoriums are tucked into other kinds of structures, such as office towers, museums, and schools. Outdoor facilities are popular, especially because of the city's magnificent summer weather.

INDOOR

The Art Place Theater–Mountain View. A black box theater seating 200 to 250, this facility may be arranged in arena style, three-quarter thrust style, or as a proscenium theater. The facility works well as a dinner theater. 3330 Sandy Plains Rd., Marietta. 509-2700.

The Coca-Cola Roxy Theater. Once a movie theater, then a cinema and draft house, today the Roxy hosts touring groups that present musical revues of folk, rock, jazz, blues, reggae, and specialty shows. Food and beer/wine service are available. Rental of the space is available for groups ranging from 500 (cabaret theater–style) to 1,000 (open-seating–style). 3110 Roswell Rd., Buckhead. 233-7699 (recorded information).

Callanwolde Fine Arts Center. Charles Howard Candler, Coca-Cola heir, commissioned Henry Hornbostel, architect of Emory University, to build a handsome Tudor-style house for Candler and his family. Completed in 1920, the house was especially designed for music, with its 3,752-pipe Aeolian organ at the heart of a unique music system. Since 1973 Callanwolde, meaning "Candler Woods," has served DeKalb County and the Atlanta area as a fine arts center. Callanwolde presents a variety of performances, including poetry readings, storytelling, and musicales. Callanwolde is also available for private affairs. 980 Briarcliff Rd., Druid Hills. 872-5338.

Center Stage Theatre. Center Stage books concerts and diverse performance events. Available for private use, it seats up to 974 in theater style. All seats are good, and none is farther than 65 feet from the stage. Good acoustics. Also housed in the structure is **Encore**, which may be booked for private functions. Lexi Halverson is general manager. 1374 W. Peachtree St., Midtown. 874-1511.

Chastain Park Amphitheatre.

Chastain hosts popular acts, rock groups, and the Atlanta Symphony Orchestra. The Fourth of July celebration is an Atlanta institution. Parking can be a problem, so come early. Bring a picnic and make it elegant or casual, but don't forget the candles. 135 W. Wieuca Rd., Buckhead. Tic-x-press: 231-5888 for performance and ticket information.

Civic Center. Seating about 4,500, the

Civic Center hosts myriad arts performances, from the Atlanta Ballet presentations to visiting performance events. The entrance gallery sparkles with massive chandeliers and dramatic lighting. A facility of the City of Atlanta, it was completed in 1967. 395 Piedmont Ave., Downtown. 523-6275.

Clayton County Performing Arts

Center. A huge stage sits in an 1800-seat facility that can be divided into three different performing areas seating groups of 250, 339, and 1211 persons. Rigid rotating walls keep sound from penetrating from one space into another. The facility is equipped to handle theatrical works and all kinds of musical productions. Owned by the Clayton County Board of Education, the facility's time is heavily scheduled for many school events, but civic and commercial organizations may schedule activities after school hours. Call Larry Volman, director, to arrange rentals. 2530 Mt. Zion Pkwy., I-75 at Exit 75-A, Jonesboro. 473-2875.

Cobb Civic Center. This 15,000-square-

foot exhibit hall, built in 1975, provides permanent seating for 2,880. Portable seating accommodates another 700, and meeting rooms seat forty people each. 548 S. Marietta Pkwy., Marietta. 528-8450.

14th Street Playhouse. Professional

actor, director, and choreographer Robert Putnam took on a difficult task when he became manager of the beleaguered facility. But in the first year of his administration, some sixty groups booked the space, and it is now home to a number of arts groups. 173 14th St., Midtown. 873-1099.

Fox Theatre. Plans to demolish this

Atlanta landmark galvanized preservationists, and today the old theater, with its star- and cloud-studded ceiling and dramatic theater organ, remains a testament to Atlanta's architectural and artistic heritage. Touring opera groups, musical theater, popular performers, and ballet groups make the Fox a must several times a year. 660 Peachtree St., Midtown. 881-2100.

Georgia-Pacific Auditorium. Located

in one of downtown Atlanta's impressive towers, this facility is an intimate (254 seats) space with superb acoustics. Adjacent to the High Museum at Georgia-Pacific (see chapter 5), it is part of the space dedicated by Georgia-Pacific to foster the arts in the working environment. 133 Peachtree St., Downtown. 652-5800.

Georgia State University Concert

Hall. Located in the university's Art and Music Building, this facility offers concerts that feature outstanding guest artists. Some are free, and some require admission. Gilmer St. & Peachtree Center Ave., Georgia State University, Downtown. 651-3676.

Georgia Tech Theatre for the Arts.
This facility opened in April 1992. Seating 1,200 people, the $7.5 million facility hosts a broad spectrum of cultural events, including performances by guest symphonies, renowned international artists, top local artists, and groups from Georgia Tech. Drama-Tech, for instance, uses the "black box" theater installed in the facility. 350 Ferst Dr., Georgia Institute of Technology campus, Midtown. 894-9600.

Glenn Memorial United Methodist Church Auditorium.
Located on the campus of Emory University, the church has an auditorium that seats about 1,200 people and has hosted some outstanding musical programs by collegiate, local, and national performers. 1652 N. Decatur Rd., south of Clifton Rd., Emory University, Northeast. Concert line: 727-6666.

International Ballroom.
Hosting national acts, the International Ballroom offers a diverse music venue for concert goers. One of the larger facilities in Atlanta, the International Ballroom seats 2500. Also available is an house restaurant, which may be used for concert functions. 6618 N. Peachtree Rd., Chamblee. 936-0447.

Kennesaw State College Howard Logan Stillwell Theater.
Located in the Continuing Education and Performing Arts Building, the facility brings to the community a variety of classical music performances by community and college organizations. P.O. Box 444, Marietta, 30061. Kennesaw State College, 3455 Frey Lake Rd., Kennesaw. 423-6151.

Lanierland.
This covered facility seats approximately 4,000 people and offers wheelchair access. Tailgating is allowed, but no alcoholic beverages are permitted inside. Country music stars such as George Jones, Conway Twitty, and the Oak Ridge Boys perform. 6115 Jot 'Em Down Rd., near Cross Roads Rd., off GA 400, Cumming. 681-1596.

Lupton Auditorium.
On the campus of an area university, the auditorium hosts performance events for the campus community. 4484 Peachtree Rd., Oglethorpe University, Brookhaven. 261-1441.

Omni.
Often the arena of choice for rock concerts, it has also hosted such events as an evening with Luciano Pavarotti. Seating from the middle down to the front is best for musical events. 100 Techwood Dr., CNN Center, Downtown. 681-2100.

Robert W. Woodruff Arts Center.
Home to Atlanta's major performing and visual arts organizations, as well as the Atlanta College of Art (see chapter 9), the center's main facilities are **Symphony Hall** and the **Alliance Theatre**. It also contains the intimate **Studio Theatre** as well as the **Richard Rich and Walter Hill auditoriums**, two smaller spaces that often host special events. 1280 Peachtree St., Midtown. 892-3600.

Seven Stages Performing Arts Center.
The facility not only houses a professional theater organization, but also serves as a performance facility for "homeless" arts groups based in

Atlanta. 1105 Euclid Ave., Little Five Points. 522-0911.

Southern Star Amphitheatre. This
Six Flags Over Georgia facility boasts a total capacity of about 12,000 seats with good wheelchair access. It attracts major country and rock stars, such as Willie Nelson and the B-52s. Some shows are free with regular Six Flags admission, others require additional ticketing. Parking lot picnics are allowed, but alcoholic beverages are not. I-20 West, Six Flags Over Georgia. 739-3400.

Spivey Hall. Clayton State College in
Morrow, Georgia (one of metropolitan Atlanta's satellite towns) took a major step forward into the world of fine arts on January 23, 1991. Itzhak Perlman, violinist, and Robert da Silva, pianist, were among the stars who helped launch the college's new Spivey Hall. A 79-pipe Italian organ, dedicated to Albert Schweitzer, was installed in 1992. The facility hosts some of the richest

performing experiences anywhere in Atlanta, and one critic has acclaimed it as Atlanta's only world-class concert hall. The Spivey International Performance Competition takes place here, as well. Tours of the hall are conducted twice weekly or by appointment. Clayton State College, Morrow. 961-3683.

Variety Playhouse. Concerts feature
local and national talent playing jazz, folk, New Age, and cutting-edge rock. Cajun bands such as nationally famous Beausoleil, jazz pianists such as Marcus Roberts, or John Wesley Harding, a cutting-edge rock group, are among the artists who have visited the playhouse. Occasionally, plays and dance events are staged here; the place is available for rental. Capacity is between 500 and 700 people, depending on how the space is configured. There's a bar, and catering can be arranged. 1099 Euclid Ave., Little Five Points. 521-1786 (show information); 924-7354 (office).

OUTDOOR

Galleria Amphitheater. Summer Sun-
day evenings bring a picnic atmosphere and a huge gathering to the Galleria. The Atlanta Symphony Orchestra and local groups such as Banks & Shane and the Freddy Cole Trio are featured. Arrive early to grab the choice spots. The free summer concert series is presented by the Jubilee Cultural Alliance, a nonprofit organization that fosters the fine arts in Cobb County. The Galleria, I-285 and Hwy. 41, Northwest. 988-9641.

Lakewood Amphitheatre. Pop, rock,
blues, and everything in between— some at bargain prices—are booked into this facility, officially known as the Coca-Cola Lakewood Amphitheatre. It has a seating capacity of nearly 20,000. Food cannot be brought inside, but may be bought at the facility. Tailgating is allowed. Parking is available on site, but MARTA (train and shuttle bus) also goes to Lakewood. Good wheelchair access. 2002 Lakewood Way, Southwest. 627-9704.

Stone Mountain Park. Random seating either on **Memorial Lawn** in front of the stone carving or around the three stages used during festivals is available for country and pop/rock concerts. The laser show and the relaxation are the main draws. Bring blankets. The concerts are free, but parking is $5 (or $20 for the season). Food is available, but picnics are permitted. No alcohol is allowed. Hwy. 78 (Exit 30-B off I-285) Stone Mountain Park Exit, Stone Mountain. 498-5600.

CHAPTER 4

Special Events

Get out your calendars! Atlanta hosts more special events than any one schedule can handle without some serious planning. This chapter lists events by the month, so you can see the year at a glance and make your plans accordingly.

The special cultural, musical, and sporting events listed here should keep you as busy as you want to be every weekend of the year. We haven't forgotten about the special fund-raising sales and other regularly scheduled shopping events, but we have included them in Chapter 6 (Shopping Around).

Be sure to call in advance for possible schedule and location changes, rain dates, and the like. Where possible, we have included some guidelines for admission prices. We label $5 and under nominal, $6 to $15 moderate, and over $15 substantial admission.

There are many more events scheduled during the year than we could possibly list here—consider this to be a mere sampling of the best. Check the weekend entertainment section of the paper or in the free weekly *Creative Loafing* for up-to-the-minute information.

WINTER

Just because it's frosty doesn't mean there aren't special celebrations in Atlanta during the winter months. St. Patrick's Day gets special attention from Atlantans, because the city's pioneers included many immigrants from Erin.

JANUARY

King Week. This annual event celebrates the birthday (January 15) and work of Dr. Martin Luther King, Jr.; the national holiday is the third Monday in January. Surrounding those dates, King Week festivities include speeches, cultural events, and entertainment, and culminate in a national parade and **March of Celebration**. For information, call the Martin Luther King, Jr., Center for Nonviolent Social Change *(see chapter 5)*. 524-1956.

Metropolitan Opera Auditions. The district competition is held on the third Saturday in January, the regional on the third Saturday in February. No reservations are required, and admission is free. The Atlanta Opera Guild *(see chapter 10)* produces the auditions. 4075 W. Paces Ferry Rd., Lovett School Chapel, Buckhead. For information, contact Betty McKemie, President, Atlanta Opera Guild, 37 Fairfield Dr., Avondale Estates. 297-9030.

Olde Christmas Storytelling Festival. Usually held during the first

or second weekend of January, depending on the dates of the Twelve Days of Christmas, this festival brings to Callanwolde a throng of storytellers from the Southern Order of Storytellers. Nationally known storytellers give evening "concerts" of storytelling, but there are also daytime events and special storytelling activities for children. Moderate admission; some discounts for seniors and children. Daytime events generally cost less than evening ones. Held at DeKalb College, central campus, 555 North Indian Creek Dr., Clarkston. 299-4000.

Peach Bowl. The date fluctuates between the last couple of days of December and the first two in January. One of the nation's most established bowl games, its credentials continue to improve, as it is now televised by the cable sports network ESPN. Festivities include a parade and other events Downtown. Ticket prices vary with location and are substantial. Georgia Dome, 285 International Blvd., Downtown. 223-9200.

FEBRUARY

Fisharama. The Georgia Wildlife Federation sponsors this show, which features hundreds of exhibitions of fishing

and boating equipment—with many items sold at discount prices. Free seminars and casting contests for children make Fisharama a family outing. Moderate admission; discounts to both seniors and children ages six to twelve; free for children under three. Atlanta Exposition Center, South Atlanta near Atlanta Hartsfield International Airport, I-285, Exit 40, Jonesboro Rd., Southeast. 929-3350.

Hispanic Festival of Music and the Arts.
Since 1990, the members of the Atlanta Virtuosi *(see chapter 3)* have produced a celebration of Spanish and Latin American music. The festival takes place in February and March, and brings to Atlanta outstanding guest artists from Hispanic countries and the United States. The music performed reflects the contributions of Hispanic culture to classical and traditional folk music. Moderate admission. P.O. Box 77047, Atlanta, 30357. 938-8611.

Mardi Gras Parade.
The Krewe of Phoenix, a nonprofit organization formed to produce this event, leads merrymakers on a delightful ramble through Downtown to Underground the Saturday prior to Fat Tuesday. Atlanta's first nighttime event is alive with illuminated floats, flambeaux, about ten walking krewes, and several marching bands. Neighborhood groups, clubs, and organizations are invited to dress in costume and enter the parade, which is televised live. Float sponsorships are welcomed and entitle the sponsor to membership in the Krewe of Phoenix. Contact Tim Lantz. Creative Events and Services, 1140 Hammond Dr., Ste. A-1120, Atlanta, 30328. 223-4636.

Southeastern Flower Show.
An annual indoor prelude to spring in all its glory opens the city's magical floral season with the largest flower show in the southeast. The show features replicas of landscaped gardens, a horticulture and flower arranging competition, and a retail gardening and shopping area where you can find interesting seeds and original art emphasizing botanical themes. An elegant preview party opens the event. Moderate admission; discounts for students and groups of ten or more. The show is accredited by the Garden Club of America. All proceeds go to the Atlanta Botanical Garden. Call for location. 888-5638.

MARCH

Atlanta Boat Show.
A happening in Atlanta for the past thirty years, the boat show is for boating enthusiasts and anyone who wishes to discover the joys of boating. Special exhibitions feature model boats, free seminars, fishing clinics, and craftsmen building vintage boats. The toy model boat show is held within the big show. Areas devoted to saltwater and underwater activities (scuba diving and snorkeling) are now included, as is an exhibition devoted to charter fishing and water travel. Moderate admission; discounts for seniors and children ages three to twelve (no charge for children under three). Watch for coupons at local dealers and in area newspapers. Georgia World Congress Center, 285 International Blvd., Downtown. 998-9800.

Atlanta Home Show. This biannual three-day event is held in March or April and October or November. It includes hourly seminars on decorating and home improvement. Hundreds of exhibits showcase accessories for the home and garden: kitchen gear, custom closets, fireplaces, woodworking tools, fencing, security systems, decking, landscaping, pools, and more. Georgia World Congress Center, 285 International Blvd., Downtown. 223-4636.

Bulloch Hall Quilt Show, "The Great Cover-Up." Two weekends and the intervening week are devoted to quilts of all kinds, both antique and contemporary. This has been a popular annual event for more than a decade. Nominal admission. 180 Bulloch Ave., Bulloch Hall, Roswell. 992-1731.

County Cork Irish Festival. A favorite Buckhead pub celebrates St. Patrick's Day with Irish music, dancing, and special Irish entertainment from noon 'til the wee hours. Traditional food and drink. 5600 Roswell Rd., The Prado, Sandy Springs. 303-1976.

Kids Fishing Event. An annual event produced by the Upper Chattahoochee Chapter of Trout Unlimited and the Georgia Department of Natural Resources gives kids a chance to try their luck at the sport. The Chattahoochee is stocked with about 2,500 trout before the event to give the junior anglers pretty good odds. Experienced anglers are on hand to give advice. This event is usually held one or two Saturdays before the opening of trout season. Additional free fishing days for kids are declared at random throughout the year, mostly in May and June, depending on the date of National Fishing Week. Free for children ages sixteen and under. Contact Chris Martin at the Georgia Game and Fish Division, Department of Natural Resources, for information. Chattahoochee River Park at Azalea Dr., off Roswell Rd., Roswell. 918-6418.

Motorcraft 500. This professional stock car race is part of the NASCAR Winston Cup Series. On this day of excitement, the noisy crowd knows how to have fun. Atlanta Motor Speedway, Hwys. 19-41 (I-75, Exit 77—Griffin), Hampton. 946-4211.

Salute to American Craft. This juried show, sponsored by the American Craft Council and produced by American Craft Enterprises, is a marketing event for craft artists who seek venues for selling their work. Artists come from all over the country, and the work presented includes textiles, ceramics, furniture, and jewelry. The preview party preceding this four-day show benefits the Georgia Trust for Historic Preservation, which contributes volunteers and organizational efforts *(see chapter 10)*. 1516 Peachtree St., Downtown. 881-9980 (Georgia Trust).

St. Patrick's Day Parade. Atlanta's Irish roots go back to its earliest days. The long-standing St. Patrick's Day tradition takes a parade down Peachtree Street and brings out the Irish (and those who wish they were) for a day of celebration. Atlanta's Hibernian Benevolent Society *(see chapter 10)* produces this parade, so it's not to be missed. Take the children. Downtown. Contact Mac McKenna, parade chairman. 449-6601.

St. Patrick's Day Parade & Festival.
This one is in Buckhead, and is produced by the Buckhead Village Merchants Association. The afternoon's merriment starts off around East Paces Ferry Road and Bolling Way.

Meandering through Buckhead Village, the parade winds up in Frankie Allen Park on Pharr Road. For all the young at heart. Creative Events and Services, 1140 Hammond Dr., Ste. A-1140, Sandy Springs. 255-5255.

SPRING

The Dogwood Festival in April kicks off the dazzling Atlanta spring, which is especially busy with festivals and events that make us all feel renewed. Arts and crafts are a major feature of many of the May events.

APRIL

Archifest.
One of Atlanta's most unusual events, Archifest is produced by the Atlanta chapter of the American Institute of Architects. It is designed to enhance public awareness of the role of architecture in daily life, and to encourage interaction among architects and between them and the public. Events include children's activities, special exhibitions, a tour of homes, and opportunities to consult with practicing architects regarding projects you may be contemplating. Many events are free. The bus tour of homes is a unique opportunity to view the designs of local architects or special historic homes. The fee for the tour is substantial. 1197 Peachtree St., Colony Square Retail Mall, Midtown. 873-3207.

Atlanta Celtic Festival.
Celebrate the Irish, Scottish, Welsh, and other Celtic cultures in this ever-expanding festival of music, dance, and food. Celtic wares and crafts are sold. Venue changes; begin to check for details in late March. Proceeds will build a Celtic Heritage Center. Nominal admission. 572-8045.

Atlanta Steeplechase.
This is an Event with a capital "E" because it appeals to just about everyone. Dress up or down; bring a bologna sandwich or a caviar spread, but don't miss the Steeplechase. Watch the races—or the people—and enjoy the antique autos that make it an outing to remember. A benefit for the Atlanta Speech School, it is usually held on the first Saturday in April. A ball held the evening before and a brunch on the morning of the event are open to those who don't mind expensive tickets. General admission is moderate, but a parking pass must also be purchased, so it's a good idea to car-pool. No tickets at the gate. Mail order only, and the tickets go fast. Mail only: Atlanta Steeplechase, 3160 Northside Pkwy., Atlanta, 30327. Event site: Seven Branches Farm, Cumming. GA 400 to Hwy. 141 (Exit 9), and follow the signs. 237-7436.

AT&T *Challenge.* This professional men's tennis tournament draws 70,000 folks to watch top stars play for a $260,000 purse. A variety of charities benefit from a proceeds pot, which raises $100,000 each year. The matches are televised, and usually appear on ESPN. Admission price ranges are substantial. ProServ, 300 Galleria Pkwy., Ste. 410, Northwest. 395-3500.

B.C. *Fest!* This annual family festival, held for two days every spring, is sponsored by the Michael C. Carlos Museum to enrich children's understanding of the history of art. The theme changes every year, but activities and films for children of all ages are always part of the fun. Carlos Museum, Emory University, Northeast. 727-4280.

Dogwood Festival. One of metro Atlanta's most multifaceted events presents parades, art shows, tours of private homes and gardens, musicales, and parties all over town. The festivities occur in early April over a period including two weekends and the intervening week. Celebrating Atlanta's luscious springtime, highlighted by the famous dogwood, the Dogwood Festival is now more than fifty years old. The big weekend takes place in Piedmont Park, and activities include hot air balloon demonstrations and the traditional hot air balloon race. Most events (except the Druid Hills Home and Garden Tour) are free. In 1992 the festival launched a bike tour through Atlanta areas that are especially rich in dogwood blooms. Participants may choose the distance they wish to cycle. 5500 Interstate North Pkwy., Ste. 505, Northwest. 952-9151.

Easter Bunny Teas. During the week before Easter, the Easter Bunny joins Atlantans at the Ritz-Carlton, Atlanta, to mingle with young guests. Music, hot chocolate, and Easter treats—created by the Ritz-Carlton's pastry chefs—are among the goodies. On Easter Saturday, the Bunny joins guests for a holiday breakfast and poses for photos with the children. Puppeteers and storytellers also entertain. Make reservations early. Admission price is moderate. 181 Peachtree St., Ritz-Carlton, Atlanta, Downtown. 659-0400.

Easter Sunrise Services. Held at daybreak, these nondenominational services occur simultaneously at both the top and the base of Stone Mountain. The dramatic event usually takes place in April but sometimes in March if Easter is early. Stone Mountain Park, Stone Mountain. 498-5600.

For Kids' Sake Day. Sponsored by WXIA, Channel 11, this annual event benefits the Georgia Council on Child Abuse. Held at Zoo Atlanta, the activities vary from year to year, but safety programs, storytelling programs, and puppetry always keep the focus on the child. Regular zoo admission is often discounted for the event. 800 Cherokee Ave., Grant Park. 624-5630; 624-5600.

Georgia Renaissance Festival. Hear ye! Hear ye! Announcing fun and frolic for one and all every weekend from late April through June—seven weeks in all—and then again in October. In the south metro area, an olde English village comes to life with fun, games, unique food, characters—meet Henry VIII (in October the star is Robin Hood)— unusual crafts, and music. Moderate admission; discounts for children ages 12 and under. Group rates. Free parking. I-85, Fairburn Exit (Exit 12). Peachtree City. 964-8575.

Indian Heritage Day. In late April, this recreated Creek Indian village comes alive. Eat fried corn bread while watching demonstrations of curing hides, arrow-making, finger-weaving, and Indian cooking. One of the Southeast Tourism Society's Top Twenty Events. Stately Oaks, 100 Carriage Lane, Jonesboro. 473-0197.

Inman Park Spring Festival and Tour of Homes. To benefit the ongoing restoration efforts of the Inman Park Neighborhood Association, residents of this Victorian neighborhood—one of Atlanta's first residential developments built after the Civil War—open their historic homes. The area is safe to walk, and the streets are closed off, allowing visitors to wander among the homes, many of which have been restored. Arts and crafts, an antique market, a street market, food, and music make the affair a treat to look forward to. It's held during the last weekend of April each year, and there's always a neighborhood parade on Saturday. Inman Park is bounded by DeKalb Avenue, Highland Avenue, Moreland Avenue, and the railroad tracks. Free and open to the public, but the tour of homes charges a moderate admission. 242-4895.

Walter Rich, of Rich's, was the founding president of the Atlanta Dogwood Festival, April 19-26, 1936. A carnival, a parade, and performances by the Metropolitan Opera, the Philadelphia Symphony, and area college choruses made up the festivities.

The Masters. OK, we know Augusta, Georgia, is a distance from Atlanta, but in early April, many Atlantans head over there for the Masters. Tickets are impossible to obtain unless you're on the mailing list, which has been closed since 1978. It used to be easy to get tickets to the practice rounds, but now a mailing list has been set up for these tickets as well. Augusta is about three hours east of Atlanta on I-20. Exit Washington Road (Exit 65), go east about two miles, and follow the signs. Augusta National Golf Club, 2604 Washington Rd., Augusta. 706-738-7761.

Peachtree Crossings Country Fair. Held twice annually (during a weekend in April and on Labor Day weekend), this newcomer to the country fair circuit showcases some very fine country crafts, good barbecue, and yummy apple dumplings. Demonstrations of country crafts and skills, activities, and lots of entertainment make these weekends merry. About 200 exhibitors showcase their wares. Nominal admission; discounts for children. Good traffic management and parking. I-85 South to Fairburn exit (Exit 12), Georgia Renaissance Festival site, Peachtree City. 434-3661.

Southside Fool's Day Road Race. Always held on the first Sunday in April, unless Easter happens to coincide (in which case it falls on the second Sunday). Held at Woodward Academy, off Rugby and Virginia Avenues in College Park, the race attracts about 300 runners. Winners in several age categories receive awards, and all participants get t-shirts. Preregistration and day-of-the-race registration are both moderately priced. For information, contact Bob Strong, athletic coordinator for the College Park Department of Recreation, which puts on the race. 3636 College St., College Park. 669-3773.

MAY

Atlanta Film and Video Festival.
Sponsored by IMAGE Film and Video Center, the festival has been held since 1977 and attracts more than 500 entries. Held annually over a five-day period, this juried competition brings to Atlanta's attention more than thirty of the most innovative independent media works from around the nation. Artists, curators, and critics comprise the jury panels. Opening night is at the High Museum of Art, and the remaining screenings are at IMAGE. 75 Bennett St., Ste. M-1, Brookwood. 352-4225.

Atlanta Peach Caribbean Carnival.
Capturing the flavor of the Caribbean without leaving Peachtree Street, this folklife festival and art show includes a marketplace selling Caribbean foods as well as arts and crafts. Entertainment fêtes—late-night parties with authentic Caribbean entertainment—a children's carnival, dance symposium, and educational seminars round out the events. A parade of marching bands with costumed dancers, stilt walkers, and music played on flat-bed trucks makes its way from Midtown to Downtown. 344-2567.

Bell South Classic. Also known as the
Atlanta Golf Classic, this major PGA event brings top players to the Atlanta Country Club. The club's course was especially designed for competition play. The classic has been an annual event for over two decades, featuring a popular pro-am match with lots of celebrities. Atlanta golfers avidly follow this tournament, so tickets go fast. Proceeds benefit Egleston Children's Hospital, which receives about a half million dollars from the event each year. About 125,000 people attend during the tournament. Admission ranges from the nominal to the substantial, depending on the day of the week—on Monday it's free, and the most expensive tickets are for Friday and Saturday. Corporate packages are available. Ample parking is based at auxiliary parking lots, and shuttle buses make the trek from the lots to the course. Atlanta Country Club, 500 Atlanta Country Club Dr., off Johnson Ferry Rd. at Paper Mill Rd., Marietta. 953-2100. Bell South Classic office (for tickets and scheduling information), 300 Interstate North, Ste. 280, Northwest. 951-8777.

Cinco de Mayo. Celebrating Mexico's
Independence Day, May 5, this event is a fund raiser for the Atlanta Virtuosi, a local chamber music group (see chapter 3). A luxurious mansion is selected as the site of the event. Following a tour of the house, a cash bar and light hors d'oeuvres precede a full authentic Mexican dinner prepared by Virtuosi member and violinist Juan

Ramírez and his brother, David, a tenor and fellow member of the Virtuosi. Traditional mariachi entertainment is part of the evening. Substantial admission. P.O. Box 77047, Atlanta, 30357. 938-8611.

Cotton Pickin' Country Fair. Although it's just a tad outside our boundaries (Meriwether County), this fair, also held in October, is popular among southsiders, but should be on everyone's "must" list. Indeed, the license plates in the parking lot indicate its popularity with all Atlantans. This fair maintains a high level of quality year in and year out, especially in the crafts department. The 35-acre site was once home to a cotton gin. Clogging, funnel cakes, and scrumptious biscuits with country ham are among the distinctive foods that enhance the appeal. The well-organized operation makes parking and getting in and out a snap. The little main street in Gay—population around 200—has some very noteworthy antique shops. Nominal admission; discounts for seniors and children; children under age three free. I-75 South to Hwy. 85. 706-538-6814.

Dobbins Air Force Base and Naval Air Station Atlanta Annual Open House. The two military facilities alternate the hosting responsibilities for this annual event. Families enjoy aerial demonstrations, bands, tours of aircraft, and the opportunity to talk with pilots. Vintage aircraft are often exhibited. Refreshments are available at this weekend event. Free admission. On the runway at Dobbins Air Force Base (off Hwy. 41) or at the Naval Air Station (off Atlanta Rd.), depending on which entity is the host. 421-5402; 421-5055

(Dobbins AFB Public Affairs); 421-5406 (Naval Air Station Public Affairs).

Gardens for Connoisseurs Tour. This Mother's Day tradition, begun more than ten years ago, opens several selected private gardens for tours benefiting the Atlanta Botanical Garden. 876-5859 (Atlanta Botanical Gardens).

Georgia Folklore by Moonlight. A magical storytelling event with local talent portraying historic characters and relating tales from days long gone. The setting, costumes, talent, and ambience make this a memorable experience. While you wait your turn for a tour of Stately Oaks, you can listen to storytellers and musicians who weave their tales and lift their voices around a large fire. Stately Oaks, 100 Carriage Dr., Historical Jonesboro (*see chapter 5*). 473-0197 (Historical Jonesboro/Clayton County).

Herb Education Day. The Chattahoochee unit of the Herb Society of America (*see chapter 10*), holds this event the first weekend in May at the Atlanta Botanical Gardens. Anyone interested in herbs should mark the calendar because this is a "must" opportunity to learn about and purchase quality potted herbs. 876-5859 (Atlanta Botanical Gardens).

Kingfest. A summer-long series running on alternate Saturdays during the months of May, June, July, and August, Kingfest presents dance, music, and theater. Each day celebrates a different musical theme, such as gospel, zydeco, blues, or rock, and the performances are then coordinated with that theme. At least one national act is included for each theme. Visual

arts and crafts are presented on the grounds, and an artists' market is a major feature. One day is dedicated to international performances and visual artists (Kingfest Internationale) and another to children (Kids' Day at Kingfest). Admission to all Kingfest events is free. All events take place at the King Center. 449 Auburn Ave., Downtown. 524-1956.

Sweetwater Fever Festival. The South Cobb Arts Alliance holds this annual festival at the historic Mable House in Mableton on the second weekend in May. The juried show looks for fine art, crafts, and photography of originality and quality. About 3,000 visitors enjoy viewing the art and making purchases. Food and entertainment. Free and

open to the public. 5239 Floyd Rd., Mableton. 739-0189.

U.S. Chef's Open. Begun in 1989, this weekend event gives professional, student, and amateur chefs the opportunity to dish up their best while vying for prizes. Exhibitors offer samples of their special goodies, and while many are products we're familiar with, occasional exotic discoveries are possible. Proceeds benefit Easter Seals and Atlanta's Table, a project that feeds the hungry in Atlanta. Moderate admission; discounts for advance purchases, and children under six are admitted free. Georgia World Congress Center, 285 International Blvd., Downtown. 223-4636.

JUNE

Atlanta Jazz Festival. Many of the best musicians—local, national, and international—perform at concerts that take place in Atlanta's city parks. Begun in the late 1970s, the festival is now one of the country's most important jazz events. The city's Bureau of Cultural Affairs produces the festival, and many corporate sponsors get on the bandwagon to support it. Grant Park is the site of the free concerts. The lunchtime brown bag concerts in Woodruff Park make it easy for downtown office workers to enjoy the festival. Most events are free, and the rest are moderately priced. 817-6815 (Bureau of Cultural Affairs, City of Atlanta).

Cabbagetown Reunion Festival. The first Saturday in June is a special day in Cabbagetown, the Atlanta neighborhood that grew up around the aban-

doned Fulton Bag and Cotton Mill. Families enjoy the old-fashioned entertainments of music, crafts, food, and storytelling. Occasionally a tour of restored homes is part of the program. Cabbagetown lies between DeKalb Avenue and Memorial Drive and is bounded by Pearl Street and Wylie Street. Downtown. No admission is charged for the festival; moderate admission for tour of homes when offered. 521-0815, Cabbagetown Revitalization and Future Trust (CRAFT, Inc.).

Georgia Shakespeare Festival. Bring a picnic supper, or have it catered, and enjoy the pre-performance entertainment with your repast as you await a fine professional company's presentation of a Shakespearean play. The theater is set up under a tent, giving a true period ambience. Concurrent with the festival, **Camp Shake-speare** invites children to get acquainted with theater (two weeks in July and two in August). The festival runs from June through August and stages three different plays. Substantial admission. On the grounds of Oglethorpe University. 4484 Peachtree Rd., Brookhaven. 264-0020.

National Pond Society Tour and Expo. The tour exhibits anywhere between thirty and forty area homes that have ponds. Exhibits include ponds enhanced with Oriental art, pop art, fish, wildlife, water gardens, waterfalls, and more. One evening tour travels to illuminated ponds. Seminars and displays continue throughout the two-day expo. Products and services for indoor ponds are also exhibited. Check with Intown Hardware (N. Highland Ave.) for tickets, or contact the society (P.O. Box 449, Acworth, 30101) for tickets. Venues change from year to year. Moderate admission; discounts for children and seniors. 975-0277.

Taste of Atlanta. It's just that...with several restaurants dishing up a taste of their best fare. This is a national benefit whose proceeds go to the Kidney Foundation. In fact, it's the foundation's largest single source of income each year. More than 50,000 people taste and sample during this three-day event. Moderate admission; children under twelve are admitted free. Prices for the nibbles range upward from 50¢. Live entertainment, children's activities, and fireworks enhance the fun. Broadcast live. Usually held in early June; locations vary. 248-1315 (Kidney Foundation).

Willie B.'s Birthday Party. The birthday of Zoo Atlanta's prize western lowland silverback gorilla, Willie B., is celebrated with African dancers and storytellers, special events, and treats for both visitors and Willie B. Regular zoo admission. 800 Cherokee Ave., Grant Park. 624-5678.

SUMMER

With all the activity going on in Atlanta, you'll have to work hard to recreate those lazy Southern summer days of yore. The Renaissance festival winds up in June, just as others are getting underway. Don't overlook Atlanta's summertime concert series—and remember, in summer's waning days, the arts and crafts scene becomes busy again with many special festivals.

JULY

Civil War Encampment. The Atlanta History Center serves as the staging ground for re-enactors demonstrating what it was like to live in a tent on a Civil War battlefield. Music, food, and other exhibitions further depict life during this period. Moderate admission; discounts for seniors and students. Children under six are admitted free. 3101 Andrews Dr., Buckhead. 814-4000.

DeKalb International Choral Festival. Established in 1990, the festival presents choruses from more than eight countries plus seven from the U.S. Sponsored by major corporations and hosted by the DeKalb Convention and Visitors Bureau, this unique event culminates with **WorldSing**, in which fifteen choral groups representing all ages perform in unison at Stone Mountain Park. International groups sing in native costume. The largest festival of its type in the world, and only the second ever held in this country, the festival won four major awards after its first year. Performances are given throughout DeKalb County, in churches and malls, and the grand finale is televised live. All daytime performances are free and open to the public, and a nominal admission is charged for evening performances. Discounts for children, seniors, and groups. 378-2525 (DeKalb Convention and Visitors Bureau).

Fantastic Fourth Celebration. Concerts of country, rock 'n' roll, and patriotic music make Stone Mountain ring on the afternoons of July 3rd, 4th, and 5th. At dark, a laser show and fireworks bring these splendid days to their close. Bring a picnic or sample the casual fare offered by food vendors at the park. Admission to the park is by day or year pass, and there is no additional charge to attend the celebration. Stone Mountain Park, Stone Mountain. 498-5702.

Georgia State Games. Created for Georgia's amateur athletes, this festival is patterned after the summer Olympics. Established in 1989 by an act of the Georgia legislature, the first games took place in 1990. The main venue for events is the Georgia Institute of Technology, although the specific events take place at various locations around the metro area. More than thirty team and individual sports attract 25,000 amateur athletes of all ages to compete in everything from archery to wrestling. This event is designed as a training opportunity for U. S. Olympians and is one of forty such state-based programs. Free admission. 1201 W. Peachtree St., One Atlantic Center, Ste. 3095, Atlanta, 30309. 853-0250.

Independence Day at Lenox Square. The Lenox Square front parking lot turns into a huge picnic area as visitors try to get ringside seats for a spectacular fireworks display. Bring lawn chairs and gather at dusk. Music (patriotic and other) precedes the nighttime dazzle: the largest fireworks show in the Southeast. Food vendors are available, but folks do bring their own munchies. 233-6767 (Lenox Square management office).

Marietta Square Independence Day Celebration. Live entertainment, carnival games, and a parade lead up to a dramatic fireworks display in the evening. Free and open to the public. Glover Park, Marietta. 528-0616.

Peachtree Road Race. A 10K race from Lenox Square to Piedmont Park draws 45,000 runners, tempted by the prize of the prestigious T-shirt, to this race. Now a national and international event with participants from all over the world, it is the official start to Atlanta's Fourth of July celebrations. A Wheelchair Division and a Master's Division (for runners age forty and over) diversify the field. To register, send a

SASE to Peachtree Road Race, Atlanta Track Club, 3097 East Shadowlawn Ave., Atlanta, GA 30305. 231-9065 (Atlanta Track Club).

Run for Life. Many events crowd the campus of Life College during the busy last Saturday in July. Starting at the square in Marietta, a 5K road race culminates at the Life campus. A 10K race starts off at Marietta High School and winds up back at the campus. Participation is open to anyone, but running clubs often field teams of runners for the road races. There's more: Family games, a "woodland walk," and a one-mile fun run are among the activities that bring about 4,000 participants and 2,000 spectators to the campus. The International Challenge Cup draws runners from foreign countries to compete with American run-

ners. Registration fees are moderate. Some proceeds benefit Open Gate, a shelter for abused children. Joe Kelly, community relations and event coordinator. 1269 Barclay Cir., Marietta. 424-0554, ext. 238.

WSB Salute 2 America Parade. Begun in 1959, it's the largest regularly scheduled Fourth of July parade in America, drawing about 250,000 viewers each year. Celebrities—usually ABC TV stars—lead the parade, which begins at Marietta Street and Techwood Drive, then turns up Peachtree Street and heads north to Ralph McGill Boulevard. Bands, clowns, floats, and, naturally, the standard cluster of politicians make up the participants. Sponsored by local television station WSB, the parade is a televised, mid-morning event. 897-7385.

AUGUST

Art in the Park. Marietta's central square becomes a three-day art gallery, displaying original paintings, photography, pottery, and other media. Food concessions keep the roving bands of art patrons well nourished. Glover Park, Marietta. 528-0616.

Atlanta International Food and Wine Festival. Originally designed to bring folks downtown to the Westin Peachtree Plaza Hotel, the festival grew into one of the largest international competitions in the world. Visitors taste wines from the United States and other countries, among them Argentina and Chile. Recently reorganized, the festival takes place in three Buckhead hotels—the Swissôtel, the Nikko, and the J.W. Marriott. Produced by the Geor-

gia Hospitality and Travel Association, 600 W. Peachtree St., Ste. 1500, Atlanta, 30308. 873-4482.

Buckarama. Based on the same concept as February's Fisherama, this event, sponsored by the Georgia Wildlife Federation, focuses on hunting and camping exhibitions, including a seminar on hunter safety. Over 35,000 attend each year. Held at the Atlanta Exposition Center near the Hartsfield International Airport, 1-285, Exit 40, Jonesboro Rd., Southeast. 929-3350.

National Black Arts Festival. This rich extravaganza of visual and performing arts reflects the cultural and artistic contributions of African-Americans to this country. The festival is held in even numbered years at various venues throughout the metropolitan area. Many events are free and open to the public. Moderate to substantial admissions otherwise; some discounting for certain groups, depending on the activity. 70 Fairlie St., Ste. 250, Downtown. 730-7315.

SEPTEMBER

Ansley Park Tour of Homes. Established in 1904 by engineer S.Z. Ruff, Ansley Park, named for its developer Edwin P. Ansley, remains one of the most attractive of Atlanta's neighborhoods. Sidewalks course through its landscaped areas, and inviting pocket parks dot the neighborhood. All this lies within sight of the rising skyscrapers of Midtown and within walking distance of the Robert W. Woodruff Arts Center and numerous appealing restaurants and shops. Ansley Park is bounded on the east by Piedmont Avenue, on the west by Peachtree Street, with Monroe Drive and 14th Street as northern and southern boundaries. Not an annual event, this tour is often held in different months. Moderate admission. In September, start checking newspapers for details.

Arts Festival of Atlanta. This nine-day paean to the arts started almost forty years ago when some folks displayed art over the clothesline in a Buckhead backyard. Since then, the Arts Festival of Atlanta has grown into a serious arts production, with its scope including both the lively and visual arts. Art by young people forms a particularly good exhibition, and there are lots of children's activities (workshops and performances). The Artists' Market is the main draw, attracting thousands to look at art and purchase fine textiles, paintings, prints, ceramics, jewelry, and leather goods. Food includes terrific corn dogs, steak sandwiches, and more cotton candy than anyone has a right to ingest. The show draws about two million people each year. Parking? Forget it. The best bet is to take MARTA to the Arts Center Station and take the shuttle, or ride to the Midtown Station and walk the two blocks to the exhibition site in Piedmont Park. Free, but donations are welcomed. At Piedmont Park, between Monroe Dr. and 10th St., Midtown. Office: 999 Peachtree St., First Union Plaza, at 10th St., Midtown. 885-1125.

Atlanta Greek Festival. For nearly two decades, Atlanta's Greek community, established several generations ago, has invited the town to celebrate Greek culture and food at the Orthodox Cathedral of the Annunciation. Entertainment (including dancing and live music), tours of the cathedral, and lots of Greek wine and strong coffee to wash down gyros and souvlaki are among the treats that attract some 40,000 of us to this wonderful festival. Parking is impossible, and side-street parking has been banned by the police. Count on the shuttle buses from the K-Mart parking lot or the Century Center parking lot, both on Clairmont Road west of I-85. Groups of senior citizens who come from retirement or other caregiving homes may enter free if they make advance arrangements. Nominal admission; discounts for children. Food items begin at $3. 2500 Clairmont Rd., Northeast. 633-5870.

Folklife Festival. One of several special events presented at the Atlanta History Center, this festival replicates the daily life of an 1840s north Georgia farming family. Traditional crafts, including candle-making, weaving, and soap making, enhance the authentic atmosphere. Regular center admission (moderate). 3101 Andrews Dr., Buckhead. 814-4000.

Grant Park Tour of Homes. This intown neighborhood was named for Colonel L.P. Grant, the native of Maine who designed the city's defenses for the Battle of the Atlanta. Now undergoing significant revival, the neighborhood's Victorian homes chiefly date from the late nineteenth and early twentieth centuries. Ever since the mid-1970s, the Grant Park Neighborhood Association has offered an annual tour of homes to encourage residents in other parts of the metro area to visit and appreciate this diverse and dynamic community. Moderate admission; discounts for children under twelve and for advance ticket purchases. 525-7004.

Gwinnett County Fair. One of the largest true county fairs in the state, it draws thousands to view the various livestock competitions throughout its ten-day run. A significant feature is the entertainment tent, where major country music groups, cloggers, and a beauty contest highlight the activities. Don't miss the fireworks. A car raffle is the big moment on the fair's last Saturday. Nominal admission; discounts for children and senior citizens. Children under age five are admitted free. Free

parking. On Johnson Rd., between S.R. 20 and 124, five miles east of Snellville. 822-7700 (Gwinnett County Extension Service).

Heritage Days. Military demonstrations, crafts, civilian encampments, entertainment, open-hearth cooking, and other activities usually focused around life in the 1860s yield a fascinating weekend. Nominal admission; discounts for children. 180 Bulloch Ave., Bulloch Hall, Roswell. 992-1731.

Montreux/Atlanta International Music Festival. Atlanta and Montreux, Switzerland, joined forces in 1988 to produce a music festival featuring a variety of styles: jazz, blues, gospel, reggae, and classical. Atlanta sends a local musician to perform at the Montreaux festival in July, and Montreux reciprocates by sending one of its talents to Atlanta for this festival. Piedmont Park is the site of the free events, but the concerts held at Chastain Park can hit the expensive category. The festival begins Labor Day weekend and lasts through some of the following week, but some years it can start in late August. 817-6815 (Bureau of Cultural Affairs, City of Atlanta).

Peachtree Crossing Country Fair. Labor Day weekend; also in April (see page 85). 434-3661.

Powers Crossroads Country Fair and Arts Festival. Held each Labor Day weekend for more than two decades, this fair attracts a good number of regular exhibitors who bring crafts and wearable art. The best exhibitors showcase authentic country crafts, including hand-sewn quilts and apple-head dolls. Food is very good at this one, with super pork barbecue and freshly made biscuits. A special section, with rides and activities costing additional small amounts, is just for children. The weather is usually warm this weekend, but the exhibits are spread out under a good stand of trees, providing a substantially cooler environment. Traffic management is excellent, and there's a baby-sitting service if you don't want to tote the toddlers. Demonstrations of a mule-powered sorghum mill, a grist mill, an apple press, black-smithing, and other crafts fill the day. Nominal admission; discounts for seniors and children under twelve. Take I-85 to Hwy. 34 (Exit 9), twelve miles west of Newnan, and follow the excellent signs. 253-2011.

> *Talk about a need for fund-raising!*
> *After the Battle of Atlanta in 1864,*
> *the city treasury contained*
> *$1.64 in Confederate money. By*
> *1867 the treasury contained a*
> *whopping $29,000.*

Sandy Springs Festival. More than a hundred arts and crafts booths, entertainment, children's activities, and demonstrations of old crafts (such as spinning, rug hooking, tatting, quilting, and basket weaving) give a lively spin to this relatively new but popular festival. The ambience represents the area's farming community life in the 1870s. Proceeds benefit the Sandy Springs Historic Community Foundation, which operates the Williams-Payne House (see chapter 5). Parking is usually not difficult. Nominal admission; discounts for children over six; children under six are admitted free. Hitson Memorial Center, Mt. Vernon Hwy. and Sandy Springs Cir., Sandy Springs. 851-9111.

Southern Food Festival. This fund-raising event, hosted by the Atlanta Chapter of the American Institute of Wine and Food (see chapter 10), showcases both traditional and contemporary cooking from all parts of the South. Sample various styles of barbecue and savor the sounds of traditional Southern music, including country and Cajun. Venue changes. Moderate admission. P.O. Box 12491, Atlanta, 30355-2491. 399-9781.

Sweetwater Valley Fine Arts and Crafts Festival. All handmade items—fine arts and crafts, plus country-style crafts—are showcased in a juried show that is similar to the "Fever" show held in the spring, also hosted by the South Cobb Arts Alliance. Food booths and entertainment. Free and open to the public. Mable House, 5239 Floyd Rd., Mableton. 739-0189.

Tour D' Town. Begun in 1986 to benefit the Atlanta City Unit of the American Cancer Society, this bike ride through the metropolitan area begins and ends in Buckhead. The tour is always held on Labor Day and is for families and individuals. In 1991, both amateur and professional categories were developed for a 1K course. Substantial admission; discount for children twelve and under. 1801 Peachtree Rd., Brookwood. 841-0700 (American Cancer Society).

U.S.T.A. Mens' 60 Clay Court Championships. Established in 1867, this is an open tournament for men over age sixty. Since 1990 this tennis event has made its home at the Standard Club in Duluth and is now sponsored by Coca-Cola. Free and open to the public. Peter Howell, head professional. Standard Club, 6230 Abbotts Bridge Rd., Duluth. 497-1866.

Yellow Daisy Festival. This huge festival attracts nearly 500 exhibitors who showcase fine country crafts. One of the biggest outdoor arts and crafts festivals in the Southeast, the Yellow Daisy Festival celebrates a unique flower and has been attracting throngs for about 25 years. Musical entertainment is usually provided by national performers. Food is available. Parking and traffic management are excellent. No admission, but an annual parking pass or nominally priced onetime pass is required at the gate. Stone Mountain Park, Stone Mountain. 498-5702.

Ye Olde English Festival. A small festival that's become increasingly popular over the years, it features English food—fish 'n' chips and Dragonslayer Stew—and spirits—including nonalcoholic brew. Storytellers, jugglers, and musicians evoke the spirit of the Bard. Folks leaving services at the synagogue across the street make their way to St. Bartholomew's for the festivities. Many children's activities make it fun for the little people. Nominal admission; children under six are admitted free. Proceeds benefit the church's charitable activities, most of which assist the homeless. 1790 LaVista Rd., Northeast. 634-3336.

FALL

The Highland Games are the high note of early autumn's festival season in Atlanta. From Halloween to the holidays, lively festivals and events make the late fall season exciting.

OCTOBER

Arts Alive. Produced by the Department of Cultural Affairs of the Atlanta Chamber of Commerce, this one-night event presents performance art at various venues throughout the city. More than two dozen performance groups participate, making Arts Alive the largest arts benefit in the city, according to the Chamber. Begun in 1986, Arts Alive benefits the Chamber's Business Volunteers for the Arts program. Patrons choose which performance to attend and then gather for a post-performance gala. Admission is substantial. 586-8536 (Atlanta Chamber of Commerce, Cultural Affairs Department).

Athens-to-Atlanta Rollerskating Marathon. This 85-mile race entices competitors from around the world. It takes at least four and a half hours (for the elite skaters) and up to seven or eight hours for the recreational skaters to travel the distance. It's run as an open road race, and all skaters must obey regular traffic laws. Yellow arrows on the road mark the course. The race runs through five different counties as it enters Atlanta, then through Avondale Estates and Little Five Points, ending at Piedmont Park. The entrance fee is substantial. Directors ask that people write before calling. Mail only: 1077 Vistavia Cir., Decatur, 30033. 634-9032.

Atlanta Home Show. Also in March *(see page 82)*. 223-4636.

Atlanta Third World Film Festival. Established in 1980, this festival presents screenings in the downtown Atlanta–Fulton County Public Library of films by producers from third-world nations. Sometimes filmmakers present lectures after the screenings. Most are free. 817-6815 (Bureau of Cultural Affairs, City of Atlanta).

Festa Italiana Italian Heritage Festival. This festival focuses on Italian culture, design, products, historic contributions, entertainment, and cuisine. Entertainment includes opera, classical music, a *commedial del arte* production, cultural exhibits, photo exhibits, and a bocce tournament. At the Galleria. Nominal admission. 988-8085.

Cotton Pickin' Country Fair. Also in May *(see page 89)*. 706-538-6814.

Decatur Heritage Festival. Held annually on the square in Decatur, the Heritage Festival presents storytellers, balladeers, clowns, and other entertainers along with artisans who display

wares for sale. It's a good opportunity to find baskets, quilts, textiles, pottery, pressed apples, homemade candles, and so on. Daytime activities free; nominal admission for the evening dance. Sponsored by several DeKalb and Decatur civic organizations. 373-1088 (DeKalb Historical Society).

Dunwoody Women's Club Tour of Homes. Always held on the first Wednesday in October, this tour benefits area charities. New and remodeled homes are usually included in this exhibition of up-to-date decorating ideas and trends. Moderate admission. 396-1548.

Festival of Cultures. The World of Coca-Cola and Underground Atlanta host a cultural event that lasts four weeks. Each weekend a different culture, most from other continents, takes the stage to present its dance, theater, and arts and crafts. The venue is usually Underground Atlanta. Free and open to the public. 523-2311 (Underground Atlanta).

Folklife Festival. This popular festival is held at the Atlanta History Center. Docents demonstrate traditional Georgia crafts, including candle-making, weaving, and soap making, to replicate the everyday life of an 1840s Piedmont Georgia farm family. Regular admission to the center (nominal); discounts for seniors over 65, children ages six to fourteen (age five and under admitted free), and students older than eighteen with I.D. 3101 Andrews Dr., Buckhead. 814-4000.

Georgia Renaissance Festival. Also in April through June *(see page 84)*.

Great Miller Lite Chili Cookoff.

For more than a decade, Atlantans have lined up to sample chili from huge, bubbling cauldrons, and to munch classic chili dogs and Brunswick stew. Around 100,000 chili chompers make the trek to savor the food and entertainment, and to laugh at the uproarious competitions. Nominal admission; children under twelve free. Nominal parking fee at the gate required, or annual parking pass. Stone Mountain Park, Stone Mountain. 498-5702.

Halloween in Atlanta.

Many fun events and activities open to celebrate this family-focused day. Proceeds benefit various charities. Below is a partial listing of our own favorites; check local newspapers for more.

Halloween Happenings. Bring the mini-monsters for a costume contest, live entertainment, and a film. Children of all ages welcome. Glover Park, Marietta. 528-0616.

Haunted Hayrides. Usually held every evening in October through the Halloween weekend, this experience is a chilling one. The creepies come out when 56 acres turn into a "haunted forest" inhabited by unearthly creatures of the night. A forty-minute hayride. Probably best for older goblins. Free refreshments. Watch for advertising. Alpharetta area.

Rhodes Hall Haunted Castle. This one got many of the other Atlanta haunted adventures rolling. The stately Victorian Amos G. Rhodes residence becomes a ghostly castle—perhaps with its own resident ghost—to benefit the Georgia Trust for Historic Preservation, which calls the house home—haunted or not. Duration varies, but usually at least one week is planned. Moderate admission; discounts for children. 1516 Peachtree St., Midtown. 881-9980.

Tour of Southern Ghosts. Costumed storytellers tell all about Southern ghosts in the main house of the Stone Mountain plantation, around the grounds, and in some of the outbuildings. Two weeks in October. Stone Mountain Park, Stone Mountain. 498-5702.

Zoo Atlanta's Great Halloween Caper. Benefiting the Atlanta Zoo, this tradition features a haunted house and many activities for children, including animal demonstrations (especially arachnids and reptiles). Usually held on the Saturday prior to Halloween, this event requires regular zoo admission plus a small fee for admission to the haunted house. 800 Cherokee Ave., Grant Park. 624-5678.

Hispanic Festival.

All events—exhibits, entertainment, food, and demonstrations—reflect and represent fourteen Central and South American countries as well as Spain. Shuttles run from the Target store parking lot on N. Druid Hills Road. Nominal admission. Immaculate Heart of Mary Catholic Church. 2855 Briarcliff Rd., south of Clairmont Rd., Northeast. 888-7839.

Jonesboro Fall Festival and Battle Reenactment.

More than 500 soldiers dress up in authentic attire and gear to present living military history demonstrations and to re-create the Battle of Jonesboro. This weekend affair also features live entertainment, arts and crafts, antiques, food, and tours of a mid-nineteenth-century plantation. Nominal admission. Stately Oaks Plantation, Jonesboro. 473-0197 (Historical Jonesboro).

Peachtree Peddler Craft Bazaar. In a suburban neighborhood near Spalding Drive and Holcomb Bridge Road in Gwinnett County, a group of crafters organize a juried bazaar featuring designer apparel and accessories, handmade gifts, and other items made by about 75 artists. 441-0416; 623-4528

Roswell Historical Society Tour of Homes. Bulloch Hall and at least five or six additional historic homes participate in this annual event benefiting the Historical Society (see chapter 5). Held during odd-numbered years. Admission is moderate. 992-1665.

St. Elias Annual Fall Festival. This Antiochian Orthodox Church holds a fascinating event celebrating the culture and culinary richness of the Middle East. Now about a quarter-century old, the festival features lots of dancing, live entertainment, tours of the church, and plenty to eat. The quality of the unusual dishes—kibbé, pickled turnips, falafel, and yummy pastries—is close to professional, and the coffee is stiff enough to fly the plane from Lebanon. Most worthwhile. Free and open to the public, with food prices beginning at a few dollars. 2045 Ponce de Leon Ave., Druid Hills. 378-8191.

Stone Mountain Highland Games. The entertainment at this annual event is decidedly the highlight of the affair. Fife-and-drum and military brass bands take to the meadows at Stone Mountain, kilts billowing and regimental falcons flapping as their music fills fine fall afternoons. The games include traditional Scottish activities, such as the caber toss, in which muscled young men toss a twenty-foot, 120-pound tree log. Presentations include highland dancing and reenactments by folks representing Oglethorpe's Scots, who founded St. Marys, Georgia. Some of the food is traditional, such as the meat pies. More than a hundred clans and societies gather to help one another with genealogy and clan history. Exhibitors sell exquisite plaid fabric and kilts, as well as books and tapes about Scotland and Celtic culture. Always held on the third full weekend in October. Moderate admission; discounts for children ages six to twelve. Stone Mountain Park, Stone Mountain. 498-5702.

Vacation World. About 300 exhibitors attract both the trade and the public to learn about short vacations as well as luxurious long ones. Prizes and travel specials, including giveaways, are part of the draw. Special features are devoted to the needs of seniors, singles, and the physically impaired. Moderate admission, with some discounts for advance purchases; children under twelve with an adult are admitted free. Georgia World Congress Center, 285 International Blvd., Downtown. 223-4636.

Wok-a-Thon. Produced by the Atlanta Chapter of the American Institute of Wine and Food, this annual taste of Pacific Rim culinary treats is a fund raiser for the Deen Terry Memorial Culinary Scholarship. The chapter bestows the prize annually on area students who are pursuing culinary careers. Atlanta's Asian restaurants provide the samples and the entertainment. Venues change, but the Hotel Nikko is the recent choice. Substantial admission. P.O. Box 12491, Atlanta, 30355-2491. 399-9781.

NOVEMBER

Atlanta Marathon and Half-Marathon.
Always run the morning of Thanksgiving, this race draws 5,200 participants for the half-marathon (thirteen miles) and about 750 runners for the full marathon (26 miles). The event starts in Lithonia and ends in Piedmont Park. Established in the early 1960s, this is the lesser-known older brother of the Peachtree Road Race held in July. Divisions are based on age groups, and the top three in each get the awards. 231-9065 (Atlanta Track Club).

"Bring Your Own Pillow" Electro-acoustic Music Concert.
Four concerts, repeating the same program, are presented in a single day to allow listeners the opportunity to attend for a brief period and then return later to catch what they missed. Produced by Composers' Resources (*see chapter 3*), it is usually held at the Georgia State University Recital Hall, Downtown, as well as other venues. Moderate admission; discounts for those who bring their own pillows. 998-7286 (Composers' Resources).

Heaven Bound.
A holiday performance of Big Bethel AME Church for more than sixty years, *Heaven Bound* is a religious musical pageant in the tradition of medieval allegorical theater. Church members perform the roles and sing in the choir. Founded in 1847, the church today holds about 1,600 persons. The performance is held on at least two nights, usually the first weekend in November. Nominal admission, and it's open to the public. 220 Auburn Ave., Downtown. 659-0248.

The Lighting of Château Élan.
Château Élan, a majestic sixteenth century-style French château, serves as an oasis for wine, food, art, and entertainment. The resort elegantly begins the holiday season with the annual Lighting of Château Élan. Visitors enjoy musical entertainment by area performing groups, and the opportunity to fill gift lists at the Holiday Gift Show. The holiday events continue through December. Château Élan also offers other seasonal events throughout the year. 100 Tour de France, Braselton, Georgia. 932-0900.

Lighting of the Great Tree.
For years, this annual rite illuminated the top of Rich's department store Downtown. Although Rich's Downtown closed in 1991, the tradition goes on, with the tree lighting now taking place at Underground Atlanta, Downtown. 523-2311 (Underground Atlanta).

A Meal to Remember.
Produced by Senior Citizen Services to benefit Meals on Wheels, Atlanta, this function is always held the first Friday in November and always at the Ritz-Carlton, Buckhead. A nationally known celebrity chef is invited to prepare a special dish for the dinner, and five well-known local chefs prepare additional courses. All chefs donate their time and ingredients to the project. Very substantial admission. 881-5950 (Senior Citizen Services).

Veterans Day Parade.
Honoring Georgia veterans of all wars, this patriotic and colorful parade is full of meaning for many. Downtown. 321-6111, ext. 6257.

DECEMBER

Candlelight Tours. Swing to the tunes of a Jazz Era holiday season, then contemplate the simplicity of an early nineteenth-century holiday celebration. That's how Christmas is welcomed at the Swan House and Tullie Smith House, both on the grounds of the Atlanta History Center. Two evenings in early December are chosen for the Candlelight Tours. Substantial admission. 3101 Andrews Dr., Buckhead. 814-4000.

Christmas at Bulloch Hall. During two weekends and the intervening week, Bulloch Hall is decorated in period holiday finery. The annual Candlelight Tour of Bulloch Hall, for which admission is moderate, recreates Mittie Bulloch's 1853 wedding to Cornelius Van Schaak Roosevelt. The Roosevelts were the parents of President Theodore Roosevelt. Nominal admission to Bulloch Hall for the Christmas events. Gift shop and tearoom. 180 Bulloch Ave., Bulloch Hall, Roswell. 992-1731.

Christmas at Callanwolde. Ongoing entertainment—choral groups and bell ringers—adds to the pleasure of shopping for special treasures in this lovely Tudor-style house. For two weeks (usually the first two in December), selected Atlanta interior designers transform the house into a breathtaking spectacle. A toy shop, sweet shop, collectibles and boutique shops, art shop, and pottery shop will boost your Christmas spirits. A shop selling gardening and nature items, in the conservatory, is run by the DeKalb Federation of Garden Clubs. The Pike Holiday Shop sells decorations for the season. Proceeds benefit the Fine Arts Center. Moderate admission; discounts for seniors over sixty and children under twelve. 980 Briarcliff Rd., Druid Hills. 872-5338.

Country Christmas. The Atlanta Botanical Gardens calls this its gift to the city of Atlanta. Always held on the first Sunday in December, this festive occasion features live entertainment and old-fashioned, natural decorations with hundreds of poinsettias. Free and open to the public. 876-5859 (Atlanta Botanical Gardens).

Festival of Lights. Beginning around Thanksgiving and continuing to Christmas Day, Newnan celebrates the holidays on the town square with bands, choral groups, a live nativity scene, Santa Claus, specially decorated trees, and more. The schedule of events varies annually, so check for exact times each year. Free and open to the public. Main Street, Newnan. 254-3703.

Festival of Trees. Beginning the first Saturday of December, the festival launches its season with a fabulous parade held in downtown Atlanta. Then, for ten days, the festival displays the work of local designers who decorate trees, designer vignettes, and (sometimes) tabletop topiary for the holiday season. The event is a fund raiser for Egleston Children's Hospital at Emory University. Festival of Trees has become popular over the past few years, especially since it moved to the World Congress Center and acquired Rich's famous Pink Pig. If possible, go after school during the week, to avoid long lines for the activities and for parking. If you must go during the weekend, try to choose the first weekend and go early in the day to avoid the same problems. Waiting for some of the activities can take as much as 45 minutes to an hour. Moderate admission; discounts for children and senior citizens. An additional fee (50¢ to $1) may be charged for some of the activities. Georgia World Congress Center, 285 International Blvd., Downtown. 264-9348.

Fidelity Tree Lighting.
Fidelity National Bank, with headquarters in Decatur, places a seventy-foot white pine with 10,000 lights and 6,000 basketball-size ornaments atop its building. On the last Friday in November, the streets in front of the bank close at 6 P.M., and the program starts around 7 P.M. Several Decatur choirs present music, including the choir from the bank's adopted school, Martin Luther King, Jr., Middle School in Atlanta. Free and open to the public. Several vendors are chosen to sell items for the benefit of area charities. 160 Clairmont Ave., Decatur. 371-5500.

Governor's Mansion Tree Lighting.
This annual lighting of a Christmas tree on the grounds of the Georgia Governor's Mansion is a splendid beginning to the holiday season. Following the lighting ceremonies, the governor and his wife receive the public. After a tour of the first-level public areas, guests usually go downstairs for refreshments. Free and open to the public. 391 W. Paces Ferry Rd., Buckhead. 261-1776.

Grant Park Learning Center Candlelight Tour of Homes.
Always held the first weekend in December (Friday and Saturday evenings), from 6 P.M. to 10 P.M., the tour selects about eight completely renovated homes in Grant Park. Refreshments are served at the Learning Center, which has been sponsoring this tour since 1980. Proceeds benefit the center. Moderate admission; discounts for advance ticket purchases; children under age twelve are admitted free. 521-0418 (Grant Park Learning Center).

Marietta Pilgrimage: A Christmas Home Tour.
This tour is always held the first weekend of December. Homes in one of Marietta's five historic districts are decorated to reflect the period during which each house was constructed. The rotation enables the tour to showcase different houses every year, and it also features six private homes, as well as six or seven public buildings. Special activities on the same weekend include **Pilgrimage Concerts**, the **Pilgrimage Art Exhibition**, and a quilt show. The Merry Olde Marietta Tea Room, set up in one of the featured buildings, sells lunch and refreshments. Proceeds benefit the Cobb Landmarks and Historical Society, which is currently restoring the 1840 Root House (Marietta's oldest extant house) and the Welcome Center. From 10 A.M. to 6 P.M. Moderate admission. 429-1115 (Marietta Welcome Center).

Memories of Christmas Past.
Beginning the first weekend in December and continuing for two to three weeks, the Mable House in Mableton becomes a Christmas House filled with antiques and decorated trees. The artists' market sells handmade items, including holiday crafts (handmade ornaments), art (originals and prints), and gifts of all kinds. Free and open to the public. 5239 Floyd Rd., Mableton. 739-0189.

Or VeShalom. For the past two decades, this Sephardic synagogue has celebrated its cultural and culinary traditions with a splendid annual festival. Sometimes held in November if Hanukkah is early, the festival is a delight and an opportunity to savor some of the community's unusual traditional foods. Pick up a copy of the sisterhood's cookbook, *Comé con gana: The Sephardic Cook,* for recipes covering these treats. 1681 N. Druid Hills Rd., Brookhaven. 633-1737.

Teddy Bear Tea. Children and accompanying adults enjoy traditional tea and hot chocolate while visiting the Macy Bear Friend at this holiday event. Held the same week as Festival of Trees, the tea includes a photo with Bear Friend and Santa at Macy's, plus tickets for the Festival of Trees. Proceeds benefit Egleston Children's Hospital at Emory University. The tea is very popular, and tickets sell out early. Moderate admission. Lobby of the Ritz-Carlton, Atlanta, Downtown. 659-0400.

Zoo Atlanta's Breakfast and Supper with Santa. These weekend events at Zoo Atlanta are extremely popular and will be repeated by public demand. After breakfast or supper, little guests climb into Santa's lap to whisper what they want for Christmas. Face-painters and storytellers enhance the activities. Moderate admission in addition to regular zoo admission. 800 Cherokee Ave., Grant Park. 624-5678.

CHAPTER 5

City Sights

Too often everyday busyness keeps us from taking advantage of our surroundings. Use this chapter to become a sightseer in your own backyard! Special adventures await the willing around every corner, from museums to historic tours to attractions like Six Flags Over Georgia and Zoo Atlanta.

If you have a little more time to explore, remember that Atlanta is only a short drive from Lake Lanier or the Georgia mountains. Atlantans don't have far to go to hike well-developed trails, explore Civil War battlefields, or pan for gold.

The entries in this chapter appeal to adults, but many of the city's sights are oriented toward children as well. Botanical gardens, museums, and historic spots all have features that tykes can enjoy. Want to catch an exhibition in the High Museum of Art? Take the sprites along, and let them explore every floor before turning them loose in the High's interactive children's exhibition.

We've tried to be as accurate as possible, but be advised that admission policies are subject to change.

ATTRACTIONS

Where to go and what to do with kids on the weekends could leave some families wondering if they're going to expire from cabin fever. It's always possible, however, to visit one of Atlanta's exemplary special attractions. Hours may change, often varying with the season, so call before going to any of these special spots.

American Adventures. This family-oriented facility features exhibits that focus on early twentieth-century themes. Bumper cars (adults must drive them for the littlest people), a carousel, a train, a mini roller coaster, a ferris wheel, a playscape, and a game room are all designed for the pleasure of children. Both indoor and outdoor activities make it easy on the older folks. There is a casual family-style restaurant. Special birthday party programs are available. 250 N. Cobb Pkwy., Marietta. 424-9283 (recorded information); 424-6683 or 424-9283 (office).

Cherokee Batting Range and Grand Prix. Go-carts reach speeds of up to twenty miles per hour, but drivers must be over ten years of age to test their skills on the facility's 700-foot track. The course snakes up and down, traveling over banked curves. Yes, there are spills and crack-ups, but safety prevails. The track has ten go-carts, so an entire family can have a crashing good time. A baseball batting range is also available (see chapter 8). 711 Bascomb Commercial Park North, Bell's Ferry Rd., Woodstock. 591-4778.

Cyclorama. This circular painting, done in 1885–1886 by German, Austrian, and Polish artists, with an accompanying diorama, depicts the 1864 Battle of Atlanta. Visitors sit comfortably on a tiered platform while a recorded narration explains the events represented in the painting. The Cyclorama was extensively restored in the early 1980s. Located in Grant Park, the structure housing the painting also exhibits the famous locomotive, **The Texas**. The gift shop features books about the Civil War. 800 Cherokee Ave., Grant Park. 624-1071 (tickets); 658-7625 (information).

Ebenezer Baptist Church. Founded in 1886, its legacy within the family of Dr. Martin Luther King, Jr., dates back to the Nobel laureate's maternal grandfather. King grew up a few blocks down the street and served this church as co-pastor with his father. Seating about 750 worshippers, the church is often crowded with visitors for the two services on Sunday. Regular tour guides, some of them volunteer members of the congregation, lead visitors through the church. A recording plays during part of the guided tour to further detail the King legacy. Donations are gratefully accepted. 407 Auburn Ave., Downtown. 688-7263.

Georgia Governor's Mansion. Finished in 1968 and designed by architect A. Thomas Bradbury during the administration of Governor Carl Sanders, it was first occupied by Governor and Mrs. Lester Maddox. Maddox began a tradition of opening the mansion to the public through a series of **Little People's Day** receptions. Today the mansion remains accessible to Georgians and tourists, who may visit the public rooms. The lighting of the Christmas tree is a favorite ceremony that brings hundreds to the mansion grounds *(see chapter 4)*. The mansion contains a superior collection of Federal period furniture, as well as eighteenth- and nineteenth-century paintings and porcelains. Guided tours are conducted Tuesdays through Thursdays, 10–11:30 A.M. Additional tour hours are added at holiday time. 391 W. Paces Ferry Rd., Buckhead. 261-1776.

Lake Lanier Islands. This huge man-made lake covers 38,000 acres, and Lake Lanier Islands is a resort covering 1,200 acres. It's all here: boating, golf, camping, fishing, tennis, equestrian sports, and water sports. Boaters can pilot everything from houseboats to pontoons, and sailing is given serious attention. The **Water Park**, with its **Kiddie Lagoon** and **Wiggle Waves**, is especially designed for small children. One-half mile of beach, ten water slides, a diving platform, paddle boats, sailfish boats, canoes, and refreshment stands enhance this facility—and all for one entrance fee. Admission is charged per car. 6950 Holiday Rd., Lake Lanier Islands. 932-7200; 932-7233 (stables).

Malibu Grand Prix. "Formula One" and "Can Am" cars (these are two-seaters) hit speeds of up to sixty miles per hour. Only licensed drivers or those over the age of fourteen who complete a special **Car Control Clinic** may take the wheel of one of these babies. Anyone over four and a half feet tall can drive a sprint car, which can reach speeds of up to 25 miles per hour. A video sports game center, miniature golf, batting cages, and bumper boats keep the crowds coming. The not-so-faint-of-heart may enjoy one of the racing events *(see chapter 4)*. 5400 Brook Hollow Pkwy., at I-85 between Jimmy Carter Blvd. and Indian Trail, Norcross. 416-7630.

Martin Luther King, Jr., Memorial, Historic District, and Center for Nonviolent Social Change. Listed on the National Register of Historic Districts, this multifaceted complex contains the tomb of Martin Luther King, Jr. Dr. King's birth home is maintained and preserved by the National Park Service. An early learning center, dining facility, gift shop, archives, and library are the major features of the complex. Tours are available. 449 Auburn Ave., at Boulevard and Jackson Sts., Downtown. 524-1956.

Monastery of the Holy Ghost. Built by Trappist monks who are especially known for bonsai plants, the monastery is located near Conyers. Brother Paul Bourne is world renowned for his award-winning work in bonsai, and Brother Francis Michael directs a wholesale and retail operation in bonsai tools and pottery. The monastery's sparkling Gothic-style architecture and picnic grounds contribute to the peaceful surroundings. Visitors are not allowed in the cloister but personal tours can be arranged for adults as well as for children above grade six. 2625 Hwy. 212, Conyers. To arrange a tour, call the Monastery Retreat House. 760-0959.

Mountasia Fantasy World. These privately owned facilities have miniature golf courses, bumper boats at two of the locations, miniature Indy car race tracks, and game rooms. Birthday adventure packages, special group rates, and fund-raising activities are welcome. A six-acre lake is part of the immaculately maintained, family-oriented facility in Lawrenceville. Three locations in metro Atlanta: 175 Ernest Barrett Pkwy., N. Cobb. 422-3440; 8510 Holcomb Bridge Rd., Alpharetta. 993-7711; 1099 Johnson Ferry Rd., Marietta. 977-1200.

Six Flags Over Georgia. This large recreational facility boasts a variety of rides and engaging things to do. Since its opening in 1967, rides continue to be added to the park, but the triple-loop **Mind Bender**, the **Georgia Cyclone, Ninja—The Black Belt of Roller Coasters**, and the water rides are top draws. If the glitz and glamour of Hollywood-style revues are more your style, check out the **Batman Stunt Show** and the **Police Academy Show**. End your day with the fireworks and laser show that lights up the night sky during the summer season. One ticket covers all activities, and children under two are admitted free. The season runs from mid-March to mid-November, but hours and days vary depending on the month. 7561 Six Flags Pkwy., Six Flags Exit (13-C from Downtown) off I-20 West, Austell. 948-9290 (switchboard); 739-3400 (recorded information).

White Water. A fun summer spot for all ages with special areas for toddlers, White Water also has a controlled wave pool, water chutes, and several other water attractions. Snack foods are sold at scattered locations, and one restaurant with a grill serves substantial fare. Season passes or day tickets are available. 250 N. Cobb Pkwy., Marietta, next to American Adventures. 424-9283 (recorded information); 424-6683 (office).

Yellow River Wildlife Game Ranch. A real winner for both children and adults, the ranch, on 24 wooded acres lying along the Yellow River, has trails to guide you among wild animal exhibits, displaying fawns, bears, mountain lions, and buffalo. Most interesting are the feeding stations, where visitors can feed the animals, many of which stroll right up to the outstretched hand. 4525 Hwy. 78, 10 miles east of I-285 (Exit 30-B off I-285), Lilburn. 972-6643.

Zoo Atlanta. Resident peacocks wander the grounds while docents conduct lectures designed to entertain and enthrall visitors. Willie B., a gorilla, made the front page of *The Atlanta Journal and Constitution*'s Sunday edition when he found a mate for the first time in his thirty-plus years of contented bachelor bliss. The majority of animals are displayed in natural habitats. The **Ford African Rain Forest** is impressive. The zoo's famous elephant, Starlet O'Hara, occasionally treats visitors to a painting session. Food facilities offer snack fare. It's a good idea to bring water containers because the concessions charge the price of a soft drink to fill one of their cups with water, and the summer heat is tough on children and adults. Parking is generous and free, but on summer weekends the zoo's popularity can make parking difficult, so plan to go early. 800 Cherokee Ave., Grant Park. 624-5600.

PARKS & GARDENS

When it comes to parks, the Atlanta area has several fine facilities—notably Piedmont Park, Grant Park, Chattahoochee River National Recreation Area, and Chastain Park. Atlantans pack them to listen to music, to play tennis, and to hike trails. Plan ahead to allow time for parking if you're attending an event at any of these facilities.

Atlanta Botanical Garden. This beautiful thirty-acre facility has several specialized garden areas. The glass-enclosed **Dorothy Chapman Fuqua Conservatory** exhibits exotic plants from all over the world in its 16,000 square feet. In the gardens, designed for demonstration, a wide variety of plants thrive in our long growing season. The **Storza Woods** is a fifteen-acre hardwood forest, a rare sight in Atlanta; its walking trails curve past many old specimens. A visitors' center holds special programs, such as Herb Education Day, presented in May by the Chattahoochee Unit of the Herb Society of America. Lectures and classes *(see chapter 9)* and garden membership *(see chapter 10)* are important activities and benefits. The gift shop sells gardening paraphernalia and other wares reflecting natural themes. Don't miss the greenhouse and its array of plants. This site is a good one for both adults and children—even the youngest ones, who find the plants and the environment fascinating. Services include a plant hotline, 888-GROW (4769). Garden members are admitted without charge, as is everyone on Thursday afternoon. Closed Mondays. 1345 Piedmont Ave., Midtown. 876-5859.

Big Trees Forest Preserve. Serenity in the midst of madness, some might say.

Located just south of the North Fulton County Government Annex on Roswell Road, this preserve offers quiet walking trails in the middle of a busy world. It was developed by the Southeast Land Trust, which is planning to build a nature center in the future. Park cars at the Annex lot. The path is clearly marked *(See chapter 10)*. Southeast Land Trust, 130 Azalea Dr., Roswell. 594-9367.

Cator Woolford Memorial Garden. This splendid little pocket park is part of the 36 acres that contain **REACH** (Rehabilitation and Education for Adults and Children), located in the former Cerebral Palsy Center, and the **Atlanta Hospitality House**, dedicated to sheltering families whose members are hospitalized in Atlanta. The property formerly belonged to a wealthy Atlanta family who wished the land and mansion to be used for community purposes. Open to the public, the garden is also available for private events. 1815 Ponce de Leon Ave., Druid Hills. 377-3836.

Chastain Park. Surrounded by some of Atlanta's most attractive residential neighborhoods, this park has an amphitheater that is famous for its concerts featuring classical, jazz, pop, blues, and rock performers. Atlantans dine on caviar picnics before the shows and light their candles as darkness falls, making any musical event a unique experience. Other Chastain facilities include the **Arts and Crafts Center** (*see chapter 9*) and the **Chastain Art Gallery**, both at 135 W. Wieuca Rd., Buckhead. Among its other features are the summer swimming facility (255-0863) at 235 W. Wieuca Rd., Buckhead, an eighteen-hole golf course, and a tennis center. For special events activities information call the Bureau of Cultural Affairs, 653-7160.

Chattahoochee Nature Center. In a simple, rustic building beside a small pond, the center's live exhibits of native wildlife make this privately funded facility a treat for both children and adults. Two nature trails and aviaries containing birds of prey are among the center's most interesting features. A small admission is charged. 9135 Willeo Rd., Roswell. 992-2055.

Standing Peachtree, an Indian village on the frontier between Creek and Cherokee lands, began Atlanta's earliest association with the peach tree. But the tree in question may actually have been a "pitch" or pine tree, not a peach tree.

Chattahoochee River National Recreational Area. This national park stretches for 48 miles from Lake Lanier to Peachtree Creek. Established in 1978, the area includes the river and 4,100 acres of land divided into fourteen land units, each with its own trails. The area attracts millions to enjoy rafting, picnic facilities, jogging, horseback riding, hiking trails, a stocked urban trout stream, and mountain bike trails (**Cochran Shoals** and **Vickery Creek** units). The Indian rock shelters and critter-watching opportunities also enhance the area's appeal. Cochran Shoals has a prepared, relatively flat three-mile gravel trail that's excellent for jogging, walking, and cycling. Parking for Cochran Shoals is available at Interstate North Pkwy., off I-285 at the river, or Columns Dr., off Johnson Ferry Rd., in East Cobb. The area is open daily throughout the year, but summer is the season for the 'Hooch. Trail maps are available at each unit or may be obtained by phone or by writing park headquarters, located off GA 400 at Exit 3 (Northridge). 1978 Island Ford Pkwy., Dunwoody, 30350. 952-4419.

Confederate Cemetery, Marietta. More than 3,000 Confederate soldiers are buried in this magnificent, peaceful spot, established in 1863 when W. H. Miller, MD, died. The last man buried here from the Confederate Soldiers' Home was the black bodyservant of a Georgia captain. Special services commemorating Confederate Memorial Day are celebrated at the cemetery on the last Sunday in April. Pick up a tour map at the Marietta Welcome Center. Powder Spring Rd., at S. Marietta Pkwy., Marietta. 429-1115.

Grant Park. The park contains the **Cyclorama** and **Zoo Atlanta**, as well as a swimming facility and recreation center with basketball courts. It is named for Confederate Colonel Lemuel Pratt Grant, a native of Maine, who designed the breastworks for the defense of Atlanta. 800 Cherokee Ave. Recreation Center, 537 Park Ave. 627-9751. Summer swimming facility, 625 Park Ave. 622-3041. For activities information, call the Bureau of Cultural Affairs, 653-7160.

Kennesaw Mountain National Battlefield Park.
Before the Battle of Atlanta, Union and Confederate forces clashed on June 27, 1864, at Kennesaw Mountain, just north of Marietta. Fortifications run for miles through the woods, and monuments mark the battle's historic moments. Maintained by the National Park Service, the 2,884-acre park offers hiking on sixteen miles of trails. A visitors' center details the history of the battle. Stilesboro Rd. and Old Hwy. 41, off Barrett Pkwy., Kennesaw. 427-4686.

Oakland Cemetery.
Established in 1850, the cemetery is still owned by the City of Atlanta. A virtual museum of privately owned Victorian funerary monuments, it contains the graves of Civil War soldiers, *Gone With the Wind* author Margaret Mitchell, golfer Bobby Jones, and Atlanta's first mayor, Moses Formwalt. Conducted tours are available. The cemetery is open daily, but hours vary with the season. No admission except for tours. 248 Oakland Ave., at Memorial Dr., Downtown. 658-6019.

Panola Mountain State Park.
The centerpiece of this 617-acre park is a 100-acre granite outcropping that recalls its neighbor to the north, Stone Mountain. At Panola Mountain visitors still find rare plants and animals native to the Piedmont region. Hiking, nature trails, guided mountain hikes on weekends, and wildflower walks are among the park's attractions. Regularly sched-

uled hikes for the public are led by rangers to protect the park's delicate environment. Groups may also arrange guided hikes. The park is designated a National Natural Landmark. 2600 Hwy. 155, Stockbridge. 389-7801.

Pickett's Mill State Historic Site.
The Battle of Pickett's Mill, May 27, 1864, was a victory for the Confederates, who prevented Union troops from out-flanking Confederate positions. Twice a month, re-enactors demonstrate weapons firing, cooking methods, and period military drills from both the Confederate and Union armies. Call ahead to find out details because the number of available volunteers determines the program's content. 2640 Mt. Tabor Church Rd., off Hwy. 381, Dallas. 443-7850.

Piedmont Park.
When the children of the families who settled Inman Park in the late nineteenth century grew up and married, they built their homes along Piedmont Avenue and in the part of the city now called Midtown. In the early twentieth century, the city limits stopped at the park's northern boundary. Host to the 1895 Cotton States and International Exposition, Piedmont Park has been, for more than twenty years, the site of the immensely popular **Arts Festival of Atlanta**, held in September *(see chapter 4)*. Visitors enjoy symphony concerts in the summertime, and it is a popular jogging spot. The park's appeal is enhanced by the tennis center, with both clay and asphalt courts and nighttime lighting (at Park Dr., 872-1507) and a swimming facility (Piedmont Ave. at 14th St., 892-0117). Located adjacent to the park is the **Atlanta Botanical Garden**. Piedmont Ave. between 14th St.

and Monroe Dr., Midtown. For activities information call the Bureau of Cultural Affairs, 653-7160.

Stone Mountain Memorial Park.

Stone Mountain is the world's largest granite outcropping. With over 3,200 acres, the park's many facilities include an antebellum plantation with its accompanying outbuildings, a petting zoo, and an antique car museum. A train travels to the base of the mountain, letting passengers off to climb it (a 1.3-mile hike) and savor the view of Atlanta's skyline. Climbers may descend by train, skylift or retracing their steps. Bicycling, hiking, canoeing, camping, ice skating, and golfing are all popular activities in this year-round facility. Presented from spring to fall, the nightly **Laser Light and Sound Show** is not to be missed. Entrance fee is by yearlong or nominal single-visit car pass, and each attraction within the park charges its own admission. Hwy. 78 (Exit 30-B off I-285), then Stone Mountain Park Exit, Stone Mountain. 498-5600; 498-5606 (Laser Show information).

Sweetwater Creek State Conservation Park. Only minutes from Atlanta's skyline, this park boasts almost 2,000 acres of wilderness. Ruins of the Civil War–era New Manchester Manufacturing Company, a textile mill, picnic shelters, a barbecue pit, fishing docks, and hiking trails are among the park's features. Fish in the 215-acre lake or in Sweetwater Creek, which flows through the park. Mt. Vernon Rd., Lithia Springs. 944-1700.

Vines Botanical Gardens. This facility, which is under the direction of the Gwinnett Parks Division, contains twelve acres located within a ninety-acre regional park. A three-acre lake and an 18,000-square-foot manor home are also part of the site, located near Grayson. Within the botanical gardens are seventeen different garden areas, containing exquisite botanical specimens and antique European statuary. 3500 Oak Grove Rd., Loganville. 466-7532.

William H. Reynolds Memorial Nature Preserve. This 130-acre nature preserve of hiking trails and picnic areas offers a bird-watching sanctuary, family programs, storytelling, and nature walks. Four miles of foot paths arranged in half-mile loops explore the preserve, and an interpretive native plants trail is wheelchair accessible. The Interpretive Center presents exhibits in nature study, and field guides are available. Specially guided nature walks may be arranged for groups. 5665 Reynolds Rd., Morrow. 961-9257.

MUSEUMS

Atlanta is building more and more museums to enhance and extend what's offered by the world-renowned High Museum of Art. Besides art, natural science is also the subject of many endeavors, and history occupies the time and interest of many of Atlanta's curators. Herewith, our favorites.

ART

Atlanta International Museum of Art and Design. The museum's mission is to exhibit art and design from diverse cultures, past and present. Supported by a coalition of corporate sponsors, the museum makes a unique contribution to the Atlanta arts environment. Exhibits have included rugs, boxes, baskets, crafts, and silver from myriad countries and cultures. 285 Peachtree Center Ave., Garden Level, Marquis Two Tower, Downtown. 688-2467.

Center for Puppetry Arts. In addition to its theater, the center houses a large museum exhibiting hand, body, rod, shadow, and string puppets from all over the world and from many periods of puppet history. The **Karagoz Turkish Shadow Play Theater** exhibit dates to the fourteenth century and represents the vitality of art in Turkish society during the Ottoman era. A giant body muppet, created by the late Jim Henson, is one of about 400 figures in the collection, which also contains more than 450 posters related to puppetry. The gift shop sells Chinese opera masks, puppets, muppets, T-shirts, and other puppet paraphernalia. 1404 Spring St., Midtown. 873-3391.

Emory University's Michael C. Carlos Museum. Designed by nationally known architect Michael Graves, this exceptional museum exhibits an outstanding permanent collection of Greek, Roman, Egyptian, Asian, and Pre-Columbian art and archaeology, the latter chiefly from Costa Rica. Egyptian coffins, Roman urns, and Greek vases, jewelry, and coins fill the display spaces. Special exhibitions usually focus on the same themes of the permanent collection, although departures, such as an exhibition on Impressionist art, do occur. Maxwell Anderson is the director. A small museum shop sells appropriately-themed books, T-shirts, posters, mugs, and reproduction jewelry. At the rear of the building, a few visitor parking spaces are available on S. Kilgo St. No admission is required, but a nominal contribution is requested.

Courses and special learning opportunities are available *(see chapter 9)*. Membership is encouraged *(see chapter 10)*. Tours are welcome with advance booking. Michael C. Carlos Hall, Main Quadrangle, 571 S. Kilgo St., Emory University campus, entrance at N. Decatur and Oxford Rds., Northeast. 727-4282.

Hammonds House. Dr. Otis Thrash Hammonds was a physician who collected works by artists of African heritage. After his death in 1985, his house, together with its art and furnishings, became a cultural facility in West End. Built circa 1857–59, the house is a fine example of Eastlake-style Victorian architecture. Hammonds House presents traveling exhibitions and openings by local and visiting artists. The permanent collection contains more than 250 works of art, mainly by African-American artists, and it includes African sculptures and masks, as well as Haitian paintings. The gift shop sells fine jewelry and crafts inspired by the art forms of Africa, and the facility is available for private affairs. Parking is available only on the street, so arrive early for openings and exhibits. 503 Peeples St., West End. 752-8730.

High Museum of Art. Named for Mrs. Joseph M. High, whose home stood on the property and served as Atlanta's first art museum, the High Museum of Art was founded in 1905 as the Atlanta Art Association. The High Museum first occupied the High home, and then expanded into an adjacent brick structure in 1955. In 1962, after the tragic loss of 122 Atlanta art patrons at Orly Airport in Paris, a fund drive began with an anonymous contribution that had to be matched by other contributions. The Atlanta Memorial Arts Center opened in 1968, housing the museum, symphony hall, the Alliance Theatre, and the Atlanta College of Art. Award-winning architect Richard Meier designed the internationally recognized High Museum of Art, which opened in 1983. Together, the two structures form the Robert W. Woodruff Arts Center.

The 135,000-square-foot museum houses the High's permanent collection, focusing on nineteenth-century American paintings and works by contemporary artists. Other important elements in the permanent collection include Italian paintings and sculpture from the fourteenth through the eighteenth centuries, the **Uhry Print Collection**, a fine collection of sub-Saharan African art, and a well-regarded decorative arts collection.

The High's rich programming includes weekend workshops for families and school-based programs that take the "trunk" exhibits to area schools. Children's tours also explore the museum. For information on the museum's workshops, lectures, and **Institute for Teacher Training** (*see chapter 9*). The museum shop sells art books, posters, art-focused souvenirs, and has a terrific section of art-focused games and toys. The atrium and two smaller spaces are available for private functions, with the larger atrium being especially popular for corporate parties, conventions, and wedding receptions. 1280 Peachtree St., Robert W. Woodruff Arts Center, Midtown. 733-4200.

High Museum of Art at Georgia-Pacific Center. In 1986, this facility opened as a branch of the High Museum of Art. Two levels of galleries occupying 5,000 square feet of space host traveling exhibitions, loan exhibitions, and selections from the High's permanent collection. The space may be rented for private functions, and docent-guided tours may be arranged by special reservation for adult groups. 133 Peachtree St., Georgia-Pacific Center, Downtown. 577-6940.

High Museum of Art, Folk Art, and Photography Galleries.

This 12,000-square-foot satellite facility of the High Museum of Art is one of the largest branch museums in the country. Located in the heart of Atlanta's business and convention district, and adjacent to the High Museum of Art at Georgia-Pacific Center, this museum offers a continuous program of changing exhibitions featuring folk art and photography. 30 John Wesley Dobbs Ave., Downtown. 577-6940.

Marietta/Cobb Museum of Art.

The permanent collection focuses on nineteenth- and twentieth-century American art, including works from the "Ash Can" School, the Hudson River School, and nineteenth-century artists from the South. **Kidsplace** is a gallery on the second floor designed to introduce children and their parents to art as a hands-on experience. Guided tours are available by appointment two weeks in advance. 30 Atlanta St., Marietta. 424-8142.

Nexus Contemporary Art Center.

When this unique arts center, founded in 1973, was forced to abandon its original location in a former elementary school building, the creative energy it generated seemed threatened. Undaunted, the former storefront cooperative gallery took everything, including the unconventional **Nexus Press**, to a 40,000-square-foot warehouse. The gallery and press occupy the renovated building. In addition to showing rotating exhibitions of regional, national, and international artists, Nexus has gathered a permanent collection of modern art. Reaching Nexus is a bit tricky; be sure to watch for the blue-and-white signs that point the way *(see chapter 10)*. 535 Means St., near Georgia Tech, off Ponders and Marietta Sts., Downtown. 688-1970.

Oglethorpe University Museum.

Growing out of the University Art Gallery, which opened in a small room a few years ago, the new museum occupies 7,000 square feet on the third floor of the university's Phillip Weltner Library. The new museum's permanent collection exhibits realistic art from diverse cultures and presents the art as a reflection of these cultures. 4484 Peachtree Rd., Oglethorpe University, Brookhaven. 364-8555.

HISTORY

APEX Museum.

The African American Panoramic Experience (APEX) is housed in the historic John Wesley Dobbs Building. Built in 1919, the 7,500-square-foot building was a school book depository. Efforts to build this unique museum began in 1978, and it moved into the Dobbs building in 1986. The museum hosts traveling exhibits from the United States and around the world, especially Africa. Before the Olympics in 1996, a 100,000-square-foot experiential exhibit building will be completed. Bethany Campbell is executive director. 135 Auburn Ave., Downtown. 521-APEX (2739).

Atlanta Heritage Row.

The Atlanta architectural firm of Richard Rothman & Associates, having drawn the master plan for Underground Atlanta, fashioned a museum out of a 7,000-

square-foot, narrow building. Atlanta Heritage Row is a showcase for six history exhibits, dozens of period-related displays, videos, and other audiovisual programs detailing the city's history. The exhibits escort the viewer from the city's earliest days to the present. *People: The Spirit of Atlanta* is a wide-screen presentation that focuses on the city's past, present, and future. Nominal admission. 55 Upper Alabama St., between Pryor St. and Central Ave., Underground Atlanta, Downtown. 584-7879.

Atlanta History Center.

A multifaceted facility that sits on 32 acres, the Atlanta History Center presents both permanent and rotating exhibits in **McElreath Hall**. Examining the history of our city, McElreath Hall exhibits materials from the center's collection that describe the Battle of Atlanta. Soldiers' uniforms, equipment, pistols and guns, period medical equipment, photographs, and costumes form the core of the collection. From time to time, selected archival photographs, costumes, and other materials are thematically arranged in special exhibitions that further explore the city's history.

Also on the grounds is **Tullie Smith House** (see page 119), with assorted original outbuildings typical of its day and culture. The center houses the **Philip Trammell Shutze Collection of Decorative Arts**, donated to the Atlanta Historical Society by Shutze, a well-known Neoclassical Atlanta architect. Special programs target both children and adults (see chapter 10). Visitors may enjoy lunch in the **Swan Coach House** tearoom (see chapter 1). A leisurely tour of the garden and woodlands, planted with native Geor-

gia specimens, a tour of **Swan House** (see page 119), and a visit to the museum shop, or a lecture series (see chapter 9) all complement an afternoon's visit. Researchers work at projects in the library/archives on the lower level of McElreath Hall.

The **Atlanta History Museum** houses an extensive collection of Civil War memorabilia gathered by the Beverly DuBose family of Atlanta; it also displays collections of folk material, costumes and textiles, and much more. Tour the 83,000-square-foot Atlanta History Museum with exhibitions on the history of Atlanta, Southern folk craft traditions, Atlanta's black upper class from 1880-1930, the Civil War, Atlanta's ethnic and immigrant communities and *Gone With the Wind*. Visitors can also enjoy a unique museum shop and the Coca-Cola cafe.

The center is open daily. Plan to wear comfortable shoes in order to enjoy the gardens and grounds. Children under six and Historical Society members are admitted free, and access to the research library, archives, and museum shop is free. 130 W. Paces Ferry Rd., Buckhead. 814-4000.

Atlanta History Center Downtown.

Opened in 1988, the downtown center houses special exhibitions that focus on Atlanta. Positioned across from the High Museum at Georgia-Pacific Center, the center serves over 15,000 visitors each year. It presents *Greetings from Atlanta*, a video describing the city's history. 140 Peachtree St., Downtown. 814-4150.

Atlanta Museum.

The former private residence of Rufus M. Rose, of Four Roses whiskey fame, is on the National Register. One of many northerners who came south before the Civil War and fought for the Lost Cause, Rose was a pharmacist who built his Victorian home around 1900. Currently owned by J. H. Elliott, an appraiser, the museum was begun in 1938 by Elliott's father. The collection is a wacky hodgepodge of memorabilia from Atlanta's past and other unrelated items, such as a lock of Napoleon's hair and Franklin D. Roosevelt's fishing and campaign hats. 537 Peachtree St., Downtown. 872-8233.

Big Shanty Museum. One of the outstanding episodes of the Civil War was the Andrews Railroad Raid, which began when 22 Union raiders stole *The General*, a locomotive, and planned to head north to destroy Confederate supply lines. Raider leader James Andrews, a Union spy, was hanged at a spot near Juniper Street, downtown Atlanta. Some of the raiders were the first recipients of the Medal of Honor, then recently created. Today *The General* is displayed in this renovated authentic cotton gin, a gift to the City of Kennesaw. The museum also contains exhibits and presents a slide film of the famous raid. 2829 Cherokee St., Kennesaw. 427-2117.

Federal Reserve Bank of Atlanta Monetary Museum. A delight for both adults and children, and a special draw for business travelers, this third-floor museum houses a history of money in all its forms. Rare numismatic items are an important feature of the collection, which also showcases the history of money and banking in America. Tours are self-guided, but groups may arrange for a guide. 104 Marietta St., Downtown. 521-8764.

Gwinnett County Historical Museum. When the original 1838 Female Seminary, a school for girls, was destroyed by fire in 1850, this charming Greek Revival structure was built in its place (1853–55). Restored in 1974 by the Gwinnett Board of Commissioners, the structure houses a museum on the second floor. Director Angela Trigg operates on a shoestring budget to preserve the donated memorabilia, which include photographs, documents, domestic articles, and clothing. The museum relies heavily on the generosity of its patrons. The first floor is available for private affairs. 455 Perry St., Lawrenceville. 822-5178.

Male Academy Museum. The first male academy of Newnan opened in 1883. Today, the facility houses the **Newnan-Coweta Historical Society** *(see chapter 10)* and an authentic collection of period clothing from the nineteenth and early twentieth centuries. Regularly changing displays draw from its permanent collection of costumes, decorative arts, and interior design. A museum shop contains items relating to Coweta County history. Guided tours are available. Donations accepted. Newnan is about forty miles from Atlanta. 30 Temple Ave., Newnan. 706-251-0207.

Museum of the Jimmy Carter Library. Minutes from Downtown, the **Carter Presidential Center** houses the **Jimmy Carter Library and Museum** and the offices of the **Carter Center**. The center is a unique cluster of nonprofit organizations devoted to alleviating conflict and human suffering around the world. Permanent exhibits in the museum include memorabilia from the life and presidency of Jimmy Carter,

Jr. Special exhibits show life in the White House and allow the visitor to walk into the Oval Office. Light lunches in the dining facility (see chapter 1) and a gift shop in the library museum enhance an all-day visit. A good spot for children. 1 Copenhill Ave., near Little Five Points. 331-3942.

The Olympic Experience. This audiovisual exhibit celebrates the 100th anniversary of the modern Olympics, which will occur when the Games take place in Atlanta in 1996. The walk-through exhibit displays maps of the sites where the events will take place. Official Olympic merchandise and collectibles are available for sale. Peachtree St. at Alabama St., Underground Atlanta, Downtown. 658-1996.

Stone Mountain Relics and Civil War Museum. Preserving the rich history of the South and its Civil War heritage, this small museum exhibits one of the finest private collections of Civil War memorabilia open to the public. Established in 1978. 968 Main St., Stone Mountain. 469-1425.

Stone Mountain Village Museum. The museum, arranged in a series of vignettes, exhibits artifacts, photographs, and memorabilia relating to the history of this charming nineteenth-century village. Mannequins are dressed in original antebellum gowns and are arranged on sets such as a porch and a kitchen. 941 Main St., Stone Mountain. 469-8045.

The Teaching Museums. What do you do with a school building that no longer meets contemporary pedagogical needs but has historical significance? Fulton County's answer to that question is to turn two such structures into museums, which opened in early 1992.

Teaching Museum North. Staffed by costumed docents who are all retired Fulton County principals and teachers, this museum offers hands-on, interactive exhibitions built inside the school's rooms. Enter a reproduced Georgia courtroom, the scene of mock trials; a log cabin, which features vignettes and demonstrations of nineteenth-century domestic life; a room devoted to recalling local life in the 1930s; and a writers' corner with a mural depicting 23 Georgia writers placed in a historic time line. The Roswell Room honors the town's mayor, W. L. "Pug" Mayberry. Refurbished and fitted with a sound system, the auditorium hosts speakers and arts programs. Jacque Coxe is the director. 791 Mimosa Blvd., Roswell. 552-6339.

Teaching Museum South. The Hapeville museum is housed in the former North Avenue Elementary School, which was designed by Philip Trammel Schutze, Atlanta's premier Neoclassical architect. The school opened in 1929, and museum director Dr. Pamela Sezgin's goal is to restore the building to its original condition. The museum focuses on the history of south Fulton County, including old Campbell County, which today lies in south Fulton. The reconstructed one-room schoolhouse, complete with wooden benches and quill pens is a favorite stop at the museum as is the **Courthouse-Constitution Room**. The Museum also displays artifacts from the county's five oldest high schools and features a nature center experience. Exhibitions of art by school children, science fairs, and traveling exhibits are among the projects planned. The 150-seat auditorium hosts performance art events. 689 North Ave., Hapeville. 669-8015.

The World of Coca-Cola. Located near Underground Atlanta and the New Georgia Railroad Depot, the World of Coca-Cola is housed in a splendid pavilion of modern design. Exhibits contain memorabilia from the fascinating evolution of this international company, whose history parallels that of post-Civil War Atlanta. A thirty-minute film documents Coke's impact around the world. Smaller children find the exhibit a bit static, but the slowly revolving bottling line gets their attention. Of course, the drink in its various forms (cherry, classic, new, etc.)

is dispensed liberally, and there's a gift shop with many reasonably priced Coke-emblazoned items for all ages. 55 Martin Luther King, Jr., Dr., Downtown. 676-5151.

ZACHOR Holocaust Center. This permanent exhibition portrays Holocaust history, and includes photographs and survivors' memorabilia. Along with the rotating exhibits, the center's programs convey the richness of pre–World War II European culture, the atrocities committed by the Nazis, and the process of rebuilding and surviving. A resource library, an audiovisual collection, and conducted tours are among the center's offerings. 1745 Peachtree Rd., Brookwood. 873-1661.

HISTORIC HOUSE MUSEUMS

Many of the distinguished older homes in the Atlanta area are still in private hands; some still belong to the descendants of the original owners. These may be open from time to time on special tours, but the houses listed below are always open to the public. Call in advance to check on times, admission, and programs. Some of these houses are available for private events, and others that may also be rented for parties are listed in Chapter 7 (Services & Resources).

Archibald Smith Plantation Home.
Archibald Smith, one of Roswell's founders, and his wife Ann Margaret Magill, came to Roswell in 1838. In 1844 Smith built his eight-room frame house out of hand-planed timbers produced on his farm. Leased by the **Roswell Historical Society** *(see chapter 10)*, the house and its outbuildings, including a corncrib and servants' quarters, contain a number of original furnishings. The family has donated more than 14,000 artifacts to the Roswell Histori-

cal Society to be displayed in the exhibits, making this one of the richest historical treasures in the metro area. The land now is the site of Roswell's Municipal Complex and public library. The house is open for public tours on a scheduled basis. 935 Alpharetta St., Roswell. 992-1665.

Bulloch Hall. A descendant of one of Georgia's early governors, Major James Stephens Bulloch built his home in Roswell in 1840, shortly after the town

was founded. The handsome temple-form Greek Revival home boasts a full-façade pedimented portico. Listed on the National Register, it was home to Martha Bulloch, mother of President Theodore Roosevelt and grandmother of Mrs. Eleanor Roosevelt. Now owned by the City of Roswell, Bulloch Hall is available for private affairs and serves as a cultural center (see chapter 9). Nominal admission. 180 Bulloch Ave., Roswell. 992-1731.

Elisha Winn House. Originally serving as Gwinnett County's first courthouse, the Elisha Winn House was the scene of the county's first election—its Superior Court met in Winn's barn! Listed on the National Register, the Winn House was built around 1812, making it the oldest surviving residence in the county. The property also held a small jail erected near the barn, so that the court's prisoners could be conveniently incarcerated. Dacula Rd., Dacula. 822-5174 (Gwinnett County Historical Society).

Gilbert House. On 500 acres of family land, Jeremiah Silas Gilbert (1839–1932), a Confederate veteran, rebuilt the home that had been burned in the Civil War. Using the materials of his land—earth and stone—and his own mortar formula, Gilbert constructed the fourteen-inch-thick walls at the rate of a foot a day and completed the house around 1866. The family lived in it for the next sixty years. Purchased by the City of Atlanta in 1971, the restored residence, containing several pieces of original furniture, also showcases period landscaping with native dogwoods, azaleas, and a vegetable garden with period plants. Schedules are erratic, so it's best to call ahead. Available for private functions. 2238 Perkerson Rd., Southeast. 766-9049.

Herndon Home. Former slave Alonzo Herndon built a fortune in barber shops and insurance. The company he founded, Atlanta Life, is today a mainstay in Atlanta's business center. Herndon's fine 1910 Beaux Arts residence is preserved along with the furnishings he collected and photographs of the Herndon family. The Herndon House reflects the kind of academic eclecticism that marked many Atlanta houses of its day: Gothic details in the staircase quatrefoils, a decidedly French style in the music room, the monumental classicism of its paired columns on the portico. A visit to the Herndon Home reveals the sophistication of Atlanta's black elite in the city's postbellum years. The house is near the campus of Morris Brown College. 587 University Pl., off Martin Luther King, Jr., Dr., Northwest. 581-9813.

Martin Luther King, Jr., Birth Home. It's a simple Queen Anne–style Victorian house built in 1894–1895 for a German-American family. In 1909, when King's mother was five years old, her father, Rev. A. D. Williams, pastor of Ebenezer Baptist Church, purchased the ten-room house. For the next 32 years, members of the family called it home. Today it is part of the two-block area designated the **Martin Luther King National Historic Site and Preservation District**, which includes the **Center for Nonviolent Social Change**. 501 Auburn Ave., Downtown. 331-5190.

Rhodes Hall. Furniture magnate Amos Giles Rhodes (1850–1928) built his Romanesque Revival residence, designed by Atlanta architect Willis

Denny, out on Peachtree Street in 1902. It contained a series of painted and stained glass windows commissioned from the Von Gerichten Art Glass Company. The windows depict the rise and fall of the Confederacy, and surround the curved mahogany staircase that leads from the first floor to the second floor hallway. At one point moved to the Georgia Archives building downtown, the windows were restored to Rhodes Hall with great ceremony in 1990. On the National Register since 1974, Rhodes Hall has been headquarters for the Georgia Trust for Historic Preservation since 1983. Rhodes Hall hosts an annual fund-raising Halloween festival that has been scaring Atlanta children and a few grown-ups since 1984 *(see chapter 4)*. Available for private affairs. 1516 Peachtree St., Midtown. 881-9980.

Robert Mable House. As a young Scot, Robert Mable (1804–1885) came to north Georgia to search for gold. The home he built around 1843 stands on Floyd Road, near Clay Road, in the Cobb County town that bears his name. During the Civil War, the house served as a hospital for wounded soldiers of both sides. Since 1984, the house has been open as an arts center for special exhibits and art classes. *(see chapter 9)*. 5239 Floyd Rd., Mableton. 739-0189.

Stately Oaks. This classic Greek Revival, antebellum house, built by Whitmel Allen in 1839, features a wide central hall, double gallery porches, and an unusual two-story, one-room wing over the original cellar. The restored original kitchen built of hand-hewn logs, an 1898 school house, and a rose garden are focal points of this histori-

cal exhibit. **The Country Store** serves as a museum shop, and the facility is open for private functions. Throughout the year, many special events take place on the property, including a reenactment of the Battle of Jonesboro. Christmas at Stately Oaks is special and other events take place during the year *(see chapter 4)*. Jonesboro, 30237. 100 Carriage Dr., Jonesboro. 473-0197.

Swan House. Listed on the National Register, Swan House, built for Mr. and Mrs. Edward Hamilton Inman, is an opulently furnished, Neoclassical-style residence designed by renowned Atlanta architect Philip Trammell Shutze (1890–1982). Furnishings include many eighteenth-century antiques as well as twentieth-century objects. The swan motif found throughout the house gives the structure its name. Docents lead regularly scheduled tours of Swan House; they focus on the landscaping, interior design, and furnishings, as well as on the historic importance of the house as a reflection of the fashion and lifestyle enjoyed by wealthy Atlantans from the early part of this century. The house and its original 22 acres became the nucleus of the Atlanta History Center in 1988, when the parcel was purchased by the Atlanta Historical Society. A tour is included with regular admission to the Atlanta History Center. 130 W. Paces Ferry Rd., Buckhead. 814-4000.

Tullie Smith House. Originally located in DeKalb County near what is today Executive Park on N. Druid Hills Road, the Tullie Smith House is a typical plantation plain-style residence built in the 1840s. Listed on the National Register, the house, together with its outbuildings (including a kitchen and smokehouse), provides a glimpse of what life was like in mid–nineteenth-century rural Georgia. Costumed docents demonstrate typical activities of the day—cooking, blacksmithing, quilting, candle-making, spinning and weaving, and basketry. The garden contains the herbs typically grown for a rural household, and the house is filled with original pieces of simple pine furniture as well as decorative and utilitarian items appropriate to the period. Regular tours are conducted, and popular annual events include a Civil War encampment with living history interpreters. A tour is included with regular admission to the Atlanta History Center. 130 W. Paces Ferry Rd., Buckhead. 814-4000.

Williams-Payne House. Built around 1869, it reflects the plain–style construction that characterizes many post-bellum homes in the rural South. Moved from its original location to the current site near the sandy spring that lends its name to today's urban community, the clapboard house was a summer cottage for the second owners, the Payne family of Dunwoody. The house is a restoration project of the Sandy Springs Historic Community Foundation. On the site are an authentic milkhouse and privy. The **Sandy Springs Festival** is held here (see chapters 4 and 10). Visiting hours are Mondays through Fridays, 10 A.M. to 4 P.M. 6075 Sandy Springs Cir., Sandy Springs. 851-9111.

The Wren's Nest. Home to Atlanta journalist Joel Chandler Harris, author of the Uncle Remus stories, this Victorian cottage is filled with memorabilia, including original furniture, wall coverings, photographs, and the great raconteur's spectacles, hat, and typewriter. Careful, ongoing renovation has restored the structure to period perfection. Activities focus on storytelling programs, making the Wren's Nest a delight for both children and adults. A museum shop stocks a wide array of Harris-related memorabilia and Uncle Remus books. Group tours may be reserved (see chapter 10). 1050 Ralph David Abernathy Blvd. (formerly Gordon St.), at Lawton St., West End. 753-8535 (fees and basic information); 753-7735 (storytelling activities and other information).

NATURE / SCIENCE / TECHNOLOGY

Antique Auto and Music Museum. On the grounds of Stone Mountain Memorial Park, this museum features antique automobiles and musical oddities. A 1948 Tucker, player pianos, and juke boxes highlight the collection. Park admission and museum admission are charged. Stone Mountain Memorial Park, Stone Mountain. 498-5690, ext. 229.

Crawford W. Long Medical Museum. Long, the college roommate of Alexander Stephens (vice president of the Confederacy), practiced medicine in the mid-nineteenth century. He made his mark in medical history by being the first to use ether as an anesthetic. (He had seen young people use it as "laughing gas" at parties.) The museum contains some of Long's office furnishings, early medical equipment, and memorabilia from World War II, when some Crawford W. Long Hospital staffers served in North Africa and Europe. 550 Peachtree St., at Linden Ave., Downtown. 686-8191.

Fernbank Museum of Natural History.

The Fernbank Museum of Natural History is Atlanta's largest museum. Fernbank has the first **IMAX** theater in Georgia, one of only 24 in the U.S. The six-story screen projects the "big picture" of natural history. The permanent exhibit, **A Walk Through Time in Georgia**, takes visitors through fifteen galleries to explore the beauty of Georgia and the chronological development of the earth. The **Spectrum of the Senses** includes 65 hands-on participatory exhibits which tease the eyes and ears into understanding scientific concepts of light and sound. To satisfy the curiosity of its youngest visitors, the museum provides **Fantasy Forest** and **Georgia Adventure**. These discovery rooms are carefully designed to teach children about their natural environment through quick, successful experiences. In addition to its permanent exhibits, the museum hosts fascinating traveling exhibitions. 767 Clifton Rd., Atlanta. 378-0127.

Fernbank Science Center.

Located in the heart of Druid Hills, one of Atlanta's classic residential areas, Fernbank is owned and operated by the DeKalb County School System. It contains a forest preserve, a planetarium, and a science exhibition displaying models of dinosaurs, bird specimens, and weather and geological presentations. The naturalist center in this facility is dedicated to Robin Harris, a civic leader and a descendant of Joel Chandler Harris, author of the Uncle Remus tales. Programs attract children and adults. For instance, Saturday morning's program, **The Sky Tonight**, takes place in the planetarium, which is the largest in the Southeast. Staff astronomers explain the position of the various constellations and other phenomena visible that night. Children under the age of five are not admitted to most of these programs. Fernbank's observatory, equipped with a 36-inch telescope, is open to the public on clear Thursday and Friday evenings.

A well-constructed trail encircles the perimeter of **Fernbank Forest**, a preserve, whose specimens are identified with markers. Part of the trail is specially equipped for the visually impaired. Cross trails enable visitors to cut through the preserve without having to walk the entire circumference, which tends to be a bit lengthy for younger children. Fernbank's greenhouses, located at 1260 Briarcliff Road, are open on Sunday afternoons, and various plants are given to visitors at that time. 156 Heaton Park Dr., Druid Hills. 378-4311.

Georgia State Museum of Science and Industry.

A museum of natural science and industry is housed on the first and fourth floors of the state capitol building. Exhibits depict Georgia wildlife in natural settings, rocks and minerals from every county, and Indian artifacts. The flags of the historic Georgia regiments from the Civil War are displayed, as is a model airplane exhibit showing the development of aviation from its beginnings to space flight. Washington St., at Martin Luther King, Jr., Dr., Downtown. 656-2846.

Lanier Museum of Natural History.

This museum is part of Gwinnett County's Parks and Recreation Division. Exhibits focus on the natural history of Gwinnett County, as well as on its cultural and historical development. The 150-foot observation tower provides splendid views of the Lake Lanier area. Classes, tours, a newsletter *(Tower Report)*, and holiday programs are among the museum's special efforts. 2601 Buford Dam Rd., Buford. 932-4460.

SciTrek, the Science and Technology Museum of Atlanta.

Opened in 1988, this unique environment was designed to enhance our appreciation of the wonders of science and technology. A complete mechanics laboratory, an optics display, a mathematics exhibition sponsored by IBM, and a special section for small children (complete with TV studio and a computer exhibit) make this museum attractive to children of all ages. More than a hundred hands-on exhibits occupy four exhibition halls and present the fundamentals of science. Live demonstrations, workshops, lectures, films, and parties make the subject of science a comfortable one for the little people. The museum shop sells books and do-it-yourself experiments. SciTrek also offers grown-ups a vital volunteer program and memberships (members are called "Trekers"). Nominal admission, with discounts for seniors and young children. 395 Piedmont Ave., Plaza Level, Civic Center, Downtown. 522-5500.

Southeastern Railway Museum.

An all-volunteer group of railroad buffs has restored old railway cars, tracks, signals, engines, and other relics. An outdoor museum, it is maintained and operated by the Atlanta Chapter of the National Railway Historical Society. Visitors can climb into the engineer's seat, walk through the cars, and explore every inch of the exhibition. Open Saturdays only. Nominal admission; discounts for seniors and children *(see chapter 10)*. U.S. Hwy 23, 3966 Buford Hwy., Duluth. 476-2013.

Telephone Museum.

Items displayed, including telephones of all sorts and sizes, tell the story of telephone's evolution from the historic moment when Alexander Graham Bell whispered, "Watson, come here. I need you." Open weekdays only. 675 W. Peachtree St., Southern Bell Center, Downtown. 529-3637.

HISTORIC TOWNS

The romance of the Old South is a mythical experience still pursued by people from all over the world. In the small, historic towns around the metro area, one gets closer to finding that elusive myth than in Atlanta, where columned houses did not prevail anyway and where so much of the postbellum city was destroyed by development and by the fire of May 21, 1917, when many of the homes from Boulevard to Highland burned.

The public may visit many metro-area homes and gardens during tours offered throughout the year—some available on a regular basis, some by appointment, and some only seasonally. Farther outside Atlanta are a few towns that, while not within our purview, deserve mention for their splendid tours at Christmas and in the spring. These include nearby Madison, only 45 miles east of Atlanta, and Athens, 65 miles east, which contain jewels of antebellum architecture and are easily visited on day trips. Times and days for regularly scheduled tours change, so call before going.

Decatur. Declared the county seat of DeKalb County in 1823, Decatur was named for Stephen Decatur, best known for suppressing the Barbary pirates in the early nineteenth century. Retaining its small-town character and charm, downtown Decatur blends old buildings with dramatic new ones. The old courthouse, housing the **DeKalb Historical Society** *(see chapter 10)*, is where you can pick up maps for walking tours. The not-to-be-missed sites include the **Mary Gay House** and the **Swanton House**. Mary Gay was a true Southern belle who defended her home against Union incursion, and the Swanton House was originally owned by Ammi Williams, one of DeKalb County's earliest settlers. Restored and open to the public, these houses are at 716 and 720 W. Trinity Place, Decatur. Maps are also available at the DeKalb Chamber of Commerce, 750 Commerce Dr., Ste. 201, Decatur. DeKalb Historical Society, Old Courthouse on the Square, Decatur. 373-1088.

Jonesboro. Scarlett's town! Her fictional Tara was nearby, and Jonesboro was a significant Georgia town during the Civil War, as the Battle of Jonesboro (August 31-September 1, 1864), was a major event following the Battle of Atlanta. With 32 historic points of interest, Jonesboro offers a rich driving tour. Clayton County Convention and Visitors' Bureau, 8712 Tara Blvd., Jonesboro. 478-4800.

Marietta. Founded before the Civil War, Marietta has carefully preserved her historic treasures. Self-guided walking and driving tours glide past 52 historic homes located in two National Register historic districts. **The Cannonball Trail** is a driving tour of Marietta Civil War sites, and you can pick up a brochure with appropriate information at the city's welcome center. The turn-of-the-century town square and the national and Confederate cemeteries are among the special places the tours present. Marietta Welcome Center, 4 Depot St., Marietta. 429-1115.

McDonough. Henry County was created in 1821 from Creek Indian land, and McDonough was established two years after the treaty ceded the territory to Georgia. This charming town was named for Commodore Thomas Macdonough, who fought in the War of 1812. Walking tours guide the visitor past the Romanesque courthouse, the public park at **Courthouse Square**, and several town monuments, including the **Globe Hotel**, the city's oldest commercial structure (now an apartment building). Several houses are antebellum. Henry County Chamber of Commerce, P.O. Box 1378, McDonough, 30253. Mailing address: 1310 Hwy. 20 West, McDonough. 957-5786.

The country's oldest black-owned newspaper, the Atlanta Daily World, *is still published in Atlanta.*

Newnan. Known as the "city of homes," Newnan boasts architectural treasures from the antebellum era—when Greek Revival was paramount—to the Victorian era and the early twentieth century. During the Civil War, Newnan was known as "Hospital City," for medical personnel treated both Confederate and Union troops there. Its Carnegie Library was the first in the nation to invite its benefactor, Andrew Carnegie, to an opening. Contact the Chamber of Commerce or the Histori-

cal Society, housed at the **Male Academy Museum**, for driving tour maps. The same tours are also comfortable for walking, if you're inclined to do so. Pick up a map at the Main Street Office, Carnegie Bldg., West Court Square. 706-254-3703. Chamber of Commerce, 23 Bullsboro Dr. (Hwy. 34), Newnan, 30264. 706-253-2270.

Roswell. Roswell King and his son, Barrington, came up from Darien, on the coast of Georgia, to explore business opportunities in the area. They founded Roswell in 1837, making it a center for textile manufacturing. Roswell's mills turned out cotton and woolen goods to supply the Confederate Army with uniforms, so the town was a prime target for Sherman's Army of the Tennessee as it marched through Georgia in 1864. The mills were burned, and many of the women and children who worked there were rounded up and sent into the Midwest. The fine old homes and the church, however, were not touched, leaving a nucleus for today's restoration efforts. Founded in 1971, the Roswell Historical Society (*see chapter 10*) saved historic **Bulloch Hall**, home to Mittie Bulloch, Theodore Roosevelt's mother, and the **Archibald Smith Plantation Home** (completed in 1846)—the society's new headquarters. The square in Roswell (*see chapter 6*) contains many fine craft shops, boutiques, and antique stores. The society has maps for walking tours, and tours led by costumed guides leave from the bandstand in the park on the square. Hwy. 120 and Hwy. 9, Roswell. 992-1665; 993-0422.

TOURS

Get to know Atlanta inside and out, both her history and her modern spirit, by touring not only established neighborhoods but also the latest enterprises. Here are a few ideas.

Atlanta Preservation Center. Walking tours of the city's historic districts—generating public awareness of Atlanta's rich architectural treasures—are a major activity of the center. From April through November, the two-hour tours cover the following areas: downtown; **West End**, including the **Wren's Nest**; the **Fox Theatre District** *(see chapter 3)*; **Underground Atlanta** and the Capitol Area; **Inman Park**, a late nineteenth-century residential area; **Druid Hills**, developed in the early twentieth century; and **Sweet Auburn**, the financial and main residential area of black Atlantans in the early twentieth century. Tours of the Fox Theatre are available year-round. See chapter 10 for information about joining the center. DeSoto Bldg., Ste. 3, 156 7th St., Midtown. 876-2040 (recorded information); 876-2041 (offices).

Chattahoochee Nature Center. Brochures direct leisurely walks through the woods and wetlands of the center. A marked trail and a boardwalk are designed to guide the visitor along the paths, whose sights are described in the brochures. Guided walks are offered on Saturdays and Sundays. 9135 Willeo Rd., Roswell. 992-2055.

CNN TV Studios. Watch news in the making in this state-of-the-art facility made famous by owner Ted Turner. Guided tours lasting about 45 minutes include the **TBS Collection**, which includes materials from the MGM/RKO film library. Groups of twenty or more are welcomed, but they should make reservations six weeks in advance. Advance notice is required for wheelchair and other special tours. 1 CNN Center, Marietta St. at Techwood Ave., Downtown. 827-2300.

Druid Hills. DeKalb County began to bloom in the early twentieth century when first Joel Hurt, developer of Atlanta's Inman Park, and then Asa Candler, founder of the Coca-Cola Company, developed Druid Hills. At the heart of its plan was the landscaping and residential design of Frederick Law Olmsted, designer of Central Park in New York City and father of landscape architecture in America. Now familiar to most Americans because of the Alfred Uhry Pulitzer prize-winning play and Oscar-winning film *Driving Miss Daisy*, Druid Hills remains a handsome residential neighborhood blending various architectural styles. Pick up a driving tour map at the DeKalb Historical Society, located in the old courthouse in downtown Decatur, and tour Druid Hills, one of several areas listed in the tour. DeKalb Historical Society, Old Courthouse on the Square, Decatur. 373-1088.

Fort McPherson. Fondly known as "Fort Mac," this nineteenth-century military installation was named for General James Birdseye McPherson, U.S.A., killed during the Battle of Atlanta. Consisting of about 500 acres, the reservation is home to the Third United States Army. The visitor will want to view **Staff Row**, a street lined with nineteen officers' residences, and **Troop Row**, containing two-story dormitory barracks. Between them lies **Hedekin Field**, the post parade ground.

Constructed between 1889 and 1910, the officers' residences have been listed on the National Register since 1974. Groups of ten to 45 may arrange tours by calling the Public Affairs office at least two weeks in advance of the desired date. Public Affairs also provides a self-guided driving tour enabling visitors to enjoy a casual drive around the area during daylight hours. Free. Fort McPherson, Southwest. 752-2028 or 752-2204.

Fox Theatre.

When English archaeologist Howard Carter discovered the tomb of Pharoah Tutankhamen, a fever of "Egypto-mania" spread across this country. Intended originally as a temple for 5,000 Shriners, the Fox Theatre, named for movie mogul William Fox, is a frenzy of architectural elements copied from Arabic buildings and monuments in many countries. The architectural firm of Mayre, Alger, and Vinour, directed by partner Oliver J. Vinour, a Frenchman, designed the architectural illusion, with its star-studded ceiling and famous **Mighty Mo** organ, which has four keyboards and 3,622 pipes. Threatened with demolition, the Fox Theatre has been lovingly cared for and protected by Atlanta Landmarks, which oversees all restoration and renovation efforts. Regular tours begin at the kiosk in the Fox arcade, directly in front of the building.

Call ahead for times. "Top-to-bottom" tours, conducted by expert guides, give an insider's view of the building, from its secret tunnel and trap door to its expansive stage and grand restored Egyptian Ballroom. 660 Peachtree St., Midtown. 881-2100.

Georgia State Capitol.

Several other cities preceded Atlanta's designation as the state's capital. Milledgeville, which had been prominent in the secession decision, was the antebellum capital; Union authorities moved the capital to Atlanta. Dedicated on July 4, 1889, the Georgia State Capitol cost one million dollars and is still famous for its gilded dome topped with a figure representing freedom. Now a National Historic Landmark, the capitol houses the governor's offices as well as many historic exhibits. A walking tour of the capitol building includes the **Senate** and **House**, the **Hall of States**, and the **Hall of Flags**, with commentary on the history of the building. The **Museum of Science and Industry**, located in the capitol, is not included in the tour. Washington St. at Martin Luther King, Jr., Dr., Downtown. 656-2844.

Historic Air Tours.

Climb aboard a four-seat Cessna 172 to explore the Battle of Atlanta from a perspective that only the legendary Union Army mascot, an eagle named "Old Abe," could have appreciated. Richard Stone's flying firm conducts several tours covering various Atlanta-related themes, and each passenger has an individual headset to hear the commentary. Daylight hours only. 1954 Airport Rd., DeKalb-Peachtree Airport, Chamblee. 457-5217.

Plantation House Driving Tour. This self-guided tour was developed by the Gwinnett Historical Society, located at 221 N. Clayton Street, off the square in Lawrenceville. Formed in 1818, the county was named for Button Gwinnett, a signer of the Declaration of Independence. At that time, the dominant architectural style of most plantation houses was "plantation plain"— two stories high and one room deep. These houses expanded by additions as families, and financial resources, grew. Most of the houses on this tour reflect that style. In general, the houses remain in private hands and are not open to the public unless otherwise indicated on the tour map, Gwinnett County Historical Society, P.O. Box 261, Lawrenceville, 30246. 822-5174.

Sweet Auburn. Atlanta's Auburn Avenue was characterized in a 1956 *Forbes* article as "the richest Negro street in the world." Lining the avenue are the buildings that represent the financial and cultural achievements attained by black Atlantans. A walking tour map, "Freedom Walk," details an exploration that begins at **Underground** and continues along **Auburn Avenue**, past **Atlanta Life**, an insurance company founded by former slave Alonzo Herndon. **Big Bethel AME Church**, founded in 1847 as the city's first black church, and the **Top Hat/Royal Peacock**, where racially mixed audiences heard the best performers in blues, jazz, and rock are also on the tour, which concludes at the **Martin Luther King, Jr., Center for Nonviolent Social Change**. The area has undergone substantial renovation, but much more remains to be done. For copies of the tour map, contact the Atlanta Convention and Visitors Bureau, 233 Peachtree St., Peachtree Center Mall, Downtown. 222-6688.

LIBRARIES

Atlanta's libraries contain unique collections that interest both the professional scholar and the casual student of local subjects. Most are attached to the city's academic institutions, but it's possible to access this richness without being a member of the student body or faculty.

Atlanta–Fulton County Public Library Central Branch. Eugene Mitchell, Margaret's father, persuaded industrialist Andrew Carnegie to give the city $100,000 for a public library built in 1902. In 1980 a bright, new building by internationally renowned architects Marcel Breuer and Hamilton Smith replaced the original Carnegie Library. The new building is a comfortable, well-lit space with good equipment, gallery spaces downstairs for special exhibitions, and a wonderful self-service lunch spot, called **Delectables** (*see chapter 1*). **Special Collections** houses the **Margaret Mitchell Collection**, containing personal papers and mementos; the **Williams Collection**, with documents pertaining to local African-American history; periodicals on microfilm; the **Georgia Collection**, with its genealogical material and reference works; and the **Ivan Allen Department**, which collects business materials. Twenty-nine branches serve the city of Atlanta. Central: 1 Margaret Mitchell Sq., at Peachtree St., Forsyth St. and Carnegie Way, Downtown. 730-1700.

Atlanta History Center, Research Library, and Archives.

The Atlanta Historical Society began collecting items related to Atlanta's history in 1926. Today, among its more than 3.5 million items are 19,000 volumes, including telephone directories, books on Atlanta and the rest of Georgia, the **DuBose Civil War Collection**, and the **Thomas S. Dickey Collection**. Books on the Atlanta campaign and military ordnance (field manuals, biographies, and regimental histories) are part of the DuBose and Dickey collections. Private papers, maps, newspapers, journals, splendid archival photographs (more than one million), some 100,000 architectural drawings and records, and around 800 manuscript collections make this the source for research on Atlanta's past, the Civil War, and modern history. In McElreath Hall, the Atlanta History Center. 130 W. Paces Ferry Rd., Buckhead. 814-4000.

Bulloch Hall.

Books and materials on the history of Roswell, surrounding counties, and Theodore Roosevelt are preserved in this fine old home (see page 117). 180 Bulloch Ave., Roswell. 992-1731.

Cobb County Central Library.

This splendid post-modern facility, designed by the Atlanta architectural firm of Stevens & Wilkinson, is one of the most comfortable libraries we've ever encountered—and that's a lot of libraries! Ample parking, wonderful lighting,

and beautiful spaces attractively arranged with good furniture make this a superb facility. Our favorite space is the **Georgia Room**, which contains a good collection of Cobb County and Marietta resource materials. The fine staff is pleasant, helpful, and knowledgeable. This one is a real benchmark against which to measure other libraries in the metro area. In addition to Central, the Cobb County Public Library System has fifteen branches. Central: 266 Roswell St., Marietta. 528-2320.

Emory Law Library.

At this time, public access is limited to use of the **U.S. Government Documents Collection**. 1722 N. Decatur Rd., at Clifton Rd., Emory University, Northeast. 727-6824.

Georgia Department of Archives and History.

Dating to 1918, when it was created by the Georgia General Assembly, the Department of Archives and History operates as a service agency for the state and local governments and for all Georgians. Preserved are records of significance for Georgia history, state agency records, genealogical sources, law publications, periodicals and newspapers, county courthouse records (on microfilm), census records, and many private manuscript collections. Also on microfilm are original land grants and plats dating from 1755 to 1909, municipal records, and county and state maps. The department also operates a resource center in Hapeville, which researchers may access by requesting particular materials at the main archives building downtown. Exhibits focus on Georgia history, and archives publications are available. The windowless, marble-block building is open to the public, but users must obtain I.D. cards, for which a valid driver's license or other photo identification must be presented. User passes are issued for one year and are renewable. Parking is expensive, so it's a good idea to plan on spending the day. The Georgia State University MARTA stop is about three blocks away. Snack area and lockers are available for the public. 330 Capitol Ave., Downtown. 656-2350.

Gwinnett County Libraries. The Lake

Lanier Regional Library System serves three counties: Gwinnett, Dawson, and Forsyth. Two special facilities in Gwinnett merit comment. The main library in **Lawrenceville** features a **Center for Special Needs**, which is specially equipped for serving visually and hearing-impaired patrons as well as those who are wheelchair bound. The **Peachtree Corners** branch houses a special business information center, whose staffers can search and fax material (for a fee) to area businesses; it provides access to Dialog Information Services, a national database containing about 350 basic programs. Six other branches serve Gwinnett County. Central: 1001 Hwy. 29 South, Lawrenceville. 822-5361; Peachtree Corners: 5570 Spalding Dr., Norcross. 729-0931.

Health Sciences Center Library of Emory University. Professional

health materials, periodicals, and books are available to Atlanta health professionals, who may purchase a membership for $50. Corporate memberships begin at a negotiable fee of $3,000 but go up from there according to the corporation's size. 1462 Clifton Rd., main floor of the former Dental

School building, Emory University, Northeast. 727-5810.

Jimmy Carter Library. The library is a

research facility open to professional history scholars studying the presidency of Jimmy Carter. 1 Copenhill Ave., near Little Five Points. 331-3942.

National Archives and Records, Southeast Region. This fascinating

facility contains federal government records gathered from eight Southern states, including North and South Carolina, Tennessee, Georgia, Kentucky, Alabama, and Mississippi. Some colonial records date from 1716, but most date from 1790, the beginning of centralized federal government. The largest single collection of court records in the Southeast is here. The **Genealogy Department** contains the federal census records from 1790 through 1920, Revolutionary War records and the period's pension files, and a national collection of all Selective Service records for soldiers who served in World War I. 1557 St. Joseph's Ave., East Point. 763-7477.

Pitts Theology Library. At present

the public may access the collection by paying a fifty dollar subscription fee. Serving and affiliated with Emory University's Candler School of Theology, Pitts is the second largest theology library in North America. The collection is especially strong in Reformation, English church history, Northern European dissertations from the seventeenth and eighteenth centuries, and African religious periodicals. The world's largest collection of such periodicals is housed in Pitts. The Quadrangle, Emory University, Northeast. 727-4166.

Robert W. Woodruff Library of Emory University. Generally restricted to university personnel, Woodruff Library may be used by non-Emory folks who apply for an $80 researcher card. It entitles the holder to check out books for four-week periods for one year. The entrance level of the library is **Shatten Gallery**, which has hosted outstanding special exhibitions. **Special Collections** on the top floor holds a treasure trove of papers, documents, and first editions of important Atlanta publications, such as *Gone With the Wind,* in English and in several translations; works by and about Ralph McGill, late editor of *The Atlanta Constitution;* and materials related to the author of the Uncle Remus stories, Joel Chandler Harris. 450 Asbury Cir., at Clifton Rd., Emory University, Northeast. 727-6868.

William Russell Pullen Library, Georgia State University. Named for the university's long-serving head librarian, Pullen Library contains a number of intriguing special collections. Most popular is the Johnny Mercer collection, permanently exhibiting memorabilia relating to the Georgia songwriter's musical career. Housed here are his Academy Award for "Moon River"—the theme from the film *Breakfast at Tiffany's,* his Grammy for "Days of Wine and Roses"—from the film of that title, and other such documents about his life and career. Approximately 1,200 titles form the **Rare Book Collection,** and some 140,000 images constitute the **Lane Brothers Photograph Collection,** depicting Atlanta from the 1930s to the 1960s. Georgia State University, University Plaza, Downtown. 651-2172; 651-2476 (Special Collections).

WINERIES

"What?" asked the astonished vintner in Québec. "Seyval in Georgia?" (Seyval is a French-American hybrid grape that makes very nice wine.) "Mais, oui, mon ami," he was assured. Georgia had a flourishing wine industry before Prohibition, but the growth of today's wineries and their ever-ascending quality has amazed many. Visit them for an interesting excursion. Most wineries are located about an hour's drive from Atlanta. The trip to Habersham, near Baldwin, takes about an hour and a half.

Cavender Castle. Decatur attorney Gerard Carty is a native of Scotland who, with wife Mindy as director of marketing, opened Cavender Castle in April 1991. The gift store, tasting room, winery, bed and breakfast inn (five rooms with private baths), and a small restaurant for lunch on the weekends make the operation unique. The winery is across the road from the Crisson Gold Mine. New Hwys. 19 and 60, Dahlonega. 706-864-4759.

Château Élan. When Irish pharmaceutical entrepreneur Donald Panoz established the winery in 1983, everyone thought he was wasting his money. "Grow *vinifera* in Georgia? Who is he kidding?" Well, Panoz has set the pace for everyone else. The state-of-the-art winery boasts a chateau-style visitors' center, free daily tours with tastings, a wine market featuring the winery's products, two restaurants, banquet facilities, and an art gallery—there's more here than a winery! In addition to the 200-acre vineyards, the 2,400-acre complex includes nature trails, picnic areas, and an outdoor pavilion for summer concerts and private bookings. Brad Hansen, winemaker and general manager, is proud of the chateau's wines. The setting is exquisite, making it perfect for weddings. An eighteen-hole golf course opened in July 1990, and the European-style health spa is open. The annual events calendar is excellent. 7000 Old Winder Hwy., Braselton. 800-233-WINE (Georgia only); 706-867-8200 (for tours); 932-0900 (Atlanta telephone).

Fox Vineyard and Winery. John Fuchs named his vineyard and winery for himself—Fuchs means "fox" in German—and he declared the establishment "dedicated to the prevention of alcohol abuse." A former Eastern pilot, Fuchs founded his winery in 1984, and he has become a well-established presence in Georgia's growing viticultural industry. A tasting room at the winery opens daily for tastings and sales. **Antebellum Rose**, made of DeChaunac, and **Ambrosia**, a blend of Orange Muscat and Seyval, are proprietary labels. Hwy. 11 South, Social Circle (I-20 East, Exit 47). 787-5402.

Habersham Vineyards and Winery. Habersham's owners, brothers Tom and Chuck Slick, established the vineyard in 1980 and the winery in 1983, and today produce seventeen different wines. The winery has thirty acres under production in north Georgia, and tasting rooms are at the winery and throughout the state. The wine is chiefly made from Georgia-grown grapes, which include varietals such as Cabernet Sauvignon and Sauvignon Blanc. The proprietary labels include **Cherokee Rose**, a semi-dry blush wine; the **Georgia Gothics**, proprietary blends recalling homemade wines made from native American grapes; and **Peachtreat**, a Muscadine blend flavored with peach concentrate. Habersham's Muscadine wine regularly wins medals in competition. A tasting room and retail store are located downtown in Underground Atlanta. 522-WINE (9463). Hwy. 365, Baldwin, 20 miles north of Gainesville. 706-778-WINE (9463).

CHAPTER 6

Shopping Around

You know where the closest mall is, but you're looking for something a little different—an antique table, the work of a local artist to hang on your walls, or maybe just a super deal at an outlet store.

An increasing number of independent merchants operate specialty shops in Atlanta, and alternative shopping opportunities, such as flea markets, abound. That's what interests us in this chapter, not the chain stores that you'll easily find all over town. We've focused on outlets, discount stores, antique shops, book stores, gift shops, specialty food emporiums, art galleries, and flea markets. For these entries, we've selected shops that in our view exemplify quality, uniqueness, and service. We've also surveyed some of the best shopping areas in Atlanta.

Still, we confess that space limitations have obliged us to omit many shoppers' favorites, including some of our own. But the stores we've listed express the spirit and variety of Atlanta shopping. Browse through these pages before you hit the stores and make the most of your shopping experience.

ANTIQUES, COLLECTIBLES, & GIFTS

Atlanta used to be a town devoted exclusively to fine English and French antiques. Today, this market is a mélange that ranges from exquisite quality antique furnishings to wacky, offbeat, twentieth-century collectibles.

Afghanistan Nomadic Rugs. Tamor Shah, from Afghanistan, is a nationally recognized authority on new and antique nomadic rugs. In addition to rugs, find antique wooden chests and bowls, myriad woven pieces, and intriguing painted wooden animals. 3219 Cains Hill Pl., Buckhead. 261-7259.

Beverly Bremer Silver Shop. Antique silver (see chapter 7). 3164 Peachtree Rd., Peachtree Plaza, Buckhead. 261-4009.

British American Antiques. Period English antiques (late eighteenth- and nineteenth-century) are comfortably displayed. Staffordshire willow transferware is a specialty. Very fair prices. 652 Miami Cir., Miami Circle Market Center, Buckhead. 231-4454.

Buckhead Antique Market. Used books, recent out-of-prints, and back issues of *Life* form an important part of the inventory. Books about the South and the Civil War are of major interest. **Mother Clutters** is a section of the store in which six dealers sell antiques and collectibles, including old records. 3107 Early St., Buckhead. 814-1025.

By Hand South. Functional pieces dominate this contemporary Ameri-

can craft shop. All of the pieces, from pottery bowls, boxes, and vases to jewelry and glasswork, are hand-crafted. Some fiberwork is also featured, especially in the form of loom throws and fiberart wall hangings. Artists from all over the country are represented. Shipping, wrapping, and a gift registry are available. 308 W. Ponce De Leon Ave., Decatur. 378-0118.

China Chasers. Some forty different brands and more than 3,000 patterns, in both china and crystal, are carried. List your desired pattern with China Chasers for a search (no fee or obligation). More than 90% of the inventory includes discontinued patterns. 3280 Peachtree Corners Cir., Norcross. 441-9146.

Consignment Guild. Finer resale and antique furniture and unusual accessories. 2833 Peachtree Rd., Buckhead. 237-8289.

Crabapple Corners. Country-style gifts and collectibles, home accessories, and braided cable rugs. 790 Mayfield Rd., Alpharetta. 475-4545.

Deanne Levison American Antiques. Specializing in period American antiques, Deanne Levison is a nationally renowned authority and dealer. By appointment only. 2995 Lookout Pl., Buckhead. 264-0106.

Denmead's Warehouse Antiquities & Curiosities.

Originally a warehouse and then a general store, Denmead's is the oldest building on Marietta's historic square. The twenty privately operated stalls purvey collectibles, antique toys, vintage jewelry and clothing, and antique furniture. 34 Mill St., Marietta. 427-6223.

Doll House Annie.

Almost all the miniatures in this shop are by American artists, and many are handmade pieces. Special items include miniature hand-blown glass accessories, china pieces, linens, rugs, silver, and chandeliers. Owners Diana and Jim Matson custom design and build doll houses, but completed doll houses and kits are available. 4371 Roswell Rd., Marietta. 971-4155.

Final Touch Gallery and Books.

Personal customer attention drives this gift and book store in Decatur; nice touches include the quarterly newsletter and the hand choosing of gifts with particular customers in mind. Beautiful custom framing is also available in the midst of the antique accessories and gift items. Browse through the books, especially the wide selection in art, gardening, and children's literature. 308 W. Ponce de Leon Ave., Decatur. 378-1642.

Garwood House.

Northern European country and Biedermeier furniture: exquisite desks, lamps, books, and handsome upholstered pieces pack this 25,000-square-foot space. Elegant displays in the showroom entice the visi-

tor into the extensive warehouse. 1510 Ellsworth Industrial Dr., Downtown. 892-7103.

Gold's Antiques and Auction Gallery.

Atlanta's outstanding antique auction house offers furnishings, glass, art work, porcelains, rugs, silver, and bronzes—just about anything you could call an antique. Consignments. 1149 Lee St., Southwest. 753-1493.

Happier Days Collectibles.

Dan Daniels has a collector's dream of Coca-Cola memorabilia, Olympic collectibles, baseball cards, auto tags, records, and magazines (_Life_ dating back to 1936; _Time_ and _National Geographic_). 5104 Jimmy Carter Blvd., Norcross. 242-9954.

Howell Mill Antiques.

A cluster of shops covers more than 15,000 square feet and houses porcelains, furniture, accessories, and tableware. 1189 Howell Mill Rd., near Huff Rd., Northwest. 351-0309.

Irish Country Pine & Travel.

Antique Irish pine furniture, old photos and prints from Ireland, and a nice selection of antique Delft pack this appealing shop. 511 E. Paces Ferry Rd., Buckhead. 261-7924.

Jim Depew Galleries.

Consignments, auctions, liquidations, and appraisals make Depew's a busy place. 1860 Piedmont Ave., Northeast. 874-2286.

Kilim Collection.

Flat-weave oriental rugs are called kilims, and that's what fills this unusual little shop. Even the aroma is unique. 22-A Bennett St., Brookwood. 351-1110.

Last Chance Trading Post. Old costume jewelry, modern and antique furniture, silver, china, pictures, books, records, and hard-to-find, unusual accessories fill this fascinating emporium. 47 Camp Creek Rd., Lilburn. 381-0782.

Laura Ramsey Antiques. Good prices on well-selected English antiques. 220 S. Main St., Alpharetta. 475-2085.

Now & Again. Antiques and collectibles from all periods, including modern pieces, are accepted for consignment. The inventory changes frequently. 56 E. Andrews Dr., Andrews Square, Buckhead. 262-1468.

Old Mill Antiques. Choice American and English antiques and collectibles fill a 22,000-square-foot space. Some crafts, books, china, and glassware are also offered, but the primary focus is on antique furnishings. 17 Augusta Dr., Newnan. 706-251-0999.

The Raven's Nest. Paintings and furniture from the early nineteenth century fill an original cotton gin. 780 Mayfield Rd., Alpharetta. 475-3647.

Rebecca's Uniques. Victorian furniture as well as some pieces from other periods make a fine setting for the display of other treasures: rare china and crystal; a nice selection of Hummel, Wedgwood, and Limoge; and porcelain teapots, antique paintings, and photographs. Interior design and consignment services. 111 N. Main St., Woodstock. 591-5738.

Simpler Times. This antique store, located twenty miles south of Atlanta in McDonough, is open to the public the last Saturday of the month; the rest of the time, only antique dealers are allowed. The majority of the pieces are of English origin. 54 Covington St., McDonough. 957-11023

Stalls, A Buckhead Antique Market. Individual stall owners may not always be on the premises, but a central management unit serves everybody. Unusual, beautiful collectibles such as antique bowling pins, baskets, and accessories are artfully displayed. Open Wednesday through Sunday. 3215 Cains Hill Pl., Buckhead. 231-9815.

Tara Relics. This is a great source for antique armaments, souvenirs, documents, books, regimental materials, and other Civil War items as well as *Gone with the Wind* memorabilia and souvenirs. 104 N. Main St., Jonesboro. 473-9307.

Three Crown Antiques. Antiques and collectibles from England, France, Germany, Holland, and the U.S. pack Three Crown's 15,000 square feet. 733 Bullsboro Dr., Newnan. 706-253-4814.

Travis Antiques and Interiors. Dottie Travis has assembled a selection of fine French and English antiques (furnishings and accessories), and offers interior design service. 12 Kings Cir., off Peachtree Hills Ave., Buckhead. 233-7207.

Tymes Furniture Company. Furniture, framed prints, lamps, and other home furnishings, all sixty percent less than most furniture retail prices. 54 Covington St., McDonough. 957-7908.

Vista Gallery. Exquisite custom framing, English and Scottish antiques, botanical prints (antiques and reproductions), and an elegant gift selection can all be found at this unique little shop. The owner takes regular trips to the British Isles to replenish her selection. Join the mailing list to receive notice of special purchases and Saturday teas. Closed Sunday. 2840 LaVista Rd., Decatur. 633-0982.

ARCHITECTURAL ANTIQUES

Atlanta architect James Means collected bits and pieces of buildings being torn down, and stored them to use in the fine Colonial-style houses he designed for clients. Reapplying architectural antiques in new structures is an Atlanta tradition that these sources, among others, help to perpetuate.

Architectural Accents. A treasure trove of exciting architectural hardware, doors, archways, mantels—items one can really use. 2711 Piedmont Rd., Buckhead. 266-8700.

The Hardware Group. Salvaged antique oak and cypress from old buildings. 641 10th St., near Northside Dr., Northwest. 240-0073.

The Wrecking Bar. In the nineteenth century, Austrian immigrant Victor Kriegshaber built this fine home, now listed on the National Register. Today, the home is the Wrecking Bar, and its 18,000 square feet contains doors, mantels, light fixtures, stained and beveled glass, and hardware, much of it appropriate to residential reapplication. 292 Moreland Ave., Little Five Points. 525-0468.

ART GALLERIES

Only three decades ago, Atlanta contained no more than a half-dozen respectable galleries. Today, the town is filled with fine galleries that attract buyers from around the world. Limiting our selection to just these few was indeed difficult.

Abstein Gallery. Works in all media by local and regional artists are showcased in one of the largest galleries in the Southeast. 558 14th St., Midtown. 872-8020.

African Connections. This African arts gallery and boutique imports its wares including a collection of traditional and ceremonial masks and handcrafted jewelry. Accessories, bags, hats, and some clothes are also available. 1107 Euclid Ave., Little Five Points. 589-1834.

Ann Jackson Gallery. Works by artists from China, Argentina, Yugoslavia, the United States, and other countries, as well as Ann's own Impressionist-style paintings fill the gallery. Gustav Denzel-style painted carrousel horses (c. 1880) handcarved in Spanish pine are special attractions. 932 Canton St., Roswell. 993-4783.

Ann Jacob Gallery. Abstract and representational modern paintings, drawings, etchings, prints, and sculpture are displayed in a comfortable, well-lit space. 3500 Peachtree Rd., Phipps Plaza, Buckhead. 262-3399.

Axis Twenty. Furniture as sculpture. Daring and adventuresome one-of-a-kind pieces from local and national artisans are displayed, as are both manufactured pieces by such fine firms as Knoll, and architectural floor lamps by architect Michael Graves. 200 Peachtree Hills Ave., Buckhead. 261-4022.

Berman Gallery. Original pottery, especially raku, by local and national artists. Rick Berman, himself a potter, also shows folk art. 3261 Roswell Rd., Buckhead. 261-3858.

Chattahoochee Flyaway. C. E. Sutton has a real feel for wildlife art, duck stamps, and decoys. All are replicated with extraordinary detail. 2326-A 4th St., Tucker. 939-4585..

Densua's. A rich and diverse collection of African artifacts includes tribal masks, textiles, and jewelry. In Rich's, 2841 Greenbriar Pkwy., Greenbriar Mall, off Lakewood Freeway, Southwest. 346-2637.

Dimensional Arts. Monumental modern sculpture is the focus, although some interesting prints are sold as well. The sculpture is designed to be placed outdoors. Some pieces are produced by rising local artists and are very well

priced. 1200 Foster St., Northwest. 355-4961.

Dorothy McRae Gallery. Works in all media by national and regional artists can be found in the contemporary fine art gallery. Openings happen about every six weeks, but browsers can wander through the art from past shows in the large warehouse behind the gallery proper. 3193 Roswell Rd., Buckhead. 266-2363.

Eve Mannes Gallery. A stunning world of modern painting, sculpture, and furniture by local, national, and international artists. This is a mecca for anyone who respects cutting-edge art. 116-A Bennett St., Brookwood. 351-6651.

Fay Gold Gallery. Contemporary paintings, photography, works on paper, prints, and sculpture—a world of modern art—has been assembled by a former painter. 247 Buckhead Ave., East Village Square, Buckhead. 233-3843.

Fräbel. The renowned German-born glass sculptor has done commissions for three U.S. presidents and other heads of state. Pristine and unique in style, many pieces are affordably priced. Lenox Square, Peachtree Center, and an open studio gallery at 695 Antone St., between Howell Mill Rd. and Northside Dr., Northwest. 351-9794.

Heath Gallery. Contemporary art from all over the world. 416 E. Paces Ferry Rd., Buckhead. 262-6407.

Illumina. Exquisite handcrafted jewelry (chiefly by American artists), and sculpture by local artists. 3500

Peachtree Rd., Ste. A-24, Phipps Plaza, Buckhead. 233-3010.

Jackson Fine Art. Twentieth-century art and contemporary photography. 3115 E. Shadowlawn Ave., Buckhead. 233-3739.

Japan Arts. Rachel Preston specializes in contemporary work from Japan, her father's homeland. By appointment only. Mail only: 93 Dunwoody Springs Dr., Sandy Springs.

McIntosh Gallery. Important contemporary Southern artists show their work in a gallery that has been a major art forum in Atlanta for two decades. 587 Virginia Ave., Virginia-Highland. 892-6228.

Out of the Woods. This shop specializes in ancient, contemporary, and ethnic art and fine crafts. The turned-wood art objects—from exquisite critters carved in exotic woods to handsome bowls and delicate pieces—Ashanti sculpture, Zuni pottery, and paintings featuring Native American themes are all appealing. 22-B Bennett St., Brookwood. 351-0446.

Ray's Indian Originals. Hopi and Zuni jewelry; original work by acclaimed Native American artists; antique pieces and Kachina dolls; historical pottery, baskets, and weavings. Open Saturdays; other times by appointment. 90 N. Avondale Rd., Avondale Estates. 292-4999.

Rolling Stone Press. Original hand-printed lithographs. 432 Calhoun St., Midtown. 873-3322.

Sandler Hudson. Contemporary paintings and sculpture, chiefly by Georgia artists, make this gallery special. 1831-A Peachtree Rd., Brookwood. 350-8480.

The Signature Shop and Gallery. Fine contemporary American craft in various media, much of it local and regional. 3267 Roswell Rd., Buckhead. 237-4426.

The Swan Coach House Art Gallery & Gift Shop. The gallery presents continuously changing exhibits; the gift shop offers handsome children's clothes and gifts, antiques, crystal, and pottery. 3130 Slaton Dr., Buckhead. Gallery: 266-2636; gift shop: 261-0224.

Vespermann Galleries. Fine contemporary glass sculpture of the highest quality sparkles in the beautifully-lit **Glass Gallery**. Next door, the **Craft Gallery** sells jewelry, hand-blown glass holiday ornaments, and other unique craft objects. 2140 Peachtree Rd., Brookwood Square, Brookwood. Craft Gallery: Ste. 240, 350-9545; Glass Gallery: Ste. 237, 350-9698.

Weinberg Gallery. This splendid gallery sells wearable art, jewelry, baskets, and extraordinary one-of-a-kind sculptural furniture by local and national artists. 2140 Peachtree Rd., Brookwood Square, Brookwood. 351-0903.

Yazum Village Art. Almost everything in this colorful, international shop is handmade. You'll find Haitian paintings, African sculptures, and clay figures from Russia in the gallery and shop located across from the High Museum. 1285 Peachtree St., Midtown. 874-8063.

ART & ANTIQUE SALE EVENTS

These are special, frequently held or annual events focusing on antiques, and you should mark them on your calendar at the beginning of each year. In addition, collectors should watch for shows held at regional malls, and check Chapter 4 (Special Events) for festivals featuring arts, antiques, collectibles, and crafts.

Atlanta Antiques Show. Held every January, May, and October, this is an exciting assemblage of dealers who vend everything from antique silver to furniture. In October, a good books section, containing titles that examine antiques and collectibles, is usually displayed as well. Contact Bud Marion of Gemshows, Inc., which manages the event. 305-565-3484.

High Museum Antiques Show and Sale. This project of the Members Guild is the largest fund-raising event for the High. Held in late November, it includes lectures, verbal appraisals, a tour of homes, and special exhibitions. Atlanta Apparel Mart, Spring and Harris Sts. Downtown. Information and tickets: 898-1152.

Salearama. This terrific flea market benefits the High Museum of Art and is usually held in February. Treasure seekers may find everything from jewelry to furniture. An elegant preview party and auction the night before start the ball rolling. Locations vary from year to year. 898-1152.

Trinity School "Spotlight on Georgia Artists." This art sale focuses on Georgia artists, but also includes artists from the Southeast. The show and sale usually take place during the second week of February. The event kicks off with a Sunday preview party and wraps up with an auction on Saturday. The show is open daily from 10 A.M. until 4 P.M. More than 1,000 pieces of art from about 150 artists make this decade-old event popular. Proceeds benefit the artists and Trinity School. 3254 Northside Pkwy., Buckhead. 237-9286.

ARTISTS

When visiting other parts of the country, we check out local art galleries for work by area artists. Too often, we hear: "Oh no, we only have work by international artists." Good thing Picasso wasn't born in Poughkeepsie! Well, we think Atlanta's artists are outstanding. Many sell or work exclusively out of home studios, while others are represented in galleries. Watch for special holiday sales that some artists hold either individually or in collaboration. Get on mailing lists, and you'll receive notice of these wonderful shopping opportunities, especially good for wearable art, jewelry, baskets, and ceramics. This list merely hints at what's available, as we've selected only a couple of representatives in each medium. Affordability was a consideration, but don't expect these folks to sell their work for nothing.

Susan Ashley. Beautiful mixed-media and watercolors. 523-7886.

Barbara Brozik. Acrylic paintings on paper, cut and woven into wall sculptures and furniture. 524-8434.

Mary Booth Cabot. Wonderful botanicals. Original paintings and limited-edition prints. 587-2587.

Nick Cook. Fine but affordable turned-wood objects, such as bowls and figures. 421-1212.

Victoria Greenhood. Handsome semiprecious stones banded in gold or silver. 875-6515.

Linda Gunshor. Delicate porcelain and raku. Among the functional pieces, the porcelain lamps are especially interesting. 874-4617.

W. Chester Old. Outrageously whimsical lamps and other utilitarian ob-jects—mirrors, candle holders, napkin rings, for instance—are fashioned from metal. 378-6602.

Joseph Perrin. Strongly geometric oils and acrylics in vibrant colors; portraits. 296-5709.

Judie B. Raiford. Original jewelry primarily designed in silver and gold. Studio: 953 Canton St., Roswell. 992-6197.

Susan Starr. Fiber art, wearable art for the holidays, and mixed-media works in which fiber plays a central role. 992-1697.

Cristina Tamames. Powerful shapes in silver and gold jewelry. 993-1034.

Misty Taylor Designs. Sterling and silver-plated jewelry, sometimes with semiprecious stones, is manufactured in Mexico. At Gallery V, 10 Elizabeth Way, Roswell. 992-4144.

Elizabeth Turk. Black-and-white portrait photographs in natural or outdoor settings. 577-3872.

Betty Wassmer. Wonderful, whimsical ceramics. 876-4814.

BOOKS & MUSIC

While these sources are outstanding for most requirements, both new and used, don't overlook some of the antique shops listed at the beginning of this chapter, or flea markets—unusual tapes (especially of international music) and out-of-print books and magazines are regularly featured at many of them.

A Cappella Books. Alongside new, used, and rare-book editions of modern literature, you'll find books on everything from baseball to hoboes and gypsies. Out-of-print and collectible books on folk, country, blues, and jazz music are another specialty. 1133 Euclid Ave., Little Five Points. 681-5128.

The Book Nook. You can trade your old paperbacks—from category to category—for other used paperbacks (romances for romances, for instance). You may also swap your old records, CDs, and books on tape. 3342 Clairmont Rd., Northeast. 633-1328.

Ageless Books. A wide variety of used books, including good Georgian, Southern, and American history books. Some antiquarian and first editions. 3369 Buford Hwy., Suite 820, Northeast Plaza, NE. 321-3369.

Architectural Book Center. Architecture, interior design, art, landscaping, and related subjects. Operated by the local chapter of the American Institute of Architects. Colony Square Mall, Midtown. 873-1052.

Atlantis Connection New Age Books. Incense permeates this small shop that sells books on astrology, crystals, and related matters. 1402 N. Highland Ave., Virginia-Highland. 881-6511.

Auto Motif. Automotive titles are amid other paraphernalia for auto enthusiasts. Parts and accessories, however, are not sold. 2941 Atlanta Rd. SE, Smyrna. 435-5025.

Barnes and Noble. More than 100,000 titles are available at each Barnes and Noble location. They cater to a variety of customers, from individuals to corporations. Both locations feature a small cafe with coffee, fruit juices, and dessert; the Buckhead site also includes a music section. 2900 Peachtree Rd., Buckhead. 261-7747; 4776 Ashford-Dunwoody Rd., Dunwoody. 393-9277.

Books & Bytes. A full-service bookstore with an emphasis on computer books and software. Children's literature, science fiction, mystery, romance, and the classics are also in good supply. 850 Dogwood Rd., Five Forks Village, Lawrenceville. 985-0812.

Books & Cases. Book lovers will find fine first editions, books on art and architecture, antique buying guides, fine multi-volume sets, bindings, antiquaria, and exquisite prints. Search service offered. 715 Miami Cir., Ste. 220, Miami Circle Market Center, Buckhead. 231-9107.

Borders Book Shop. The staff knows its inventory, and special-order service is prompt. Discounts and sales are great. 3655 Roswell Rd., at Piedmont Rd., Tuxedo Festival, Buckhead. 237-0707.

Charis. Feminist themes, including lesbian topics and women's issues. The inventory of 11,000 titles includes children's books specifically chosen for their anti-racist, anti-sexist perspective. 419 Moreland Ave., Little Five Points. 524-0304.

Criminal Records. This Little Five Points music store describes itself as "wacky but lovable." All kinds of new music on cassette and CD, but they only buy and sell used CDs. Comics, posters and magazines galore. Ask about the "all-green" policy. 466 Moreland Ave., Little Five Points. 215-9511.

The Dependable Bookman. Woody Bates specializes in books about Asia—reference, art, history, botanical—and books by and about Lafcadio Hearn, an American author who lived in Japan. Mail order only; four catalogues each year. 4010 Beechwood Dr., Atlanta, 30327. 237-0529.

Dollar Bookstore. Judy and Charlie Dollar's discount bookstore carries books on tape (also for rent), discounted software, used books, and maps. Dollar also rents best sellers. 1050 E. Piedmont, Marietta. 565-8696.

Engineer's Bookstore. Founded in 1954 to serve Georgia Tech students, this bookstore now provides technical reference, building codes, and computer books to the expanding professional community in Atlanta. 748 Marietta St., Midtown. 221-1669.

First World. A large inventory of books covers black history, from Africa to the New World. 677-1/2 Cascade Ave., near Langhorn Ave., Southwest. 758-7124; Underground Atlanta. 681-2042.

Hobbit Hall Children's Bookstore. Carrying a full line of classics and new publications, Hobbit Hall stocks books for all kids, from toddlers to young adults. Nationally recognized authors and illustrators visit this lovely converted house monthly. Besides sponsoring special events in local schools, Hobbit Hall provides activities and food for kid's birthday parties, and conducts a creative summer camp in its back yard play area. 120 Bulloch Ave., Roswell. 587-0907.

International Records. Good values on an extensive collection of fine CDs and tapes that embrace all kinds of classical, jazz, and popular music—some of it hard to come by. 231 Peachtree St., Peachtree Center, Downtown. 584-5490.

David McCord, Bookseller. McCord specializes in books on African American subjects, Americana, Southern and regional subjects, and photographica. By appointment only. P.O. Box 54071, Civic Center Station, Atlanta, 30308. 873-3495.

The Nature Company. Books on the environment, maps, fine art, and New Age music on CDs are all part of a fascinating inventory. 3393 Peachtree

Rd., Lenox Square, Buckhead. 231-9252; 4400 Ashford Dunwoody Rd., Perimeter Mall, Dunwoody. 551-0266; 114 Lower Alabama St., Underground Atlanta, Downtown. 525-3131.

Old New York Book Shop. For more than twenty years, Cliff Graubart and Howard McAbee have specialized in first editions. The collection ranges over two floors of an old house. 1069 Juniper St., Midtown. 881-1285.

Opus 1. Opus 1 supplies educational organizations and individuals with classical sheet music and books of music to instruct young performers. Catalog sales. Hours vary seasonally. 315 W. Ponce de Leon Ave., Ste. 421, Wachovia Bank Bldg., Decatur. 378-1132.

Outwrite. The bookstore and coffee shop carries a complete line of lesbian and gay literature in a comfortable atmosphere. The coffee shop offers a variety of brews and baked goods. 931 Monroe Dr., Suite 108, Midtown Promenade Shopping Center, Midtown. 607-0082.

Oxford Book Stores. One of the largest and best independent bookstores in the country, and open 'til the wee hours Friday and Saturday nights, Oxford at Buckhead is nearly three times larger than the original at Peachtree Battle. The coffee shop, **Oxford Espresso Cafe** (266-8250), and the art gallery, **The Arts Connection** (237-0005), are added delights. 360 Pharr Rd., Buckhead. 262-3333. This is a bookstore you can spend the day in! **Oxford at Peachtree Battle**, the oldest store, also keeps late-night hours and includes a coffee shop. 2345 Peachtree Rd., Peachtree Battle Shopping Center, Buckhead.

364-2700. The smaller **Oxford at West Paces** is at 1200 W. Paces Ferry Rd., W. Paces Ferry Shopping Center, Buckhead. 364-2488.

Oxford Too. A rainy day kind of place, it houses remainders, first editions, and backstocks of old *Gourmet* and *Life* magazines. **The Collectors' Corner** focuses on modern first editions, many of them signed. Good used paperbacks and used records. Downstairs is **Oxford Comics and Games** (233-8682). 2395 Peachtree Rd., near Peachtree Battle Shopping Center, Buckhead. 262-3411.

The Science Fiction & Mystery Book Shop. The open gracious atmosphere and well-organized space makes it a pleasure to browse here. Approximately 14,000 active titles are available and many of the featured specialty magazines can't be found anywhere else. No used books. 2000-F Cheshire Bridge Rd., Midtown. 634-3226.

Shrine of the Black Madonna. A cultural center that also sells reproduction African jewelry and other items, it is principally a bookstore. 946 Ralph David Abernathy Dr., West End. 752-6125.

Soul Source. African and African-American subjects. Frequent special events (readings and musicales). Downstairs, the **Soul Source Café** nourishes students on salads and sandwiches. 118 James P. Brawley Dr., Atlanta University Center, West End. 577-1346.

Southern Highlands Books. Good Georgiana, Southern, and American history books, as well as architecture and art books make this store a good source for these subjects. Military history, especially Civil War and World War II, is a strong suit. 1800 Century Blvd., NE. 320-7862..

The Tall Tales Bookshop. Hardbacks and paperbacks, with literature a specialty. The knowledgeable staff is adept at securing special orders, even of modern first editions. 2999 N. Druid Hills Rd., Toco Hills Shopping Center, Northeast. 636-2498.

Tower Records. If it's not at Tower, it's probably not worth having. The CDs hail from around the world (Argentina to Zimbabwe), and reproduction 45s with hits from the '50s and '60s supplement extensive classical, jazz, and rock sections. 3400 Woodale Dr., #200, Around Lenox Shopping Center, Buckhead. 264-1217.

Wax-n-Facts. Before Little Five Points became cool, Wax-n-Facts was bringing music lovers into the area. The eighteen-year-old establishment features new and used albums, cassettes, and CDs and music-related magazines, newspapers, and T-shirts. It can get pretty crowded, but there are some real finds tucked away in the bins. 432 Moreland Ave., Little Five Points. 525-2275.

Wuxtry. This funky store is a standard stop for alternative music lovers. If you're searching for hard-to-find music, the Wuxtry staff will go out of their way to locate it for you; they even offer international mail order. Buy, sell, or trade your used items, or select from the assortment of new music. 2096 N. Decatur Rd., Decatur. 329-0020.

Yesteryear. You'll find out-of-print Georgiana, American history, modern first editions, maps, and Civil War books, as well as old cookbooks, art, architecture, decorative arts books, and fine prints. Loads of atmosphere and helpful assistance. 3201 Maple Dr., Buckhead. 237-0163.

BOOK SALE EVENTS

Like the art and antique sales, these are special annual events that raise money for certain organizations and charities. They are worth placing on your calendar at the beginning of each year if chasing out-of-print books is one of your personal pursuits.

American Association of University Women Book Fair. An annual fall event, this is a mecca for book collectors, browsers, and just plain readers. 279 Buckhead Ave., Buckhead. 261-7646 (book room); 355-1861.

Atlanta Antiquarian Book Fair. Over seventy dealers from around the U.S. and Britain—the "old book people"—converge on the Gwinnett Civic Center for a weekend in late October, offering a huge selection of rare and out-of-print books; a must-see for dealers and anyone who loves books. Special exhibits, signings, and lectures round out the show, which benefits the Georgia Adult Literacy Program. Sponsored by the Georgia Antiquarian Booksellers Association, 3666 Clairmont Rd., Chamblee, GA 30341. 457-2919.

Brandeis University National Women's Committee Book Sale. Always held in May at Toco Hills, it is a treasure seeker's nirvana. Run by volunteers to benefit the libraries at Brandeis University, in Massachusetts. Call for information. 231-6211.

Friends of the Library Book Sale. This benefit for the Atlanta–Fulton County Library is usually held in the spring. Most books sell for between 50¢ and $2. 1 Margaret Mitchell Sq., Downtown. 730-1700.

Goodwill Secondhand Book Sale. During the first week in February, Goodwill holds the largest secondhand book sale in the Southeast. Northlake Mall, at the intersection of I-285 and LaVista Road in DeKalb County, is the scene for this popular annual event. More than 200,000 titles in about forty categories, including mystery, science fiction, cooking, religion, comics, and juvenile fiction are available. Proceeds benefit the corporation's job training programs. Goodwill Industries: 2201 Glenwood Ave., Atlanta, 30316. 377-0441.

CULINARY

Atlanta now has a great deal more to offer in the way of markets and bakeries than it had just a few years ago. Specialties include the exotic as well as fine Southern products. (We often send packages containing barbecue sauce and Vidalia onion relish to friends around the country.)

BAKERIES

Bernie the Baker. Atlanta's only authorized Kosher baker, Bernie Idov sells traditional Jewish-style breads and baked goods. Superior poppy-seed pastry strip and pecan-raspberry torte. 3015 N. Druid Hills Rd., Toco Hills Promenade, Toco Hills Shopping Center, Northeast. 633-1986.

The Bread Market. Robert Fisher and his daughter, Lori, have learned their craft from one of the best: Nancy Silverton of the La Brea Bakery in Los Angeles. Using Silverton's recipes, this team produces European-style

breads, baguettes, and focaccias in a huge French oven. 3167 Peachtree Rd., Buckhead. 816-8600.

Buckhead Bread Company. Attached to Pricci (see chapter 1) an Italian restaurant, the bakery produces breads, pastries, and other baked goods. The bakery's $50,000 Tibiletti oven is the only one like it in this country. 500-A Pharr Rd., Buckhead. 237-8396.

Fiesta. Remarkable Latin American pastries. The first location also serves authentic Mexican dishes. 2714 Shallowford Rd., Chamblee. 986-9916; 2581 Piedmont Rd. (actually on Sidney Marcus Blvd.), Lindbergh Plaza, Buckhead. 233-9332.

The Finishing Touch Bakery. Extravagant and elegant desserts and pastries. Cakes and sweets made by special order. Desserts sold at **Sweet Stuff**, a dessert and coffee shop (*see chapter 1*). 1409-A N. Highland Ave., Virginia-Highland. 873-9933.

The German Bakery. The owners of this European bakery have been in business over thirty years. The German-inspired atmosphere makes choosing from the European breads and the birthday and coffee cakes even more fun. The small gourmet food section features imported items. 2914 White Blvd., Decatur. 296-4336.

Goldberg and Son. Splendid bagels, bialys, and traditional Jewish treats are baked on the premises. Closed Mondays and all Jewish holidays. Also has a small deli. 4383 Roswell Rd., Roswell-Wieuca Shopping Center, Buckhead. 256-3751.

Henri's. This full-line, from-scratch bakery and deli offers Danish and French pastries, assorted breads (like six grain, pesto, whole wheat, and nonfat recipes), tortes, and birthday cakes. They've been in business over 65 years in Atlanta, and have built a loyal clientele. 61 Irby Ave. Buckhead. 237-0202; 999 Peachtree St., Midtown. 875-1922; 6289 Roswell Rd., Sandy Springs. 256-7934.

International Bakery. Wonderful baklava and other fine Greek pastries. Also Greek olive oils, pastas, imported cheeses, and ready-to-use phylo dough for your own baking. 2165 Cheshire Bridge Rd., Northeast. 636-7580.

Maison Robert. Wonderful French pastries made by a Frenchman married to a good ole gal from Mississippi. Holiday treats—stollen, for instance—and custom chocolates are to swoon for. Tearoom. 3867 Peachtree Rd., Cherokee Plaza, Brookhaven. 237-3675.

Masada Bakery. This wholesale bakery makes whole-grain breads and sells the overproduction in a small retail space at the bakery. Special deals on Mondays. 1660 NE Expressway Access Rd., between Exits 31 and 32, Northeast. 320-0452.

My Bakery. Old-fashioned recipes yield light, delicious breads, sweet rolls, cookies, and desserts. Blackberry jam, jellies, and relishes are made in season. Homemade hard candies are made for the holidays. 1604 Hwy. 92, Woodstock. 924-6000.

The Royal Bagel. Voted best in Atlanta for the last five years by *Atlanta* magazine, this is also a favorite of the entire Peachtree Publishers' staff. Thirteen kinds of bagels are available with assorted spreads to eat in or take out. Generous salads, soups, and sandwiches are also available. The full-line bakery offers cookies, pastries, and cakes as beautiful as they are delicious. All the baking is done on the premises. 1544 Piedmont Ave., Ansley Mall, Midtown. 876-3512.

Swissôtel Breads. Executive Pastry Chef Christoph Bruehwiler has done so well with his house bread, Walliser, and farmer's bread that, by popular demand, they are now sold in the hotel's gift shop. 3391 Peachtree Rd., Swissôtel, Buckhead. 365-0065, ext. 2482.

Tropical Delite. Wonderful West Indian baked goods. The meat patties, spicy or not, come off tops. Traditional Jamaican fruitcake, dark and fragrant, is a holiday treat that must be ordered in advance. 2136 Candler Rd., Decatur. 284-1878.

Willie's German Bakery. Worth the trip for sourdough rye, six-grain, and Bavarian farmers' bread. Wonderful pumpernickel and poppy seed strudel must be ordered in advance. Look for special traditional German holiday treats. Call ahead to reserve. 4808 Flat Shoals Rd., Decatur. 987-3298.

MARKETS

Agnes Gift Shop. We don't know who Agnes is, but this is one of the nicest Oriental markets in the city. The produce is especially good. 5210 Buford Hwy., Doraville. 457-7911.

Arthur's Kosher Meat Market and Deli. Two locations offer not just meat, but also frozen products, takeout, deli, and groceries. 2166 Briarcliff Rd., near LaVista Rd., Northeast. 634-6881; 120 Copeland Rd., off Roswell Rd., just inside I-285, Sandy Springs. 252-4396.

Atlanta State Farmers Market. A true farmers market. Each stall is operated by a different vendor, and most sell items in large lots only. Many Atlantans join forces, buy large quantities, and divide the take and the cost. Fine produce, Christmas trees at holiday time, honey, homemade preserves, relishes, and jellies make the trip worthwhile. 16 Forest Pkwy., Forest Park. 366-6910.

Burger's Markets. The first market opened about sixty years ago, and now there are 25 throughout Georgia. The original family operates them all, including the seven found in Atlanta's outlying suburban areas (Douglasville, Marietta, Powder Springs). Daily deliveries of fresh fruit and vegetables are displayed on wooden planks, and the seafood and meats are fresh. Original market: 6631 Bells Ferry Rd., Woodstock. 924-2247.

Coffee Plantation. Not only coffee, but all the accessories coffee drinkers could possibly want. Two locations: Toco Hills Shopping Center, N. Druid Hills Rd., Northeast. 636-1038; 4920 Roswell Rd., Fountain Oaks Shopping Center, Sandy Springs. 252-4686.

The Cooks Market-Café. Unique grocery items, including the specialties of local producers, takeout, and prepared foods are attractively displayed. Special items ordered in advance, such as game, are received the next day. 2770 Lenox Rd., Plantation Heights, Northeast. 364-0900.

Costa's Pasta. This family-run operation purveys pastas (some stuffed) freshly made on the premises, homemade sauces, domestic and imported cheeses, and Italian meats. Bring your own pan and have it filled with lasagne. Oven-ready dinners. 2145 Roswell Rd., East-lake Center, Marietta. 971-2771.

Country Fed Meat Co., Inc. Beef, chicken, and seafood are available wholesale to the public. Get a quarter cut, a half cut, or a whole steer packaged and wrap-ped for the freezer. 633 Roberts Dr., Riverdale. 991-5888.

DeKalb Farmers Market. From the exotic to the ordinary—it's all attractively displayed in this 100,000-square-foot market. Besides produce and groceries, there's fresh fish, both offbeat and ordinary. Great Lakes whitefish, pike, and shrimp with their heads left on (a miracle!) are among the unusual items that show up from time to time. Tanks display live rainbow trout, lobsters, and Dungeness crab. If all that food is making you hungry, stop by the cafeteria; you can eat in or take out. 3000 E. Ponce de Leon Ave., Decatur. 377-6400.

> The ridge in Atlanta, on Peachtree Street near Macy's, Downtown, is a signal watershed where rainwater that drains down the west side of the street winds up in the Gulf of Mexico, and water on the east side flows into the Atlantic Ocean.

Dinho Market. A large, well-kept market devoted to all manner of Asian foods, Dinho's provides groceries to Atlanta's Asian restaurants. 5379 New Peachtree Rd., Chinatown Mall, Chamblee. 454-8888.

East 48th Street Market. Italian specialties—wine, cheese, pastries, bread, salamis and sausages, and olive oils—present an ambience perfumed with the scent of fine things to eat. Catering, baskets, takeout, and cooking lessons _(see chapter 9)_ are offered. 2462 Jett Ferry Rd., at Mt. Vernon Rd., Williamsburg at Dunwoody Shopping Center, Dunwoody. 392-1499.

El Rinconcito. A 25-year fixture in Atlanta, it has all kinds of Hispanic food products displayed attractively. Cheerful help in English. 2845 Buford Hwy., Clock Tower, Northeast. 636-8714.

Harry's Farmers Market. Three locations bring unique produce, meats, seafood, baked goods to die for, and unusual grocery items—and don't forget a well-stocked wine shop—to the 'burbs. The meat department features fresh rabbit, frozen game, beefalo, Coleman's all-natural beef, and the market's own sausage. The seafood department is huge, and offers only the freshest items, from salmon to squid. The bakery is known for its wonderful breads and cookies. Buy a cup of gourmet coffee for 25¢ to sip while you shop—it's easy to spend hours here. One sign that points to outstanding quality, value and selection: restaurant chefs often shop here.

The Harry's in Gwinnett County is the smallest of the three at "only" a bit over 60,000 square feet, but contains basically the same array of products, except that its wine selection is limited. The original, and largest, location: 1180 Upper Hembree Rd., Alpharetta. 664-6300; 2025 Satellite Pointe, Duluth. 416-

6900. New in '94: 70 Powers Ferry Rd., Marietta. 578-4400.

Hoa Binh Seafood Market. A Vietnamese market selling wonderful barbecued pork and duck, Oriental food items, fresh meat, and fish. It's not the cleanest market, but close your eyes to the unswept floor. If you want fresh duck (with the head on!), this is one of the few places to get it in town. We know chefs who shop here. 2216 Cheshire Bridge Rd., Northeast. 636-7165.

International Farmers Market. An 80,000-square-foot operation, this market gets much of its seafood and produce directly from producers rather than through brokers. The market claims to have the largest tanks east of the Mississippi River for holding live fish and seafood in a retail operation. A bakery and a takeout section round out the offerings. 5193 Peachtree Industrial Blvd., Chamblee. 455-1777.

J.J.'s West Indian Mart. Carole Johnson's warm, friendly greeting makes a visit here all the more delightful. Besides Caribbean groceries—fresh callaloo (similar to spinach), canned goods, and drinks—cooked meals, featuring Caribbean specialties, are served in the market. 3429 Covington Dr., off Covington Hwy., Decatur. 288-7865.

J. Martinez. Estate-grown Blue Mountain coffees and other Jamaican and West Indian specialty items are sold in a fine, well-arranged shop. Sip some freshly brewed Jamaican while you browse. A corporate gift catalog and special packaging are available.

3230-A Peachtree Rd., Buckhead. 231-5465.

Kim Sun Market. A large Korean market with general Oriental grocery items, this shop also has some wonderful barbecue to take home. The man who makes it doesn't speak English, but he gets his point across with sign language. 5038 Buford Hwy., Chamblee. 457-2492.

Lindsay Farms. Simply scrumptious Southern-style items, such as a Savannah rum cake, the best pickled Vidalia onions, and wonderful marmalades, preserves, and relishes are sold under Ann Lindsay's private label. Catalog and mailing services. 4794 Clark Howell Hwy., College Park. 305-0620.

Marietta Farmers' Market. A true farmers market, reminiscent of the one at Union Square in New York City, the Marietta version consists of a dozen or so trucks that gather daily during the week. The number doubles on the weekends. Locally produced fresh fruits and vegetables are sold. Parking lot by The Depot, Historic Marietta Square, Marietta.

Municipal Market of Atlanta. At this Atlanta institution, stall owners sell everything from whole pigs, a specialty of **Hardeman's** (659-6308), to trapped rabbit and salt-cured chicken—stuff absolutely no one else has. This is not for the faint of heart, but the adventurous will enjoy it. 209 Edgewood Ave., Downtown. 659-1665.

New Garden Bake Shop & Deli. Really good Italian sausage, homemade cheesecake, cannoli, pastries, and Italian bread. 6135 Peachtree

Pkwy., Ste. 610, Market Place at Peachtree Corners, Norcross. 447-0858.

Nippan Daido. This nifty Japanese grocery store offers rice, shiitake mushrooms, tuna, pickled ginger, wasabi, and Japanese beer. 2390 Chamblee-Tucker Rd., Chamblee. 455-3846.

Norcross Oriental Market. Unusual Thai and Chinese grocery items such as kefir leaves (essential in Thai cooking), mild, flavorful Thai white vinegar, and fresh lemon grass are attractively displayed. 6065 Norcross-Tucker Rd., off Jimmy Carter Blvd. at Singleton Rd., Norcross. 496-1656.

Nutrition Naturally. This grocery-store-sized operation has some of the lowest prices in town on packaged health products, frozen foods, supplements, and drinks. No produce. 1799 Briarcliff Rd., Sage Hill Shopping Center, Northeast. 872-2297.

Nuts 'N Berries. This market's reputation stems from good prices, a large inventory, and a fine little cafe serving tasty vegetarian dishes. 4568 Peachtree Rd., at Ashford-Dunwoody Rd., Brookhaven. 237-6829.

Quality Kosher Emporium. A charming staff supplies everything from cut-to-order meat to party trays. Sandwiches are terrific. 2153 Briarcliff Rd., Northeast. 636-1114.

Rainbow Grocery. The granddaddy of health-food stores, Rainbow Grocery sells organic produce, grains, frozen foods, and takeouts. A cafe serves tasty, good-for-you dishes. 2118 N. Decatur Rd., at Clairmont Rd., Decatur. 636-5553.

Sausage World & Deli. Former Braves catcher Biff Pocoroba oversees a world of sausages: Italian (five kinds); kielbasa, bratwurst, bangers, Swedish potato sausage, chorizo, and fresh andouille. Special orders are available. 5363 Lawrenceville Hwy., Lilburn Square, Lilburn. 925-4493.

Sevananda. Serving as the "Piggly Wiggly" in *Driving Miss Daisy*, Sevananda is a cooperative that has built a loyal following over the years. It offers produce, vitamins, dairy products, and other health-oriented items at good prices. Substantial herbal section. 1111 Euclid Ave., Little Five Points. 681-2831.

Shields Market. Shields has been a fixture in Decatur for nearly half a century. Sawdust covers the floor, and meat hangs on hooks in an old-time cooler. The meat selection includes hanging beef—beautifully cut to order—hams, pork, turkeys, and fresh, ice-packed chicken. 143 Sycamore St., Decatur. 377-6897.

Tailgate Market. The North Fulton Extension Service runs a market out of nineteen pickups filled with home-grown fruits and vegetables. Fall and winter bring homemade jellies, pickles, and preserves. Saturday mornings, from 7 A.M. to noon. Wills Rd., Wills Park, Alpharetta. On Tuesdays and Thursdays, most of the same group is at Mt. Vernon Presbyterian Church on Mt. Vernon Rd., Sandy Springs.

Taj Mahal Imports. It's a pity you can't bottle the aromas of these Indian and British foods in a store packed with curries, chutneys, Basmati rice, mincemeats, mustards, and pickles. 1594-G Woodcliff Dr., Briarcliff Shopping Center, Northeast. 321-5940.

Taste of Britain. The Camerons sell canned goods, frozen Cornish pasties, other traditional British treats, and Danish bacon. Get on the mailing list to attend one of the store's special events, such as a haggis tasting. 73 S. Peachtree St., Norcross. 242-8585.

Taste of Europe. In addition to unusual smoked and cured meats (the smoked pork chops are heavenly!), Taste of Europe offers flavorful prepared dishes for takeout, good lunches, and corporate catering. 6631 Roswell Rd., Abernathy Square, Sandy Springs. 255-7363.

PICK YOUR OWN

Depending on the season, local farmers invite folks to pick or gather their own fruit. In the late summer and fall, the apples ripen in North Georgia. Berries carry the day in the farming areas south of the city. For peaches, head into the middle of the state; you can get there in a couple of hours. To check for locations and seasons, as well as for advice on what to bring to haul your fruit home, ask for copies of the *Farmers and Consumers Market Bulletin*, published by the Georgia Department of Agriculture. It prints the seasonal list, and it's free. 19 Martin Luther King, Jr., Dr., Downtown. 656-3722.

FASHION DESIGN & TAILORING

You may not think of Atlanta as a fashion design center. But a little looking reveals that we've got some fine young designers who are beginning to make names for themselves. Many have graduated from the local campus of the American College of Applied Art (see Chapter 9 (Expanding Your Mind)), which has a fine fashion design program.

Anthony Liggins. Liggins says his clothes are for women who are "conceptually clever and experimentally humanistic." Visit the studio and showroom by appointment. 254 E. Paces Ferry Rd., Ste. 203, Buckhead. 842-0621.

Bill Hallman. Hallman, a native of Vietnam, designs comfortable clothes for young professionals, mostly male.

He also sells lines designed by others, such as Wayne Van Nguyen. Hallman's Antenna line features clubby women's clothes at moderate prices. 1054 N. Highland Ave., Virginia-Highland. 876-6055.

Bonnie's Boutique. Stunning high-fashion evening garments, many imported from Italy, are trimmed with crystals, beads, and stones. Custom-designed dresses average around $900, but beautiful, machine-stitched dresses ($150 to $400) are values. The designs are so classic you'll wear them into the next century. Sizes up to 14, but special orders for larger and petite sizes are available. 1 Galleria Pkwy., Galleria Specialty Mall, Northwest. 850-0595.

Emily Redwine. Custom-designed women's clothing, from wedding dresses to cocktail dresses, casual attire, and business suits. By appointment only. Mail only: 63 Avery Dr., Atlanta, 30309. 876-5018.

Francesco Tailors. Custom-made men's suits from a fine collection of fabrics. Not inexpensive (suits start at $850 and average around $1,200), but unique designs custom-fit the client. Alterations only under special circumstances. 3098 Piedmont Rd., Gallery of Fabrics Bldg., Buckhead. 237-8644.

J. Reynolds. Three lines are offered: better cocktail dresses, suits, and formals, priced between $200 and $600; prom and bridesmaids dresses, with sequins, ruffles, and beading, retailing from $150 to $300; and hand-beaded, brightly colored pageant and evening gowns, costing between $600 and $900. The warehouse shows held several times a year are great for finding samples, damaged, or one-of-a-kind dresses. 985 Ponce de Leon Ave., at N. Highland Ave., Virginia-Highland. 881-6398; 250 Spring St., Midtown. 521-3431.

Knox Clayton. A native of Costa Rica, Clayton has been at F. Alonso for fifteen years creating custom fashion designs, from formal wear to sports wear. 110 E. Andrews Dr., Cates Center, Buckhead. 233-8431.

Morse Designs. As a girl, Debra Morse learned to sew in order to fit her own tall frame fashionably. In Atlanta since 1980, Morse Designs sells directly to the public by appointment. Makeup and accessories counseling and "closet therapy" are à la carte services. P.O. Box 12388, Atlanta, 30355. 872-7234.

Wayne Van Nguyen. Designing men's and women's fashions for the artistic set, Vietnam native Van Nguyen retails his line in shops around the country, and in Atlanta at Bill Hallman. Custom-designed suits (for both men and women) are available at the studio. By appointment only. 254 E. Paces Rd., Ste. 203, Buckhead. 842-0621.

FLEA MARKETS

Longtime Atlantans fondly recall one of the city's first flea markets in an old discount store on the spot where the Lindbergh MARTA station is now located. This one started our love affair with flea markets, where one can find everything from produce to bonsai, clothes to furniture, rugs to toys. Most are open only toward the end of the week and/or the weekend, so check with that special vendor you plan to visit before going.

Atlanta Antique Center and Flea Market. On Fridays, Saturdays, and Sundays this former Sears warehouse is transformed into a bustling center offering collectibles and quality antiques from knowledgeable dealers. Totaling 80,000 square feet, it houses 154 dealers, a restaurant, and a candy booth. No admission. 5360 Peachtree Industrial Blvd., Chamblee. 458-0456.

Georgia Antique Center and International Market. Some shops are open all week, and most open at 11 A.M. This rambling, climate-controlled, 140,000-square-foot facility houses 200 dealers. Snacks and sandwich vendors. No admission. 6624 NE Expressway, Norcross, at Jimmy Carter Blvd. exit. 446-9292.

Gwinnett Flea Market. The week begins on Wednesday in this former furniture outlet, which houses over 200,000 square feet of space. Most dealers focus on new merchandise rather than antiques and collectibles. Fast food vendors. No admission. 5675 Jimmy Carter Blvd., at I-85, Norcross. 449-8189.

Kudzu Flea Market. This market opens Friday, Saturday, and Sunday at 11

A.M., although some merchants open a bit earlier. Early twentieth-century collectibles, including furniture and accessories, make the place a treasure trove. 2874 E. Ponce de Leon Ave., Decatur. 373-6498.

Lake Acworth Antique & Flea Market. James Little started this market out of a fruit stand, back in 1971. Since then it has merged with the adjoining Yesteryear Flea Market owned by Bill Abernathy to cover about twelve acres. Some stalls are in buildings, while other dealers operate out of pickup trucks and vans. One large building holds nothing but crafts. The hodgepodge has a definite international flavor. Snack bars and rest rooms. Saturdays and Sundays only. Parking is 50¢. 4375 Cobb Pkwy., at Hwy. 92, Acworth. 974-5896.

Lakewood Antique Market. This is a superior way to spend a day on the second weekend of each month, beginning at 9 A.M. Friday and Saturday, and 10 A.M. on Sunday. The nominal admission is good for the entire weekend. Dealers sell everything from quality antiques and collectibles to genuine junk. The seven exhibition buildings cover about seven acres. Food vendors and a restaurant. Take I-75 to Lakewood Freeway (exit 88E), and follow the signs. 2000 Lakewood Way, Southwest. 622-4488.

North I-85 Twin. Imagine your basic drive-in movie theater: where the cars usually park, one finds vendors who pay $20 a day to set up shop on Saturdays and Sundays. Some arrive as early as 2 A.M. to set up their merchandise: junk, produce, memorabilia, collectibles, or tapes of music from other cultures. Some merchandise is new, although often imperfect, and occasionally perfects may be found. Lots of military surplus. A concession stand does a brisk business in hot dogs and fries. I-85 Access Rd. between Exits 33 and 34, Shallowford Rd. and Chamblee-Tucker Rd., Northeast.

Scott Antique Market at the Atlanta Exposition Center. This is an ideal spot to search for serious antiques and collectibles, including furniture, silver, crystal, and porcelain. The 160,000-square-foot center houses more than 800 quality dealers. Another 200-plus dealers set up on five acres outside. It's open during the second weekend of every month. The nominal admission is good for the entire weekend—Friday, Saturday, and Sunday beginning at 9 A.M. Take I-285 to exit 40, Jonesboro Rd. 3650 Jonesboro Rd., Forest Park. 361-2000.

Yesteryear Flea Market. Bill Abernathy is James Little's neighbor in the flea market business. They share the same twelve acres and the parking (50¢) and sell the same kind of serendipitous stuff. Saturdays and Sundays. 4337 Hwy. 92 NW, at Cobb Pkwy. (Hwy. 41), Acworth. 974-6259.

HANDMADE ITEMS

Unique, finely crafted furnishings and other objects need not cost a ransom. Covering a few of Atlanta's resources in handmade treasures, this list hints at the depth and breadth of what's available in several areas.

FASHION

MCM. This German firm specializes in leather goods, such as designer handbags, luggage, and accessories. Handmade in Munich, the bags are priced from about $170 and up. Apparel and fragrances are also available. The friendly, knowledgeable staff neither hovers nor pushes. 3393 Peachtree Rd., Promenade Wing, Lenox Square, Buckhead. 261-4762.

Tom James. The men's shirts are well made, and the fabrics are beautiful. 900 Circle 75 Pkwy., Smyrna. 612-8779; 2800 N. Druid Hills Rd., Ste. A-100, Northeast. 636-0900.

FURNITURE & ACCESSORIES

The Downeaster. Using plans from the Smithsonian Institution and the Seaport Museum at Mystic, Connecticut, Joe Anastasia designs and produces replicas of model ships. Preferring basswood, mahogany, teak, and walnut, he draws the templates and cuts the wood by hand. Repairs *(see chapter 7)*. By appointment only. Mail only: 425 Grenock Cir., Atlanta, 30328. 393-1789.

Fragile. This shop offers unusual ceramics, glassware, flatware, geometric Mikasa and Sasaki tableware patterns, lively art-studio ceramics by Kevin Goehring of Tampa's Square One, hand-painted ceramics from Deruta of Italy, and Sasaki stainless flatware. Bridal registry. 175 Mt. Vernon Hwy., Sandy Springs. 257-1323.

Irish Crystal Company. This is a wonderful source for fine, hand-cut Irish crystal and handmade linens. While not cheap, they are less expensive than many well-known lines of similar items. 3168 Peachtree Rd., Peachtree Plaza, Buckhead. 266-3783.

Moss Blacksmith Shop. A seventh-generation blacksmith, former volunteer fire chief Ken Moss re-creates items in metal, or designs original pieces. Moss has done historic restoration for architects and for the Roswell Historical Society. His iron gates and fences grace many of Atlanta's plush homes. Metal repair *(see chapter 7)*. 1075 Canton St., Roswell. 993-2398.

The Rocker Shop. Beautiful handmade rocking chairs of cane and wood. 1421 White Cir., Marietta. 427-2618.

Silks & Such. Handsome handmade pine furniture, including deacon benches, desks, and chests. The jams and jellies are delicious, and the silk and dried flower arrangements are lovely. 1934 Hwy. 92, Woodstock. 926-9855.

JEWELRY

Let's Knot. Leanore Block incorporates pieces of gold and silver and other unusual materials to craft custom hand-strung designs. She also performs expert restringing. Call for an appointment. 3202-B Paces Ferry Pl., Buckhead. 266-2440.

Geode. Handsome one-of-a-kind jewelry designs from local and national jewelry artists are displayed in a captivating space. 3393 Peachtree Rd., Plaza Level, Lenox Square, Buckhead. 261-9346.

Georgia Gold & Gems, Inc. Using gold panned in Georgia, near Villa Rica, and stones imported from Latin America, goldsmith Mitch Ingram refines the metal, cuts the stones, and designs one-of-a-kind pieces. Some antique and estate jewelry. 52 Galleria Pkwy., Galleria Specialty Mall, Northwest. 955-7095.

Lauderhill's Jewelers. Lauderhill's will design an entirely new piece, sometimes even using a customer's gems. Customers may have rings, bracelets, pins, and necklaces redesigned. 3000 Old Alabama Rd., Haynes Market Shopping Center, Alpharetta. 442-0048; 2090 Dunwoody Club Dr., Dunwoody. 396-0492.

Middleton & Lane. Norma Lane has a degree in fine art, with a specialty in jewelry. She applies her training and practices it with conviction and style to design custom pieces. Repair, too *(see chapter 7)*. 5022 Vernon Oaks Dr., Dunwoody. 396-0062..

MUSICAL INSTRUMENTS

Walter Bishop. Bishop builds harpsichords by hand, using museum drawings. He also will build them from Zuckermann kits. By appointment only. Mail only: 1859 Westminster Way, Atlanta, 30307. 325-4735.

Robert Cunningham. Psalteries and Celtic harps. Cunningham makes harps in all sizes, from lap harps to floor harps. It takes about three months to complete a harp, and a month or so to make a psaltery (either the ancient, plucked psaltery or the more modern, bowed psaltery). By appointment only. Mail only: 446 Clifton Rd., Atlanta, 30307. 373-0955.

Handcrafted Dulcimers. Burge Searing specializes in mountain and hammered dulcimers, plus accessories required to learn the time-honored technique of playing this haunting Appalachian folk instrument. Lessons, tapes, and books. 913-J S. Main St., Stone Mountain. 469-5529.

OUTLETS & DISCOUNT CENTERS

Years ago, we shopped on a budget by purchasing samples after a season was over. Salesmen sold off these samples in their apartments and in rented mart spaces, and we learned about them by word of mouth. Today, the industry has organized this effort, selling merchandise in large warehouses that are open on a regular basis. Some, however, are open only sporadically or on weekends, so check before going.

ART & CRAFT SUPPLIES

Binders Art Center. Founded more than forty years ago, Atlanta-based Binders manages to hire staffers who have taken at least a crack at drawing and painting. Their knowledgeable assistance makes it easy to select items, and the prices are very attractive. Locations are all over the metro area and in Duluth, Sandy Springs, and Southlake. Main store: 2581 Piedmont Rd., Lindbergh Plaza, Buckhead. 233-5423.

Michael's. Packed to the rafters with discounted craft and art supplies,

Texas-based Michael's has a location in nearly every part of the north metro area. They're in Dunwoody, Kennesaw, Marietta, Stone Mountain, Tucker, and Duluth. Atlanta original: 2131 Pleasant Hill Rd., Mall Corners Shopping Center, Duluth. 497-1694.

BOOKS

Chapter 11. "Prices so low, you'd think we were going bankrupt" is the motto of this local chain. Books are generally discounted at 11%, and bestsellers are discounted at up to 30%. The art books are splendid values. Special orders and helpful staff. You'll find these bright yellow stores in strip malls all over—there are currently eight locations with more on the way. Original store: 6237 Roswell Rd., Sandy Springs. 256-5518.

Book Warehouse. Overruns and remainders (unsold books) abound, but no semblance of order governs the display. All books are new, and the proceeds benefit cancer research at Emory University. 1831 Peachtree Rd., Brookwood. 352-8000; 5370 Highway 78, Stone Mountain. 498-8077.

FABRICS

Calico Corners. Selling drapery and upholstery fabrics, Calico Corners draws people from all over the metro area for quality and discount prices. The knowledgeable staff can make referrals to talented custom sources. 4256 Roswell Rd., Sandy Springs. 252-7443.

Forsyth Fabrics and Furniture. Upholstery and drapery fabrics, many from European sources, at wholesale prices. Rolls of fabric are stacked to the ceiling, and customers may take a two-inch sample. Trim, custom pillows, and furniture are available. 1190 Foster St., off Howell Mill Rd., near Downtown. 351-6050.

Gail K. Fabrics. In a labyrinthine, freestanding building that feels like a

flea market, fine fashion fabrics are sold wholesale to the public. By buying out whole lots, Gail K. makes prices very attractive. Search service. 571 Armour Cir., Midtown. 876-8853.

Karen's Decorative Fabrics. Designer drapery and upholstery fabrics (P. Kaufmann, Waverly, Anju Woodridge), for both indoor and outdoor applications, are sold at great discounts. 3000 Old Alabama Rd., Alpharetta. 664-4090.

Textile Warehouse Co. One of Atlanta's largest fabric selections, the firm also deals in gifts, pictures, and rugs. Services include custom drapery, upholstery, slip covers, and blinds. 4312 Chamblee-Tucker Rd., Market Plaza, Tucker. 938-3343.

FASHION

Accessories

Scentsations. Designer fragrances at an average 30% discount off regular prices. Friday, Saturday, and Sunday only. Inside K&G Liquidators *(see below)*, 1777 Ellsworth Industrial Blvd., Northwest. 355-2584.

Apparel

Alpharetta Bargain Store. Open since 1959, it sells men's, women's, and children's clothing at greatly reduced prices. We've heard stories about the designer dresses friends have found here for peanuts. 131 S. Main St., Alpharetta. 475-5062.

The Gap Warehouse. The chain's private-label discount store offers men's, women's, and children's clothing at nearly a 50% discount. I-75/85 S. to Lakewood West exit, then exit Greenbriar Pkwy., and turn right at the first traffic light. 3065 Headland Dr., East Point. 349-8600.

K & G Liquidation Center. Men's clothes by name designers. Bargains such as Ralph Lauren's Chaps wool button-down shirts priced at $20 make the place attractive to all kinds of shoppers. Women's apparel is sold too, but seems less interesting and occupies less of the square footage. No refunds, but exchanges are accepted within a limited time after purchase. 1777 Ellsworth Industrial Blvd., Northwest. 352-3471.

Loehmann's. Shopping at Loehmann's requires patience, a sharp eye, many return trips, and raw persistence. The payoff? Designer garments for women at rip-off prices. The three locations include Sandy Springs, Loehmann's Plaza on Briarcliff Road, Northeast, and the Atlanta original: 2460 Cobb Pkwy., Smyrna. 953-2225.

Macy's Close Out. The center carries merchandise from the regular Macy's stores. When an item is discounted 50% at a regular store, the center may purchase it for sale. After one week, it is reduced another 25%, then 50% more after two weeks. If it's still there after three weeks, the item is reduced by 75%! A $500 designer suit could go for $125. Imagine 14,000 pairs of shoes, all selling for less than 50% of their original cost! The clothes are jam-packed, though, so be prepared to take your time and be willing to dig through piles and racks. 3576 Memorial Dr., Avondale Mall, Decatur. 288-3882.

The Men's Wearhouse. There's just no denying the quality of the merchandise, which includes ties, pants (racks of them), suits, shirts, and accessories for men. And the location we sampled (Buckhead) offered very professional, personal, and friendly service. Myriad Atlanta locations: Buckhead, Duluth, Kennesaw, Roswell, Sandy Springs,

Smyrna, Stone Mountain, Northlake, and Southlake. Buckhead has the most merchandise: 3255 Peachtree Rd., at Piedmont Rd., Buckhead. 264-0421.

Old Sarge Army-Navy Surplus. Popular for more than thirty years as a source for outdoor gear, Old Sarge also stocks hunting and camping equipment, tarps, rainwear, U.S. and foreign military clothing (for adults and children), and military collectibles. Sporting equipment and accessories are also important to the inventory. 5316 Buford Hwy., Doraville. 451-6031.

The Oops! Co. Second, or what is sometimes called "flawed," men's and women's sports apparel from the very top manufacturers. These lines are usually sold through catalogs. Included are sweaters, jackets, coats, slacks, and shirts, plus some knits and novel-

ties. 3675 Satellite Blvd., Ste. 560, at Pleasant Hill Rd., Gwinnett Market Fair, Duluth. 497-9324; 1425 Market Blvd., Ste. 525, King's Market, Holcomb Bridge Rd. at GA 400, Roswell. 552-0035.

Stone Mountain Handbags Factory Store. This outlet is packed with leather handbags, briefcases, makeup pouches, coin purses, and other small items made of leather. Handbags that cost about $300 in stores elsewhere in the U.S. sell for 20% to 50% less. 963 Main St., Stone Mountain. 498-1316.

Woodstock Outlet. This old-fashioned outlet store stocks just about anything—men's, women's, and children's clothing, hardware, wall coverings, window treatments, rugs, and furniture. It operates like a general store and carries modestly priced items. 5643 Bells Ferry Rd., Acworth. 591-7126.

Second Hand & Consignment

Another Chance. Women's clothes on consignment. Everything from casual to evening clothes and accessories are sold in a 3,000-square-foot shop. 1420 Roswell Rd., Eastside Plaza, Marietta. 977-1685.

Best Dressed. Men's and children's apparel, along with some women's and maternity items, are found in this quality consignment shop. Baby equipment (carriages, strollers) is also available. Will consider outright purchases rather than consignment. 220 Sandy Springs Cir., Sandy Springs Shopping Center, Sandy Springs. 256-5100.

Elegance. Women's clothes, sizes 4–10, represent the good designer labels. Also available are costume jewelry and good vintage stuff that is hard to find as well as new items from the Apparel Mart in Downtown. Prices run from $15 to $170, and about 20% is new merchandise. The elegant space is fitted with fine embellishments—chandeliers and hardwood floors—and classical music fills the air. Afternoons only. 3330 Piedmont Rd., Piedmont Peachtree Crossing, Buckhead. 233-8996.

Fantastic Finds. Women's consignment and samples. The many designer clothes are part of a good, varied selection that includes accessories and some gift items. 220 Sandy Springs Cir., Springs Landing Shopping Center, Sandy Springs. 303-1313.

Nearly New Shop. Atlanta's Junior League raises money from donations of often very stylish duds and other items. The proceeds benefit various charities. Designer apparel may include a St. John's knit suit, Ungaro suits, Lillie Rubin designs, and others. 2581 Piedmont Rd., Lindbergh Plaza, between Sidney Marcus Blvd. and Morosgo Dr., Buckhead. 233-6639.

Play It Again. This quality resale shop offers great bargains on fashionable duds and evening attire. Most items seem to suit the smaller sizes, and glamour is the game. 273 Buckhead Ave., Buckhead. 261-2135.

ReRuns Fashion Boutique. A consignment boutique with samples and costume jewelry. In the Roswell location, the **Baby Room** is a separate space stocked with cribs, high chairs, strollers, swings, playpens, toys, and myriad baby stuff. Many designer labels and consignment goods. The three locations include Alpharetta, Marietta, and the original: 1066 Canton St., Roswell. 992-6711.

Stefan's Vintage Clothing. Beautifully preserved, good-quality clothing from the turn of the century to the early 1960s. The inventory offers men's suits and coats, women's dresses (both dressy and tailored), hats, bow ties, suspenders, jewelry. No shoes. 1160 Euclid Ave., Little Five Points. 688-4929.

Shoes

AJS Shoe Warehouse. We know people who haunt this place regularly, picking from among the 15,000 pairs of shoes typically in stock. When you're done with the shoes, check out the handmade jewelry and handbags. 1788 Ellsworth Industrial Blvd., Downtown. 355-1760.

Bennie's Shoes. A 15 to 60% discount on top lines of men's shoes: Rockport, Bass, Florsheim, Footjoy, and Allen Edmonds, to name a few. The locations are in Smyrna, Norcross, and the original: 2581 Piedmont Rd., on the Sidney Marcus Blvd. side of Lindbergh Plaza, Buckhead. 262-1966.

FOOD

American Fare. It's HUGE! This almost overwhelming store carries fancy food items as well as ordinary groceries; clothing (Gitano clothes for children); toys; televisions and other electronics; small appliances; bedding and linen. It gives fresh precision to the expression "one-stop shopping." 1701 Mountain Industrial Blvd., at Hwy. 78, Stone Mountain. 938-0151.

Smith Institutional Foods. Institutional-sized containers of foods and paper products are sold at a discount. In back, specialized products are packed for retailers, and sometimes retail shoppers can pick up a small portion. 2786 E. College Ave., Decatur. 377-1728.

FURNITURE & ACCESSORIES

Mathews' Furniture Galleries. This may be Buckhead's best-kept secret. Floor samples of fine furniture lines are sold at savings up to 65% off original retail. Among those often available are Baker, Hickory-White, Council Craftsman, Southwood, and Fairington. Mathews is a registered Council Craftsman dealer, and also carries John Widdicomb, Karges, and Kindel. Design services. 1240 W. Paces Ferry Rd., West Paces Ferry Shopping Center, Buckhead. 237-8271.

Peachtree Quality Salvage. This place stocks everything from nuts and bolts to designer clothes. Household goods, stereos, cosmetics, fabrics (good lines such as Waverly, Jay Yang, and Robert Allen), and children's clothes are yours for the choosing. One of the two stores in Roswell deals only in buying, selling, and trading computers. There's also a shop in Mableton as well as the corporate office: 2016 Atlanta Hwy., Cumming. 523-4871 (Atlanta telephone).

Wall-Bed International. Twin to king-size wall-installed beds are perfect for recreational or second residences of minimal space. 1841 Warren Pl., Norcross. 447-6504.

HOME

Home Depot. This Atlanta-based firm has mushroomed into a national phenomenon. It offers not only the materials for do-it-yourself home repair, remodeling, gardening, and landscaping, all at great prices, but also a knowledgeable staff, classes (*see chapter 9*), and videos. The stores are jammed on weekends, so shop during the week if at all possible. To determine which of the thirteen metro locations is most convenient for you, call 433-8211. The main office is 2727 Paces Ferry Rd., Vinings.

4-Dollar Wallpaper. Every wallcovering in the store costs only $4 for a single roll, and the choice of thousands, many by fine designers, is overwhelming. 5192 Brook Hollow, Norcross. 729-8383.

Richards Variety Store. In the same location since 1958, this unique store is jammed with both the unusual and the ordinary—everything from good-looking faux Chinese jardinières to dinnerware. The back of the store is a discount hardware center. 2347 Peachtree Rd., Peachtree Battle Shopping Center, Buckhead. 237-1412.

KITCHEN

Lechter's. Five locations around town, mostly in malls—with more being added all the time—offer discount kitchen gear. Designer tea kettles go for less-than-designer prices, and a ridged cast-iron frying pan costs $16 when a similar item, at fancier spots, sells for about twice that price. Picture frames and other home accesories, too. Market Square, Northeast. 325-

0358; Perimeter Mall, Dunwoody. 395-7555; Shannon Mall, Union City. 969-1619; Southlake Mall, Southeast. 961-

2367; Town Center, Kennesaw. 425-8333.

MUSICAL INSTRUMENTS

Baldwin Family Music Center. Name-brand pianos, organs, and electronic instruments—new and used—are offered at great prices. 1871 Cobb Pkwy., Marietta. 952-7982.

Southern Keyboards Pianos and Organs. The main showroom, one of the largest in the Southeast, features pianos, organs, and keyboards from Kawai and Roland. Southern is a good source for used pianos. Main showroom: 1898 Leland Dr., Ste. B, Marietta. 953-0938.

NURSERIES/FLOWERS/GARDENING

Fiori Flowers. The firm's slogan is, "for those in search of distinctive gifts"—which include traditional and exotic flowers, fruit and gift baskets, and chocolates at wholesale prices. Delivery throughout the metro area. 950 East Paces Ferry Rd., Buckhead. 365-0044; 420-A Armour Dr., Northeast. 872-9796.

Flowers From Holland. A European-style wholesale/retail flower market in the heart of Atlanta. The large selection of unusual exotic flowers comes from all over the world, especially Holland, South America, and Hawaii; prices are per stem. Don't look here for stuffed animals or balloons; this is strictly upscale and elegant. Available for weddings and commercial accounts. Retail: 3393 Peachtree Rd., Lenox Square, Buckhead. 233-0081.

McGinnis Farms. This wholesale nursery opens to the public on Thursday, Friday, and Saturday. Look for discounts of 25 to 40%. McGinnis offers popular trees, plants, and flowers as well as the exotic flora and fauna. 5610 McGinnis Ferry Rd., Alpharetta. 740-2820.

The Plant Plant. Not exactly the real McCoy, these silk plants fool the eye with lifelike realism. Imagine a ficus that never drops its leaves, a fake Christmas tree that looks *real,* or a Ming arelia that never dies. Perfect for those of us who commit planticide. 500 Lindbergh Dr., Buckhead. 237-5504.

Stenger's Crossties & Landscape Material. On a huge plot of land in north Fulton County, Sonny Stenger has assembled such a huge collection of crossties that, he says, it's impossible to miss it. Also handles decorative stone and delivers firewood. 13225 N. Hwy. 9, Alpharetta. 664-7152.

SPORTING GOODS

Atlantic Billiard Corp. Showroom. Direct from the manufacturer to the consumer come pool tables, accessories, and collateral items (bumper pool, pinball machines, and juke boxes). Discount prices. 6950 Peachtree Industrial Blvd., Ste. F, Norcross. 446-0101.

Gorilla Golf Outlet. Southsiders recommend it as tops in the area. The outlet sells all major lines of golf clubs, such as Ping, Hogan, Bullet, Ram, and Maxfli; bags by Taylor-Made, Miller, and Mizuno; men's PGA Tour clothing; a full line of Footjoy, Dexter, and Etonic shoes; and all golf accessories. Club repair. 7447 Hwy. 85, Riverdale. 997-1708.

Pro Golf Discount of Atlanta. Excellent golf equipment, clothing, and accessories are sold at great discounts. Name brands in clubs, bags, shoes, and clothes. The four locations include Stone Mountain, Marietta, Roswell, and the original: 5810 Buford Hwy., Doraville. 455-8809.

The Sports Authority. A warehouse filled with everything for the sports enthusiast—equipment for skiing, hunting, camping, tennis, golf, rollerblading, kyaking, canoeing, rafting, and every other sport we haven't mentioned. Locations include: 3450 Steve Reynolds Blvd., Duluth. 418-9354; 2963 Cobb Pkwy., Smyrna. 955-6662; 3221 Peachtree Rd., Buckhead. 814-9873.

SPECIALTY SHOPPING AREAS

Clusters of shops abound in Atlanta, sometimes in a restored village in one of metro Atlanta's suburban towns, at other times in structures specifically designed as shoppers' emporiums. They may focus on specific shopping themes, such as antiques or art, or may contain an array of boutiques and specialty stores. We have listed some shops individually under their various categories, but cannot list them all. So we direct you to the areas, knowing you'll discover many unique resources within each one.

INSIDE I-285

Atlanta Decorative Arts Center. Atlanta architect John Portman's ADAC, a world of Oriental rugs, antiques, rich fabrics, and unique accessories, is a design resource center. Customers must accompany their designers, as ADAC is open only to the trade, but the annual sample sale in the spring is open to the public. Many of the establishments at ADAC also have retail operations. 351 Peachtree Hills Ave., Buckhead. 231-1720.

Atlanta Outlet Park.

Twenty-two outlet stores form a shopping area in Atlanta's warehouse district. Men's and women's wear, lingerie, accessories, fabrics, children's wear, sportswear, lighting fixtures, jewelry, perfumes, and even a **Macy's** warehouse store are among the outlets. On Fridays and Saturdays all shops are open, but some operate weekdays. Maps available at the shops list what inventory each store carries. Exit Howell Mill Rd. off I-75, proceed to Chattahoochee Ave., and follow the signs. Northwest.

Bennett Street.

Oh, what a street this is! Running west off Peachtree Street, it's lined with antique shops, art galleries, and Oriental rug shops. Prices range from the perfectly affordable to the very expensive. **TULA** is a warehouse that a local artist turned into studio work space. Today, TULA contains about 45 art galleries and artists' studios purveying art of all kinds—textiles, pottery, oils, and acrylics. Get on the gallery mailing list so you can attend openings. 75 Bennett St., Brookwood. 351-3551.

Brookwood Square.

Adjacent to Bennett Street, Brookwood Square contains galleries, furniture and clothing stores, gift shops, a piano establishment, restaurants, and the Atlanta location of **Myers Carpet**—one of Dalton, Georgia's, most well-known carpet manufacturers (352-8141). 2140 Peachtree Rd., Brookwood.

Buckhead Village.

The epicenter of Buckhead Village lies on Peachtree Road, at its intersection with East and West Paces Ferry Roads and Pharr Road. Within two miles of this point one can furnish a mansion and assemble a wardrobe suitable for royalty, dine on food fit for a shah, arrange exquisite flower displays, pull a pint at a pub, play billiards, or sip sherry at afternoon tea. **East Village Square**, between Buckhead Avenue and Pharr Road, contains galleries, restaurants, and shops. The former residences of **Paces Ferry Place**, running north off West Paces Ferry Road, now contain chic shops, and all justify spending the better part of a day right there. On Buckhead's western edge lies **Andrews Square**, and around the corner are the antique-filled shops of **Cains Hill Place**.

During both World War I and the Depression, Rich's accepted cotton for merchandise, crediting the value of the bales at a price slightly above market prices. Also during the Depression, the city treasury ran out of money to pay its teachers. Rich's suggested that the city pay them in scrip, which Rich's cashed at full value without obliging the teachers to spend the money at the store.

Chamblee.

Two important shopping features that make Chamblee special are **Antique Row** and **Chinatown Mall**. More than 200 dealers operate in Antique Row. Parking is good, and walking from shop to shop is the best way to take it all in. The shops line Chamblee's Peachtree Road, accessed by turning southeast off Peachtree Industrial Boulevard onto any of the side streets, such as Broad Street or Chamblee-Dunwoody Road. The Chamblee Antique Dealers Association has produced an excellent map, available at any of the shops.

Chinatown Mall, with shops, businesses, markets, and restaurants reflects the success Asians have enjoyed in Chamblee. Retailers carry gifts, furniture, clothing, and food. Near the MARTA Chamblee station, Chamblee-Dunwoody Rd. and New Peachtree Rd. 5381 New Peachtree Rd., Chamblee, Northeast. 458-4624.

Downtown. Despite the lamented closing of Rich's downtown store, the city's core offers some good shopping. **Peachtree Center**, John Portman's high-rise blend of offices and shops, presents over fifty retailers. It's directly across from Macy's refurbished downtown location.

Little Five Points. This intown neighborhood shopping area is more bohemian by suburban standards than Virginia-Highland, itself no stranger to the funky. Here, in the heart of Atlanta's most diverse neighborhood, you'll find well-established galleries cheek-by-jowl with funky boutiques, bookstores, and clothing stores that sell vintage apparel. Little Five Points invites walking and shopping and, most certainly, people-watching. The intersection of Moreland Avenue and Euclid Avenue is its heart.

Miami Circle Market Center. Located off Piedmont Road near East Wesley Road, Miami Circle is a street name that has come to be identified as a major decorative arts resource area. Firms doing business here generally welcome customers without their designers. Contact John Tribble, who handles questions at 261-3224. Northeast.

RIO. This inspired piece of Art Deco architecture by that talented group of Florida architects, Architectonica, is located at the intersection of Piedmont and North Avenues. Shops, restaurants, and night spots. 595 Piedmont Ave., Downtown. 885-9902.

2300 Peachtree Road. Developed by antique dealer Jane J. Marsden, 2300 occupies the site of the handsome 1929 Brookwood Hotel (now demolished). Suggesting an Italian shopping area, it houses design firms, galleries, antique shops, and myriad design-related firms. Marsden's own treasure-packed shop, loaded with French, English, and continental antiques, is, of course, on the premises. Call Mike Willis for information on shops. 2300 Peachtree Rd., Brookwood. 355-1288.

Underground Atlanta. Restored in the 1960s, Underground Atlanta closed but then came back to life with all motors running on June 15, 1989. Its specialty retailers now number over 100. Numerous restaurants, night clubs, and a new food court, are enclosed within 200,000 square feet of space. Pushcart merchants sell everything from T-shirts to original art in the **Humbug Square Street Market** at Lower Alabama and Pryor streets. The tilt toward tourist trinkets is banished from today's Underground. Serious shoppers will find much to satisfy their demands. Underground is also the site of the small museums, **Atlanta Heritage Row** and the **Olympic Experience** (see chapter 5), as well as an increasing number of festivals and special events. Combine your trip there with a visit to the World of Coca-Cola museum, across the street, for a full day's adventure. MARTA (Five Points is the stop) is the most sensible way to get there. 523-2311. Downtown.

Vinings. Located near Cumberland Mall, Vinings was once a popular summer village for Atlantans, but now finds itself surrounded by office towers. The contrast between the gleaming, modern high-rise buildings and the fragile, century-old structures gives the impression that the new is swallowing up the old. Today, the town contains shops and restaurants, but the quality of the antiques varies. **Vinings Jubilee**, at 4200 Paces Ferry Road, is an attractive, easy-to-get-around-in shopping emporium. Northwest.

Virginia-Highland. Virginia-Highland has undergone a vigorous revitalization, making it a haven for upscale residents and art-driven emporia. It now beckons walkers and shoppers, who come for antique and collectibles browsing, book buying, and art gallery shopping. The intersection of Virginia Avenue and North Highland Avenue is where to begin. Northeast.

OUTSIDE I-285

I-85 Corridor. Along both sides of I-85 north of North Druid Hills Road to around Jimmy Carter Boulevard in Norcross lie some spectacular shopping opportunities, most of them discount or special-priced. **Dawson Boulevard**, which runs south of Jimmy Carter along the east side of I-85 North, presents a mecca of stores offering wholesale and discount prices, chiefly on furniture. Watch out, though, because some stores sell at retail the same item that another may offer at a wholesale price. Example: the price of a steel-tube bunk bed set ranged in three different locations from $199 to $399.

Marietta. This antebellum town has rediscovered and restored its main square. Surrounding charming Glover Park at the core of the square are shops, restaurants, and the well-regarded Theatre in the Square (see chapter 2). **The Depot** is another area that's been redeveloped with a view toward attracting the kinds of shops and restaurants that appeal to upscale folks. Many of the Marietta shops offer antiques, and some artists' studios are tucked into the upper floors of buildings around the square.

Park Place. Dunwoody's most introspective shopping area sits across the street from Perimeter Mall, withdrawn from the mayhem on Ashford-Dunwoody Road. Two arms encircle a comfortable plaza, ringing it with shops and dining establishments. Some of the shops represent national chains, while others are either second-store locations for Atlanta retailers or the sole locations for fine independent merchants. 4505 Ashford-Dunwoody Rd., just north of I-285, Dunwoody.

Roswell. The residents of Atlanta's suburban, antebellum towns have Roswell to thank for establishing the standards by which all other such towns are to be measured for charm and quality shopping. Roswell's historic square and the houses lining **Canton Street** offer shops of all kinds, including many galleries of both traditional and modern art. In addition to antique shops, Roswell has boutiques that sell clothing for women and children. The **Roswell Mill**, a renovated historic mill, has a wonderful selection of artists' studios, unusual shops, restaurants, and night spots, and is the site for many festivals, special events, and a summer concert series. Take GA 400 to Holcomb Bridge Rd. (Exit 4-B), to Hwy. 9, and turn left into Roswell.

Stone Mountain Village. Gathered along the railroad tracks, the village is a collection of nineteenth-century façades housing antique shops, clothing stores, artists' studios, and a Civil War museum. Savor the sound of a passing train while you shop. At Christmas, enjoy some of the finest window displays we've seen anywhere. Take Hwy. 78 (Exit 30-B off I-285) to the Stone Mountain Business District exit. Stone Mountain Welcome Center: 879-9511.

CHAPTER 7

Services & Resources

Both longtime residents and newcomers need guidance to find the perfect service provider who can make solving life's little problems a breeze. Or maybe you need information—a listing of Atlanta's alternative newspapers or small, specialty video stores. This chapter can guide you to the information and services you need.

Look inside for a listing of recycling centers and services, caterers to handle any size event, landscapers, shopping services, event photography, and day spas. Obviously this list is not inclusive; we can only suggest the variety of expertise and service available in Atlanta.

We intend this information as a guide rather than a guarantee, so please check references before committing your money and time to anyone's care.

And please let us know about any especially wonderful services or resources you may know about for our next edition!

ALTERATIONS & TAILORING

When you need expertise in this area, it's usually at a crisis hour: You're going to a friend's wedding, and your one and only appropriate outfit needs to be taken in (if you're lucky!). Here are some folks to rely on in these times of desperation.

Alterations and More. Margaret Scsaszny (CHUS-ney) has been doing fine, professional alterations on men's and women's clothing for more than eight years. 8610 Roswell Rd., Ste. 650, Loehman's Plaza, Dunwoody. 642-7019.

Pete's Custom Tailor and Alterations. Pete Theofanidis is a native of Greece. Pete was trained in Paris and once worked for Neiman-Marcus. Now that he's in business for himself, his fifty years' experience gathers praise-heaping clients who bring him both pesky, small jobs (fixing button holes) and large ones (alterations on leather, suede, and fur). 6309 Roswell Rd., Ste. 2-F, Sandy Springs Plaza, Sandy Springs. 256-3653.

Saul's Reweavers & Alterations. In business since 1940, these folks perform miracles. Saul's staff knows how to hide their repairs, and work is ready when promised (but do allow sufficient time, as they are busy—for good reason!). Two locations: 175 Mt. Vernon Hwy., Sandy Springs. 252-0888; 20 Pharr Rd., Buckhead. 266-8611.

ALTERNATIVE NEWSPAPERS

These alternative papers offer a variety of perspectives on Atlanta life, with information on politics, culture, and activities around town.

Creative Loafing. Atlanta's most popular (free!) paper for finding out about community and cultural events. Complete with listings of live music, classifieds, and an extensive calendar of events. 688-5623.

Southern Voice. With a readership of 44,000, *Southern Voice* is the leading gay and lesbian weekly for the Southeast. 876-1819.

Etcetera. A weekly magazine, *ETC.* provides news, entertainment and political information for the gay community. 525-3821.

Alternatives. A monthly newspaper with articles focusing on environmental, social, and holistic health issues. 303-1873.

Oz. A bimonthly magazine focusing on art, film, photography, and other creative disciplines. In addition to providing articles and reviews, *Oz* serves as a communication vehicle for artists and art enthusiasts. 633-1779.

Planet Atlanta. An internationally focused monthly newspaper with articles pertaining to business, art, culture, and personality profiles. 378-6486; 816-5551.

ARCHITECTURE & CONSTRUCTION

This is a *huge* area, so we've had to make some tough choices. For information on area architects, call the Atlanta chapter of the American Institute of Architects (873-3207) in Midtown. They'll send you a free copy of the AIA "Project Preference Survey," a listing that shows what kinds of projects member architects prefer to do. For information about homebuilders, call the Homebuilders Association of Greater Atlanta (938-9900), in Tucker.

American Building Services. Bob Stampler is a true local character. During his Saturday radio programs, 8 to 10 A.M. on WGUN, 1010 AM, and 11 A.M. to 1 P.M. on WQXI, 790 AM, he tells listeners the best way to fix up their homes. A fun-loving guy, Stampler is dead serious about fine detailing in his construction projects. Call him for decks, additions, kitchen and bath design, and general remodeling. 975 Chattahoochee Ave., Atlanta. 377-3393.

Bath Style. These folks can work with your designer, plumber, architect, or contractor to develop plans for the dream bath you've always wanted. The firm's showroom consultants will sketch the layout and assist in the selection of fixtures. 6885 NE Expressway, Doraville. 368-8419.

California Closet Company. Organize your closets and garage the easy way. These custom planners will do free home consultations, but you can choose a do-it-yourself kit to complete your design. Everything is made of fine wood products. 1009 Mansell Rd., Roswell. 993-6622.

Design Galleria Ltd. Specializing in fine custom cabinetry, this firm handles imported cabinetry in both contemporary and traditional styles. Design Galleria offers a turnkey operation, providing everything from an initial needs assessment to installation. 351 Peachtree Hills Ave., Ste. 234, Buckhead. 261-0111.

W. Lane Greene. An architect who specializes in historic restoration, Greene has spent more than a dozen years doing this kind of work. He personally conducts much of the basic preliminary research that such projects require. One of his recent projects was the restoration of the Wren's Nest *(see chapter 5)*. Greene works for private individuals as well as foundations and groups trying to save important buildings. 650 Miami Cir., Ste. 2, Buckhead. 237-1861.

Headfirst Builders. Mike Head handles general remodeling, and does baths and decks especially well. Interior and exterior painting is another specialty. 101 Cimarron Pkwy., Dunwoody. 668-0123.

Kitchen Fronts of Georgia. Can't afford to knock the kitchen down and rebuild? Call this fourteen-year-old firm to replace the fronts of old cabinets. They'll install new counter tops, drawer fronts, hinges, and framework. Senior citizen discounts and free in-home estimates are available. 3264 Shallowford Rd., Chamblee. 455-3139.

KitchenSmith. Gone is the little space that the firm used to devote to kitchen gear. In its place, supporting the firm's very fine kitchen design talent, are displays of closet equipment, built-in drawers and other storage space, and supremely elegant bath equipment. KitchenSmith ably designs both traditional and modern kitchens and baths, but they really take flight in the modern mode. 3098 Roswell Rd., Buckhead. 261-3098.

William G. Moffat. With an M.A. in history, Moffat has been a historic preservation planner for six years. Now operating as a preservation consultant, he prepares National Register nominations and conducts "rambles"—tours of historic districts designed either as educational adventures to look for old houses hidden in the byways or for folks who seek houses to restore. He also prepares tax credit applications for historic buildings (both residential and commercial). Although not residing in our general area of operation, he comes to Atlanta if needed. 185 Woodland Way, Athens. 706-548-7326.

Moon Brothers. Karl deSantos, John Duncan, and Mark Fosner are the Moon Brothers. All three are architecture graduates from Ohio University, and deSantos and Fosner hold master's degrees in architecture from Georgia Tech. Historic restoration, new construction in the modern mode, and modernizing older houses are typical projects of the Moon Brothers. The rationale for the firm's name? Don't ask. 1662 McLendon Ave., Candler Park, Northeast. 377-6006.

Marion Orsborn Construction. Orsborn is a retired IBM executive who, as a part-time contractor, has built a reputation for honesty and excellent work. His firm primarily does interior remodeling, additions, and bathroom and kitchen updating. Mail only: 905 Heards Ferry Rd., Atlanta, 30328-4727. 255-3019.

Outdoor Architecture By Jeffrey Johnson. Jeffrey Johnson has specialized in decks, gazebos, sun rooms, screened porches, cabanas, and similar outdoor structures since 1982. Projects are warrantied for five years. 1188 Mountain Park Rd., Woodstock. 992-3834.

Sahara Japanese Architectural Woodworks. Toshihiro Sahara began his apprenticeship in Sukiya-style construction in Tokyo in 1947. (Sukiya craftsmen construct post-and-beam houses using natural woods, hand tools, and age-old classic techniques.) All wood surfaces are finished by hand plane, achieving a stunning luster. Sahara's reputation and work load have grown since he started his Atlanta business in 1988. Gracing a number of Atlanta homes and offices are his custom-made lamps, shoji screens, and furniture. 1716 Defoor Pl., Northwest. 355-1976.

Sawhorse. An award-winning company known for large, dramatic house renovation projects, Sawhorse has also settled into a design-build mode scaled to handle $25,000 to $75,000 projects with speed and quality. Example projects include attics, kitchens, bathrooms, additions, and expansions. Architect on staff. 731 Highland Ave., near Little Five Points. 522-4542, 523-7335.

SpaceMakers Closet Interiors. This Atlanta-based firm individualizes the family closets, but it doesn't stop there: SpaceMakers designs garages, pantries, laundry and sewing rooms, and special built-ins for work areas. The showroom is open to the public. 1750

Enterprise Way, Ste. 105, Marietta. 952-3455 (Cobb/Fulton); 840-9099 (Gwinnett/DeKalb).

Wollaston Smith International. A. Wollaston Smith III studied architecture at Georgia Tech and applies his training to the special design needs of kitchens and baths. He is a source for high-end cabinet systems from Europe (Snaidero) and the U.S. (Woodmode). Smith also knows a fine local manufacturer who produces quality, budget-conscious cabinets. Also a source for unusual appliances, Smith can obtain whatever appliances a customer might want at wholesale prices. The firm recently won a national design contest from DuPont Corian. Smith's book, *The Environmental Home and Living Complex,* is his treatise on residential home design. 3762 DeKalb Technology Pkwy., Doraville. 451-7677.

ART SERVICES FOR THE HOME

Ornament and fine detailing distinguish many Atlanta homes. Here's where you'll find the unique artists who can execute faux finishes, good woodworking, and ornamental iron. Also listed are artists and framers, as well as appraisers of art objects and art consultants, the latter usually listed only by telephone number as they primarily work from the home.

ART APPRAISERS

Beverly Bremer Silver Shop. Appraisals on antique silver. 3164 Peachtree Rd., Peachtree Plaza, Buckhead. 261-4009.

Hardy & Halpern. A team of professionals with superior credentials, Hardy & Halpern appraise fine art and antiques. Areas of expertise include an-

tiques, furniture, porcelain, pottery, silver, collectibles, glass, and fine art (prints, drawings, paintings, sculpture). The principals are well schooled in art history, and have long been active in the Atlanta arts scene. Plaza Towers, 2575 Peachtree Rd., CU 7, Buckhead. 261-4447.

Stone Mountain Relics. Appraisals of Civil War memorabilia and collectibles, especially Confederate items *(see chapter 5)*. 968 Main St., Stone Mountain. 469-1425.

ART CONSULTANTS

Specialists who help their clients find quality artwork, usually in certain fields—are listed only by telephone number, as they chiefly work out of their homes.

Barkin-Leeds, Ltd. Temme Barkin-Leeds, MA, specializes in work by contemporary Southern artists, but also offers a wide variety of art consulting services. 351-2880.

Clark Fine Art. Kitty Clark Manson consults on traditional and contemporary art. 351-2007.

Davis-Moye and Associates. Dorothy Moye consults on contemporary art, especially fiber. 377-2116.

The Camille Love Gallery. Camille Russell Love specializes in work by contemporary African-American artists. 691-9205.

Ray Ketcham Gallery. Deals in nineteenth- and early twentieth-century American and European paintings. 255-8745.

Marianne B. Lambert. Consults on contemporary art, especially from the South. 435-5180.

Local Color. Owner Arlene Howard consults on most periods of art and within all budgets. 256-3491.

ARTISTS & FRAMERS

Awalt Woodcarving. Chad Awalt makes antique furniture reproductions in most popular period styles. Large pieces as well as mirror and picture frames are part of his stock in trade. By appointment. Mail only: 4731 Sterling Acre Ct., Tucker, 30084. 493-1750.

Ivan Bailey. An ornamental iron artist of unusual talent, Bailey does residential work, including fences, outdoor sculpture, fountains, light fixtures, and table bases. One client's forty-foot balcony railing has seven octopuses "holding hands," their tentacles twining between the railing supports. By appointment. Studio: 887 W. Marietta St., Downtown. 874-7674.

The Brier Patch. Deborah Stokes, a professional artist and art teacher, designs and paints stencils for walls, floors, furniture, and floor cloths. She also paints original designs on ceramic tile. By appointment only. Mail only: 11034 Bethany Rd., Alpharetta, 30201. 343-8864.

Caroline Budd Picture Framing. In the business for more than twenty years, Caroline and crew design wonderful frames that respect artwork. Budd is frequently the framer chosen by many artists, and she knows good restoration specialists. 458 Plasamour Dr., Northeast. 872-8446.

Clymer Door Co. Extraordinary ornamental cut and beveled glass for windows and front doors earns David Clymer raves, not only for the quality of his workmanship but also for leaving a clean work site. 530 Kensington Farms Dr., Alpharetta. 475-9429.

Furaha's, A Picture Frame Place. Furaha Moye and George Whitehead combine their considerable talents to offer high-quality framing for a reasonable cost. Whitehead has a degree in fine art from the University of DC, and Moye has been in the framing business for twenty years. Custom services include museum mounting, shadowboxing, restoration, and painted bevels. 976 Piedmont Ave., Midtown. 881-8672.

Oh So Faux. Imagine fake windows or a door painted on a wall—or a fork painted on a floor! Charles Sligh's firm not only does faux finishes but also silver and gold leafing, repair of metal-leaf, painted sisal and cloth floor coverings, wall and ceiling murals, and trompe l'oeil. Sligh recommends consulting with your designer to obtain these services, but you may contact him directly. 349 Peachtree Hills Ave., Ste. B4, Atlanta Decorative Arts Center (ADAC), Northeast. 233-4120.

Painted Finish. Barbara Lehman's decorative painting of walls, woodwork, and furniture (including faux finishes) is becoming legendary. She also does decorative floor painting and paints cloth rugs. 4501 Ashburn Walk, Marietta. 971-4029.

Saye Tiles. Executive secretary of the National Organization of Stencil Artisans League, Susan Saye does watercolor, stenciling, and custom tile painting, all made to order. For example, the tile design may be an intricate bonsai tree for kitchen backsplash, or a four-inch-square tile pattern for an office building. Mail only: 3459 Havalyn La., Doraville, 30340. 457-5195.

Sewell Stained Glass. Randy Sewell does commissioned work only, so all designs are original. Contemporary (abstract) or representational designs are installed in finished doors, windows, and specially designed pieces. By appointment only. Mail only: 38 Muscogee Ave., Atlanta, 30305. 239-9130.

Thomas H. Williams. The telephone book indicates he is both sculptor and woodworker, but his woodwork *is* sculpture. Kitchen cabinets, front doors, stairways, and even garage doors are so distinctive that you don't even have to check for the signature at the bottom. Williams also makes custom furniture and, indeed, extraordinary sculpture. By appointment. Mail only: 3502 Cold Springs Lane, Chamblee, 30341. 458-3376.

REPAIR & RESTORATION

Atlanta Doll Hospital. Antique and contemporary dolls are repaired and refurbished, and their missing parts are replaced—including hair for those that have gone bald from hugging. And get this: There's an emergency room for repairing the doll whose "mommy" just can't be without it even for a night. Repair of miniature doll house furniture, if all parts are supplied, is another line. 2000 Cheshire Bridge Rd., Northeast. 248-1151.

The Downeaster. Joe Anastasia repairs model ships, after doing extensive research *(see chapter 6)*. Mail only: 425 Grenock Cir., Atlanta, 30328. 393-1789.

Estes-Simmons Silverplating, Ltd. Expert silver artisans re-plate and re-store silver and gold pieces. They remove dents; repair pewter, brass, and copper; and replace broken pieces on metal items. 1050 Northside Dr., Downtown. 875-9581.

Moss Blacksmith Shop. Re-creation, design, and repair of ironwork (see *chapter 6*). 1075 Canton St., Roswell. 993-2398.

Silver-Craft Co., Inc. A legend in the world of silver restoration, Hugh Thompson specializes in restoration plating and repair of sterling, copper, pewter, and brass. The governors' mansions of Georgia, Alabama, Florida, and Mississippi are among his clients, as are some of Atlanta's posh, private clubs. 3872 Roswell Rd., Buckhead Court, Buckhead. 231-3297.

CULINARY

Southerners love food, but often don't have time to prepare complicated dishes. Atlanta's fine caterers help fill this void, and there's lots of takeout (see Chapter 1 (Dining Out)) and other services that ease the at-home cooking burden.

CATERERS

Affairs to Remember Caterers. The firm's elegant displays have made Affairs a legend among Atlanta caterers. Most impressive of all is its dessert buffet, a seemingly mile-long table laden with deep, dark, mysterious chocolate desserts of all kinds. Can do Kosher. 680 Ponce de Leon Ave., Virginia-Highland. 872-7859.

Bill Wilson's Barbecue. Wilson serves delicious pork and other meat that's smoked for at least eight hours and then hand chopped. By appointment only. Especially good for festivals, craft shows, and company bashes. Mail only: 2643 East Piney Point Dr., Douglasville, 30135. 489-2855.

Camerron. Lee Chadwick insists that food must look good, taste good, and stay good-looking throughout an event. She refuses to push pâté because, she says, after it's been hacked at for a half-hour, it looks too messy to meet her criteria. The delightful, down-to-earth proprietor and pleasant staff are thoroughly professional. Request off-premises catering, or reserve her events facility. 5510 Chamblee-Dunwoody Rd., Shops of Dunwoody, Dunwoody. 698-8888.

Chef for a Night. The big client is coming for dinner, and you need smashing food as well as waiters and bartenders. Call Laurie Luntz's Chef for a Night and relax. Her crew buys the groceries, prepares and serves the food, and even cleans up. The fare can range from French to Vietnamese because the client designs the menu. Intimate dinners and large cocktail parties are readily accommodated. Reserve well in advance. Mail only: 1601 Emory Rd., 373-0750.

Cloudt's. No, it's not the same company it was when owned by the late Frank Cloudt. It's as good or better under new owner Michael Safari, who's reinstated some of the old people and recipes. Among the latter, folks may recognize the tea biscuits, marinated shrimp, French chicken with brandy, cream, and scallion sauce, the famous pound cake, and lemon bars. 4064 Flowers Rd., Doraville. 455-6600.

Mark Fitchpatrick. Fitchpatrick is becoming famous for his special events cakes of all kinds. Wedding cakes are a tour de force for this inventive bakery designer. One client reports that hers not only was gorgeous but also tasted heavenly. By appointment only. 457-1439.

Grant Park Mansion. The forte is Country French and European styling, but a classic Southern party buffet is within the realm of possibility. Based in Grant Park Mansion. 603 Boulevard, Grant Park. 627-5474.

Linda Easterlin Catering. Linda Easterlin plans each event with the client so that each party has individuality—no formula menus for her. Atlanta families have relied on her to cater their special events for twenty years. We're nuts about her jalapeño corn muffins. By appointment only. Mail only: 3832 W. Nancy Creek Ct., Atlanta, 30319. 255-5146.

Lowcountry Barbecue Catering. Taste the flavors of Charleston and Savannah with lowcountry-style barbecue, or cook a whole pig in the old style. Bennett Brown's firm handles small to very large events with great flair. 2000 S. Pioneer Dr., Smyrna. 799-8049.

Plaza Catering. They're doing a lot of the big, splashy parties these days, but they can also handle smaller events for ten or more guests. At one 1991 party, five chefs and twenty cooks created an evening to remember at the Georgia Governor's Mansion. A division of Westin Peachtree Plaza Hotel. Special attention to kosher. 210 Peachtree St., at International Blvd., Downtown. 589-7471.

Proof of the Pudding. Owned by four partners, Proof operates out of the Carter Presidential Center and handles all of the events there. Proof also caters a lot of sporting events, especially golf tournaments. Both set menus and custom-designed catering are available, and Proof can assist with every detail, including the flowers. Can handle kosher. Their **Gourmet To Go** service offers corporate box lunches and platters, delivery, and service. 489 Courtland St., Downtown. 892-2359.

Rupert's. Chef Jason Spencer caters events held at the Buckhead restaurant or elsewhere. The superior pasta bar, serving handmade ravioli, tortellini, and capellini, is sumptuous. The tiny tarts and handmade chocolate truffles are outstanding desserts. In addition to catering, Rupert's can take care of musical entertainment, floral needs, and logistics. The size of the party is no impediment. 3330 Piedmont Rd., Buckhead. 266-9835.

A *Southern Tradition.* This outfit provides either party planning or standard catering services for everything from informal gatherings and picnics to intimate dinners or elegant receptions—all in the "Southern tradition." Staff designers can handle decorations, flowers, invitations, and other incidentals as well. Choose from such dishes as crab cakes prepared at table, turkey on sweet potato muffins, jambalaya, and Southern caviar (black-eyed peas and capers). Native Atlantans Dorothy Haynes and Mitchell Bowling are comfortable with parties that number from two to 2,000. 1901 Montreal Rd., Ste. 104, Tucker. 491-7277.

Tuohy's Catering. Inventive food artfully presented, Tuohy's treats—and they're definitely delicious—may take a slightly Pacific Rim twist (for example, pork tenderloin with lime and ginger). Associate Chef Don Law also prepares dishes that reflect his interest in Southern cooking. Each client may construct individual menu plans for catering "as you like it," as Tuohy's says. 442 Armour Cir., 875-3885.

SHOPPING & DELIVERY

Aisle 1. Too busy to shop? Get everything but beer, wine, and liquor, which can't legally be delivered in Georgia, by giving Aisle 1 your shopping list. Call in your order, FAX it, or leave a standing order. You'll have it the next day for a small fee. A retailer sans storefront, Aisle 1 sells out of a catalog, but customers can make special requests. 5495 Jimmy Carter Blvd., Norcross. 448-2063.

Cooks Market. John Cook can order special items, such as game, and have them in-house the next day. The market will deliver groceries, and customers can FAX in their orders (*see chapter 6*). 2770 Lenox Rd., Plantation Heights Shopping Center, Northeast. 364-0900.

DECORATING & DESIGN

Referrals to area designers are available from the American Society of Interior Designers (ASID.), Georgia Chapter, 231-3938. The International Society of Interior Designers (ISID.), 261-4895, and the International Furnishings and Design Association (IFDA.), 365-0433, will also help you locate design expertise.

Gandy/Peace, Inc. Charles Gandy and William Peace have formed one of the city's most innovative firms, winning awards for some of the most exciting work we've seen. Gandy, an author and former professor of design at Auburn University's School of Architecture, commands the respect of his colleagues, who elected him national president of ASID. in 1988. Peace graduated from the University of Kentucky with a degree in interior design and has studied architecture. This is a splendid team for all interior design needs. 3195 Paces Ferry Pl., Buckhead. 237-8681.

Oetgen Design, Inc. John Oetgen, a graduate of Georgia State University's interior design program, has quickly grown into one of Atlanta's foremost designers. Oetgen's witty sense of pat-tern and design have led him to craft some of Atlanta's most unusual residential interiors. A second endeavor, **John D. Oetgen Fine Antiques**, features European antiques and unusual accessories. 2300 Peachtree Rd., B-109, Buckhead. 352-1112.

VanTosh & Associates. About two decades of experience backs this full-service interior design firm. Known for both commercial and residential work, Jill Vantosh can design interiors for everything from crisp, modern spaces to more traditional model homes for builders and developers—an award-winning aspect of the firm's work. Vantosh's strength is her ability to blend seemingly disparate pieces—drawing from traditional and modern styles—to design for the client and the space. 1477 Spring St., Midtown. 881-6074.

FASHION DESIGN

See Chapter 6 (Shopping Around) for custom-designed fashions from Atlanta's own up-and-coming fashion designers.

FURNITURE SERVICES

That antique or collectible unearthed at a local flea market may need restoration, pieces damaged during the great move need repair, and sometimes Atlanta's humidity gets to our furniture—never mind what the kids and the family critters can do! Here are a few folks to call in these events.

Aaron's Lamp & Shade Center. Besides selling lamps and shades, Aaron's will create a lamp from a favorite vase, figurine, or jar. 3529 Northside Pkwy., Buckhead. 231-2160.

Bits and Pieces Antiques. For more than fourteen years Johnny Crawford, a self-taught artisan, has been practicing his craft, producing authentic period and stylistic reproductions: Chippendale, Art Deco, and Biedermeier, among others. Crawford can design to your specifications or reproduce from a photo, and will hand carve many details. 3345 Main St., College Park. 766-5299.

Freemanville Woodworking Shop. Have you ever wanted to make your own furniture, but found the cost of equipment too expensive? Richard Graham invites people to use his woodworking shop and tools to make anything from rolltop desks to frames, and he'll teach you if you're a novice (*see chapter 9*). He has been making and selling furniture for almost twenty years. These are private one-on-one sessions, so call for an appointment. Mail only: 15970 Freemanville Rd., Alpharetta, 30201. 475-5452.

Furniture Restoration Specialists. In business for more than a decade, Jeff Forsyth restores, refinishes, and repairs antiques, and can replace and repair carvings on furniture. He can re-veneer and repair laminates, repair and repaint wicker furniture, and strip and repaint metal furniture. Forsyth is also skilled at converting furniture from one use to another, such as making an armoire into an entertainment center. 1706 Darwin Rd., Smyrna. 434-3335.

The Furniture Shop. The Gavalas family has been in the furniture repair business since Papa Tony Gavalas came to Augusta, Georgia, from Greece around 1932. The family, including Tony's great-grandson, Victor, continues the tradition—repairing furniture, restoring antiques, stripping, and, especially, hand carving. Custom-designed furniture, including home entertainment centers, conference tables, and reproduction designs, is a specialty. 102 Fairground St., Marietta. 422-5899.

Georgia Best Table Pads and Accessories. Judy Keith's crew measures for your table pads at your home or office. Pads are made of heavy-duty vinyl in seven different wood-like finishes as well as black and white. Mail only: 2557 Riverglen Cir., Atlanta, 30338. 455-4775.

Myers Dickson Upholstery, Inc. At this 35-year-old firm, the work is excellent, and the prices are fair in the extreme. However, once you've placed your order, stay in touch to make sure nothing falls through the cracks (designers and longtime customers keep this place very busy). Pickup and delivery are available. 2868 Franklin St., Avondale Estates. 498-2442.

Roswell Clock & Antique Co. Excellent reputation for repairing movements of antique clocks, whether wall, mantel, or grandfather. Restoration of cabinets is another line. 955 Canton St., Roswell. 992-5232.

Sunlighting Lamp & Shade Center. Operating from two workrooms totaling 6,000 square feet of space, Carolyn and Stephen Uhl's well-established Atlanta firm repairs lamps and shades, and turns vases, figurines, and just about anything else you could imagine into lamps. The firm also makes shades from a customer's fabric or wall covering, or from one of the firm's more than thirty in-stock fabrics and papers. 4990 Roswell Rd., Sandy Springs. 257-0043.

Traditional Irish Antique Restoring. John O'Callaghan restores antiques and preserves authenticity by bringing back the original finish. O'Callaghan studied in Ireland with a master craftsman who had, in turn, studied at the Glenstall School of Art, which was a famous, respected craft school. A search service is available. Impressive client list. 1200 Foster St., Old Murray Mill, Northwest. 352-2631.

Richard Weems Master Restorer. After nearly three decades of working at furniture restoration, Weems specializes in restoring chairs, but can handle caning, rushing, wicker repair, or woodworking needs. Weems still personally restores every antique. He makes it clear, however, that he does not do refinishing. 6336 Ferry Dr., Sandy Springs. 843-8563.

Woodpride. This is the outfit that *Atlanta* magazine readers have often designated "Best in Atlanta" in the furniture refinishing category. Pieces are hand-stripped before being refinished, and special care is taken with antiques and heirloom pieces. Pickup and delivery are available. 2802 Piedmont Rd., Buckhead. 237-5417.

GIFTS & MAILING

You need these people at holiday times to send special gifts to relatives "up Nawth" so that you can wow them with the quality of Southern food products: delicious marmalades, country ham, and preserves and mixes for making *real* cornbread (not that Yankee stuff with—gasp—sugar in it).

Amoré Baskets. Sandra Moore designs standardized gift baskets for all major holidays, customized gifts to meet most needs and budgets, and balloon bouquets for all occasions. Telephone orders only; orders may be delivered the same day, if needed, throughout metro Atlanta. Nationwide shipping available. 740-8660.

Blooming Cookies, Flowers, and Baskets.
Stuck on a stick, like a flower, Blooming Cookies are baked fresh daily, then shipped immediately to anywhere in Atlanta, the U.S., or overseas. Cookie flowers come in various fun containers such as a personalized, hand-painted terra-cotta pot. Call for a catalog of ideas. 502 Amsterdam Ave., Virginia-Highland. 876-2200.

Creative Celebrations, Inc.
Since 1980, this Stone Mountain firm has specialized in handsome, customized gift arrangements of Georgia food products. Fine coffees, teas, spices, and gourmet gift foods of all kinds are available, as is shipping. 923 Main St., Stone Mountain. 469-5889.

Hunter Horn Plantation.
Pack a gift box with perfect tender ham and stunning champagne mustard or a juicy smoked turkey with extraordinary cranberry relish. Other goodies to choose from include cakes and preserves. You can order some of the best smoked hams and turkeys you've ever tasted from this Savannah-based firm. 800-476-1812.

Lindsay Farms.
An extensive catalog offers a wide array of delicious Georgia gourmet products, including scrumptious Savannah Rum Cake, the best pickled Vidalia onions, and wonderful marmalades, preserves, and relishes. You can send these items any-

where through the reliable, prompt mailing service. Also offered are handmade, Georgia-produced art items, furniture, and gifts. 4794 Clark Howell Hwy., College Park. 305-0620.

Mostly Chocolate.
Louise Magnuson and Katherine Wunder mold chocolates for all occasions and holidays. The pair designs chocolates to order, such as company logos, and customers may choose patterns in the white or dark chocolate. Shapes include anything from Thanksgiving turkeys to Santas; every detail is hand-painted on in colored chocolate. Will ship anywhere in the U.S. or abroad, except in summer. By appointment only. Mail only: 8155 Habersham Waters Rd., Dunwoody, 30350. 394-3806.

Gift Express.
For more than a decade, Riedy Gimpelson has specialized in designing gift baskets with specialty food items—like Country Thymes mustards, preserves, and relishes from South Carolina, potpourri, ceramics, baby gifts, and picture frames. Gimpelson operates out of her home by appointment. Mail only: 200 Colewood Way, Atlanta, 30328. 255-5249.

Touch of Georgia.
Now in four locations, Touch of Georgia is a terrific source for Georgia goodies—grits (real ones, stone ground and delicious), preserves, good baking mixes, splendid sweets, and relishes. Good mailing service and gift wrap. Original location: 4400 Ashford-Dunwoody Rd., Perimeter Mall, Dunwoody. 394-5048; office, 578-9453.

HOUSEHOLD

These are some service providers whom we or friends whose judgment we trust have used over the years to handle household repairs and maintenance. A word of advice regarding any labor that could be dangerous, such as roofing, tree work, gutter work: get proof of insurance before letting anyone work on your property. A contractor should provide you with a copy of an insurer's certificate as proof.

APPLIANCES

Bob Carroll Appliance Co. If you hate waiting all day for appliance service and delivery—you know, they say, "anytime between 8 A.M. and 6 P.M." and they get there at 5:59 P.M.—call this outfit. Appointments are scheduled, and the crew arrives on time. 2122 N. Decatur Rd., at Clairmont Rd., Decatur. 634-2411; 396-2411.

Georgia Service Center. Repair of all kinds of small appliances—mixers, blenders, toasters, and the like. Two locations: 5366 Buford Hwy., Doraville. 455-1716; 4719 Lower Roswell Rd., Marietta. 971-1836.

Home Maintenance Company. Mark Houck has been in the appliance fix-it business for years. He works on all makes of appliances (washers, dryers, stoves, refrigerators), replaces burned-out motors in attic fans, installs hot water heaters, and so forth. And if it's out of

his league, he'll tell you before wasting your time (and his). 612 Valley Brook Rd., Decatur. 292-7558.

The Husband Helpers. Cindy Waters and her crew install kitchen appliances of all kinds—disposals, dishwashers, cook tops, gas and electric ranges, gas dryers, compactors, and wall ovens—and will haul off old appliances. Mail only: 9365 Cain Cir., Gainesville, 30506. Atlanta telephone: 381-9021.

The Vac Shop. Danny and Alice Powell repair all kinds of vacuum cleaners. Call to find the closest hardware store or Kroger store where you can drop off and pick up your vacuum. They have set up a network of more than thirty such spots throughout Atlanta, so one is sure to be handy. 679 Atlanta St., Roswell. 641-3024.

CARPET & FLOORING

Don Adair Carpets. Not just for carpet installation, Don Adair's teams can install all types of hardwood and vinyl

flooring. The crews are neat, fast, and super-pleasant. 1091 Center St., Mableton. 948-4059.

Enhance Home Services. Elizabeth Stubbs' slogan is "The Enhance Advantage;" her firm specializes in installation, refinishing, pickling, and polishing of hardwood floors. Installation and carpet cleaning (both steam and dry cleaning) are additional services, so with one firm, you can meet all your floor surfacing needs. 60 Shawnee Lane, Marietta. 565-3808.

Marble and Tile Services. Carlos Diaz' firm installs and repairs marble and tile floors, counters, fireplaces, and par-quet floors. His crews do extremely neat work, and will re-grout bath and floor tiles. These folks understand detail. Mail only: 1635 Pirkle Rd., Norcross, 30093. 279-7181.

Wood Floors by J. Douglas. This twenty-year-old firm focuses on quality installation and refinishing of wood floors, especially oak strip, plank, parquet, and exotic woods. Sanding, finishing, pickling, and custom designs. 2644 Mountain Industrial Blvd., Tucker. 493-9130.

CHIMNEY SWEEPS

Chimney Service Company. Jim McPherson is a nationally certified chimney sweep who promises no mess. Besides cleaning chimneys—important for preventing dangerous buildups in flues—he also offers critter removal, leak repair, capping, and damper installation and repair. He also cleans ducts and air purification systems. Mail only: 385 Birch Rill Dr., Alpharetta. 751-8976.

Conscious Cleaning. Repairing and installing dampers, chimney caps, and glass fireplace doors as well as getting the soot off your flue will keep down the risk of chimney fires. Livtar Khalsa has been in business since 1977. 112 Millbrook Cir., Roswell. 993-6683.

Custom Chimney Sweeping. Jim Morson arrives in top hat and traditional costume to do a chimney cleaning inspection. He can cap a chimney, repair the firebox, or rebuild a fireplace. Mail only: 1588 Sheridan Dr., Marietta, 30066. 435-3021.

CHRISTMAS TREES

Grinch Christmas Tree Co. The company's slogan is "Come steal one from us." Randy Steinbrenner and Arthur Griffin will sell the tree, deliver it, and set it up. The Grinch group deals in Fraser firs—which hold their needles and are considered the best holiday trees—as well as Douglas and Noble firs. Trees may range from two to 25 feet in height, and delivery is available throughout the metro area. Mail only: 3727 Peachtree Rd., Apt. 9, Atlanta, 30309.

Rusty Smith's Christmas Tree Delivery. The freshest and fullest trees, ranging from seven to twelve feet in height, are delivered and set up using your stand or one he can provide. Service area is North Metro. Mail only: 685 Barrington Way, Roswell, 30076. 993-2681.

CLEANING

A-Aall Personal Cleaning Service.
For the past decade, the company has been cleaning houses for clients who want regular service or a single visit. Some regular clients have one room cleaned each week, called a "mini-spring-cleaning." Windows—cleaned inside and out—carpet and furniture cleaning, and ultrasonic blind cleaning are among the firm's talents. 3972 Clairmont Rd., Chamblee. 457-1331.

Acme Carpet and Drapery Cleaning, Inc.
A family-owned firm for more than a quarter-century, Acme cleans all kinds of household items: carpets, rugs, draperies, even the kids' favorite stuffed animals. Feather pillows get new down and new covers. If you bring in your drapes and rugs, you'll get a discount, but they will pick them up at your home, return them, and re-hang them—and they come on time! 525 W. Howard Ave., Decatur. 377-1734.

Goldarm European Cleaning.
Having arrived here from Chicago in 1987, Goldarm employs maids who are new immigrants from Poland. The same person comes to a client's house each time, and the job includes cleaning chandeliers, polishing silver, washing windows inside and out, plus regular cleaning. Goldarm handles all transportation of workers and operates in all sections of the city. Fully insured and bonded. Call Richard Darmstaedter.

Mail only: 885 Barnes Walk Ct., Lilburn, 30247. 381-9298.

Fiber Clean of Atlanta.
Carpet, upholstery, and drapery cleaning and restoration are the firm's general areas of expertise, but owner Tom de Gregareo specializes in cleaning fine fabrics, such as antique satin and Oriental rugs. 2121 New Market Business Park, Ste. 146, Marietta. 951-0038.

Houndstooth Carpet & Upholstery Cleaning.
Houndstooth offers extremely reasonable prices and prompt service by cheerful, professional people who clean rugs, carpets, upholstered furniture, drapes, and ducting. 2781 Clairmont Rd., at Briarcliff Rd., Northeast. 320-1625.

I.A.Q. (Indoor Air Quality).
The firm specializes in cleaning air ducts. Founded in 1986 and now merged with the Duct Doctor, this firm is the largest duct-cleaning company in the South. One of the principals of the Duct Doctor is a well-known Atlanta allergist; another has served as an officer of American Allergy Consultants. 3150 Gateway Dr., Norcross. 446-1764.

MR. Clean/MR. Shine.
Louis Llop does more than clean windows. He gets them sparkling inside and out, then goes on to the gutters, the chandeliers, and the exterior (outside pressure washing). He's been around town for

over ten years. 3440 Keswick Ct., Chamblee. 451-0100.

Sharian. Purveyors of Oriental rugs in Atlanta for six decades, Sharian also cleans rugs—both Oriental and ordi-

nary—and will pick up and deliver (extra charge). Storage, appraisal, and restoration of antique Oriental rugs are specialties. 368 W. Ponce de Leon Ave., Decatur. 373-2274.

DOMESTIC PERSONNEL PLACEMENT

A Friend of the Family. This firm provides child and companion care in the home, on a permanent or temporary basis. In business since 1984, Judi Merlin's company has served more than 6,000 clients in the Atlanta area. The 1,400 screened and qualified care givers are all over 21 and drive. 895 Mt. Vernon Hwy., Sandy Springs. 255-2848.

KADAN Agency. Linda Kadan has ten years' experience in placing professional homecare personnel. Candidates are carefully screened, polygraphed when necessary, bonded, and insured. Long-term and temporary homecare personnel handle housekeeping (home or office), child care, house sitting, and nonmedical elder care (either live-in or daytime). By appointment only. Mail only: 5014 Mt. Vernon Way, Dunwoody, 30338. 396-8997.

DRAPERIES & SHUTTERS

Calico Corners Fabrics. One of Atlanta's most popular sources for upholstering, drapery, spreads, padded headboards, and custom-made pillows, Calico Corners is also a splendid source for fabrics. 4256 Roswell Rd., Sandy Springs. 252-7443.

The Louver Shop. Custom-made, all-wood construction shutters, stained or painted. 4619 Poplar Rd., Pine Lake, 30072. 292-1436.

The Shutter Shoppe. Quick delivery on custom-made plantation and traditional-style shutters, available in basswood or aspen (both are durable, with smooth finishes that accept stains and paints well). Detailed, precise workmanship. Free in-home estimates; prices include installation. 9345 Industrial Trace, Alpharetta. 410-9525.

EXTERMINATION

Georgia Department of Agriculture, Division of Entymology & Pesticides. So you've gotten three

different stories from two different pest control firms and can't be sure what's eating your house alive? Call these guys if you are in a quandary about the service you have received or are planning to get. They don't have the staff to handle every possible situation, but will give an objective opinion when you have a conflict you can't resolve. 19 Martin Luther King, Jr., Dr., Downtown. 656-3641.

Patterson Exterminating Co. Prompt, professional, personal, and humane service in the handling of both insects and rodents. For instance, when dealing with roof rats, they place chemicals out of harm's way for children and pets. When wild critters invade—birds, squirrels, and the like—Patterson makes a special effort to trap and release, not kill. 3319 Burk Dr., Chamblee. 457-8026; 455-7226.

GUTTERS & ROOFING

American Gutter and Home Improvement Co. Bob MacLaurin installs and repairs gutters and down spouts. He also does roofing. Ask about other home improvement services. Special discounts are available for senior citizens. 4372 Hwy. 78, Lilburn. 979-9748.

Roofing Repair Specialists. Talk to Randy Edwards, field supervisor of this excellent roofing company, about repairing and installing roofing of all types, including slate, cedar, tile, fiberglass, and flat roofs. (The firm is certified to install continuous-membrane, flat-roof systems.) Look to them for copper flashing, chimney caps, entry, and bow window covers—all custom fabricated on site. 506 Clifton Rd., Candler Park, Northeast. 924-9922.

HEATING & COOLING

Atlantis Heating and Cooling. Mike Johnson troubleshoots heating and air conditioning problems. Johnson, in business since 1984, likes to say he's not just a "parts changer." He has a reputation for being meticulous, but the result is a job done right the first time. Installation and maintenance. Mail only: 1002 Sycamore Dr., Decatur, 30033. 378-1653.

Temperature Design and Control. Dealing with both the installation and repair of heating and air conditioning systems, Bob Johnson works for the big developers on large contracts and for us little guys needing the same service at a fair price. The courteous personnel work all over the Atlanta area and provide prompt attention. 560 Mt. Zion Rd., Oxford. Atlanta phone: 688-3511.

INSULATION & WEATHERIZING

Atlanta Weatherization Experts. Joe Garvey specializes in replacing windows and doors as well as installing insulation. He also does small construction jobs, orders doors or windows that the customer selects from one of several catalogs, accepts delivery, installs, paints, and—a big one for us—leaves a clean work site when finished. Mail only: 399 Stonewood Dr., Stone Mountain, 30087. 469-5776.

LANDSCAPING

Art Marble & Stone Co., Inc. This is a good source for excellent masonry, landscaping, and marble installers. The place offers a superior selection of marble, building stone, flagstone, fireplace equipment and gas logs, and other accessories for the home. 5862 Peachtree Industrial Blvd., Chamblee. 458-2331.

Aqua Irrigation Systems. We sometimes hit dry spells around here in the summer. Many homeowners install underground sprinkler systems to keep their lawns green without the hassle of hoses. This firm installs and repairs all such systems and irrigation pumps. 240 Cranfill Rd., Marietta. 424-4402.

Concrete Services Group. Scott Bartlett's firm specializes in restoring concrete driveways and laying new ones. Installing patios, walkways, foundation slabs, and stamped and tinted concrete are other specialties. 2127 Powers Ferry Rd., Marietta. 951-8856.

Dorough Landscape Co. Doug Dorough's degree in horticulture and design is from Auburn University, and he is one of Atlanta's most respected landscape designers. Awards and honors seem to waft his way, deservedly. A separate division handles a full range of landscape maintenance services for both residential and commercial clients. 5444 Lawrenceville Hwy., Lilburn. 921-6485.

Environmental Artisans. Brian Hodges is a landscape architect whose company does landscape design and installation. Call on him for retaining walls, grassing, grading, planting, and drainage. The design and installation of poolscapes is a particular focus. Services offered in all sections of Atlanta. 2748 Peeler Rd., Dunwoody. 458-9586.

Georgia Forestry Association/Urban Forestry Headquarters. Call these people when someone rings your doorbell and says your trees have "oak wilt," but the arbors in question are Bradford pear trees! County extension agents can also help, but additional services from the Urban Forestry people include advice on how to protect your valuable trees from damage and pests. 500 Pinnacle Ct., Norcross. 416-7621.

Goodman and Associates. Residential garden design, ponds, waterfalls, outdoor lighting, and swimming pools are Will Goodman's stock-in-trade. He does not install landscapes, but can recommend those who do. 488 Kennesaw Ave., Marietta. 421-9865.

Griffith Landscape Services. Sam Griffith handles small jobs that typically don't interest large firms, such as cleanup, sod and small shrub installation, trimming, lawn mowing, and tree-cutting. His card trumpets, "No job too small." He's also an excellent painter, both interior and exterior. Mail only: 2314 St. de Ville, Atlanta, 30345. 634-7482.

Hardscapes, Inc. Mike Nicholas does all kinds of outdoor projects in brick or stone—pool decking, walls, mailboxes, walkways, waterfalls. He also specializes in building garden accessories, such as benches, birdbaths, and brick fixtures. Mail only: 7337 Covington Hwy., Lithonia. 482-2550.

Hastings Nature & Garden Center. Long Atlanta's prestige gardening expert, Hastings offers outstanding design and planning consultation services. A big asset is that the firm specializes in Southern gardens. Services include lawn installation and renovation, specialty water areas (fish ponds, for instance), perennial gardens, lawn and garden lighting, and seminars on a variety of gardening subjects. 2350 Cheshire Bridge Rd., at Lindbergh/Lavista, Northeast. 321-6981.

Hercules Tree Service. Adam McMahon can handle all your tree-care needs, including topping, trimming, and pruning. He specializes in dangerous tree removal. 3255 Jett Ferry Ct., Dunwoody. 394-7428.

Proland, Inc. President Nathan Thompson has been in business here for twelve years. Proland's comprehensive service includes landscape design and installation; grounds management; building of patios, decks, and retaining walls; and irrigation systems. A busy man! 6121 Bluestone Rd., Sandy Springs. 250-9097.

Tony's Tree Service. Tree removal and trimming; garden planting and general landscaping; gutter cleaning, repair, and installation; design of islands in driveways; and lawn aeration are all part of Tony Womack's established business. P.O. Box 394, Silver Creek, 30173. 438-4414.

Tuff Turf, Inc. Wade Smith and his ten-person crew do residential landscape installation and maintenance, continuing the tradition started by Wade's dad more than twenty years ago. Serving north metro by appointment. Mail only: 925 Gantt Rd., Alpharetta, 30201. 664-2514.

Robert Walker Concrete Work. More than thirty years' experience makes this company tops in concrete patios and driveways. Brick, stone, and block work are also a part of the business. By appointment only. Mail only: 1078 Wimberly Rd., Atlanta, 30319. 231-0035.

LIGHTING

Lamp Glow Industries, Inc. If you still have one of those inefficient, costly, gas-fueled yard lights, consider switching to electricity. Lamp Glow will convert the light to a REALITE system that uses nine kilowatt hours of electricity per month, as opposed to the fourteen to twenty therms per month used by gas lights. A photoelectric cell turns the lamp on at dusk and off at dawn. 819 Pickens Industrial Dr., Ste. 1, Marietta. 514-1441.

PLUMBERS

Bill John Plumbing, Inc. In business more than fifteen years, Bill John does remodeling and repair work that involves every type of plumbing. 5250 Hwy. 9, Alpharetta. 475-4722.

E.H. Housworth Plumbing. Prompt service by appointment. They get there when they say they will, and the job is done right the first time. P.O. Box 48807, Atlanta, 30362. 945-4717.

Leroy's Plumbing Co., Inc. Charming and always smiling, Leroy Piper is highly recommended by folks who've used him for all types of plumbing repairs and remodeling. North Fulton and East Cobb areas only. 112 Norcross St., Roswell, 30077. 993-3993.

REFINISHING

Lowe Glass Co. All kinds of glass and mirror needs, both automotive and household, are met, but the best service offered is the re-silvering of mirrors. 4783 Peachtree Rd., Chamblee. 457-0288.

Unique Refinishers. Ron Kott re-glazes bathtubs, tile, and sinks. He specializes in refinishing antique tubs and sinks. 5171 Hwy. 20, Sugar Hill. 945-0072.

JEWELRY DESIGN & REPAIR

Losing a pearl earring doesn't mean you have to throw out the other one; the remaining bob can be matched to perfection. Great-grandmother's rubies can be reset in a design of modern inspiration. Jewelry repairs and custom-designed jewelry are precious services.

Adamark Jewelers. Mark Geller specializes in silver-plating as well as repair and polishing of silver, copper, and brass. 6136 Roswell Rd., Sandy Springs. 252-1185.

Fowler Jewelers. Jeannette and Sam Fowler have been caring for Atlanta's jewelry for more than 36 years in the same location. Watch repair is a specialty. 6125 Roswell Rd., Sandy Springs. 255-2480.

Grace Carmody Design Studio. Carmody will custom design or redesign one-of-a-kind pieces, such as baby spoons, rattles, and anniversary gifts—often in contemporary, bejeweled designs. She also teaches jewelry design at the North Arts Center in Dunwoody. Mail only: 3355 E. Terrell Branch, Marietta, 30067. 953-0173.

Jewelry Artisans, Inc. Choose the shape of your custom design from hundreds of wax models. Recycle old gold and antique gems in new settings, or choose from a gem collection that they claim is the largest in the city. 6690 Roswell Rd., Sandy Springs. 255-6268; 3529 Chamblee-Tucker Rd., Chamblee. 458-5805.

Knox Jewelers, Inc. On-premises artisans specialize in jewelry design and repair. They will also custom design new settings for your old gems. 180 Allen Rd., Ste. 107, Sandy Springs. 252-2256.

Let's Knot. Specializing in pearl maintenance, Leanore Block restrings pearls, updates clasps, adds pendants, and attends to whatever a fine strand needs. She also crafts custom-made signed jewelry *(see chapter 6)*. 3202-B Paces Ferry Place, Buckhead. 266-2440.

A *Step Above*. These specialists can do all kinds of repairs, even on costume jewelry, and can repair practically anything in metal. 5022 Vernon Oaks Dr., Dunwoody, 30338. 396-0062.

Silver Rose Fine Jewelry. Somehow, repairs that seem to be a major labor elsewhere turn out to be a breeze at Silver Rose. They call you when it's ready, so your favorite necklace doesn't get lost getting fixed. 7706 Spalding Dr., Spalding Corners Shopping Center, Norcross. 448-1747.

MUSICAL INSTRUMENT SERVICES

Whether you need the family grand tuned, the piano moved to a new home, or your guitar restrung, you can find the right specialists in Atlanta.

Emile Baran Violins. Repair of all kinds of bowed stringed instruments. A Decatur institution. 117 Clairemont Ave., Decatur. 377-3419.

Gentle Giant Piano Movers. Michael Buckner moves pianos and organs so gently that they don't know they've budged. With almost twenty years' experience, Buckner has been at this calling full-time for the past seven years. Mail only: 330 Stoney Brook Dr., Douglasville, 30143. 949-6088. Or call Piano Gallery, 351-0550.

King Band Instrument Repair Service. Established in 1929 by Eddie King of Buffalo, New York, the business has been expanded by King's son Charles and his partner, Jay Himmel. They also repair school instruments for area school systems. P.O. Box 1417, Decatur, 30030. 373-1050.

Piano Gallery. Floridian Andy Williamson trained at the New England Conservatory of Music in piano technology; he further honed his piano repairing and tuning skills at Tanglewood, the Boston Symphony's summer home. In Atlanta since 1988, Williamson is based at the Piano Gallery, the source for Steinway, Weber, and Boston pianos. 2140 Peachtree Rd., Brookwood Square, Brookwood. 351-0550.

PARTY & WEDDING SERVICES

Atlanta is a great place for a special event or wedding. Facilities such as restored historic homes make handsome settings for large, elegant affairs. We've chosen some special sources for this listing.

ENTERTAINMENT

For musicians other than those listed below, see chapter 3.

David C. Cooper. Call him when you want something different. Cooper Music Productions can provide a Russian trio playing balalaikas, Yugoslavian music, or a bluegrass band. The **World Music Consort** (Asian music, for instance) and the **Atlanta Brass Works** (a brass quintet) may also be booked. Mail only: 976 Fourth Blvd., Decatur, 30030. 288-9512.

Bob Geresti Classical & Contemporary. Solo or with a companion, Geresti and his portable piano offer classical or contemporary music for parties, receptions, and weddings. Call for a free demonstration tape. Mail only: 180 W. Putnam Ferry Rd., Woodstock, 30188. 928-1056.

Bob Henson's Band. For weddings, parties, and private functions, Bob Henson can provide anything from a single instrument to a fourteen-piece band (the **Continentals**). Mail only: 2756 Northbrook Dr., Doraville, 30340. 938-6898.

Deedi Henson, Harpist. Henson performs classical or contemporary music for private affairs, weddings, and conventions. She can also arrange for ensembles that combine harp with flute,

violin, or cello, or all four together. Mail only: 2756 Northbrook Dr., Doraville, 30340. 939-3180.

Jeff Justice. This wonderful comedian specializes in private parties, with magic and humor for adult audiences. The material is always appropriate and never off-color. Justice appears regularly at such clubs as The Punch Line and A-Comic Cafe. P.O. Box 52404, Atlanta, 30355. 262-7406.

Margaret Perrin. Pianist Margaret Perrin has been entertaining Atlantans at parties for several decades. Lively and talented, she can swing in a heartbeat from big band to classical, pop to rock. Perrin tailors the music to the occasion, and may arrange to have other musicians perform with her, according to the client's wishes. Mail only: 1546 Cooledge Rd., Tucker, 30084. 939-4112.

Shoal Creek Band. Honestly, one of the best bluegrass and folk music groups we've heard in a long time— and we know of at least one wedding they've done. The band members all grew up in the fifties and sixties, so they have a good idea of how bluegrass, folk, country, Irish, and gospel music are supposed to sound. Mail only: P.O. Box 338, Dahlonega, 30533. 706-864-7817.

Mary Sue Taylor, Pianist. A jazz pianist, Taylor performs with her trio in many of Atlanta's jazz clubs. Alone or with other musicians, she does a variety of musical formats for private affairs. She also teaches piano to beginners and advanced students. Mail only: 280 Hollyberry Lane, Roswell, 30076. 641-7170.

Kay Watkins, Storyteller. Watkins is terrific at parties for small fry, espe-

cially those ages four to ten. She has performed at Six Flags, Callanwolde, the YMCA, several camps, and for numerous private clients. Mail only: 571 Terrace Ave., Atlanta, 30307. 373-1335.

World Artists. Lynn Carpenter McConnell's unique agency represents various musical groups that are available for private functions. Included are **Troika Balalaikas**, **Atlanta Brassworks**, and a Celtic music group that plays traditional Irish music on traditional instruments. Mail only: 2005 Chesterfield Dr., Atlanta, 30345. 634-1595.

FACILITIES

Please see the historic homes listed in Chapter 5 (City Sights) for other facilities that welcome private events.

The Academy of Medicine. This handsome, restored Neoclassic building by renowned Atlanta architect Philip Trammell Shutze is on the National Register of Historic Places. Above the rotunda hangs the Czechoslovakian crystal chandelier that once was part of the *Gone With the Wind* movie set. The academy has been the setting for many grand Atlanta events. The dining room seats eighty, but can accommodate up to 150 for buffets and cocktail parties. 875 W. Peachtree St., Midtown. 874-3219.

The Ansley Inn. An elegantly restored Tudor mansion, this 17,000-square-foot residence caters to corporate needs. An executive conference room, a formal, twelve-seat dining room, and its reception capacity for as many as 350 make the inn an attractive temporary corporate headquarters. 253 15th St., Midtown. 872-9000.

Ashley Oaks. Historic Ashley Oaks' fourteen rooms are tastefully furnished with antiques, Waterford crystal, silver, and oil paintings. Built in 1879, the house can accommodate up to fifty people for banquet dinners and lunches. Up to 150 can be served at receptions. 144 College St., Jonesboro. 478-8986.

Burge Plantation. A.G. "Sandy" and Betsy Morehouse make available this splendid 800-acre antebellum plantation and house, located about 45 miles from downtown Atlanta, for corporate and convention use. The facility includes a conservatory, covered pavilion, croquet course, baseball field, tranquil surroundings, and more. Still a private home, it has been in the same family since 1809. From April through September, this estate is available for rehearsal dinners, weddings (ceremony, reception, and all), reunions, company picnics, and executive retreats for groups of twenty to 2,000. Rte. 1, Morehouse Rd., Mansfield, near Conyers. 787-5152.

Catalpa Plantation.
Located about forty miles from downtown Atlanta, the **Goodwyn-Bailey-Smith House** was the 1991 winner of the Georgia Trust for Historic Preservation's Honor Award for restoration, and took second place for restoration from the National Trust. It is also on the National Register of Historic Places. Owners Renae and Rod Smith deserve all the credit because their modifications respect the structure and spirit of the original plantation house. Available for private affairs held outdoors, Catalpa can accommodate about eighty for a sit-down dinner on the grounds. The Smiths can arrange the catering, or clients may arrange their own. Private and group tours (maximum of about forty) are also welcome. 2295 Old Poplar Rd., Newnan. 253-3806.

> In 1860 Dill & Raspberry opened a fine art gallery, offering camera photography services, painting supplies, and restoration services. Located on Whitehall Street, the establishment advertised that its photographs were "of artistic merit, and no humbugging."

Flint Hill Plantation.
Built in 1835, this distinguished plantation plain-style house was given the Mt. Vernon touch some sixty years ago, with white columns having replaced an interim Victorian look. Today the house and its lovely one-and-a-half–acre garden are the scene for weddings, business meetings, and civic functions. Flint Hill can seat up to 250 people for sit-down dinners, or accommodate up to 500 stand-up guests throughout the house and garden. Managed by Magic Moments, which also handles Primrose Cottage (see below). 539 S. Peachtree St., Norcross. 263-7669.

Fox Theatre.
Within Atlanta's most exciting landmark, three areas are available for private events. Dinner dances may be held on the stage, and there's also the colorful yet subdued and just plain wonderful **Egyptian Ballroom**—a one-of-a-kind space with most unusual themes. Finally, the **Grand Salon**, with its red and gold richness, is perfect for cocktail buffets prior to private theater showings. 660 Peachtree St., Midtown. 881-2110.

Glenridge Hall.
Built in 1929 as an English country manor house and still a private residence available for special events, Glenridge Hall made a cameo appearance in the film *Driving Miss Daisy*. Much of the original property still surrounds the house with exquisite natural splendor. Conservator Joseph Mayson welcomes corporate cocktail parties and entertaining. He reserves the right to approve caterers, florists, and entertainment. One room can handle fifty people for a seated banquet, and the splendor of the great hall, with its 34-foot vaulted ceiling and baronial fireplace, make receptions memorable. There is a total of 6,000 square feet of interior party space. The 2,500-square-foot exterior terrace may be tented to accommodate about 200 people for

a seated affair. Rules: no smoking inside, and no spike heels. Mail only: 6615 Glenridge Dr., Atlanta, 30328. 394-0261.

Glenwoods. The 1918 English manor house once sat in a parklike setting that even contained a vineyard. The Neel Reid–designed, seventeen-room residence almost lost the battle of the bulldozer, but was rescued and, despite the loss of the surrounding eight acres, holds a firm place among Druid Hills' elegant homes. The interior was totally renovated in 1933 by Phillip Shutze. After 23 years of effort, Alyse Corcoran Baier has restored Glenwoods to its former luster. Today, the residence is available for corporate parties and weddings. 1632 Ponce de Leon Ave., Druid Hills. 378-6064.

Grant Park Mansion. Built in the late nineteenth century, the house exudes all you would expect of Southern charm, elegance, and grace. Inside are five handsomely appointed rooms furnished with fine period antiques, crystal chandeliers, Oriental rugs, and elegant window treatments. The facility can handle 200 guests for an indoor reception, or seventy for a seated dinner. This is a no–smoking establishment. 603 Boulevard, Grant Park. 627-5474.

Houston Mill House. In the late 1880s, Major W. J. Houston built a dam and water-powered gristmill on property near Emory University. Builder Harry J. Carr constructed his family's fieldstone home on the property in the 1920s. Purchased by Emory University in 1959, Houston Mill House became a hospitality and entertainment center in the 1970s. Lunch is served during the

week, and the house is available in evenings and on weekends for university programs, private affairs, weddings, and parties. Two bed-and-breakfast rooms are located on the second floor. Epicurean Catering is the exclusive caterer for buffet and banquet service. 849 Houston Mill Rd., near Emory University, Northeast. 727-7878.

Lovejoy Plantation. Legend holds that the lady of the house, standing on the stairway, fired on a Yankee deserter who came to plunder the place. Sound familiar? Built in 1836, Lovejoy Plantation, located about thirty miles south of downtown, is home to Betty Talmadge, former wife of Georgia's former senator, Herman Talmadge. Antiques and memorabilia, free-ranging critters, and 1,200 acres of farmland make this a true glimpse of the old South. Savor a "Magnolia Supper" or a barbecue with Southern delicacies. The Talmadge special suppers are a hit with corporate and private patrons alike. Lovejoy. 478-6677.

Marlow House. A charming Victorian house that was originally (in 1887) a boarding house, the Marlow House opened in 1983 as a bed-and-breakfast inn. Its public rooms, accommodating 200 for a reception and 125 for a seated dinner, may be rented for weddings, special events, and corporate entertaining. 192 Church St., Marietta. 426-1881.

Oak Hill Plantation. Surrounded by five lovely acres, this restored, 5,000-square-foot Greek Revival home lies within thirty miles of downtown Atlanta. Furnished with fine, period American antiques, including a Duncan Phyfe sofa, American Connecticut pieces, and French Empire and English Regency furnishings, the private residence is open for tours by appointment. Owner Gail Talmadge Notti welcomes weddings and parties at the home, and can handle everything from the invitations to the birdseed for the bridal send-off. The house can accommodate sit-down dinners for fifty people as well as an outdoor barbecue for 650. Mail only: 267 Jonesboro Rd., McDonough, 30253 (Exit 71, off I-75 south). 957-1582.

Primrose Cottage.
Roswell's first permanent home was built in 1839 by Roswell King, the town's namesake, for his daughter, Elisa Hand. The facility can seat 125 dinner guests, or accommodate 500 for a stand-up reception that uses both the house and the grounds. Primrose occupies a romantic site behind an old white fence in quaint, historic Roswell. Managed by Magic Moments, which also handles Flint Hill (see above). 674 Mimosa Blvd., Roswell. 594-2299.

Rock Springs Farm.
Hire a farm and throw a picnic. For a minimum charge, you can fish, hike, picnic, play croquet or softball, pitch horseshoes, or go on a hay ride. Equipment is available for all of these activities. At dusk, enjoy a large bonfire. Available from March through October. Rock Springs Rd., Exit

> Henrietta Cuttino Dozier (1872–1947) was born near Jacksonville, Florida, but was reared and educated in Atlanta. Known as "Harry," she was Atlanta's, Georgia's, and Florida's first licensed woman architect, and was a founding member of the Georgia chapter of the American Institute of Architects. Disappointed at not being able to get work in Atlanta, Dozier returned to Jacksonville, where she designed many fine residences.

46 (Hwy. 20, Buford) off I-85 north, Lawrenceville. Office: 125 Perry St., Lawrenceville, 30245. 963-0973.

Stanley House.
A handsome, Queen Anne residence built in 1895 for Woodrow Wilson's aunt, the Stanley House today operates as a bed-and-breakfast inn, along with its companion, the Marlow House (see page 195). It is also a good setting for special events and weddings, as it can hold up to 65 people (depending on the configuration) for a seated event and 125 for a cocktail event. Catering. Your own alcoholic beverages may be served. 236 Church St., Marietta. 426-1881.

Warren Farm Country Inn.
With a gazebo and pavilion on eighteen landscaped acres, this 6,000-square-foot, formal Victorian house is furnished with Victorian-style pieces in the front rooms, and nineteenth-century antiques in the back. It can accommodate from fifty to 1,500 guests, and the staff will coordinate all aspects of events. Turn your catering, flowers, music, and guest list over to them and be a guest at your own bash. The inn lies within thirty miles of downtown Atlanta. 5809 Warren Farm Rd., Powder Springs. 439-6075.

FLORAL DESIGNERS

Bailey's Florist & Gifts. Born in Hiroshima, Japan, Hisako Holland began studying Ikebana flower arranging at age fifteen. At 21, she studied the fine Japanese art of making handcrafted silk flowers, and she has since studied with Mary Takashashi, a California-based Japanese flower artist who frequently visits Atlanta to teach. In 1990, Hisako and her husband, Dave, bought Bailey's, near their home in Conyers. She continues to produce fine Japanese flower arrangements and handcrafted silk flowers within a full-service floral shop. Conyers is lucky—and not far from Atlanta. 1815 Hwy. 138, Conyers. 760-8711.

Forrester's Flowers. For almost ten years, Joe Underwood has owned this Atlanta institution, which has been here for forty years. Forrester's has its own greenhouses, making it a ready source for all kinds of floral material. One of the largest florists in Atlanta, Forrester's can handle many styles of floral design, making it a good choice for large events. 2070 Cheshire Bridge Rd., Northeast. 325-0333.

Hamilton House. Ronnie Stewart and crew design traditional arrangements, but they shine when it comes to modern and avant-garde styles. Decorative accents and gifts are also available. Services include gourmet baskets, weddings, parties, and banquets. 7732 Spalding Dr., Norcross. 447-4469.

Haskett-Schneider Designs. From miniature Victorian-style bouquets to large dramatic arrangements, unusual floral and plant designs are arranged to customer specifications for weddings, parties, and special events. The pair offers full floral service, including city-wide delivery. 375 Pharr Rd., Ste. 301, Pharr Plaza, Buckhead. 266-1515.

Marvin Gardens. Avant-garde and English floral arrangements with an Art Deco flair are designed for special events, weddings, and intimate parties. Also offered are accessories, gourmet baskets, exotic plants, and gifts. In business more than twelve years. 3205 Paces Ferry Pl., Buckhead. 231-1988.

RENTALS

All Event Rentals. This young company was an instant success on the party materials rental circuit. Rent portable bars and beverage fountains, barbecue grills, candelabra, wedding arches, raffle equipment, tents, audiovisual systems, and even cribs for overnighting little guests—they left nothing out. 3067-A N. Peachtree St., Duluth. 476-1659; 1744 Connally Dr., East Point. 761-4116.

C. C. Whittier Bridal Salon. Here the bride, her mother, and her attendants will find everything they need—for rent or sale. Gowns that retail for as much as $3,500 or as little as $250 are available for sale, and rentals run from $100 to around $600. 480 E. Paces Ferry Rd., Ste. 5, Buckhead. 266-1146.

Evening Sensations. Formerly Overnight Sensations, this shop rents high-fashion dresses, in sizes four to sixteen, for parties and balls. Great costume jewelry, too. 4920 Roswell Rd., Fountain Oaks Shopping Center, Sandy Springs. 250-0711.

Grande Entrance. "Borrow" a special designer gown for an evening, a wedding, or a special event. Extensive rentals include costume jewelry. Shoes are sold in sizes ranging from two to 22. 3330 Piedmont Rd., Buckhead. 842-0211.

Suburban Rental. Everything you'll need to throw the shivaree—tents, tables, cloths, dishes, glassware, chafing dishes, and platters. 6110 Bluestone Rd., Sandy Springs. 256-3848.

SPECIAL TOUCHES

Golden Touch Wedding Services. The Reverends B. G. and W. G. Hurd are an unusual husband-and-wife team who will perform the customized wedding ceremony you've always dreamed about, anywhere you choose to hold it. Mail only: 105 Bent Grass Dr., Roswell, 30076. 992-4575.

Yellow Rose Carriage Service. The Schwartz Vis-à-Vis Carriage, the Cadillac of carriages, is drawn by a registered, matched pair of grey quarter horses. The name comes from the firm's custom of giving the guest of honor a yellow rose. The carriage's passenger area is weather protected. Serving all areas except downtown. Mail only: 952 W. Sandtown Rd., Marietta, 30064. 499-9719.

PERSONAL & HEALTH

When the brain needs some time off, check out some of these day spas, massage therapists, and physical trainers for relief and self-improvement. This section also addresses selected specialized needs, such as sources for assisting older or infirm family members.

Certified Nurse Midwives. A certified nurse-midwife (CNM) is a primary care provider for normal maternity, newborn and well-woman gynecological care. Nurse-midwives attend women during delivery in hospitals or birthing centers. Some nurse-midwives also attend home births. In any setting, the provision for the safety of mother and baby is a primary concern. Nurse-midwifery services are covered by most private medical insurance carriers. Midwife Associates, 2500 Hospital Blvd., Roswell. 664-1000. Midwife Maternity Center, 1001 Thorton Rd., Lithia Springs. 292-8899. Or call your local hospital for a nurse-midwife closest to you.

Jeanne's Body Tech. One of the most highly regarded aerobic and exercise operations in the city, Jeanne's Body Tech starts business very early in the morning. The facility has a comfortable, well-lit aerobics area, a weight room, a pro shop with exercise fashions, and free babysitting in the morning and afternoon. Locker rooms and showers. 334 E. Paces Ferry Rd., Buckhead. 261-0227.

Natural Body. Using all natural products to soothe away stress and anxiety, Natural Body offers facials, massages, wraps, manicures, everything you need to feel pampered and cared for in the most natural way. Popular with both men and women, Natural Body has two spa locations: 1402-2 North Highland Ave., Virginia-Highland (spa and retail), 237-7712; 3209 Paces Ferry Place, Suite 1, Buckhead (salon and spa), 872-1039. Natural Body retail stores offer a full line of cruelty-free imported products and provide gift basket services. 1403 North Highland Ave., Virginia-Highland. 876-9624.

Noëlle The Day Spa. Float your cares away with a day of body massage, facials, and luxurious treatments. Walk out feeling glamorous. For both men and women. Sunday hours. Gift certificates. 3619 Piedmont Rd., Buckhead. 266-0060.

Pierce Program. Increase your energy, decrease stress, focus your mind and strengthen your body with Vini Yoga. Instructors recommend Vini Yoga as a natural remedy for back and shoulder pains, high blood pressure, headaches, asthma, overeating, and smoking. Pierce's **Pregnancy Program** is very popular and focuses on strengthening pelvic muscles to help the expectant mother carry her unborn baby. The Pierce Program offers private and group lessons. All programs are geared towards meeting individual needs. Program costs range from $85-$100. 1764 North Highland Ave. NE, Virginia-Highland. 875-7110.

Spa Sydell. Serving both men and women, Spa Sydell is famous for excellent skin, body, and nail care, body massage, and makeup consultations. Two locations: 3060 Peachtree Rd., Buckhead Plaza, Buckhead. 237-2505; 1259 Cumberland Mall, Marietta. 801-0804.

Dr. Sylvester Cain Memorial Sick Room Equipment. The Norcross Women's Club operates this resource center; they lend sick room equipment for the Norcross community. Available equipment includes electric beds and wheelchairs. A $10 donation helps to keep the equipment in good working order. 65 N. Peachtree St., Norcross. 449-4756.

T.L.C. Nursing Services and Elder Care. TLC President Robert Williams believes that adult day care is a better solution to some health management problems and one that costs less than long-term hospitalization or in-home or resident care. One woman we know places her Alzheimer's-afflicted husband at TLC two days a week so that she can paint—and preserve her peace of mind. Program participants enjoy a hot meal, aerobics, bingo, dancing, crafts, and other activities. Available services include physical and speech therapy; in-home care is also offered, but costs more than day care. 475 Hembree Pl., Roswell. 442-9266.

PETS

From cats to canaries to canines, pets come in various forms and furs—all needing care from time to time. Here are some specialists who provide just the right loving touch.

The Cat Sitter. Linda Bagne knows how to treat your friendly feline, and will come to your home to care for your cat(s) on whatever schedule you determine. Bagne guarantees that her critter clients get thirty minutes of individual attention. She'll also bring in the mail and newspapers, and will water your plants. Serving north Atlanta. P.O. Box 232, Roswell, 30077. 594-1010.

Critter Sitters. You will have an interview to meet your sitter and know who is caring for your pets. Thirty sitters and a 24-hour answering service provide organized, comprehensive, and responsible care, directed by Jeffrey R. Lauterbach. Sitters also bring in your mail and newspapers, alternate the lights lit in your home, and learn your alarm systems to enhance protection while you're away. Call for appointment. 377-5475.

For Cats Only. Mike Kopley loves cats and they're what he specializes in. Of course, he'll also take up your newspapers and mail while he's there if you wish. Security awareness comes naturally to Kopley, who once worked with the Atlanta Police Department's Thor unit. By appointment. Mail only: 2103 Defoors Crossing, Atlanta, 30318. 351-7657.

Pet Sitting by Ann. One friend still recalls the tenderness Ann Bowers showed her beloved dog in the last days of its life. A registered nurse, Bowers will tend pets while you're away, run them to the groomer, and take them out for a walk or a run. She'll also bring in the newspaper and mail, water the plants, and alternate the lights. Insured and bonded. Service area principally intown and northern suburbs. By appointment. Mail only: 568 Park Dr., Atlanta, 30306. 897-1820.

PHOTOGRAPHY

Covering both stills and videos, these folks make event and wedding photography a specialty. A few do specialized photography.

PORTRAIT

John and Mary Photographers. John and Mary Beavers do weddings (about fifty to sixty yearly) and portraits. Mary enjoys photographing babies and mothers. They are happy to network with video people to arrange videos for weddings as well. By appointment only. 393-8355.

Hatfield Image Maker (HIM). For many years, Warren Hatfield has done portraits and events (a specialty) for major Atlanta firms and foundations. He is also a well-known portrait and wedding photographer. By appointment only. Mail only: 3140 Rockingham Dr., Atlanta, 30327. 355-0498.

VIDEO

Custom Video Productions. Robert Gupton turns old home movies into videos by transferring them—whether 8 mm, 16 mm, slides, or prints—onto VCR cassettes. Film may be done with or without sound. 1826 Meadowood Dr., Marietta. 971-8013.

L–T Video Productions. Larry Troutman has more than seventeen years' experience in filming videos for parties, weddings, and sporting events. His transfer service repackages old home movies and slides into a videotape—a great gift idea. He also films home fur-

nishing inventories for insurance purposes as well as the increasingly popular video wills. Mail only: 2916 Hillwood Dr., Lawrenceville, 30244. 921-4994.

The Video Editor. Want to cut what you don't like from your home videos or rearrange the sequence of events on tape? Video Editor's editing suites are available at an hourly rental rate. If you can operate your camera, you can do your own editing, and a technician will show you how. 5975 Roswell Rd., Hammond Springs Shopping Center, Sandy Springs. 256-4108.

POOL SERVICES

In Atlanta we enjoy our pools for a greater portion of the year than do folks in many other parts of the country. But special requirements in pool construction and maintenance go with our climate, soil, and ordinances. Here are some people who can keep you out of the deep end.

Artistic Pools. A well-regarded firm with a lengthy track record for award-winning design, Artistic specializes in design and construction, repair, and maintenance. Artistic's **Pool and Patio Shop** has an extensive accessories inventory. 3884 N. Peachtree Rd., Chamblee. 458-9177.

Atlas Pools & Spas. Everything from vinyl-lined pools to custom-built gunnite pools, spas, and decks. People who know about pools usually name Atlas when asked for a recommendation. Maintenance programs available. 6100 Peachtree Industrial Blvd., Doraville. 451-3700.

Masterpiece Pools. DB-2000 Construction does all kinds of design and construction projects for both commercial and residential clients. Its pools division designs and builds not only water-

scapes and pools but also companion amenities (lighting, decks, and exterior structures). Robert and Terry Colwell, uncle and nephew, combine extensive experience in construction and water projects. The firm's client list includes a number of well-known Atlanta residents. 5025 Winters Chapel Rd., Norcross. 393-9655.

Peach State Inc. David Martin's company does everything for your pool except build it, including installing spas and wooden decks. The firm repairs both vinyl and concrete pools, replaces tiles, and repairs or replaces pumps, heaters, and assorted pool equipment. Pool renovation and monthly or weekly maintenance service are the focuses. The retail shop offers one of the most extensive pool accessory lines in the area. 325 S. Atlanta St., Roswell. 998-0062.

RECYCLING

Community Recycling. An all volunteer program, Community Recycling provides recycling for paper, newspaper, magazines, colored glass, aluminum, corrugated cardboard and steel cans. Located in Little Five Points, behind Sevenanda, Community Recycling has also set up a bulletin board

with recycling information. 1111 Euclid Ave. 681-2831.

International Farmer's Market. Recycling bins inside for newspaper, glass, and aluminum. 5193 Peachtree Industrial Blvd., Chamblee.

Kroger and *Publix*. These supermarkets recycle plastic bags, plastic milk jugs, and two-liter plastic bottles at all locations, and at some, brown paper bags and styrofoam food containers as well.

REI-Recreational Equipment Inc. Behind their store, REI provides a recycling center for everything but plastic. 1800 NE Expressway, Brookhaven. 633-6508.

Southern Recycling. If you've been frustrated by the city's limited recycling pickups, Southern Recycling can solve your problems. They offer three programs, one for businesses and two for residential areas, including apartments. For $8 a month, anyone without city services (pickup) can receive weekly pickup of aluminum, tin, steel, plastics one through six, glass, newspapers, junk mail, magazines, office paper, corrugated cardboard, and chip board. The supplemental program picks up everything listed above that the city doesn't every two weeks for $5 a month. There is a one time $5 fee for the mesh bags used for pickup. 50% of the profits are donated to local charities. Call 351-5155 for details.

SHOPPING SERVICES

Many of us swear we're "born to shop," but for those who hate it, here are some people to call.

A *Friend of the Family*. This firm will do all kinds of shopping—for personal items, groceries, you name it. Just let A Friend know what you need. 895 Mt. Vernon Hwy., Sandy Springs. 255-2848.

Phipps at Your Service. A hostess will shop, wrap, and ship gifts without charge—no joke! You call or fax what to get, who it's for, and what the card should say. There's no minimum, and no tipping. Is this too good to believe, or what? 3500 Peachtree Rd., Buckhead, Concierge Center, Phipps Plaza, Buckhead. 262-0992.

SPORTS EQUIPMENT REPAIR

Given the importance of sports in this town, especially participation sports, getting the equipment fixed is as crucial to a happy life in Atlanta as a good day at the Steeplechase.

Bicycle South. Repair of all brands of bicycles. Custom frame work. 2098 N. Decatur Rd., at Clairmont Rd., Decatur. 636-4444; Bicycle South Gwinnett. 3500 Gwinnett Place Dr., Duluth. 623-6014.

Cycleworks. Repair of all kinds of bicycles. 1570 Holcomb Bridge Rd., Roswell. 993-2626; 3455 Peachtree Ind. Blvd., Duluth. 476-4945.

Golf Repair North. Repair of antique and modern woods, irons, and putters. 20 N. Main St., Alpharetta. 475-7717.

TRAVEL SERVICES

We all know good travel agents, and we can't begin to list all the ones we know or that our friends know. The folks listed here are travel planners who arrange special trips, or provide auxiliary service assistance.

Atlanta Luggage Repair. Even women' purses come under their purview. But generally, this is the place to repair luggage, briefcases, garment bags, totes—that kind of stuff. 5207 Buford Hwy., Doraville. 457-5312.

Travel Opportunities. Take short trips with your current and future friends. The Cobb County Parks, Recreation, and Cultural Affairs Department offers half-day trips and excursions. Urban explorers will enjoy outings such as a day's visit to Bulloch Hall in Roswell, a mountain living tour of LaPrade's (a mountain fishing camp), two days at Biltmore Estate (the Vanderbilt home in Asheville, North Carolina), or Christmas in Williamsburg, Virginia. A small charge is levied for non–Cobb County residents. Some two dozen trips are planned in any quarter of the year, and may cost anywhere from $1 up. 1792 County Farm Rd., Marietta. 528-8818.

Wills International Travel Service. Take China. Carolyn Lee Wills loves to, and she makes exotic vacations simple, easy to enjoy, and affordable. After 25 years with Eastern Airlines, Wills specializes in organizing trips to China for small Atlanta groups. After eight visits through the years, she has made all the right contacts, and will take the uncertainty out of your visit to the land of the Forbidden City. **Ixtapan Spa Dream** is another Wills specialty. Why pay over $1,000 a day to unwind at some très chic Western resort when, for less than that, you can stay for an entire week in this Mexican mountain setting? It's located just 65 miles southwest of Mexico City in a flower-filled environment blessed by an eternal springtime climate. 1447 Peachtree St., Ste. 1009, Midtown. 885-1050.

VIDEO RENTAL

Everyone knows about Blockbuster Video, but there are specialty video stores scattered around the city that offer something a little different.

Entertainment ToNite. Entertainment ToNite's specialty feature is their 2,000-3,000 laser disc selection. Although laser discs have never become as mainstream as video tape, they are far superior in picture quality. However, Entertainment ToNite has only one laser disc player for rent. Their "5 movies for 5 days for $5" is a popular video rental rate. 2088 N. Decatur Rd., Decatur. 633-1008.

Movies Worth Seeing. Dedicated to film buffs seeking those hard-to-find and unusual movie titles. Movies Worth Seeing carries an unparalleled selection of foreign, classic, cult, silent, independent, art, documentary, and experimental films. Their New Release section contains hundreds of exceptional titles. Guaranteed to have movies you've never heard of, Movies Worth Seeing also offers a selection of audio books and will assist in placing special video orders. 1409 North Highland Ave. NE, Morningside. 892-1802.

Versatile Video. In addition to their 14,000 movie title collection, Versatile Video rents video games, computer software, audio books, camcorders, VCRs, and TVs. Other services include VCR repair and transferring tapes to work in foreign video players. Established in 1981, Versatile Video is Atlanta's oldest video store. 5575 Chamblee-Dunwoody Rd., Dunwoody. 393-8838.

CHAPTER 8

Sports & Recreation

Looking for some fun and friendly competition? Or perhaps you prefer to watch others compete? Either way, Atlanta can keep you busy with its professional, collegiate, and amateur sporting events, as well as a variety of recreational activities.

The Atlanta Braves, known as "America's Team," whip the city into a baseball frenzy every summer. If you prefer touchdowns to home runs, the Georgia Dome is the place to be, as the home of the Atlanta Falcons. Hockey fans follow the Knights, while the Hawks rack up the hoops at the Omni. But don't forget to cheer on your favorite college teams. While records vary every season, Georgia Tech, Georgia State, and the University of Georgia regularly rank nationally in several sports programs.

But suppose you are interested in participating yourself in all this activity. No matter what your chosen recreation might be, you can find it in this guide and do it in Atlanta. So fish, bowl, rock climb, ice skate, hike, camp, checkmate your chess partner—and have fun!

METRO AREA DEPARTMENTS OF PARKS AND RECREATION

CITIES		COUNTIES	
Alpharetta	442-0105	Cherokee	479-1953
Atlanta	817-6788	Clayton	477-3766
Decatur	377-0494	Cobb	528-8800
Douglasville	920-3008	DeKalb	371-2631
East Point	765-1080	Douglas	920-7129
Hapeville	669-2136	Fayette	461-9714
Marietta	528-0615	Fulton	730-6200
Roswell	641-3766	Gwinnett	822-8840
Smyrna	431-2842	Henry	954-2031
		Rockdale	785-5922
State of Georgia	**656-3530**		

ARCHERY

Buckskin Archery. This equipment and service shop has a 4,000-square-foot, five-star range that's approved by the national Field Archery Association. The range also serves as a base for archery clubs, and some organizations are open to children ages seven to seventeen. Call Buckskin for club information in your area. 2396 Cobb Pkwy. (I-75 north to Exit 116—Barrett Pkwy.), Kennesaw. 425-2697.

BASEBALL & SOFTBALL

AMATEUR

Cherokee Batting Range. Hone your skills in five baseball and two softball batting cages, or on practice pitching ranges. Open daily *(see chapter 5)*. 711 Bascomb Commercial Parkway, North Bell's Ferry Rd., Woodstock. 591-4778.

McDivot's Driving Range. Nine stations offer a choice of pitching speeds, and players have unlimited "outfield" to swing for at this center, open daily. A golf driving range is also on site. 1360 Upper Hembree Rd., Roswell. 740-1674.

Softball Country Club. Established in 1985, this unusual facility has just undergone a change in ownership, which has brought an infusion of money for renovation and improvement. More of the same is planned. Right now, the clubhouse has a sports bar atmosphere with a big-screen TV, beer on tap, and indoor spectator seating. Softball leagues for both men and women, as well as coed leagues, play tournaments every weekend, starting in late February. Tournaments sometimes benefit specific charities. Ask to be included on the mailing list. 3500 N. Decatur Rd., Scottsdale. 299-3588.

COLLEGIATE

Georgia Institute of Technology. Ranked number one in the nation in the 1994 preseason, **Yellow Jackets** baseball is a pretty good bargain with season tickets ranging in price from $40 to $55. A Senior Citizen discount allows for a $25 season ticket, while general daily admission is just $3 for adults. Tech has earned nine straight trips to the NCAA Baseball Tournament and the Yellow Jackets alternate day games with quite a few 7 P.M. starts under the lights at Chandler Baseball Stadium on campus. Mail only: Georgia Tech Athletic Association Ticket Office, Atlanta, 30332-0455. 894-5447

Georgia State University. Baseball started again in 1992 after a six-year hiatus. University Plaza, Downtown. 651-2071 (Sports Information).

University of Georgia. Winners of both the 1987 and the 1990 College World Series, the baseball **Bulldogs** play at Foley Field, one of the top ten collegiate facilities in the country. Tickets are nominally priced. Some of these kids could wind up in professional baseball, and you will have seen them back when. P.O. Box 1472, Athens, 30613. 706-542-1231.

PROFESSIONAL

Atlanta Braves. What can we say? Winning three straight division championships have made the Braves the most popular attraction in town. Buy your tickets early! 521 Capitol Ave., Downtown. 577-9100 (tickets), or through TicketMaster.

BASKETBALL

COLLEGIATE

Georgia Institute of Technology. Season tickets are issued on a priority giving system through the Alexander-Tharpe Fund (894-5427) and are difficult to come by because this is the darling college team of the Atlanta area. The **Yellow Jackets**, under coach Bobby Cremins, have achieved a national reputation for success and have earned invitations to eleven straight post-season Tournaments. If you are interested in a particular game, call the Georgia Tech Ticket Office to see if tickets have been returned for resale. The games are held in Alexander Memorial Coliseum, better known as "The Thrillerdome" on the Georgia Tech campus. The **Lady Jackets** women's basketball team has also established a level of success, having won the NWIT national title in 1992, hosting the women's Final Four in 1993, and earning a trip to the NCAA Tournament that year as well. Tickets are available for home games at Alexander Memorial Coliseum by contacting the Georgia Tech Ticket Office, Atlanta, 30332-0455 (894-5447).

Georgia State University. Someone cracked that it would be a cold day in perdition before the GSU **Panthers** would get into the NCAA tournament. Well, they did it in 1991, and Georgia State's interim president, Sherman Day, declared a "snow day" in the middle of spring to celebrate. The Panthers are making their move, and it should be great fun to watch this ever-improving team on the march. The **Lady Panthers** make their mark in women's basketball as well. GSU Sports Arena, Decatur & Collins Sts., Downtown. 651-2071 (Sports Information).

University of Georgia. The basketball **Bulldogs**, who number NBA All-Star Dominique Wilkins among their alumni, have recently been in the NCAA tournament and were the 1990 SEC champions. They count four of their alumni among the NBA's first-round draft players. Coach Hugh Durham, homing in on his 500th win, has taken two teams to the Final Four, his 1972 FSU team and his 1983 Georgia team. Many big games are sold out. Not outdone by their male counterparts, the **Lady Bulldogs** are one of the country's most successful women's basketball teams. They've made three trips to the women's Final Four and claim two recent gold medal Olympians. The University of Georgia Coliseum, with a capacity of over 11,000, is the home court for both teams. P.O. Box 1472, Athens, 30513. 706-542-1231.

PROFESSIONAL

Atlanta Hawks. The Hawks are sparked by the grace and spirit of many players, including the brilliant play of Mookie Blaylock, Ken Willis, and recently acquired Danny Manning. Play is at the Omni Coliseum, 100 Techwood Dr., Downtown. Offices are at 1 CNN Center, South Tower, Ste. 405, Downtown. 827-3800; Tickets: 827-DUNK.

BICYCLING

Cerrato Bicycle Company. Rides every Sunday and Thursday cover 28 to 36 miles, all within the city limits. Some participants complete part of a ride— others, the whole enchilada. Ride at your pleasure and leisure. Cyclists range from beginner to experienced. The trips leave from a point across the street from the Brookhaven MARTA Station, Peachtree Rd. at Dresden Dr., Brookhaven. 7 Jones St., Norcross. 417-1821.

Cycle South. During daylight savings time, groups ride on Monday and Tuesday evenings. Monday's 25-mile road ride, with up to 25 riders, includes many beginners. Tuesday's ride is a ten-mile trail ride, and all cyclists are experienced riders who love the rugged terrain. 7210 Hwy. 85, Riverdale. 991-6642.

Dick Lane Velodrome. From late April through October, cyclists compete at this outdoor facility in Grand Prix Series races, which include pursuit races, unknown distance runs, two-person runs, and sprint races. The oval velodrome offers banked curves similar to those of an auto-racing track. This track measures one-fifth of a mile and is unique to Georgia. Before it opened in 1974, a group of local cyclists tapped Dick Lane, then director of parks for East Point, to design bicycle riding trails. Site of the 1984 U.S. Olympic trials; a nominal entrance fee is charged. 1889 Lexington Ave., Sumner Park, East Point. 765-1085.

Free Flite Bicycles. The **Wild, Wild West Ride** is a 65-mile trek that goes north one Sunday each month. The distance makes it advisable for experienced riders only. For others, the first- and third-Saturday rides of 35 miles offer shorter options for both beginners and experts. On Thursday evenings during the summer, a 35-mile ride at a 24-mile-an-hour pace interests experienced riders. 2800 Canton Rd., Marietta. 422-5237.

Georgia Bicycle Motocross (BMX) Association. This group is part of the national Bicycle League. Participants may enter races throughout the year; points earned in one state transfer to competitions held in another, as this is a national sport. Riders range in age from three years to adult; each race is categorized accordingly. Tracks are in Albany, Powder Springs, Newnan, and Peachtree City. Ruth Asci, contact. Mail only: 2153 Elder Mill Rd., Senoia, 30276. 706-599-8420.

REI-Recreational Equipment Inc. Just inside the entrance is a posting board with information about outdoor activities, including bicycling groups. 1800 NE Expressway Access Rd., between Exits 31 and 32, I-85, Brookhaven. 633-6508.

Roswell Bicycles. One Sunday a month, during winter and fall, thirty- and fifty-mile rides head through north Fulton and Cherokee counties and attract racer types—though intermediates also participate. A thirteen-mile ride for beginners rolls out on Sundays all year long, and during daylight savings time, thirty-mile rides pedal out two evenings a week. Check out the mountain trail riding. 670 Houze Way, Roswell. 642-4057.

Skate Escape Bike Shop. Renting bicycles, roller skates, and rollerblades, Skate Escape is located across from Piedmont Park, where you can put your rented two-wheeler to work. This full-service bicycle shop, open since the 1970s, rents cruiser and ten-speed bicycles, and sells both all-terrain and road bicycles. 1086 Piedmont Ave., Midtown. 892-1292.

Southern Bicycle League. To promote recreational touring, racing, mountain biking, bicycle safety, and commuter bicycling, the league offers several events throughout the year. Regularly scheduled tours with varying degrees of difficulty and length are frequently run at Stone Mountain Park; some are out of state. Formed around 1974, the league has 4,000 members. It publishes **Freewheeling**, a magazine that appears 11 times a year and is available through local bike shops. 1285 Willeo Creek Dr., Roswell, 30077. 594-8350.

Stone Mountain Park. *(See chapter 4).* The park's excellent roads and trails make this the perfect bicycling spot for a family outing. Stone Mountain. Bicycle rentals: 498-5600, ext. 301.

BILLIARDS

Please see the "Billiards and Sports Bars" section of Chapter 2 (Night Life) to find many of Atlanta's finest billiards parlors.

BOATING

Lake Lanier Islands. Lake Lanier Islands is a state-operated resort. Here, visitors may rent fishing boats, ski boats, pontoon boats, houseboats, and party boats. Several marinas offer slip rental and other related services. The season runs from March through mid-November. 6950 Holiday Rd., Lake Lanier Islands, Buford. 932-7255.

Lanier Sailing Academy. This academy rents sail boats in addition to teaching sailing. 8000 Holiday Rd., Lake Lanier Islands, Buford. 945-8810.

BOWLING

Express Lanes. The latest equipment from Brunswick—automatic scoring—has been installed as part of a $1,500,000 renovation. A large, comfortable lounge is insulated from the sounds of the 32 Anvilane synthetic bowling lanes. 1936 Piedmont Cir., Midtown. 874-5703.

Jim Maxey's Bowling and Trophy Shop. This 24-lane facility has state-of-the-art equipment. Maxey is a registered member of the Professional Bowling Association's Hall of Fame. Snack bar and lounge. 5640 Peachtree Ind. Blvd., Chamblee. 458-7050.

Suburban Lanes, Inc. Also a Jim Maxey facility, this 32 lane alley has a fairly extensive game room and Redemption Center. Take advantage of their competitive lane price at $8 per hour or $19.95 for three hours. 22619 North Decatur Rd, Decatur. 373-2514.

BOXING

Don Wade Boxing Training Center. The Knights boxing team, which is based here, is the only international boxing team in the U.S. Wade is working to place metro Atlanta youth in the Olympics. This nonprofit organization presents boxing programs for exercise and self-defense, and views boxing as a deterrent to drug abuse among young people. The center has been operating since 1976. 2350 Ventura Rd., Smyrna. 432-3632.

CAMPING

Lake Lanier Islands. The camping facilities here include more than fifty tent sites and 300 spots on six hookup sites that accommodate forty-foot RVs. 6950 Holiday Rd., Lake Lanier Islands. 932-7270.

REI-Recreational Equipment Inc. REI is a major source for information about camping sites and groups. 1800 NE Expressway Access Rd., between Exits 31 and 32, I-85, Brookhaven. 633-6508.

CANOEING

Evening Float. Every Tuesday evening from April through September, the Chattahoochee Nature Center leads early evening "floats." The relaxing, two-hour excursions offer a great opportunity to enjoy the flora and fauna that make up the river's ecosystem. Basic strokes and safety are taught before the start of each float. Children at least eight years old are welcome with adults. Canoes, paddles, and life jackets are provided. 9135 Willeo Rd., Roswell. 992-2055.

Georgia Canoeing Association. This volunteer group *(see chapter 10)* has acted as a regular booster for the sport for more than 25 years. Every weekend brings more trips the group has organized for all levels of skill. The 1,100 members boast of three or four potential Olympians in the club. A monthly newsletter details the activities and is available at Go With The Flow (4 Elizabeth Way, Roswell; 992-3200) or by calling the association: 2923 Piedmont Dr., Marietta; 421-9729. Also available at REI-Recreational Equipment Inc. 1800 NE Expressway Access Rd., between Exits 31 and 32, I-85, Northeast. 633-6508.

Southeastern Expeditions. This professional team guides rafting, canoeing, and kayaking trips down the Chattooga River in North Georgia and the Ocoee River in East Tennessee. With twenty years' experience, they know how to safely share the thrill of these sports with individuals or groups. Minimum age is ten years old. Reservations required. Tours conducted April through October. 2936-H N. Druid Hills Rd., Northeast. 329-0433.

CAVING

REI-*Recreational Equipment Inc.* Information on caving is posted on a bulletin board just inside the entrance. This is a major networking source for caving organizations, as well as for equipment. 1800 NE Expressway Access Rd., between Exits 31 and 32, I-85, Brookhaven. 633-6508.

CHESS

U.S. *Chess Federation.* A growing "sport" in our city, chess is represented by five chess clubs. Four of them are in the Atlanta area, and all welcome beginners and masters as new members. Tournaments take place almost every month, with major regional tournaments occurring about six times a year. Located in Decatur, Forest Park, Cobb County (two), and Ft. Benning (Columbus), the five clubs are part of the U.S. Chess Federation. You may also see a game or two being played in the upstairs coffee shop, **Cup & Chaucer**, at Oxford Book Store, Peachtree Battle. The Georgia Chess Association has a floating telephone number and address, depending on who is president. U.S. Chess Federation, 186 Rte. 9W, New Windsor, NY, 12553. 914-562-8350.

CRICKET

Atlanta *Cricket Association.* Seven teams play each Sunday, May through October. Fields are located in Smyrna, College Park, and Cedar Shoals. Cricket in Atlanta dates to about 1985, when a group of gentlemen from Commonwealth countries—England, India, Pakistan, Jamaica, the West Indies, and South Africa, among others—decided it was time to introduce cricket to our town. Membership is open, so if you would like to play and don't know how, David Thomas, president of the Georgia Cricket Association, says the members will teach you. Visiting teams from Columbus and Augusta, and from towns as far away as DC and New York, come to play in knockout tournaments. David Thomas, contact. Mail only: 4660 Bush Rd., Duluth, 30136. 263-6460.

CROQUET

Atlanta *Mallet Club.* This organization, associated with the U.S. Croquet Association, represents a sport that's a popular choice with several major Atlanta charities for their fund-raising events. Following the sport's traditional fashion, spectators and participants don their whites for the matches. Atlanta has gone over the moon for croquet, and you'll find folks playing

<td></td></td>

<td></td>

it in backyards and parks, as well as private clubs. Some members of the Atlanta Mallet Club have approached the caliber of tournament play. Membership dues are substantial and include membership in USCA. Pinckney Purcell, contact. Mail only: 2513 Kingscliff Dr., Atlanta, 30345. 939-7829.

EQUESTRIAN

Atlanta Horse Center. Horses are boarded, trained, and conditioned. The facility includes a covered arena, 110' x 210', as well as thirty acres with one-and-a-half miles of trails *(see chapter 9).* 1795 Corn Rd. SE, Smyrna. 434-3731.

Lake Lanier Islands Stables. This year-round facility conducts trail rides from 11 A.M to 3 P.M., Wednesday through Sunday. The rides last between 45 minutes and one hour. Beginners are welcome. Horses are paired with the rider's experience. 6950 Holiday Rd., Lake Lanier Islands. 932-7233.

Sweet Sunshine Equestrian Center. This is an inside center, but if you board your horse here, you'll have access to 200 acres of trails for riding *(see chapter 9).* 14295 Birmingham Hwy., Alpharetta. 343-9807.

Vogt Riding Academy. See chapter 9. 1084 Houston Mill Rd., Northeast. 321-9506.

FENCING

Atlanta Fencers' Club. See chapters 9 and 10. 40 7th St., Midtown. 892-0307.

Fayette Fencing Academy. See chapter 9. 330 N. Fayette Dr., Fayetteville. 461-3809.

FISHING

Whether you use one of the guide services listed below or go angling on your own, you must have a current state fishing license. These are available in many fishing shops and major stores such as K-Mart.

Bill Vanderford's Guide Service. The oldest fishing guide service in the area, Vanderford's shows folks a good time all year long. The service has forty qualified guides. Lane Chesser is a well-regarded member of Vanderford's guide crew and she's also his partner. Bass is the primary interest, and most fishing is done on Lake Lanier. The service provides all equipment and rain and foul weather gear, as well as boats. Vanderford, the owner, is the author of three books on the subject of fishing, the most recent being *Secrets to Fish-*

ing Lake Lanier. He is the outdoor editor for the *Daily News* and *Outdoor Life* magazine. 2224 Pine Point Dr., Lawrenceville. 962-1241.

Chattahoochee Fishing Guide Service.

Gene Lancaster leads fishing trips on Lake Lanier and its tributaries in search of largemouth bass—striped, black, spotted, and white—and crappie. When the water is clear, he runs river trips. Lancaster can arrange loaner tackle, boat rental, and rain gear; he supplies the know-how. P.O. Box 1563, Gainesville, 30503. 706-536-7986.

Chattahoochee River.

Fishing is allowed on a wide stretch of the river, which is designated a trout stream—though bream, catfish, and other species also abound in its waters. Fishing is permitted year-round from the Roswell Road Bridge at Hwy. 9, downstream to the I-285 West Bridge. North of the Roswell Road Bridge—up to Buford Dam—fishing is permitted from the last Saturday of March through October 31. On the part of the river between Hwy. 141 and Hwy. 20, only artificial lures may be used. 399-8070.

Georgia Department of Natural Resources, Game and Fish Division.

Anglers have a haven in the North Georgia area, where excellent bass, trout, and other types of fish are available. One of the best sources for complete fishing information is their pamphlet on Georgia's sport fishing regulations and sites. 2070 US Hwy. 378, Social Circle, 30279. 918-6400.

Lake Lanier Islands.

This state park offers excellent fishing for large- and small-mouth bass, stripper bass—some have weighed up to fifty pounds—and a variety of other species. Many anglers believe that winter is the best season for catching the "big ones." 6950 Holiday Rd., Lake Lanier Islands. 932-7255.

FOOTBALL

COLLEGIATE

Georgia Institute of Technology.

The Yellow Jackets took the town by storm in 1990 when they brought home the national championship. Single-game seats and season tickets go for substantial prices. Georgia Tech Ticket Office, Atlanta, 30332-0455. 894-5447.

University of Georgia.

The Bulldogs have won ten SEC championships and been invited to thirty bowls representing sixteen different contests. They are the fifth most bowl-active college football team in the country. Two Heisman Trophy winners have come from this team: Frank Sinkwich in 1942 and Hershel Walker in 1982. The Bulldogs don't lack for audience support, so it's hard to get tickets for most of the big games. Sanford Stadium, renovated and expanded to hold over 86,000 fans, is the fourth-largest on-campus facility in the country. P.O. Box 1472, Athens, 30613. 706-542-1231.

PROFESSIONAL

Atlanta Falcons. Head Coach June Jones hopes to take Falcons football straight from the Georgia Dome to the NFL playoffs—again. During the six weeks of training camp (late July through August), fans are welcome at the training center to watch the team run drills. Spectators may occupy field bleacher seats for these practices. After regular season play begins, the training center is closed to the public. Tickets go on sale in July. Falcon Inn and Conference Center, I-85 and Suwanee Rd., Suwanee. 945-1111; Tickets: 950 E. Paces Ferry Rd., Buckhead. 261-5400.

GOLF

COURSES

Bobby Jones Golf Course. Perhaps the most famous of the city's public courses is the one named for golf great Bobby Jones, a native of Atlanta. This eighteen-hole championship course features varied terrain, creeks, and tree-lined fairways, and it's close to downtown. Designed and built in 1932, it occupies a portion of the site of the Battle of Peachtree Creek. The American Golf Corporation operates the city's four eighteen-hole courses under a leasing arrangement. Snack bar; open daily. 384 Woodward Way, Atlanta Memorial Park, Northwest. 355-1009. For reservations, 355-1833.

Champions Club of Atlanta. An eighteen-hole, par-72 course designed by Steve Melnyk and D. J. DeVictor, it has a practice driving range, putting green, and chipping area. Restaurant and lounge facilities. Open daily, except Christmas. 15135 Hopewell Rd., Alpharetta. 343-9700.

Cross Creek Country Club. An eighteen-hole executive course (par 54) with a public dining facility, Cross Creek is a condominium-affiliated course. The all-day fee allows golfers to stay until the daylight goes. Snack bar and lounge. Closed Mondays. 1221 Cross Creek Pkwy., Northwest. 352-5612.

Eagle Watch Golf Club. This eighteen-hole, par-72 course designed by Arnold Palmer is known for its wide fairways and water on twelve holes. The pro shop was voted one of the top 100 in America by *Golf Shop Operations* magazine, a publication of *Golf Digest.* Restaurant; closed Mondays. 3055 Eagle Watch Dr., Woodstock. 591-1000.

Fox Creek Executive Golf Range. John LaFoys designed this eighteen-hole, par-61 course (no par five holes). The driving range has both matte and grass tees, and there are practice putting greens and chipping areas. Open every day except Christmas. Snack bar. 1501 Windy Hill Rd., Smyrna. 435-1000.

Lake Lanier Islands Golf Club. This resort's eighteen-hole, par-72 course was built in 1989. Designed by Joe Lee, it has thirteen holes over water and offers accuracy off the tee. It's challenging from the championship tee, but easy for the average golfer from the regular tees. Take I-85 north to I-985 to Exit 2 (Friendship Road), and follow the signs for four miles. Open daily. 7000 Holiday Rd., Lake Lanier Islands. 945-8787.

Lake Spivey Golf Club. A PGA 27-hole golf course, with each nine having a par 36 rating, it has a practice driving range. Snack bar and lounge. Open daily except Christmas. 8255 Club House Way, Jonesboro. 477-9836.

The Links Golf Club. A challenging, par-seventy, Scottish–style course designed by Terry Anton and Jack Gaudion, the Links is privately owned but open to the public. "Waterloo" is the par-four, number thirteen hole, with a 420-yard link over water. The course also offers a lighted driving range, a putting green, and a **Wee Links** area, where children have priority on all tee times during the summer months—this unique nine-hole golf course was built especially for golfers ages six to sixteen. Memberships available. Open daily. GA Hwy. 54, Jonesboro. 461-5100.

> The Heisman trophy is named for Johann Wilhelm Heisman, a Pennsylvanian who was Georgia Tech's innovative football coach from 1904 to 1919. Heisman's 1917 team won the national championship, and his 222-0 win over Cumberland the previous year stands as the highest recorded score in college football.

Orchard Hills Golf Club. One of the area's few Scottish-style courses, with rolling hills and few trees, Orchard Hills provides a different golfing experience. Designed by Don Cottle, Jr., it is a par-72 course. Restaurant and snack bar; open daily except Christmas. 600 E. Hwy. 16, Newnan, Exit 8 on I-85 South. Atlanta telephone: 880-9414.

Southerness Golf Club. This course rests in a beautiful setting by the South River, on an old cotton plantation built about 1822. The original plantation house still stands at the club gates. Hand-mowed, bent-grass greens, plus greens containing seven other grasses, make this course stand out from others open to the public. Only sixteen sand bunkers, but several grass ones. Snack bar and lounge; open daily except Christmas. 4871 Flat Bridge Rd., Stockbridge. 808-6000.

Stone Mountain Park Golf Course. *(See chapter 5.)* These two eighteen-hole courses designed by Robert Trent Jones opened in the late 1960s and have grown in popularity with each passing season. *Golf Digest* annually rates this course among the top 75 public courses in the country. Open daily except Christmas. Stone Mountain. 498-5717.

Stouffer Pineisle Resort. The resort's eighteen-hole, par-72 course opened in 1974. Designed by (Gary) Player, Kirby, & Associates, it sits on an island surrounded by 38,000-acre Lake Lanier. With eight holes on the border of the island, it offers splendid views on a very hilly and winding course. Take I-85 north to Exit 45 (I-985/Lake Lanier Pkwy.) and follow the signs. Open daily. 9000 Holiday Rd., Lake Lanier Islands. 945-8921.

Sugar Creek Golf Course. This eighteen-hole course hosts many local tournaments. A driving range and putting green are on the site. You may carry your bag on this course, and reservations are required on the weekends only. Club rentals. 2706 Bouldercrest Rd., Southeast. 241-7671.

PRACTICE RANGES / PUTTING GREENS

McDivot's Driving Range. This driving range has seventy lighted tees, twenty of which are covered for all-weather play. **McDivot's Golf Center** teaches both indoors and outdoors. Special lessons are available using videotape to analyze a student's swing as well as how to improve it *(see chapter 9).* A state-of-the-art miniature golf course *(not* the kind with little animals and cartoon characters) is an additional draw. Snack bar. Open 9 A.M. to 10 P.M. daily. 1360 Upper Hembree Rd., Roswell. 740-1415.

SPECIAL PLAY PASSES

American Cancer Society Golf Card. Play approximately sixty golf courses in Georgia for one minimum fee, with proceeds from the card going to the American Cancer Society. Your local society office will have information about this program. P.O. Box 190429, Atlanta, 31119. 816-7800.

Golf Privilege Card. Offered by the American Lung Association–Atlanta, this card is good at one of more than 65 golf courses in Georgia and waives the greens fees, but you do have to rent a cart. It is available for a moderate donation to the American Lung Association–Atlanta, and the price goes down when you purchase five or more cards. Call the Lung Association–Atlanta to check on limitations and restrictions that may apply to the course you choose. 723 Piedmont Ave., Midtown. 872-9653.

FLYING DISC GOLF

Professional Disc Golf Association. Believe it or not, this sport is growing in Atlanta. It is played with all sizes of "Frisbees", or flying discs, which are specially weighted for this unusual game. Atlanta boasts four eighteen-hole disc golf courses. The course looks like a regular golf course—without the manicured greens—and the game is played by similar rules. Players toss the disc into a basket-shaped container instead of hitting a ball into a hole. Some players carry as many as a dozen differently weighted discs. These folks get serious about this game, but they do have fun, and they welcome beginners. The international tournaments are run by the Professional Disc Golf Association, and one takes place in the Atlanta area every year. The four county parks with flying disc golf courses are Redan Park, Lithonia, DeKalb County; Oregon Park, Marietta, Cobb County; Wills Park, Alpharetta, Fulton County; and Chastain Park, City of Atlanta. **Identified Flying Objects** is the source for all appropriate paraphernalia. 1164 Euclid Ave., Little Five Points. 524-4628.

GYMNASTICS

University of Georgia. The women's team is consistently rated as one of the top two or three teams in the country. It won national titles in 1987, 1989, and 1993. A nominal admission is charged to watch their meets in the Georgia Coliseum. P.O. Box 1231, Athens, 30613. 706-542-1231.

HANDBALL

Atlanta Team Handball Association. This sport has recently begun to receive recognition in Atlanta because of the fervor surrounding the Olympics. Led by former Olympian (1972, Munich) and Olympic coach (1976, Montreal) Dennis Berkholtz, the Atlanta Academy of Team Handball is open to interested persons of all ages. The managers of the U.S. Olympic Training Team for both men and women have moved to Atlanta. Contact Dennis Berkholtz. No permanent address has yet been established. 350-8930.

HIKING & BACKPACKING

Most hikers trek to one of two or three locations in North Georgia and North Carolina, such as the Cohutta Wilderness Area, Rabun Gap, and Neal's Gap on the Appalachian Trail. For a full description of the park areas listed below, see Chapter 5 (City Sights).

Chattahoochee River National Recreation Area. Several units are known for dense woods, steep bluffs, rock outcroppings, and varied terrain where beaver, muskrat, mink, weasel, raccoon, and assorted resident birds gather. The most popular areas include **Medlock Bridge**, **Jones Bridge**,

Island Ford, Vickery Creek, Gold Branch, Johnson Ferry, Cochran Shoals, Sope Creek, and **Palisades East and West.** Most of the areas lie along I-75, near I-285 north to Roswell. The National Park Service has full information on each spot and can send maps and details. 1978 Island Ford Pkwy., Dunwoody, 30350. 399-8070.

High Country Hikes. One of High Country's most popular hikes is the one-day trip that begins in Brasstown Bald, at the mouth of the Chattahoochee River. A naturalist accompanies the group to enrich the experience by pointing out interesting flora and other natural phenomena. 4400 Ashford-Dunwoody Rd., Perimeter Mall, Dunwoody. 391-9657.

Panola Mountain State Conservation Park. Guided three-mile hikes every Saturday and Sunday, from Memorial Day through Labor Day, begin at 10 A.M. During the other months, the hikes begin at 2 P.M. A Georgia forest ranger guides the hike, which is preceded by a presentation describing the experience. This trail is open only to guided tours. Three shorter self-guided trails provide alternatives to the mountain hike. Small state park parking fee. 2600 Hwy. 155, Stockbridge. 389-7801.

REI-Recreational Equipment Inc. Networking among the hiking and backpacking organizations is made easy at REI, where a posting board contains information on local groups. 1800 NE Expressway Access Rd., between Exits 31 and 32, I-85, Brookhaven. 633-6508.

Sweetwater Creek State Conservation Park. Three-mile and six-mile loops, plus a three-mile history trail glide easily through a lovely park. But these are more hikes than walks, so be prepared with the proper footwear. Small parking fee. Open daily. Mt. Vernon Rd., Lithia Springs. 732-5871.

KAYAKING

Go With the Flow Sports. From May to September, Go With The Flow offers lessons and trips to nearby rivers. Weekend courses that include a dry session are offered monthly, and equipment can be supplied. Sea and touring kayaking, done in seaworthy touring kayaks on large lakes or rivers, are also taught, but for these you must have your own gear. Go With The Flow, 4 Elizabeth Way, Roswell. 992-3200.

REI-Recreational Equipment Inc. This sports outfitter is also an excellent source of information on whitewater activities. 1800 NE Expressway Access Rd., between Exits 31 and 32, I-85, Brookhaven. 633-6508.

LACROSSE

Atlanta Lacrosse Club. Always seeking new members, the club is most interested in experienced players, but is open to those who want to learn the game. Atlantans play lacrosse in the spring, usually from late February through June, with tournament play in October. The Atlanta club is a member of the Southeast Lacrosse League.

Mail only: 111 Linkside Ct., Woodstock 30188. 926-6920 (adults); 587-6112 (youth).

MARTIAL ARTS

Choi Kwang-Do. *(See chapter 9.)* Headquarters: 4327 Wade Green Road, Ken-nesaw. 795-0010.

Joe Corley American Karate Studios. *(See chapter 9.)* Main location: 11060 Alpharetta Hwy., Roswell. 642-5500.

MOTOR SPORTS

Atlanta Motor Speedway. Stock car racing on the NASCAR circuit attracts about 122,000 to the races in March and November. The speedway has a high-banked oval, asphalt track. With beautifully landscaped grounds, it offers grandstands, fifty acres of infield for tailgating and viewing, and corporate suites. Barbecuing on enclosed fires is permitted. The speedway's total area exceeds 500 acres. 1500 Hwy. 41, Hampton. 946-4211.

Malibu Grand Prix. This is a race track on which you can test your skills and improve them, or even learn how to race. Racing leagues are planned for all four seasons. *(See chapter 5.)* 5400 Brook Hollow Pkwy., I-85 between Jimmy Carter Blvd. and Indian Trail, Norcross. 416-7630.

Quarter Midget Racing. Boys and girls ages five to fifteen drive race cars that are scaled down to one-quarter the size of full midget race cars. Races are held every two weeks between April and October. Members of the

Metro Atlanta Quarter Midgets of America take part in various races and exhibitions, including races against other clubs from areas such as Orlando and Huntsville. They also participate in pre-race shows at NASCAR events. These cars, which are not home-built or go-carts, can reach speeds of up to thirty miles an hour. Safety rules prevail, and the association is proud of its record. The few accidents that do happen cause only a few bruises and scratches. For information, contact the Metro Atlanta Quarter Midget Racing Association, P.O. Box 48, Powder Springs, 30078. Track location: 1773 County Farm Rd., Marietta. 528-2458.

Road Atlanta. Stars race at this major motor sports facility. Real stars. Like Paul Newman. Located in scenic natural surroundings, Road Atlanta twists and turns through beautiful mountain landscapes. Top racing stars participate in about thirty racing events annually. 5300 Winder Highway, I-85 North at Hwy. 53, Braselton. 881-8233.

RACQUETBALL

Georgia State Racquetball Association. A popular Atlanta sport, racquetball attracts about 800 men and women to this association. Courts are usually located in commercial or private clubs, as well as in the YMCAs around town. RA-sanctioned matches are held year-round for all levels of play. Association members meet during the state championships. Contact Mike Brooks, president. P.O. Box 72574 Marietta, 30007. 988-9130.

RAFTING

Equipment rental for whitewater rafting is available at several locations around the metro area, but many change by the season. Two regulars seem to stick around and have rafts available generally from May through October. If you're a winter bunny, they may make arrangements for an off-season rental. During the regular season, a shuttle is available, for a fee, to take you back to your car at the end of your run at I-75 and Hwy. 41.

Atlanta Rent-A-Raft. 1337 Powers Ferry Rd., Marietta. 952-2824.

Chattahoochee Outdoor Center. 1990 Island Ford Pkwy., Dunwoody. 395-6851.

REI-Recreational Equipment Inc. Check out the groups that conduct rafting expeditions through the information available at this sports outfitter. 1800 NE Expressway Access Rd., between Exits 31 and 32, I-85, Brookhaven. 633-6508.

Whitewater Rafting. Several groups lead guided tours of the Oconee river. To learn more about this sport, contact **High Country Outfitters**. Check for early season discounts and special rates for groups of ten or more. 4400 Ashford-Dun-woody Rd., Perimeter Mall, Dunwoody. 391-9657.

Wildwater Rafting. Seasoned, trained professionals conduct guided tours down the **Ocoee** (Tennessee), the **Chatooga** (Georgia and South Carolina border), and the **Nantahala** (North Carolina) **Rivers**. Put-in locations for all three rivers are within a two-and-a-half-hour drive from Atlanta. The company also rents kayaks for unguided trips. In business since 1971, this outfitter really knows the rapids. P.O. Box 100, Long Creek, S.C., 29658. 800-451-9972.

ROCK CLIMBING

High Country Outfitters. North Georgia's **Mount Yonah** and nearby **Sandrock**, in Alabama, offer excellent rock climbing. Clinics held on Wednesday evenings precede weekends at one of the above sites. Beginners are welcome. A qualified guide leads the expeditions. 4400 Ashford-Dunwoody Rd., Perimeter Mall, Dunwoody. 391-9657.

REI-Recreational Equipment Inc. Again, REI is one of Atlanta's best sources for information about climbing, as well as equipment. 1800 NE Expressway Access Rd., between Exits 31 and 32, I-85, Brookhaven. 633-6508.

ROWING

Atlanta Rowing Club Boathouse. Protecting the river while enjoying its use is one of the goals of the Atlanta Rowing Club, established in 1974. Its 165 members are devoted to promoting the sport, and they sponsor regat- tas as well as hold their own events. Dick Alcock is president. The boat house is on Azalea Drive, one-half mile south of Hwy. 9, 500 Azalea Dr., Roswell. 993-1879.

RUGBY

Five teams compete in the Atlanta area. Clubs are open to new members, whether experienced in rugby or not. There's also a women's team, the **Harlequins**. Call High Country Outfitters for information. 4400 Ashford-Dunwoody Rd., Perimeter Mall, Dunwoody. 391-9657.

RUNNING & WALKING

Atlanta has many 5K and 10K races in addition to a marathon—we can't begin to discuss all the running competitions that confront the serious runner. Most benefit charities, and all travel interesting routes. Please see chapter 4 for some of the bigger running events.

Atlanta Track Club. This nonprofit organization is dedicated to promoting health and fitness through road racing, cross country, and track in a spirit of fun and competition for all ages. This is one of the largest running clubs in the country, and it stages a variety of events each year, all open to the public. **Wingfoot**, the club's monthly magazine, contains articles of interest for runners. 3097 E. Shadowlawn Ave., Buckhead. 231-9064.

Chattahoochee River National Recreational Area. Cochran Fitness Trail
winds for three miles through a beautiful wooded area that runs parallel to the river. It's perfect for running, walking, or cycling. Entrances are on both New Northside Drive and Columns Drive, Sandy Springs. Several other areas in the vast national park are for running, walking, or hiking. 1978 Island Ford Pkwy., Dunwoody, 30350. 394-8324; 399-8070.

Georgia Walkers. Affiliated with the
Texas-based American Volkssports Association (founded in Germany about 1980), this group promotes walking, as well as swimming and bicycling. They hold 10K noncompetitive walks in which participants set their own pace. Walks start between 8 A.M. and 1 P.M., and finish between 4 and 5 P.M. Participants receive event and record books in order to monitor their individual progress. One activity, the **Volksmarch**, is a walk through a scenic or historic area over a premarked route that allows participants to travel at their own pace. This is an excellent family activity. Walks are planned throughout the year in the metro area, as well as in the North Georgia mountains. Nominal annual dues. Duncan Brantley, president. Mail only: 6524 Revena Dr., Morrow, 30260. 961-0109.

Hammond Park. This handsome,
wooded half-mile walking path is level and perfect for anyone who prefers walking in a parklike atmosphere to walking in a neighborhood. 705 Hammond Dr., Sandy Springs. 303-6180.

Shopping Center Walking. We're
surprised to learn this doesn't go on everywhere else in the country, but folks in other regions are amazed that many Atlantans avoid inclement weather by walking in the safety and security of the suburban shopping mall, especially during early morning hours. Lenox Square, for example, fairly hums with the rhythm of folks who are out there walking before the shoppers show up. Check with your closest area mall to learn what time it opens for this kind of activity.

Stone Mountain Park. Two loop
roads of five and eight miles encircle this massive rock, offering challenges for runners and walkers. The adventurous may charge up the steep hill on the eight-mile trail, but the view at the top is enough to make you want to stop and enjoy. Stone Mountain. 498-5600.

SAILING

Lanier Sailing Academy. See chapter 9 for information on sailing courses
taught at the school. The academy also rents sailboats, varying in size from fourteen-foot Sunfish to 32-foot cruisers, equipped, if you wish, with a captain for the day. Open daily, but sailing is postponed when storm warnings are in effect. 8000 Holiday Rd., Lake Lanier Islands. 945-8810.

SCUBA DIVING

Sea Sports Scuba. This is one of the main resources in Atlanta for scuba diving, a sport that is growing five times faster than snow skiing. This training center holds classes at its in-store classroom as well as at three SwimAtlanta pools located in Lilburn, Roswell, and Buckhead. The center is certified by the Professional Association of Diving Instructors (PADI). The course director is a physician, and instructors are licensed nurses and paramedics. The courses taught range from basic open-water certification to such specialties as underwater photography. All students learn CPR. Trips to Florida are part of most courses, some of which are approved for college credit. Adults and children from age twelve participate, and snorkeling classes begin with children as young as eight. 11240 Alpharetta Hwy., Ste. 200, Roswell. 664-9176.

SHOOTING

Cherokee Rose Shooting Resort. Granted, this facility is just outside the area we cover in our book, but it is a terrific place, and we felt it was worth an entry. Ten exciting, challenging shooting games make this the ultimate shooting entertainment: sporting clays, one of the hottest games in the nation today; **European Five Stand Sporting Clays**, where the targets shot are controlled by a computer; **Super Sporting Clays**, a multi-station course for small-gauge shotguns that's great for beginners; **DoveTowers**, the ultimate in pass shooting; **BunkerTrap**, a multi-thrower game; **GattlinGuns**, fast and furious shotgun shooting; skeet, the traditional American clay target game shot on seven stations with targets thrown high and low; and, finally, **StarShot**, a championship game available at only three other locations in the U.S., and made popular on ESPN. Open daily. Reservations are requested. 895 Baptist Camp Rd., Griffin. 706-228-2529.

Wolf Creek Trap and Skeet Range. Selected as the site for the 1996 Olympic Games shooting events, Wolf Creek is a public facility owned by Fulton County. The facility has already hosted the U.S. Open and U.S. Armed Forces Championships. The manager, Dan Mitchell, is a champion all-American skeet shooter, and the former captain of the U.S. Navy Skeet Team. Mitchell is also at home on the trap field, and Wolf Creek offers such programs as league shooting, "learn-to-shoot" classes, and many registered events. A shooting activity that is becoming very popular is called "sporting clays." Targets are set up in the woods, making the shooting a tougher challenge, and the target release delays are staggered. 3070 Merk Rd., Southwest. 346-8382.

SKATING

ICE SKATING & HOCKEY

Atlanta IcePlex. Jack Burton owns and operates this ice arena located just across from the Gwinnett Civic and Cultural Center. 2200 Satellite Blvd., Duluth. 813-1010.

Atlanta Knights. Professional ice hockey is back with a vengeance after a dry spell that started back in the 1980s when the Atlanta Flames moved to Calgary. The Knights of the International Hockey League began their first season in 1992, and proceeded to win the Turner Cup in 1994. Nearly a half-century old, the IHL is the top developmental league for the National Hockey League; it's comparable to the Triple A farm league in baseball, which feeds players into the professional system. Most players are in their early twenties, and hail from around the globe. Atlantans are responding with enthusiasm to ice hockey's comeback, and are making season tickets a hot item. The Omni Coliseum, 100 Techwood Dr., Downtown. 525-5800; Tickets: 525-8900.

Parkaire Olympic Ice. This is the home of the **Atlanta Figure Skating Club**, associated with the U.S. Figure Skating Association. Lessons are available *(see chapter 9)* and hockey leagues are set up for all ages. The rink may be rented for private parties, and a popular sport at these bashes is **Broom Ball**—played with a puck but *without* skates. Go figure! Open daily. Rentals available. 4880 Lower Roswell Rd., Parkaire Mall, Marietta. 973-0753.

Stone Mountain Park's Ice Chalet. This year-round facility is open daily and offers a regulation-size rink for both amateur and professional play. Several youth and adult ice hockey leagues practice and play here, and fifteen coaches give patch and freestyle lessons, beginning with three-year-olds *(see chapter 9)*. Affiliated with the U.S. Figure Skating Association and the International Skaters Institute of America, the rink opens as early as 5 A.M. for lessons and scheduled practices. Stone Mountain Park, Stone Mountain. 498-5729.

ROLLER SKATING & IN-LINE SKATING

Atlanta Peachtree RoadRollers. An outdoor skating club that welcomes both in-line and conventional skaters, this group advocates safe street skating practices similar to bicycling. Members meet for weekly social skates through Midtown, skating to the pace of the slowest skaters. More advanced

"rolls" are scheduled throughout the week. Rental equipment is available at High Country Outfitters; skaters meet at the Rio Shopping Center. Call High Country Outfitters for information. 4400 Ashford-Dunwoody Rd., Perimeter Mall, Dunwoody. 391-9657.

SKIING

Atlanta Ski Club. Notwithstanding the fact that Atlanta is a Southern city without peer, it still boasts the second-largest ski club in the nation. The Atlanta Ski Club is always open to new members, both experts and novices. About 25 regular trips, twenty additional downhill skiing trips, and six cross country ski trips keep members busy each year. The club's ski school helps members improve their skills, whether they are beginners or advanced skiers. Many members join the club to participate only in the camaraderie afforded by the adventure trips, social events and programs, and charity benefits. Other activities include hiking, camping, rafting, hot air ballooning, and beach trips. This group is half singles and half marrieds, and represents nearly every age group. 6303 Barfield Rd., Sandy Springs. 255-4800.

SOCCER

All-American Indoor Soccer. This facility offers a full indoor program during all four seasons of the year. 4710 Lower Roswell Rd., East Cobb. 578-6001.

Atlanta Magic. Established in 1991, the Atlanta Magic are proving themselves as the city's professional soccer team. National indoor champions for two years in a row and reaching the Southeastern Division outdoor finals, the Magic field players from all over the country. Their season runs year round, playing outdoors March to August, and indoors October to February. In addition to their pro-team are two minor leagues and the **Lady Magic**, a women's amateur program. While still searching for a home pitch, the Magic play most matches in Roswell and Marietta. 600 Village Trace, Bldg. 23, Suite 300, Marietta. 955-4484.

Fayetteville Soccer Center. Play is held indoors and outfoors, depending on the season. 215 Robinson Dr., E. Fayette Industrial Park, Fayetteville. 460-8785.

Georgia State Soccer Association. Soccer is one of the largest organized sports for youth in Atlanta; many leagues are organized for both adult men and women, as well. The association is open to beginners through professionals, and four excellent indoor/outdoor private facilities provide top-notch programs. These facilities operate on a four-season schedule. 3684 Stewart Rd., Doraville. 452-0505.

Rockdale Youth Soccer Association (RYSDA). This volunteer group, dedicated to soccer for more than twenty years, has several outdoor fields and recently opened an indoor facility. 1780 Old Salem Rd., Conyers. 483-0284.

The Soccer Academy. This was the first indoor facility in the metro area, but it now has outdoor fields as well. 327 Arcado Rd., Lilburn. 925-4404.

SWIMMING

Dynamo Swim Club. Based at both the Dynamo Community Swim Center and the Mountain Park Pool, the club was established in the '70s to promote competitive swimming. The club's 500 members include several world-ranked swimmers. The pools are available for recreational swimming at a nominal fee. Mountain Park Pool, Five Forks Trickum Rd., Lilburn; Dynamo Community Center, 3119 Shallowford Rd., Chamblee. 457-7946 (club); 451-3272 (community center).

SwimAtlanta. Fielding a team to the Junior National and Senior National championships, plus seven swimmers to the Olympic trials, makes this one of Atlanta's premier swim clubs. SwimAtlanta offers class instruction for beginners starting at six months of age. Adult beginners are accepted, and classes are also offered in water aerobics. Instruction is offered in three Atlanta locations: 324 Holly Ridge Dr., Lilburn. 381-7946; 795 Old Roswell Rd., Roswell. 992-7946; 1160 Moores Mill Rd., Northwest. 508-8887

TENNIS

Tennis classes and clinics grow like flowers in this town. Consult the beginning of this chapter for a list of city and county recreation departments, most of which operate tennis facilities as well as pocket parks with courts.

AMATEUR

Atlanta Lawn Tennis Association. ALTA is the largest locally organized tennis program in the nation: its membership totaled more than 73,000 at the end of 1993. The association oversees competitive matches for women, men, and youth. 1140 Hammond Dr., Sandy Springs. 399-5788.

Eastlake Indoor Tennis-Racquetball Center. Six indoor and three outdoor tennis courts host ALTA teams, interclub tournaments, and round-robin play. This is the only center we found with a computerized match-making service for those who do not

have a partner. Ball machines, lessons, and an on-site restringing service are all available. Eastlake is open to the public, but low-cost memberships are available. 2573 Alston Dr., Southeast. 373-3500.

Peachtree World of Tennis. This private club's facilities are open to the public, and it has eight indoor courts, heated and air conditioned, as well as eighteen outdoor courts. The club fields 28 ALTA teams for men, women, and juniors. It has been the site of many professional tournaments, including the men's Grand Prix, the women's

Virginia Slims, and the Federation Cup Play (the women's equivalent of the men's Davis Cup). Ball machines and lessons from the club pro are all avail-able. The club is on a tree-studded site and also offers three swimming pools. 6200 Peachtree Corners Cir., Norcross. 449-6060.

COLLEGIATE

University of Georgia. Most of the area colleges field tennis teams, but the University of Georgia, in Athens, has hosted the NCAA Men's Tennis Championships sixteen of the past eighteen years and hosted the NCAA Women's Tennis Championship in 1994. The Bulldog tennis stars were the national champions in 1985 and 1987, and were runners-up in 1989, 1991, and 1993. Mikael Pernfors, a native of Sweden, was the NCAA individual champion in 1984 and 1985. He's now on the professional tennis tour. Matches are played in the sixteen-court **Dan Magill Tennis Complex** on campus. Matches are free and open to the public. 542-1621 (Sports Information).

PROFESSIONAL

Professional tennis events are listed in Chapter 4 (Special Events).

Atlanta Thunder. Professional World Team Tennis made its debut in Atlanta in the summer of 1991. In its first year of play, the team's attendance averaged 2,600 spectators per match, clearly appealing to Atlanta's many tennis buffs. As we go to press, the team's permanent "home" facility has not yet been determined. Bjorn Borg is the team's marquee player. Tickets are moderately priced. Ken Small, Jr. is general manager. Mail only: 1720 Peachtree St., Ste. 1022, Mid-town. 881-8811.

VOLLEYBALL

Georgia State University. Look out for the women's volleyball team! They won the Trans American Athletic Conference in 1991. Admission to the games is free and they are open to the public. The GSU Sports Arena is home court. Decatur & Collins Sts., Downtown. 651-2071 (Sports Information).

Good Ol' Days. Yes, this is the same favorite watering hole we've all grown to love. But at the Sandy Springs location you'll find two sand volleyball courts. Avid players know that they're available, and on Monday nights, pickup tournaments yield gift certificates to the victors. 5841 Roswell Rd., Sandy Springs. 257-9183.

CHAPTER 9

Expanding Your Mind

Chapter Eight guided you through all kinds of physical activity, but what if your brain needs some exercise too? In a city with such a variety of undergraduate and graduate institutions, opportunities to increase your education abound, whether you're working toward a degree or just thirsty for knowledge.

But all sorts of less conventional classes are available as well. Always wanted to create the perfect soufflé? Fly a helicopter? Dance a tango? Get your Black Belt? Build a tree house? Speak Japanese? Whatever your goal (or your children's goals)—enrichment, advancement, profit, fun, or academic degrees—Atlanta has the resources to get your brain in gear.

LEARNING AS RECREATION

ART AND RECREATION CENTERS

County and municipal recreation centers are usually directed by the applicable department of cultural affairs, or, sometimes, department of parks, recreation, and cultural affairs. While we cannot list all the centers, we've chosen a few for your convenience. If we've missed the one closest to you, check the blue pages in the Southern Bell business directory and look for these departments under the applicable city or county jurisdiction. The following list combines both centers operated by public entities and those run by private interests, but the latter may not offer the sports and fitness-related activities that the public ones do. Some of the publicly operated centers are heavily involved in teaching art, while others tilt toward the purely recreational activities.

Abernathy Arts and Crafts Center. A division of the Fulton County Department of Parks and Recreation, this center no longer teaches crafts despite retaining the word in its name. Instead, classes focus on teaching fine art: painting, drawing, sculpture, pottery (both handbuilt and wheel), tapestry weaving, stained glass, jewelry, and handmade paper. A small gallery exhibits student and instructor work only. 254 Johnson Ferry Rd., Sandy Springs. 303-6172.

The Art Place–Mountain View. Located in the Sandy Plains Road/Shallowford Road area of Cobb County, off I-75, the Art Place–Mountain View houses seven classrooms, a gallery, a workshop area, and a 200-seat "black box" theater, the only one in the county. Events include classes, workshops, theatrical productions, concerts, festivals, and gallery exhibitions. Summer programs for children, year-round programs for all ages, and per-

formances of all kinds are scheduled. A facility of Cobb Parks, Recreation, and Cultural Affairs, it is adjacent to the Mountain View Library. This is the first of several such centers to be developed in Cobb, and all are named "The Art Place," followed by a location tag line. 3330 Sandy Plains Rd., Marietta. 565-9541 or 528-8808 (Cultural Affairs).

ART Station. This nonprofit, professional arts organization produces, exhibits, and celebrates the visual, literary, and performing arts. It is also an instrument for arts education, focusing on Southern, especially Georgia, artists. ART Station also works to make art participation available to citizens in all segments of society. Classes in the visual and performing arts, writing, theatrical productions (both Station-produced and produced by outside organizations), and exhibitions are all part of its activity. The ART Station is backed by individual memberships

Expanding Your Mind ———————— **233**

(see chapter 10) and foundations, as well as state, county, and municipal authorities. Located in Stone Mountain Village. Mail: P.O. Box 1998, Stone Mountain, 30086; 5384 Manor Dr., Stone Mountain. 469-1105.

The Atelier. Combining a work place and teaching center for artists (many of whom rent studio space at the facility and meet prospective purchasers there by appointment), the Atelier has become a fixture in Atlanta's art scene. The gallery allows artists based at the facility to exhibit their work, which is for sale to the public. 857 Collier Rd., at Howell Mill Rd., Howell Mill Village Shopping Center, Northwest. 355-6710.

Callanwolde Fine Arts Center. Operated by the Callanwolde Foundation, the center offers workshops focused on the arts. Fiction and poetry courses are designed to develop the serious writer, whether beginner or advanced. Photography is the subject of another series of workshops, and other visual arts classes are designed to attract students of all age groups and levels of ability. Dance and acting are among the performance arts taught, and the numerous crafts activities include tatting and making lace on a hand-held shuttle. Program Director Thadria Garma can answer questions about the center's activities. 980 Briarcliff Rd., Druid Hills. 872-5338.

Chastain Arts Center. Operated by Atlanta's Bureau of Cultural Affairs, the center is located on the grounds of Chastain Park. The focus is on visual arts, ranging from fiber to graphic arts to pottery. Classes are offered to both adults and children. Adults enjoy floor-loom weaving, frame making, paint-

ing, drawing, jewelry making, and making pots by hand or on the wheel, as well as printmaking and stained glass instruction. Children enjoy the **Artventures** program, which features a different, fun activity each week, such as jewelry making and hand and wheel pottery. 135 W. Wieuca Rd., Chastain Park, Buckhead. 252-2927.

Chinese Community Center. Many aspects of Chinese culture are taught to both the Chinese community in Atlanta and those interested in Chinese culture. Shadow boxing, traditional Chinese dance, and language are among the courses taught. A senior citizens center is very active, and the library contains volumes written in Chinese as well as Chinese periodicals and newspapers. 5377 New Peachtree Rd., near Chinatown Mall, Chamblee. 451-4456

Clayton County Recreation Centers. Classes for children and adults cover such diverse subjects as ceramics, karate, dance, sign language, tennis, and aerobics for pregnant women. Special activities are available for seniors who live in Clayton County. The centers are located in Jonesboro, Riverdale, and North Clayton. The **Wilma W. Shelnutt Senior Adult Center** (477-6044) has programs for Clayton County residents who are over 55 years of age. 849 N. Battle Creek Rd., Jonesboro. 473-5788. The Jonesboro Recreation Center: 101 Lake Jodeco Rd., Jonesboro. 473-5797.

Cobb Senior Center. Arts and crafts, ballroom dancing lessons, square dancing, and bridge are among the many activities directed by the center. Seniors can also join the dance club (and swing to live music) or the golf club. The **Cobb Senior Games** is an athletic program. The center was formed in 1987 and is now a model for other areas. Bernice Coleman is program director. 1885 Smyrna-Roswell Rd., Smyrna. 801-5320. Austell Senior Citizen's Center: 5580 Powder Springs Rd. 819-3200. Acworth Senior Citizen's Center: 917-5170. Kennesaw Senior Citizen's Center: 424-8274.

DeKalb County Recreation Centers.
Dotted throughout the county are myriad recreation facilities, including picnic shelters, golf courses, tennis centers, and swimming pools. Classes include instruction in all kinds of sports, including tennis, karate, golf, and bowling, and all are also offered for the mildly to moderately mentally challenged. Preschool and youth classes in arts and crafts, chess, and ballet and tap dance fill the centers. The complete list of workshops, camps, tournaments, contests, and special events is too long to enumerate here. The DeKalb recreation program won a 1989 Governor's Award for Excellence. Recreational, Parks, and Cultural Affairs Department, 1300 Commerce Dr., Room 200, Decatur. 371-2631.

Douglasville/Douglas County Cultural Arts Center.
The historic Roberts-Mozley House, listed on the National Register of Historic Places, is home to a growing cultural arts center in a thriving suburban Atlanta town. Several groups meet here to explore and enhance their sphere of interest: **Douglas Poets in Focus** promotes the enjoyment of poetry writing and reading; the **Douglas County Writers' Group** fosters fiction and nonfiction writing;

and members of the **Sweetwater Camera Club** share an interest in photography. Art and theater groups are also active at the center, as is the historical society. The county's council for the arts is based here. 8644 Campbelton St., Douglasville. 949-2787.

East Roswell Recreation Center.
Classes include everything from T-shirt drawing to beginning ballet for physical fitness. Newcomers will especially appreciate the course in Southern gardening. 9000 Fouts Rd., Roswell. 594-6134.

Gilbert House Center.
Atlanta's Bureau of Cultural Affairs directs the Center, which offers art classes, cultural programs, and workshops focused on creative activities. A free, special program for seniors is **Walking for Wellness**. Classes include knitting, rug-making, silk-screening, and special workshops just for the holidays. (See chapter 5.) 2238 Perkerson Rd., Southeast. 766-9049.

Mable House.
An early nineteenth-century residence (see chapter 5) built by Scottish immigrant Robert Mable, for whom Mableton is named, is now a resource center for the visual and performing arts, operated by the **South Cobb Arts Alliance**. Classes in watercolor, pastels, drawing, and writing are offered for both children and adults, and the center holds monthly art exhibitions. Two annual festivals that feature arts and crafts are held on the grounds (see chapter 4). 5239 Floyd Rd., Mableton. 739-0189.

Pinckneyville Arts Center.
Classes and workshops cover all kinds of artistic media, including drawing, stained

glass, watercolor, creative writing, story-telling, wood carving, calligraphy, and portraiture. Special classes for children include art, sculpture, acting, and magic. 4300 Holcomb Bridge Rd., Norcross. 417-2215.

Roswell Visual Arts Center and Community Activity Building.

North Fulton County's mushrooming population has created a demand for and interest in community-supported arts. Reflecting that fact, the Roswell Visual Arts Center opened in 1990, offering the community a state-of-the-art studio and gallery. Classes range from painting to pottery, with more than 45 different workshops exploring a variety of subjects that appeal to both children and adults. Prices are very reasonable. The high-school-level student art competition attracts young artists from five north Fulton high schools. The winner receives a small scholarship. Totaling more than 4,000 square feet of space, the center is gaining a steadily increasing audience for its activities. 10495 Woodstock Rd., Roswell Area Park, Roswell. 594-6122 or 641-3760.

Soapstone Center for the Arts.

Founded in 1978 as "The Arts in South DeKalb," this center was renamed in 1988 and continues to provide cultural services to the residents of south DeKalb County. One of the county's "designated art centers," as is Callanwolde, Soapstone serves over 70,000 people annually through vigorous outreach programs. One of these is an exhibition program in South DeKalb Mall, and another sends exhibitions to area schools. People are enrolled in painting, drawing, dance, photography, pottery, playwriting, and, creative writing classes. Soapstone is building a theater program that will consist of one- and two-person shows and a "performance cafe" that will present readings. Ariel Williams serves as executive director. 2853 Candler Rd., Decatur. 241-2453.

Southeast Arts Center.

Supported by the City of Atlanta's Bureau of Cultural Affairs, the center offers a variety of classes covering ceramics, pottery, jewelry making, sewing, and more. 215 Lakewood Way, Southeast. 658-6036.

Spruill Center for the Arts.

Year-round classes for both children and adults cover the visual, performing, and literary arts. About 6,000 people attend the classes each year. Private instruction is also available (at all levels) for bassoon, clarinet, oboe, saxophone, tuba, and other instruments. Courses in art appreciation, marketing, and calligraphy round out one of the busiest schedules on the Atlanta arts calendar. Check out the summer camps for young people interested in performing and visual arts. Some camps are offered for children as young as age five. 5339 Chamblee-Dunwoody Rd., Dunwoody. 394-3447.

CRAFTS & SEWING

Atlanta Dolls & Miniatures.

Classes teach participants everything about how to build and finish a doll house, from wiring, laying hardwood floors, and wallpapering to shingling a roof. *(See chapter 6.)* 2000-B Cheshire Bridge

Rd., Cheshire Pointe Shopping Center, Northeast. 248-1151.

Bulloch Hall. Classes in calligraphy, quilting, basketry, open-hearth cooking, gardening, folk art, drawing and painting, and herbs provide insight into early nineteenth-century life. *(See chapter 5.)* 180 Bulloch Ave., Roswell. 992-1731.

Calico Quilter. This fabric supply and teaching store offers a distinctive selection of fabrics and a knowledgeable staff that likes to give individual attention. Classes include machine and hand quilting, for both beginners and advanced students. Quilters often give seminars in such subjects as basic appliqué, machine piecing, the double wedding ring pattern, making a heartwarming jacket, and high-tech tucks. Call for a schedule and inclusion on the mailing list. 14 Elizabeth Way, Roswell. 998-2446.

The Ceramic Cottage. Buy a piece of unpainted ceramic, some paints and other supplies, and paint to your heart's content. They'll fire the finished piece. Instructions and a workshop are provided. Charlotte Price has one of Atlanta's most unusual hobby operations. 1042 Lindbergh Dr., at Cheshire Bridge Rd., Northeast. 233-4826.

The Needle Nook. Everything you need to make needlework a breeze, including the expert advice. Arlene Jacobson sells supplies and accessories for knitting, crochet, needlepoint, counted cross stitch, latch hook rugs, and embroidery. 2165 Briarcliff Rd., Briar-Vista Shopping Center, Northeast. 325-0068.

The Needle Patch. The Needle Patch offers quilting supplies, cotton fabrics, and instruction in the art of quilting. 239 E. Crogan St., Lawrenceville. 995-1516.

Sew Magnifique. Exquisite fabrics and accessories as well as sewing and knitting machines are sold here, but it's also a center for learning to sew. Machine classes, lectures and demonstrations, and hands-on classes attract beginning, intermediate, and advanced students, who may also learn pattern drafting, chanel techniques, tailoring, and other skills. 3220 Paces Ferry Pl., Buckhead. 237-0955.

Wood Creek Knitting. This is the source for lessons in how to design knitted wear. Owner Judy Holloway also teaches hand and machine knitting. Knitting machines, fine yarns, patterns for both hand and machine knitting, and knitting equipment are sold. 3241 Lakecrest Dr., Dacula, 30021. 945-6764.

COOKING & WINE

Diane Wilkinson's Cooking School. Trained in Paris at the Cordon Bleu, Wilkinson has been a cooking instructor since 1973. Between her own classes, she studies with many European chefs, among them Marcella Hazan, Michel Guerard, and Guenter Seeger. She emphasizes technique, insisting that all good cooking begins with the basics—good stocks and sauces. Wilkinson also organizes and conducts gastronomic tours to various parts of France, Italy, and the US. Mail only: 4365 Harris Trail, Atlanta, 30327. 233-0366.

East 48th Street Market. Students

learn to cook the wonderful Italian dishes served in area restaurants. Each session has a different menu, and participants taste the finished dishes after the demonstration. Classes are held at the Dunwoody store. *(See chapter 6.)* 2462 Jett Ferry Rd., Williamsburg at Dunwoody, Dunwoody. 392-1499; 6701 Peachtree Ind. Blvd. 446-8256.

Janet Gaffney's The Art of Cooking.

A food stylist and well-known local gourmet, Gaffney offers classes for the holidays and other special times. The menus are healthful, yet maintain good flavor, and include both traditional and contemporary dishes. Sessions cover entertaining and serving tips—such as proper wine service— and each class ends with a dinner party. Mail only: 464 W. Wesley Rd., Atlanta, 30305. 215-564-4033.

Kitchen Fare. At Kitchen Fare, Laura

Shapiro and her mom, Gert, have assembled one of the finest assortments of kitchen gadgets anywhere. In the demonstration kitchen area of this fine shop, well-known local chefs regularly teach classes that range from the basics of white sauces to making pasta from scratch. Classes are held in the evening, from 7 P.M. until 9:30 P.M. Students receive printed recipes and enjoy a follow-up tasting session. 2385 Peachtree Rd., Peachtree Battle Shopping Center, Buckhead. 233-8849.

Mr. C's Cooking Castle. Established in

1975, the Cooking Castle's cooking school is taught by Cassius Chapman, CEC, and includes a variety of subjects. Cake decorating for beginners, Italian cooking for diabetics, and cooking without fat are among the subjects dealt with in depth. Most courses are taught in the evening. Out-of-towners love Chapman's classes in Southern cooking, which are especially designed for the visitor and conclude with a good Southern lunch. Mr. C's Cooking Castle also publishes a bimonthly newsletter that contains recipes, tips, food-related news, and a schedule of upcoming classes; subscription rate is nominal. P.O. Box 81261, Chamblee, 30366. 2243 Brockett Rd., Tucker. 455-7304.

Nathalie Dupree. Cooking and teach-

ing have long been important in Dupree's life. When she finished studies at the London Cordon Bleu, she began teaching cooking lessons at Nathalie's Restaurant in Covington, which she and her former husband then co-owned. After serving as lead teacher for the Rich's Cooking School, she began a PBS television program and continues to teach cooking in a private kitchen. Apprentices spend about three months learning the basics. Other students take extremely expensive week-long courses, sometimes on a one-on-one basis, that are designed to fill in the gaps and teach the refinements—aspic and puff pastry, for instance. Write to Nathalie Dupree c/o Georgia Public Television: 1540 Stewart Ave., Atlanta, 30310. 881-6299.

Ursula's Cooking School.

Ursula Knaeusel has been teaching cooking in Atlanta since 1971, and hers is now the largest independent cooking school in the country, with nearly 600 students every quarter. European-trained in both restaurants and home economics, Knaeusel teaches "cooking around the world"—everything from appetizers to desserts. Morning and evening classes are available. The moderately priced series of four demonstration classes includes all ingredients. Some participation classes are also available. The adjacent **Oak Tree House** (876-3439) is available for parties and private affairs. 1764 Cheshire Bridge Rd., Northeast. 876-7463; 876-3439.

Wine Sips.

Since 1978 Atlanta wine educator Anita LaRaia has been teaching about wine and bringing depth and organization to the study of wine. Professionals—both future sommeliers and salespeople—as well as serious amateurs are eligible to take the basic diploma course, **The Wine School**, a six-week session meeting one evening a week. Students receive in-depth course books with study guides, and the course contains lectures, slide presentations, and tastings. Participants learn to identify grape varieties and regions, as well as good values and great wines. In addition, LaRaia offers short sessions at area colleges and is available for private wine lessons and privately held tastings. P.O. Box 52723, Atlanta, 30355. 901-9433.

DANCE

Ballroom & Folk

Atlanta Cajun Dance Association.

Make reservations to take beginning, intermediate, and advanced Cajun dance classes, and learn the Cajun two-step, the traditional Cajun waltz, and the Cajun jitterbug. ACDA also teaches beginning Cajun dance workshops before all ACDA-sponsored dances, which take place at least twice a month at the Knights of Columbus Post 660 (2620 Buford Hwy. NE). Many of Louisiana's best Cajun bands and the local Cajun bands Hair of Dog and Atlanta Swamp Opera perform. Newsletter available. *(See chapter 10.)* Mail only: 2704 Laurelwood Rd., Atlanta, 30360. 451-6611.

Mulligan School of Irish Dance.

Founded in 1974, this family-owned school teaches traditional Irish step dance, focusing on jigs, reels, hornpipes, slip jigs, and set pieces. Ceili dances—group dances that were probably the source of square dancing—are a special interest. Children as young as five and adults are welcome in the family-oriented classes, which emphasize development of character rather than competition. **Ceili Dance Nights** are covered-dish supper evenings for families. The school has produced champion dancers, but the focus is on developing poise, confidence, and agility in participants. Classes are held in Marietta and

Buckhead. Mail only: 4265 Meadow Way, Marietta, 30066. 926-9059; 426-5521.

Royal Scottish Country Dancing Society.

We were amazed by how many branches this group has around the state and region—but then Celtic culture is at the root of Southern culture. Classes for beginners as well as for advanced intermediate dancers are held at assorted metro area churches, recreation centers, and clubhouses. Children's classes convene at the **Decatur School of Ballet**. Classes for all levels meet in the evenings. P.O. Box 33905, Decatur, 30033. 982-9438.

Square Dancing.

A popular activity for fun and aerobic exercise, square dancing takes a good bit of time to learn. Most basic courses last about 26 weeks, and the optional, advanced course goes on for another 24. We've listed some locations around the metro area, but if we haven't named one close to your home, chances are good that someone at one of these numbers will know of a class near you. **Cathedral Squares:** Cathedral of St. Philip, 2744 Peachtree Rd., Buckhead. 874-0320. **Dixie Squares:** All Saints Catholic Church, 2443 Mt. Vernon Rd., Dunwoody. Activities building: 668-9954. **Lads and Lassies:** Henry General Hospital, Stockbridge. 474-3391. **Shufflin' Shoes:** North Arts Center. 938-4342 or Wendell Ward at 688-0628. **South Cobb Yellow Rocks:** South Cobb Community Center, Lions Club Dr., Mableton. 489-9901. **Y Knot Club:** Fullers Park Gym, 3050 Robinson Rd., Marietta. 509-2737.

Village Clogging Center.

Clogging lessons for children and adults attract students from all over the metro area. The center teaches traditional clogging, a mountain dance, and combines it with modern dance into a unique blend. Exhibition teams known as the **Dixie Dolls** range in age from three to adults. The center has enjoyed more than a dozen years of local popularity. 751 Main St., Stone Mountain Village, Stone Mountain. 498-5953.

Classical

Academy of Sports.

A complete curriculum in ballet, tap, and jazz dance culminates in an annual recital. 5020 Snapfinger Woods Dr., Decatur. 981-8000.

The School of the Atlanta Ballet, Inc.

Dorothy Alexander founded this school in 1920, when she also established what is now the company. The school is affiliated with the country's oldest regional professional ballet company. Joanne Lee directs the school. It operates in two locations: The Downtown location is reserved for career-oriented performers, who must audition for the school, and the Marietta location teaches adult beginners as well as children. Robert Barnett is owner and president. Class cards yielding tuition savings are the best way to pay for adult classes. 477 Peachtree St., Downtown. 874-8695; 2215 Roswell Rd. NE, Marietta. 303-1501.

Atlanta Tap and Dance Center.

Linda Bruehl directs a unique dance resource center where children and adults (ages two to sixty) can enjoy the rhythm and beat of tap dancing. A friend to Gregory Hines and other well-known tap dancers, Bruehl also teaches ballet and jazz, but tap is where her heart is. Bruehl advocates DANCE—Develop and Nurture Cultural Enlightenment—because she believes dance should develop creativity, foster a solid sense of self, help us adapt to the environment, and enable us to use movement as a form of social expression. The students, who come from all walks of life, learn tap dance for personal pleasure and for aerobic and physical benefits. 2741 LaVista Rd., at Oak Grove Rd., Decatur. 634-9494.

Ballethnic Dance Company.

This company offers educational workshops, classes, lectures, and demonstrations. Ballethnic's mission is to incorporate classical ballet with a mix of modern and ethnic dance styles. *(See chapter 3).* P.O. Box 7749, Atlanta, 30357-0749. 933-9050.

Dancer's Studio Backstage.

Children and adults study ballet, pointe, jazz, modern, or tap as well as acting, piano, and voice. The staff of fourteen, directed by Jonnie Kelley, includes a number of professional dancers. The studio's four teaching areas are equipped with raised hardwood floors, dressing rooms, and a reception area. **Kinderdance** is a program that accepts three-, four-, and five-year-olds. The studio's performance company is **Atlanta Dance Unlimited** *(see chapter 3).* 8560 Holcomb Bridge Rd., Ste. 118, Alpharetta. 993-2623.

Decatur School of Ballet.

Established almost a half-century ago, this is the oldest ballet school in DeKalb County. Classes for both children and adults run regularly through the nine-month season (September through May). Special summer programs are also offered. Beginning with movement instruction for children ages three and four, the curriculum includes classical ballet, choreography, tap, jazz, modern, folk, and ballroom dance. This is the official school of the **Beacon Dance Company** *(see chapter 3).* 102 Church St., Decatur. 378-3388.

Lee Harper & Dancers Studio.

Founded in 1980 by Lee Harper and Jan Duffy, the studio specializes in a contemporary approach to classical dance training. To foster an understanding of the joy of movement, the program teaches youngsters from the age of three posture, coordination, a sense of rhythm, and self-confidence. With this foundation, the children then learn ballet, jazz, tap, and musical theater dance. **DancerKids**, the "invitation only" junior company for Lee Harper and Dancers, has its own training program, including the study of ballet, jazz, and modern. Through independent study, the **Just Us Dancers** (a scholarship performing company comprised of talented teens) choreograph and direct their own work in modern dance. *(See chapter 3.)* 721 Miami Cir., Ste. 106, off Piedmont Rd., Buckhead. 261-7416.

Room to Move.

Amy Gately directs the Room to Move dance company and teaches ballet and modern dance, chiefly at Callanwolde. *(See chapter 3.)* P.O. Box 8555, Atlanta, 30306. 847-0453.

Rotaru Ballet School. Pavel Rotaru of International Ballet Rotaru *(see chapter 3)* adds another dimension to classical ballet as presented in Atlanta. His school offers Kirov training for all levels, beginning through professional as well as adult ballet classes for nonprofessionals. The facility is substantial—10,000 square feet—and is equipped with resilient sprung floors. 6000 Peachtree Industrial Blvd., at Holcomb Bridge Rd., Norcross. 662-0993.

Ruth Mitchell Dance Studio. Many of the studio's students, including Janie Parker, have gone on to professional careers. As a professional with the Houston Ballet, Parker won a gold medal in the 1982 International Ballet Competition. Classical ballet training is offered to preschool children and beginners through age ten. Intermediate to advanced professional classes are given for all ages. Tap, modern, jazz, theater dance, and adult dance classes for exercise and conditioning are also offered. Ruth Mitchell founded the school in 1956, after studying in New York at the School of American Ballet and at Ballet Arts. *(See chapter 3.)* 3509 Northside Pkwy., Buckhead. 237-8829; 81 Church St., Marietta. 426-0007.

Terpsichore Dance Expressions. Pronounced "Terp-*sick*-o-reh," the school is named for the Greek muse of choral dance and song. The school and its companion company, **Terpsicorps Theater Company**, were founded in 1982 by Atlantan Patsy Bromley, who began studying ballet at age five with Ruth Mitchell. After a career-ending injury, she returned to Atlanta and now enjoys success as a teacher. Her students regularly snap up the best scholarships and have wound up in the professional corps of some of the world's finest companies: for example, Rebecca Metzger and Albert Evans are now with the New York City Ballet. Terpsichore also welcomes youngsters who have no designs on becoming stars as well as folks who wish to learn jazz dance as a mode of exercise. 1843 Cheshire Bridge Rd., Northeast. 874-8755.

Total Dance Theatre. Ongoing classes in modern dance, creative movement, tap, and more form the core of the school founded by Terrie Axam-Austin, who also founded the dance company of the same name *(see chapter 3).* Some classes are designed for beginners (both children and adults), and include floor gymnastics and jazz. Creative movement for the little ones begins at age four. 168 Trinity Ave., Downtown. 892-8486.

DRAMA

Actor's Express. Chris Coleman, artistic director of Actor's Express, teaches classes for adults. Coleman focuses on Meisner technique, and other instructors teach movement, voice, auditioning techniques, children's classes, and

special workshops. King Plow Arts Center, 887 W. Marietta St., Downtown. 607-7469.

Alliance Theater School. Developed in 1979 to provide a professional center for the study of drama, the Alliance Theater School offers programs to train professional actors, playwrights, technicians, and administrators. Programs are also offered for students and community members who wish to enhance their skills in dramatic expression. Members of professional performing artists' unions are eligible for a discount, as are students, Alliance subscribers and guild members, and members of the High Museum of Art. Programs for children begin at the kindergarten level with **Creative Dramatics**, which allows children to explore self-expression and experience an awakening to theatre. 1280 Peachtree St., Woodruff Arts Center, Midtown. 898-1131.

Callanwolde Fine Arts Center. Many classes and workshops on the dramatic arts. *See Arts Centers, above.* 980 Briarcliff Rd., Druid Hills. 872-5338.

Jeff Justice's Comedy Workshops. Justice, a professional comic, conducts a six-week course that covers such basics of comedy as joke-telling skills, formulas for joke writing, coping with stage fright and hecklers, and how to handle the professional stage. Students write a five-minute comedy routine and then, after two rehearsals, a graduation performance is held at The Punch Line *(see chapter 2)*. Open to anyone over eighteen; students include accountants, lawyers, physicians, dentists, homemakers, and anyone who wishes to enhance his or her joke-telling skills. Class size is limited to fifteen. P.O. Box 52404, Atlanta, 30355. 262-7406.

Stage Door Players Theater School. This theater school for young teens to adults takes a hands-on approach to the basic technical aspects of set construction, lighting, sound, set changes, and direction. The school also teaches basic acting classes that use theater games and exercises to develop a monologue for presentation. Adults who want to give acting a shot or who seek to enhance their basic communication skills will find these classes full of inspiration. 5339 Chamblee-Dunwoody Rd., North DeKalb Cultural Center, Dunwoody. 396-1726.

D O - I T - Y O U R S E L F

American School of Paperhanging Arts. Courses of study can lead to certification in paperhanging arts—yes, there is such a thing! The school occupies a Greek Revival mansion built in the 1800s in the town of Commerce, about an hour north of Atlanta. The program is open to participants above eighteen years of age, and no prior knowledge of wall covering installation is required. The program is usually completed in eleven weeks, depending on the pace of each student. 450 Little St., Commerce. 706-335-5010 or 800-633-2796.

Freemanville Woodworking Shop. Learn how to work with wood by using a master's tools and benefiting from his personal instruction in a privately owned shop. Owner Richard Graham offers all the equipment a student could need to make anything from a picture frame to a rolltop desk. *(See chapter 6.)* 15970 Freemanville Rd., Alpharetta. 475-5452.

Highland Avenue Hardware. Basic and advanced courses in woodworking include finishing, joinery, and the fundamentals of using woodworking tools. Lathe-turning, wood carving, and woodworking as art attract many students. About fifteen to twenty different classes are offered twice a year, enrolling about forty students per class. Classes meet in the warehouse behind this beautiful re-creation of an old-time hardware store. 1045 N. Highland Ave., Virginia-Highland. 872-4466.

Home Depot. "How-to" classes for the do-it-yourselfer include refinishing and installation of kitchen cabinets, ceramic tiles, ceiling fans, wall coverings...you name it. The staff provides excellent help. *(See chapter 6.)* Corporate headquarters: 2727 Paces Ferry Rd., Vinings. 433-8211.

National Institute of Home Builders. For more than a decade, Tom Harrison has taught people how to build their own homes. Topics include how to obtain construction financing, the basics of good home design, construction alternatives—slab foundations, crawl spaces, or full basements, for instance—and related issues. This home study course is a good way to learn how to communicate with a builder or general contractor. It's also a good idea for real estate agents, mortgage bankers, and others who work collaterally with the residential housing industry. P.O. Box 723248, Atlanta, 30339. 257-1211.

Southface Energy Institute. How do you figure out which heating system best suits your needs? What are radiant heat barriers? What's the latest on radon? Southface addresses these and other questions about home energy conservation at its center in a once-abandoned Victorian home located at 158 Moreland Avenue. Self-guided tours (free), guided tours for groups (nominal fee), and monthly seminars (free) are the best ways to find answers to these and other energy-related questions. The **Home-building School** offers courses exploring energy-efficient construction. These courses are offered in a variety of formats: nine-day courses, weekend courses, and a short-course series. Memberships bring additional benefits, such as a quarterly journal and discounts on services. The library has up-to-date information on a variety of energy subjects. P.O. Box 5506, Atlanta, 30307. 525-7657.

GARDENING & NATURE

Atlanta Botanical Garden. Year-round classes on how to grow both decorative and culinary plants make the Botanical Garden a busy place. Flower arranging, propagating your own cuttings, and other gardening issues are the subjects of seminars and workshops. Programs such as vegetable gardening are also available for children, and some classes accept six-year-olds. **Herb Day** in May is always a good time to learn about growing herbs. Look for occasional classes given by the Herb Society of America, Chattahoochee Unit, as well as for interesting lectures throughout the year. *(See chapter 5.)* 1345 Piedmont Ave., Midtown. 876-5859.

Chattahoochee Nature Center. Programs for school-aged youngsters cover the shapes, colors, and sounds of nature. Serious discussions of forest and river ecology are held for high-schoolers. Longer (one- and two-hour) programs examine Native American culture and birds of prey in our part of the world. Children should dress in old clothes, as they may get muddy. *(See chapter 5.)* 9135 Willeo Rd., Roswell. 992-2055.

Fernbank Science Center. Planetarium shows are open to the public for a nominal fee, and on Saturday mornings **The Sky Tonight** is free. *(See chapter 5.)* Children's planetarium programs presented at holiday times and during the summer are fascinating, and very small fees are charged for these. 156 Heaton Park Dr., off Artwood Rd., off Ponce de Leon Ave., Decatur. 378-4311.

Garden Party. This unusual garden store offers specialty courses at least twice a month in such subjects as plant identification, perennials, ponds, lighting, general gardening, and composting. 488 Kennesaw Ave., Marietta. 421-0245.

Hastings Nature & Garden Center Seminars. Highly specialized horticulturists, nature writers, and photographers are among those who conduct these free seminars that take place throughout the year. Learn more about birds and how to create friendly habitats for them. Discover how to plan and plant your garden for each season, and study tree care, herbs, and more. Seating is on a first-come, first-served basis, so get there a little early. 2350 Cheshire Bridge Rd., Northeast. 321-6981.

Vines Botanical Gardens. Educational programs include various gardening workshops, special programs for children (including an astronomy class), and an experimental environmental program that is operated in conjunction with the Gwinnett County Public School System. *(See chapter 5.)* 3500 Oak Grove Rd., Loganville. 466-7532.

HEALTH & WELLNESS

These days, most medical centers offer courses that deal with the personal health issues many of us confront: weight loss or maintenance, and nicotine addiction, for example. We've listed some of the largest programs and some of the specialized ones, but check your local hospital for specifics on the courses available in your area.

DeKalb Medical Center. At the **Wellness Center**, various courses offered throughout the year deal with assorted personal health issues, such as nicotine addiction, weight loss, stress management, and self-defense for women. 2701 N. Decatur Rd., Decatur. 501-2222.

Northwest Georgia Healthcare System. Offering a variety of community classes such as first aid, adult

CPR, pediatric CPR, and smoking cessation. Youth social classes include **Babysitting, At Home Alone**, and basic aid. Also offered are a variety of other aerobic and aquatic classes for everyone from infants to seniors. The Northwest Georgia Healthcare System includes: Cobb Hospital, Kennestone at Windy Hill and Marietta, RT Jones, Douglas General, and Paulding Memorial. Education Service Line: 793-7000.

Piedmont Hospital. The **Stop Smoking Institute** and a **Weight Watchers** class both meet at the hospital and are open to the public. The **Fit to Learn** program consists of seminars on various health-related topics, and it's open to members of the **Piedmont Hospital Health and Fitness Club**, which anyone can join. Individual and family memberships are available and are fairly expensive. Most classes meet in a building across the street from Piedmont Hospital; underground access connects the two facilities. 2001 Peachtree St., Ste. 100, Brookwood. 605-1965.

Scottish Rite Children's Medical Center. The education department offers a variety of courses, including its nationally recognized babysitting course. **Safe Sitter** teaches eleven- to fifteen-year-olds how to be better babysitters. **Shapedown**, a weight management course for children or teens and their parents, a stop-smoking clinic for teenagers, pediatric CPR, and many other informative workshops focus on the needs of both children and care-givers. Some courses are open to professionals only; one very popular course instructs teachers on how to recognize health problems. A course on child abuse attracts attorneys, physicians, social workers, and teachers. Fees range from nominal to fairly expensive, and for some courses the fee structure is graduated according to the participant's profession. 1001 Johnson Ferry Rd., Sandy Springs. 250-2148.

Senior Health Plus. If you are 55 and over you may be interested in joining Cobb Hospital and Medical Center's Senior Health Plus club. A free membership includes a range of benefits such as a 25% discount at the hospital cafeteria, nutritional information and exercise classes. You'll also receive a quarterly newsletter *Senior Edition Plus*, and have the opportunity to attend monthly **Friday Forum** educational seminars. 3950 Austell Rd. SW, Austell. 732-3970.

LANGUAGES

Alliance Française d'Atlanta. The Atlanta alliance is part of the worldwide network, but it's an independent, American branch. This member-supported cultural association and school (the latter founded in 1963) offers many different activities. French language classes are available during day and evening sessions for fourteen different levels of study. **Business French** and **French at Your Desk** are special programs. *(See chapter 10.)* 1360 Peachtree St., One Midtown Plaza, Ste. 200, Midtown. 875-1211.

Casa Cultural Iberoamericana.
Native speakers, most of them retired professors, conduct private and group Spanish-language classes in the evenings. Most courses run for eleven weeks, and each class lasts two hours. Classes are limited to seven students. 3133 Maple Dr., Ste. 10, Buckhead. 237-7899.

Chinese Community Center.
Beginning and advanced classes in Mandarin Chinese are taught by native speakers, and a language laboratory is part of the facility. Classes are held in the evening for adults, most of whom are non–Chinese Americans. Chinese classes for children—usually for Chinese American children who want to maintain their language skills—are offered on Saturdays. 5377 New Peachtree Rd., near Chinatown Mall, Chamblee. 451-4456.

Goethe-Institut Atlanta.
Twelve-week German language classes of all levels meet once a week for three-and-a-half hours. Conversation, literature, modern Germany, and business German are among the additional special programs. Students may take the exams for the **Deutsche Sprachdiplom**, which is accepted by all universities as fulfilling a language entrance requirement. Opportunities to study at Goethe-Institut centers in Germany may be arranged through the Atlanta office. The Institut is also a resource center designed to foster appreciation for German culture, and offers, among other things, a fine film program (see chapter 3) and a lending library. 400 Colony Sq., Midtown. 892-2388; 892-2316.

Irish Arts of Atlanta.
Among the activities of this group is the teaching of Gaelic, a project the outfit has been doing for the last several years. (See chapter 10.) Contact Bernard Lane, chairman. Mail only: 1288 N. Morningside Dr., Atlanta, 30306. 873-5621.

Japan America Society of Georgia.
The society's fundamental approach to teaching Japanese goes across the board: speaking, hearing, reading, and writing. Classes are taught at the society offices. (See chapter 10.) 225 Peachtree St., Ste. 710, South Tower, Downtown. 524-7399; fax 524-8447.

Japan Services.
Business Japanese from a practical perspective is taught in two ten-week courses. Focus is on translation, interpretation, typesetting, and desktop publishing. Cultural and social situations are also discussed, as are aspects of Japanese business practices that may seem unusual to us. Mail only: 93 Dunwoody Springs Dr., Atlanta, 30328. 393-1955; fax: 393-2466.

Japanese Learning Center.
The **Japanese for Busy People** program gets right to the heart of the matter, and students also learn Japanese etiquette for various social situations. Classes are taught at the Williamsburg Village Shopping Center, 2779 Clairmont Rd., Ste. F-1A or F-7, at Briarcliff Rd., Northeast. Center office: 180 Allen Rd. Northeast. 256-6958.

Language Services International.
Native speakers instruct people in business, government, and industry in over 200 foreign languages. Language Services International custom designs the courses. Private, semiprivate, and small-group lessons are offered and

may be scheduled flexibly. An **English as a Second Language** program is also available. Classes may be arranged at off-premises locations. Language Services International is also a source for expert technical and legal translation. 2256 Northlake Pkwy., Ste. 309, Northlake Executive Center, at I-285 and Northlake Pkwy., Tucker. 939-6400.

M U S I C

Atlanta Music Center. Keyboard and violin lessons for all ages are the core of this professional music school, in operation since 1975. Its certified instructors are active in many forms of music performance around the city. Classes for kids teach singing and keyboard. 4051 Hwy. 78 at Killian Hill Rd., Lilburn. 979-2887; 5509 Chamblee-Dunwoody Rd., Dunwoody Village, Dunwoody. 394-1727; 1205 Johnson Ferry Rd., Woodlawn Square, Marietta. 977-0003.

Jan Smith Studios. Singers learn how not to destroy their voices when singing rock, rhythm and blues, and heavy metal. The studio has about ninety students, men and women of all ages over thirteen years old.. 1727 Clifton Rd., Ste. 228, Northeast. 633-3840.

Neighborhood Music Schools. Kristin Wendland, PhD, directs this outstanding community outreach program, established in 1990 as a nonprofit organization to teach vocal and instrumental music throughout the state. Numerous sites dot the metropolitan area, mostly in churches and schools. **Kindermusik** classes are offered for tots as young as eighteen months. These require the participation of a parent or caregiver and teach singing, movement, and basic instrumental skills. Sessions last for thirty minutes for children up to age two, 45 minutes for three year olds, and an hour for children ages four and five. Also taught are courses in composition and music appreciation for adults as well as private lessons. P.O. Box 55169, Atlanta, 30308. 651-1111.

Piano Gallery. Private piano lessons for children and adults require no previous knowledge of music. Classes for children begin at age four. Intermediate levels are also taught for both adults and children. Lesson prices are moderate for both groups. 2140 Peachtree Rd., Ste. 125, Brookwood Square, Brookwood. 351-0550.

Southern Keyboards. Moderately priced private and group piano lessons are given for beginners—both adults and children. Advanced classical piano and voice are also taught. 1898 Leland Dr., Ste. B, Marietta. 953-0938.

PHOTOGRAPHY & VIDEO

Also see Art and Recreation Centers, at the beginning of this chapter, for instruction in many media.

IMAGE Film/Video Center. IMAGE cosponsors screenings with other film organizations, maintains a library of current media periodicals and video art, conducts workshops, and sponsors an annual Southeastern screenwriting competition, a recently added activity. *(See also chapters 3 and 4.)* 75 Bennett St., Ste. M-1, Brookwood. 352-4225.

Southeastern Center for the Arts. Adults study basic and intermediate photography in classes and workshops. Professional training programs are also offered, and courses include camera technology, darkroom technique, and human figure photography, as well as nature, night, and video photography. Mature youngsters (some as young as age eleven have participated) may be eligible for **Point and Shoot**, a program intended for amateurs, but check for approval prior to registration. The center is affiliated with the Rocky Mountain School of Photography in Missoula, Montana, which conducts a ten-week professional program and a series of workshops. 1935 Cliff Valley Way, Northeast. 633-1990.

SELF-DEVELOPMENT

Fearless Flyers. Classes or individual instruction help those with a fear of flying to overcome their phobia. Dr. Burt Bradley, a well-known local psychologist, and his associates also offer classes and individualized instruction designed to help clients handle a number of other phobias and problems, including smoking. 1549 Clairmont Rd., Ste. 107, Decatur. 982-0327.

National Archives Southeast Region. Workshops in genealogy teach participants how to use the federal records housed in the Southeastern branch of the National Archives. Workshops take place six or seven times a year, and are also held on military history, black genealogy, black history, and how to research these subjects. Nominal fee. *(See chapter 5.)* 1557 St. Joseph's Ave., East Point. 763-7477.

Role Models. Weekend seminars designed to train students in modeling are taught by professionals who explain the many facets of professional work. Topics include technique, runway, TV commercials, print work, and "the business of the business." Students may view videotapes of their progress, and makeup artists are available for consultation (additional fee). P.O. Box 55107, Atlanta, 30308. 578-2331.

Taggart's Driving School. Students from ages fifteen to 87 have successfully completed Taggart's driving course, which uses dual-controlled automobiles. (In fact, Taggart's claims to have the largest fleet of fully dual-controlled cars in the nation.) Instructors give individualized lessons, taking special care with nervous and older students. Free door-to-door service. 3566 Lawrenceville Hwy., Tucker. 934-2144.

TeachMeSports. Entertaining seminars about the "Big Three" major league sports teach rules, terms, offense, defense, scoring, and stats plus the local scene and league structures. Classes, which take place during the appropriate season, include active discussions and many surprises. TeachMeSports claims that these seminars have business, family, and social benefits because they enable participants to relate better to their bosses, coworkers, and spouses who love the games. This is the way to beat the "sports widow" syndrome—join 'em! Mail only: 848 Bonnie Glen Dr., Marietta, 30067-7167. 973-3442.

SPORTS

Please see Chapter 8 (Sports & Recreation) for more resources.

Canoeing & Kayaking

Georgia Canoeing Association. The association holds beginner and intermediate training clinics in canoeing, kayaking, flat water, and river safety as well as clinics for trip leaders. Participants must have their own equipment, but equipment rentals are available at either REI or Go With The Flow. Classes are held in late spring and summer, and children's classes are available as demand requires (usually in the late spring). P.O. Box 7023, Atlanta, 30357. 421-9729.

Go With The Flow Sports. A two-day course in whitewater kayaking could lead to a dynamite summer. Supplies and equipment are provided. About once a month (May through September), courses in touring kayaking, which include overnight trips, are offered. Both courses are taught at Go With The Flow. 4 Elizabeth Way, Roswell. 992-3200.

Equestrian

Atlanta Horse Center. The center teaches Western and English riding and dressage to all ages. Horses are available for lessons. 1795 Corn Rd., Smyrna. 434-3731.

Sweet Sunshine Equestrian Center. This indoor center specializes in dressage, hunter jumping, three-day eventing, and stadium jumping for both children and adults. Instruction is available for individuals and groups. Special clinics in various disciplines are also offered. The center has horses available, or you may take lessons on your own horse. 14295 Birmingham Hwy., Alpharetta. 343-9807.

Vogt Riding Academy. This family-owned and-operated school has been in business in Atlanta since 1954. Classes in dressage and combined training are taught from the beginner to the Grand Prix levels. Group instruction rates are moderate, and private instruction is also available. 1084 Houston Mill Rd., Northeast. 321-9506.

Fencing

Atlanta Fencers' Club. Owner Gene Gettler has twenty years of experience and is a four-time Southeast fencing champion. He is also an instructor at Emory University and DeKalb College. The club offers individual and group lessons. Equipment is provided for the classes. *(See chapter 10.)* 40 7th St., Midtown. 892-0307.

Fayette Fencing Academy. The Fayette Fencing Academy is certified in all three fencing categories—foil, epée, and sabre. It currently has students who rank nationally. Wolfgang Finck, owner, was reared on fencing by his grandfather, a German national champion. Finck teaches in Alpharetta and at Concourse Athletic Club in Buckhead, and instructs at Clayton State College. Classes are taught to all age groups, both sexes, and to beginning or Olympic-level athletes. The school has been in operation since 1986. 330 N. Fayette Dr., Fayetteville. 461-3809.

Fishing & Hunting

Fish Hawk. Have you wanted to master the fine art of fly fishing ever since you saw *A River Runs Through It*? Fish Hawk, Atlanta's oldest fly fishing store, offers classes teaching the A to Z of fly fishing every year from April to October in Dillard, Georgia. Experts will guide you from setting up your line to casting as you learn the entomology of the rivers. A one day class offered Saturdays costs $99 or splurge on a three day class for $325. 279 Buckhead Ave, Buckhead. 237-3473.

Project WILD. This teacher education program is for youth leaders in scouting, church programs, and preschool, and anyone else who works with children. Participants learn how to teach youngsters about the wild. For teachers in all grades, the program includes wild aquatic subjects, and the popular **Oh Deer** program teaches how food and shelter play an important role in a deer's life. Contact the Georgia Department of Natural Resources to find out when courses are given in a location convenient to you. 2111 Hwy. 278, Social Circle, 30279. 918-6416.

Wildlife Resources Division Hunter Safety Certification. Held in all Georgia counties, the six-hour course, which usually meets two nights or six hours on a single Saturday, teaches basic hunting safety tips. Subjects include such matters as how to carry a gun safely, how different weapons work, how to obtain a license, and what to wear. 2070 Hwy. 278, Social Circle, 30279. 918-6409.

Flying

CBFC. Founded in 1977 and known as the Charlie Brown Flying Club, the school is a Part 141 FAA- and VA-approved flight school, not a club. A fleet of fourteen aircraft and a staff of six full-time and six part-time instructors keeps the school airborne. Participation in the "club" entitles members, many of whom are student pilots, to discounts on airplane rental rates and all pilot supplies. 3987 Aviation Cir., Fulton County Airport, Northwest. 696-2233.

Epps Aviation. Professional, FAA-approved pilot programs for private and professional pilots as well as wheelchair pilot training are among the opportunities at Epps Aviation, which has been in operation for more than 25 years. The flight instruction staff consists only of full-time professionals, and includes an FAA flight examiner. DeKalb-Peachtree Airport, Clairmont Rd., Northeast. 458-9851.

Peachtree DeKalb Flight Academy. This FAA-approved Part 141 school is also approved by the Georgia Department of Labor, and teaches students to fly fixed-wing aircraft. Peachtree teaches students who are studying to be both private and airline transport pilots. In business for more than eighteen years, Peachtree is the second-oldest flight school in Atlanta. It also offers ground school courses through Mercer University. 1 Corsair Dr., Chamblee. 457-8223.

Golf

The Golf Academy of Georgia. Do you miss those crucial two-foot putts, or hit a "dogleg" to the left when the fairway is straight? The Golf Academy offers lessons that may provide the key to a happier golfing experience. State-of-the-art technology emphasizes body motion, and much of the instruction is done without the student ever touching a club. Owner and chief instructor Richard Hall teaches handicappers of all levels. 15135 Hopewell Rd., Alpharetta. 664-6417.

McDivots Golf Center. This state-of-the-art facility teaches golfing. *(See chapter 8.)* 1360 Upper Hembree Rd., Roswell. 740-1415.

Gymnastics

Academy of Sports. Ballet, tap, jazz dance, gymnastics, and karate lessons are offered year-round. The gymnastics programs for both boys and girls teach the fundamentals in the standard events. The complex includes a 10,000-square-foot gymnasium and two dance studios equipped with first-rate gymnastic equipment, a spring-loaded, carpeted floor for tumbling, and hardwood floors for dancing. 5020 Snapfinger Woods Dr., Decatur. 981-8000.

Atlanta School of Gymnastics. A member of the U.S. Gymnastic Federation, this school boasts among its graduates Kathy Johnson, a Bronze medal winner in the 1984 Olympics, and Kevin Davis, a member of the 1988 US Olympic team. All equipment and instruction meet Olympic standards. Owner Tom Cook was an NCAA rings champion. Competitive teams for all ages participate in regional meets. 3345 Montreal Station, Tucker. 938-1212.

Gym Elite. Totaling 23,000 square feet, Gym Elite is the largest gymnastics facility in the Southeast. Several of its students have been state champions, regional qualifiers, and national competitors. The school's method, developed by coach Dick Mulvihill and David Day, the center's owner, is called **Show Me Gymnastics**—it is now used in more than 26 countries. Former Olympic champion Olga Korbut no longer coaches here, but she is still affiliated with the Norcross-based gymnastics school. A preschool program for children ages two and up introduces youngsters to gymnastics. Cheerleading is also taught. 5903 Peachtree Industrial Blvd., Norcross. 448-1586.

Martial Arts

Choi Kwang-Do. This is the world's fastest-growing martial art; its international headquarters is based right here in Atlanta. Adults and children learn self-defense, discipline, and self-esteem—the kids' **Black Belt Club** program is especially strong in these areas. It's a great way to get an aerobic workout, is gentler on the body than some other forms of martial arts, and emphasizes individual achievement rather than competition. Seventeen locations in the area; world headquarters is 4327 Wade Green Rd., Kennesaw. 795-0010.

Joe Corley American Karate Studios. Almost every shopping center on every corner has an outfit teaching karate and other martial arts. Corley's studios, however, also teach **Kenpo**, an ancient Chinese art of self-defense that is especially useful for women. The many studio locations include Sandy Springs, Marietta, East Cobb, Lilburn, Norcross, and, soon, Fayetteville, Douglasville, and Conyers. Main location: 11060 Alpharetta Hwy., Roswell. 642-5500.

Polo

Chukkar Farm Polo. Well-known Atlanta restaurateur Jack Cashin is famous in the world of polo and owns Chukkar Farm, which is also the home of the **Scuppernong Polo Club**. The farm's polo school introduces men, women, and teens to the fundamentals of the sport. Beginners must know how to ride a horse, and must bring their own riding boots. Everything else is provided, including tack, polo ponies, and practice hitting cages. Classes for beginners teach the rules of the game, hitting techniques, strategy, positioning, and other basics. Lessons lasting from three to four hours are available. Students who progress

to the next level must acquire all necessary personal gear. 432 Liberty Grove Rd., Alpharetta. 664-1533.

Sailing

Lanier Sailing Academy. For more than twenty years, the academy's certified instructors have taught proper sailing techniques to their students. Practical and basic sailing, advanced sailing, and coastal cruising classes are offered, and junior classes for children ages ten to sixteen are held

in the summer. Students enjoy rental discounts and free annual passes to Lake Lanier Islands and are eligible to join the school's sailing club. The academy is an American Sailing Association Training Facility. 8000 Holiday Rd., Buford. 945-8810.

Skating

All-American Skating Center. Owned and operated by Jack Burton, who also owns the Stone Mountain Figure Skating School, this facility teaches rollerskating to groups or individuals. Competitions are fierce. 5400 Bermuda Rd. at Hwy. 78, Stone Mountain. 469-9775.

Go With the Flow Sports. One of the newest sports on the block is in-line skating, an activity for the energetic and rubber-limbed. In-line skates can be rented here, and an instructional course is taught. 4 Elizabeth Way, Roswell. 992-3200.

Parkaire Olympic Ice Arena. Private and group instruction in figure skating is offered, and the **Georgia Amateur Hockey Association** teaches youth hockey to about 300 youngsters. A men's hockey league, which also numbers about 300, operates clinics for youth and adults. Fifteen figure skating professionals are on staff, and four international coaches take students all over the world to compete. Eleven "gold

test" professionals (USFSA-certified) are among the instructors. 4880 Lower Roswell Rd., Parkaire Landing Shopping Center, Marietta. 973-0753.

Stone Mountain Figure Skating School. This school has been around since 1984, but is now owned and operated by Jack Burton instead of by Stone Mountain Park. Group and private lessons offer both patch and freestyle instruction. All instructors were competitive skaters and were at least bronze medalists in international events. Some have instructed Olympic skaters; Don Laws, who coached Olympic Gold Medalist Scott Hamilton, is now the school's director. Its precision skating teams have competed internationally and took first place in Sweden (Precision Team Competition) in 1990. They also skated in the 1991 Macy's Day Parade. P.O. Box 778, Stone Mountain, 30086. 498-5730; 469-9599.

WRITING

For more information on writing classes and resources, see the art centers listed in the beginning of this chapter; see also chapter 10.

The Atlanta Writing Resource Center. Designed as a stimulating work environment for writers, the center encourages writers of fiction and nonfiction to explore its extensive library and clearinghouse service. Special programs target troubled teens, literacy skills, computer literacy for writers, and the fundamentals of creative and technical writing. A poetry competition and a writer-in-residence program are just two of its special features. Membership is nominal. 750 Kalb St., near Grant Park. 622-4152.

Callanwolde Fine Arts Center. Many classes and workshops cover all aspects of creative writing, including poetry and storytelling. 980 Briarcliff Rd., Druid Hills. 872-5338.

LECTURE SERIES

Lectures can provide a meaningful way to change pace, keep abreast of developments in a field other than one's own, and stir the mind with fresh perspectives. Check the newspaper's leisure section for current offerings.

Atlanta Historical Society. The Atlanta History Center in Buckhead hosts the **Aiken Lectures** which examine the roles that African-Americans played in the history of Atlanta and the Southeast in general prior to 1940. In the **Livingston Lectures**, held at the Atlanta History Center in Buckhead, contemporary historical figures present their views on a variety of current topics. The biannual **Elson Lectures** are educational and scholarly historical presentations by contemporary experts. 3101 Andrews Dr., Buckhead. 814-4000.

Conversations at the Carter Center. A series of six programs highlights the activities of the Carter Center at the Jimmy Carter Library. Lecture topics have included a discussion on world health challenges led by Executive Director William H. Foege, and a lecture on the art of conflict resolution led by Dayle E. Spencer and William J. Spencer, two associates with the Carter Center. A nominal fee is charged, and the lectures are open to the public. 1 Copenhill Ave., near Little Five Points. 420-5128.

Fernbank Science Center. On the second and fourth Wednesday of each month, a film or lecture on space science or astronomy is presented. Other lectures on scientific topics are offered throughout the year, and are open to the public. 156 Heaton Park Dr., off Artwood Rd., off Ponce de Leon Ave., Decatur. 378-4311.

High Museum of Art. Frequent lectures related to ongoing exhibitions are a regular part of the museum's offerings. 1280 Peachtree St., Woodruff Arts Center, Midtown. 733-4444.

NONCREDIT & CONTINUING EDUCATION

Some of these courses offer professional development CEUs (Continuing Education Units) while others are strictly for meeting new people and sifting through new experiences.

GENERAL

Atlanta College of Art. The college's noncredit, continuing education programs in art annually serve close to 2,000 adults and children (including preschoolers). More than seventy quarterly classes attract both beginners and professional artists or designers who wish to study drawing, painting, photography, print-making, computer graphics—even furniture design—to name a few of the offerings. Weekend workshops explore photography, handmade paper and offer instructive studio and gallery tours, among other topics. 1280 Peachtree St., Woodruff Arts Center, Midtown. 733-5200.

Atlanta Continuing Education Information System. ACES is a consortium of public and private institutions of higher and vocational or technical education; it offers noncredit and continuing education programs, and publishes a quarterly list that cross-references courses available in the Atlanta area. A subscription is charged. Georgia State University, Downtown. 651-3450.

Atlanta History Center. Workshops and classes cover a variety of topics, and teacher recertification courses are held in the summer. 130 West Paces Ferry Rd., Buckhead. 814-4000.

Clayton State College. Languages, software skills, and several certification programs are among the continuing education courses offered. Especially exciting are the programs for youngsters: **Kid's College**, held on Saturdays, teaches young students everything from beginning drawing to word processing. The **Preparatory School of Music** introduces musical ideas to tykes as young as eighteen months, accompanied by their parents. Adults may also take beginning piano and string classes. Outreach programs are held at county high schools in Rockdale, Henry, Clayton, and Fayette counties. 5900 N. Lee St., Morrow. 961-3550.

DeKalb College. In addition to academic and technical programs, Dekalb College also offers continuing education in subjects ranging from tap dancing and basic programming to Oriental cooking. The **Life Enrichment** programs, especially designed for active seniors, include arts and crafts, creative writing, and flower arranging. Among the recreation opportunities are scuba diving and yoga, and for the little people ages six to fourteen, there's a baseball spring training camp (551-3128). Central Campus: 555 N. Indian Creek Dr., Clarkston. 244-5050.

Emory University. Evening at Emory has become a way for Atlantans to meet people, learn something about the city, study foreign languages, and gain enrichment in a variety of pursuits. Study another language; learn how to renovate an old house; figure out how to meet your significant other within the upcoming year— these are among the possibilities offered by this wide-ranging program, which offers more than 150 different classes. 1540 Clifton Rd., Northeast. 874-0999.

Assistant Marshall C.H. Chandler did a census for Fulton County in 1860. The county's population of 11,572, of whom 7,741 lived in the City of Atlanta, included exactly two college students and twenty teachers. Three others were studying law, one dentistry, and eleven medicine.

Georgia Institute of Technology. Georgia Tech takes its continuing education seriously. Short courses (one to five days) allow professionals in various technical fields to update their knowledge and to acquire knowledge in collateral fields. In general, courses focus on architecture, engineering, management, and computer science. The **Language Institute** offers intensive English to international students as well as to business and professional people. 225 North Ave., Midtown. 894-2400.

Georgia State University. A variety of continuing education opportunities for adults is presented at Georgia State's North Metro Center. Computer, communication, and management skills as well as personal and professional development are among the program's strengths. One especially useful program serves the burgeoning immigrant population in Atlanta by enhancing the English skills of new residents. Day and evening classes are available. Continuing education units may be earned in some areas. **The Explorer** is the university's personal enrichment program. Some parts of this program are taught at the North Metro Center, some at the main campus downtown. Discounts for senior citizens (over age 62). North Metro: 1140 Hammond Dr., at Peachtree-Dun-woody Rd., Corporate Campus Office Park, Dunwoody. 551-7307; University Plaza, Downtown. 651-3456.

High Museum of Art. The High Museum offers various courses in the history of art, in European and American decorative arts, and other art topics. The **Institute for Teacher Training**, directed by the museum's Department of Education, offers workshops and courses; the latter enable participants to fulfill Georgia's requirements for teacher certification renewal. 1280 Peachtree St., Woodruff Arts Center, Midtown. 898-9508.

Michael C. Carlos Museum. Four full-time curators often lecture and present seminars and workshops to the public. Films, lectures, symposia, and concerts are presented in conjunction with traveling exhibits and the permanent collection. Monthly Saturday-morning workshops for children are connected to the museum's exhibitions and offer hands-on participation; for example, during **Hysterical Headwear** the children actually make hats after viewing a headwear exhibition. **Dig It** is a two-day summer program that introduces children through age eighteen to archeology. Fees are reasonable for both museum members and the public. 571 S. Kilgo St., Emory University, Northeast. 727-4282.

Oglethorpe University. In addition to being a vibrant institution, Oglethorpe University offers a variety of continuing education and evening programs, called **Learn and Live**. Students may study literature, learn the basics of wine enjoyment, unravel the mysteries of art history, or pursue the fundamentals of historic preservation. The language courses include the unusual: Arabic, Swedish, and Dutch, for instance. Personal enrichment and professional development are available during the evening hours, and a noncredit certificate program in management is offered. 4484 Peachtree Rd., Brookhaven. 364-8383.

Scottish Rite Children's Hospital. Professionals may earn continuing education units in a variety of courses focused on the health needs of children. 1001 Johnson Ferry Rd., at Meridian Mark Rd., Sandy Springs. 250-2148.

Southern College of Technology. Continuing education credits may be earned (one credit per ten hours of class) for engineering courses designed for professionals. There are also more than thirty computer classes, open to everyone. The school is an authorized **AutoCAD Training Center**, and the landfill operators certification training program meets the state's requirements. The EIT refresher class prepares engineers to take the state exam; it meets on Saturdays for several consecutive weeks. Russian and Japanese are also taught. 1100 S. Marietta Pkwy., off I-75 (Exit 112), Marietta. 528-7240.

SENIOR ADULT CLASSES

The general listings elsewhere in this chapter also contain information of interest to people over fifty. The following programs are entirely devoted to meeting the needs of this expanding population.

Cobb Senior Center. See page 233. 1885 Smyrna-Roswell Rd., Smyrna. 801-5320.

High Museum of Art. The **Seniors Create** art class is taught at various senior centers in the metro area and sometimes at the High Museum itself. The classes are designed to introduce participants to the basics of art, and to foster creativity and group interaction. 1280 Peachtree St., Woodruff Arts Center, Midtown. TDD—898-9502; 898-9570.

Life Enrichment Services. Classes for people fifty and over cover everything from nutrition to art. 1340 McConnell Dr., Decatur. 321-6960.

Senior Health Plus. *See page 245.* 3950 Austell Rd., SW, Austell. 732-3970.

Senior University, Emory University. Founded in 1979, Emory University's Senior University currently is patterned after similar programs at other universities, notably Duke and Harvard. The program explores topics such as humanistic medicine and education, theater, ornithology, language study, and history. Emory University, Northeast. 874-0999 (Community Education).

POST-SECONDARY EDUCATION

Atlanta's academic institutions offer young people a wide variety of educational opportunities. But the youngsters are not the only ones looking for this kind of education—one of the most popular post-retirement activities these days is acquiring another degree, or starting a long-dreamed-of career in another field. For example, one man we know studied anthropology after retiring from a utility company! Atlanta's many fine academic institutions welcome these nontraditional students as well as the young ones.

ACADEMIC

Agnes Scott College. Affiliated with the Presbyterian Church, Agnes Scott College is a four-year, liberal arts college for women. The college is especially responsive to women whose educations have been interrupted. (One such student is in her 80s!) Scott's **Global Awareness Program** offers every student the opportunity to live and study in another culture. Its library houses an extensive collection of documents relating to American poet Robert Frost and to alumna Catherine Marshall, widow of Peter Marshall, chaplain of the United States Senate in the 1940s. 141 E. College Ave., Decatur. 638-6000.

American College for the Applied Arts. Offering both associate and baccalaureate degrees in fashion merchandising and design, interior design, commercial art, and business administration, the college also has campuses in London and Los Angeles. It is an accredited, coeducational college whose Atlanta campus has an international student body that represents about 25 countries, in addition to nearly every state in the US. 3330 Peachtree Rd., Buckhead. 231-9000.

Atlanta College of Art. The oldest private art college in the Southeast, the Atlanta College of Art is next door to the High Museum of Art. A founding member of the Woodruff Arts Center, the college is dedicated to delivering art and art education to the public. Its gallery exhibitions, visiting artists lectures, and continuing education classes are open to the public and complement an undergraduate academic program that is two-thirds studio arts and one-third liberal arts. The college's primary mission is to serve its undergraduates. But there's more—with a grant from the Georgia Council for the Arts, the college developed the **Georgia Artists Registry**, housed in the college library. Containing slides and computerized information, the registry allows collectors, decorators, and others to search for specific kinds of artists throughout the state. The public may use the fine arts library by special arrangement. 1280 Peachtree Rd., Woodruff Arts Center, Midtown. 898-1165.

Atlanta University Center. Operating as a nonprofit corporation, the center is a consortium that provides support services to six traditionally African-American private colleges. For example, it raises funds for the dual degree program in Engineering, which enlists the cooperation of area technology institutes. This five-year program enables AUC undergraduates to earn both a bachelor's degree and an engineering degree. 111 James P. Brawley Dr., Southwest. 522-8980.

Brenau University. Part of the Gainesville-based private women's college of the same name, the coeducational university was founded in the 1970s to allow students to work full-time while earning academic degrees, both undergraduate and graduate. Evening and weekend

classes make achieving these goals more convenient. Majors include business administration, education, criminal justice, interior design, and nursing. The M.B.A. and the M.Ed. are the two graduate degrees offered. The **Weekend College**, established in 1986, allows working adults to pursue their goals on Friday evenings, Saturdays, and/or Sunday afternoons. 6745 Peachtree Industrial Blvd., Doraville. 446-2900; 820 N. Cobb Pkwy., Marietta. 426-5555.

Clark Atlanta University. Formed in 1989 by the merger of Clark College (founded in 1869) and Atlanta University (founded in 1865), the new institution combines undergraduate education with graduate programs in business administration, education, arts and sciences, library science, and social work, among other subjects. James P. Brawley Dr. at Fair St., Northwest. 880-8000.

Clayton State College. One of the metro area's most attractive campuses, its lovely trees shelter impressive buildings, including the internationally renowned **Spivey Hall**, an outstanding performance facility (*see chapter 3*). A unit of the University System of Georgia, the college was founded in 1969 as a two-year institution and became a four-year college in 1986. One unique program is a major in fine instrument making. 5900 N. Lee St., Morrow. 961-3400.

DeKalb College. Part of the University System of Georgia, DeKalb College has three locations throughout DeKalb County, in addition to off-campus activities at three public high schools and an affiliation with the Gwinnett Univer-

sity System Center. Regular academic programs offer two-year degrees, and both the **Gwinnett Tech** center and the central campus offer technical programs. Central campus: 555 N. Indian Creek Dr., Clarkston. 299-4000.

Emory University. Boasting an extraordinary campus whose original buildings were designed by renowned architect Henry Hornbostle, Emory University grew in size and substance partly because of an early, hefty endowment from Asa Candler, founder of the Coca-Cola Company. Emory draws students from every state and all over the world to its undergraduate and graduate programs. Especially well known are the **Schools of Theology**—the university is affiliated with the Methodist Church—**Law**, and **Medicine**. Its **Michael C. Carlos Museum** *(see chapter 5)* is developing an international reputation. The **Institute of Liberal Arts** grants doctorates to students who structure an interdisciplinary and individualized course of study. **Emory at Oxford College** in Covington is a two-year liberal arts college affiliated with Emory University. 1380 S. Oxford Rd., between Clifton Rd. and S. Oxford Rd., Northeast. 727-6123.

Georgia Institute of Technology. Part of the state's university system, century-old "Georgia Tech" is known for its traditional engineering and science programs. But its **College of Architecture** is quickly gaining an international reputation, partly because of the success of alumnus John C. Portman, Jr. The building construction program, based in the College of Architecture, is unique to the area. The **Center for Education Integrating Science, Mathematics, and Computing (CEISMC)**, ties together business and educational community resources, both public and private. These programs enrich elementary and secondary students' experiences in math and science and support teachers of those subjects in grades K through twelve. Georgia Tech also offers a graduate program that uses video-based instruction; a master of science degree in several engineering fields may be earned via videotape. 225 North Ave., Midtown. 894-5185.

Georgia State University. Originally the Georgia Tech Evening, Georgia State University today boasts a student body numbering more than 24,000. The **College of Business Administration** and the **College of Law** both attract evening and part-time students, as well as full-time day students. The doctoral programs in psychology, English, and sports science, the master's programs in historic preservation and community counseling, and the programs in the **Cecil B. Day School of Hospitality Administration** are among its most highly regarded offerings. University Plaza, Downtown. 651-2000.

Gwinnett University System Center. The exploding population of Gwinnett County, where nearly half of the residents have attended college, makes it ideal for this consortium-style institution. In 1987, the Georgia Board of Regents assembled resources from the University of Georgia in Athens, Georgia State University, and DeKalb College to develop a center that would readily serve the needs of this growing community. The center offers education, business administration, and core curriculum courses, and both graduate and undergraduate work may be pursued. 1301 Atkinson Rd., Lawrenceville. 995-2196.

Kennesaw State College. A unit of the University System of Georgia, Kennesaw State College has developed a reputation for its small classes and resulting individualized attention to students' needs. Originally a two-year college, it expanded to a four-year institution in 1979, and now has a student body numbering over 12,000. Kennesaw has the nation's first undergraduate degree program in professional sales and is the largest four-year college in the university system. Named in *US News and World Report* as an up-and-coming regional college, Kennesaw offers M.B.A. programs for both experienced professionals and "regular" students. 3455 Frey Lake Rd., Kennesaw. 423-6000.

> During World War II, the government located the Centers for Disease Control (CDC) in Atlanta to conduct experiments that might lead to a cure for malaria and related diseases. The similarity between Georgia's swamplands and the Pacific Islands was thought to enhance the fruitfulness of research. The CDC is still headquartered here.

Life College. Founded in 1974 as Life Chiropractic College by Dr. Sid E. Williams, the college now includes a **School of Chiropractic** and a **School of Undergraduate Studies**. A nonprofit institution, Life offers graduate courses that can lead to a doctorate in chiropractic or a master's in sports health science. Undergraduate studies lead to a B.S. in **Nutrition for the Chiropractic Sciences** or a B.B.A. with a major in management and minors in

athletic coaching or training. A diploma program for chiropractic technicians is also offered. Other graduate programs are being developed on this private, coeducational, suburban campus in northwest Atlanta. Admission and information: 1269 Barclay Cir., Marietta. 424-0554.

Mercer University. Mercer University holds classes at various state prison facilities, and inmates may earn college degrees. The university offers an M.S. in **Health Care Policy and Administration**, an M.S. in **Technology Management** (for managers who work in technical fields in industry and government), and other graduate programs. Equipped with research facilities, Mercer's **Southern School of Pharmacy** is one of the top schools of its kind in the Southeast. Many graduate programs are taught on evenings and weekends to accommodate the working student. 3001 Mercer University Dr., off Chamblee-Tucker Rd. at I-85 (Exit 34), Northeast. 986-3000.

Morehouse College. The American Baptist Home Mission Society established this liberal arts college for men in 1867 as the Augusta Institute. Classes were held in the basement of the Springfield Baptist Church in Augusta, Georgia. In 1879, it moved to Atlanta and changed its name twice, finally becoming Morehouse College, named for Henry Lyman Morehouse, an officer in the Mission Society. Claiming the late Dr. Martin Luther King, Jr., among its famous graduates, Morehouse College is a fixed star in Atlanta's education firmament. Its student body, numbering over 3,000, represents most of the states as well as many foreign countries. 830 Westview Dr., Southwest. 681-2800.

Morehouse School of Medicine. Established in the early 1970s as an affiliate of Morehouse College, the medical school became independent of Morehouse in 1981. Today it is a four-year institution with special interests in family practice, public health, and preventive medicine. The School of Medicine's first president, Dr. Louis Sullivan, became the US Secretary of Health and Human Services under President George Bush. Although predominantly designed to encourage minorities to enter medicine, applications from all races and national origins are encouraged. 720 Westview Dr., Northwest. 752-1500.

Morris Brown College. Another of Atlanta's traditionally African-American liberal arts colleges, coeducational Morris Brown was established in 1881 and today serves about 2,000 students. Recent alumni include an air force general as well as executives in local companies. Perhaps its most well-known program is hospitality administration, and its paralegal/prelaw program is also strong. 643 Martin Luther King, Jr., Dr., Northwest. 220-0140.

Oglethorpe University. Chartered in 1835 on a campus at Midway near Milledgeville (then the Georgia capital), the institution bears the name of the state's founder, General James Edward Oglethorpe. The Civil War interrupted instruction and decimated the student body. When it relocated to Atlanta after the war, the school held its classes in a large mansion on the site of Atlanta's present city hall. Oglethorpe moved to its new, Gothic-style campus on Peachtree Road in north Atlanta in 1915. Oglethorpe University is proud of its small student body and its focus on liberal arts education. *The National Review College Guide* lists it among America's top fifty liberal arts schools. The graduate programs target teacher education. 4484 Peachtree Rd., Brookhaven. 261-1441.

Reinhardt College. Founded in 1883 as a school affiliated with the Methodist Church, Reinhardt is a two-year school with a four-year business program. A transfer program for students in nursing is affiliated with Emory University. The school's **Academic Support Office** specializes in assisting students who have learning disorders. Numbering about 800 students, Reinhardt offers day programs at the main campus and evening study at satellite centers (North Fulton, Waleska, and Chatsworth). Despite its small size, Reinhardt fields six intercollegiate sports for men and women. North Fulton Center at Roswell. 587-2849. 140 Hwy 140 Georgia. Atlanta line, 928-0222.

Southern College of Technology. Founded in 1948, Southern College of Technology is a senior residential college in the university system of Georgia. Located on a 232-acre campus in

Marietta, Southern Tech serves some 4,000 students in day and evening classes. The **Schools of Architecture, Management, Engineering Technology,** and **Arts and Sciences** offer a wide variety of degree programs. Graduate programs are offered in selected fields. 1100 S. Marietta Pkwy., off I-75 (Exit 112), Marietta. 528-7222 (Public Relations) and 528-7281 (Admissions).

Spelman College. Spelman was founded in 1881 by Sophia D. Packard and Harriet E. Giles, two missionaries from New England who came South to establish a school for black women. In 1894, the liberal arts college was named for Lucy Henry Spelman, mother-in-law of benefactor John D. Rockefeller. The college offers a new interdisciplinary program that combines any two seemingly disparate fields, and has special strengths in fine art. 350 Spelman Lane, Northwest. 681-3643.

PROFESSIONAL & TECHNICAL

Two-year academic curricula may lead to an Associate of Arts (A.A.) degree. But many post-secondary institutions also offer diploma programs, which are shorter and more closely focused on limited areas of study.

Art Institute of Atlanta. The Institute prepares students for careers in visual communications, photography, interior design, fashion marketing, and music entertainment management. Two-year programs in these fields lead to the Associate of Arts degree. Diplomas are awarded following successful completion of continuing education courses in applied photography, design principles and production, and residential planning and retailing. The School of Culinary Arts offers an A.A. degree. 3376 Peachtree Rd., Buckhead. 266-2662.

Atlanta Area Technical School. Operated by the Atlanta Board of Education, the school offers programs in many career choices, including accounting, child development, culinary arts, electronics, mechanical drawing,

practical nursing, and welding. Degree options are available in concert with Atlanta Metropolitan College. 1560 Stewart Ave., Southwest. 756-3700; 4190 Northside Dr., Tuxedo Center, Northwest. 842-3117; admissions, 756-3880.

Bauder College. The curriculum prepares students for careers in fashion design, interior design, and fashion merchandising. All programs lead to Associate of Arts degrees and blend classroom study with "real world" exposure. Founded in 1956, Bauder claims that it places more than eighty percent of its graduates within the industry. 3500 Peachtree Rd., Phipps Plaza, Buckhead. 237-7573.

Brown College of Court Reporting and Medical Transcription.

For more than two decades, nationally recognized Brown College has been training students in court reporting and medical transcription. The college asserts that, since 1972, more than 97% of its graduates have been successfully placed within their respective professions. Candidates for admission must have at least a high school diploma and must pass tests in spelling, grammar, punctuation, vocabulary, and typing. Day and evening classes are available. 1100 Spring St., Ste. 200, Midtown. 876-1227.

DeKalb Technical Institute.

Operated by the DeKalb County Board of Education, the institute offers diploma and associate degree programs in business areas such as accounting and secretarial studies. Fashion merchandising, entrepreneurship, information processing, and marketing management are other areas of concentration. Day, evening, and weekend classes are taught at both the main campus and at several other area locations. 495 N. Indian Creek Dr., Clarkston. 297-9522.

Devry Institute of Technology.

Offering bachelor of science degrees in electronics engineering technology, computer information systems, business operations, and accounting, as well as an associate degree of applied science in electronics, the institute conducts both day and evening classes (although not all programs are offered in the evening). Equipment and facilities are continuously upgraded to meet contemporary business needs. Based in Chicago, Devry has eleven campuses in North America.

The Atlanta campus claims that it places approximately ninety percent of its students upon graduation. The student body currently numbers about 3,000, drawn largely from the Southeast. 250 N. Arcadia Ave., Decatur. 292-7900.

Georgia State University North Metro Center.

A facility for all kinds of learning opportunities, this center offers a certificate program in office administration that takes three or four quarters to complete. Continuing education and other credit and noncredit programs are also offered. 1140 Hammond Dr., Corporate Campus III Office Park, Dunwoody. 551-7307.

Gwinnett Technical Institute.

The institute is a public, post-secondary school operated by the Gwinnett County Board of Education. Its more than 41 programs include data processing, office technology, marketing, health sciences, and technical and trade curricula. Classes are taught mornings, afternoons, and evenings at the institute and several other area locations. Associate degree and diploma programs are available, as are continuing education courses, seminars, and workshops. The institute claims a 99% placement rate. The modern facility occupies a fifty-acre campus and is easily accessed off Hwy. 316 and Hwy. 120, via I-85. 1250 Atkinson Rd., Lawrenceville. 962-7580.

Massey Business College.

This college has been serving the Atlanta business community for more than forty years. Graduates demonstrate a high (ninety percent) placement rate after completing programs in such areas as business administration, secretarial studies, computer operation, and word processing. Associate degrees and diploma programs are available in day and night programs. 120 Ralph McGill Blvd., Downtown. 872-1900; 5299 Roswell Rd., Sandy Springs. 256-3533.

Micro Center Computer Education. Introductory, intermediate, and advanced courses in standard software programs, such as Lotus and dBase, as well as PageMaker, Quark and Ventura for desktop publishing, are taught for IBM, IBM compatibles, and Macintosh. Look for free, hands-on seminars. 1221 Powers Ferry Rd., Powers Ferry Plaza, Marietta. 859-1545.

The Portfolio Center. Founded in 1979 to serve the needs of commercial artists, photographers, writers, and others who fill the ranks of the advertising production industry, the Portfolio Center has developed a national reputation for its outstanding programs. Agencies all over the country recruit from the Portfolio Center, which maintains an active placement office. The center serves some 300 students in five programs: art direction, copywriting, graphic design, illustration, and photography. The courses take about two years to complete and lead to a professional diploma. Courses are primarily postgraduate, and although it is not a requirement, most students already have a college degree in some liberal arts field. The center is housed in a former warehouse area, part of which is now a studio and gallery center called TULA *(see chapter 6).* West off Peachtree St., between Mick's and Brookwood Square. 125 Bennett St., Brookwood. 351-5055.

School of Culinary Arts. A division of the Art Institute of Atlanta *(see page 263).* 3376 Peachtree Rd., Buckhead. 277-1341.

SPEAKERS' BUREAUS

Companies, organizations, and institutions will find these sources handy when planning special events for guests or when seeking ways to enhance their staffers' knowledge.

Atlanta Preservation Center. The speakers' bureau for the center presents talks about the center's mission and history. A slide presentation can be given on all of the center's tours *(see chapter 5).* The **Inman Park Heritage Education** unit explores the old neighborhood and is especially appropriate for school groups and neighborhood associations. **Stories We're Sharing** is a speakers' bureau program that covers Reynoldstown, South Atlanta, and Mozley Park. Free. The DeSoto, Ste. 3, 156 7th St., Midtown. 876-2040.

Fernbank Science Center. Director Mary Hiers will refer you to the appropriate person to address these and other subjects: environmental and nature issues, astronomy, and geography. 156 Heaton Park Dr., off Artwood Rd., off Ponce de Leon Ave., Decatur. 378-4311.

High Museum of Art. Need someone knowledgeable about art-related themes to address your business, club, or organization? Such a talk, illustrated by appropriate slides, would be useful to a group planning a trip to another country or to a business wanting to introduce its staff to another country through its art before doing business there. Topics could also include contemporary art trends or current exhibitions at the High. The nominal tax-deductible fee is waived for senior citizen centers. Reservations are required. 1280 Peachtree St., Woodruff Arts Center, Midtown. 733-4444.

TRAVEL

Employment in the travel industry constitutes a popular primary—as well as secondary—career choice. In the past two decades, Atlanta has seen a phenomenal growth in the number of travel-related businesses based here. These are some sources for entry into the travel industry.

Advanced Career Training School of Business and Travel. Full-time resident programs are available for students seeking work in the travel industry and in business. With campuses in both Atlanta and Jacksonville, this ACCET-accredited school was founded in 1975. Its curriculum is designed to combine classroom work and hands-on experience with airline, cruise, and travel agency industry requirements. Day and evening classes are offered, and state-of-the-art computer equipment is used in instruction. Ask about financial aid. 1 Corporate Square Ste. 110, (North Campus), Northeast. 321-2929; 7322 Hwy. 85, Ste. 2 (South Campus), Riverdale. 991-9356.

Executive Travel Institute. Day and evening classes are available for students, who must have a high school diploma or its equivalent, such as a GED. A writing sample and personal interview are required. The curriculum contains the courses required to work in travel agencies, the airlines, the cruise and tour industry, the hospitality industry, or other such organizations. Executive is recognized by the Career College Association and is licensed by the state of Georgia. 5775 Peachtree-Dunwoody Rd., Bldg. E, Ste. 300, Dunwoody. 303-2929.

Omni School of Travel. A program offered by Omni Career Institute, the travel and tourism curriculum is designed to equip students with the technical and professional skills required for employment in the travel industry. The course covers agency structure, geography, and domestic and international fares, as well as ticketing, reservation procedures, and other subjects appropriate to securing placement in the industry. 1150 Hammond Dr., Ste. A-1190, Sandy Springs. 395-0055.

CHAPTER 10

Getting Involved

To close our residential guide to Atlanta, we've chosen a sampling of organizations that could use your involvement. Whether you are interested in volunteering your time for a charitable organization, training as a docent at a museum, or joining a garden club, you can find the information you need in the following pages. Help others and your city by taking an active part in Atlanta.

Many groups charge dues, so we have included a scale based on annual membership fees. If these charges range from nothing to $20, we have labeled them nominal. Moderate translates as a fee from $20 to $40, while $40 and up is marked substantial. Corporate memberships are often quite substantial, while many organizations have discounts for families, students, and older members. Our listing does not include professional associations or lobbying groups.

THE ARTS

Volunteers in service to the arts are sorely needed as businesses and government make less of their precious resources available to arts organizations. In addition, joining some of these organizations will offer outlets for exploring your own talents in the arts. See also the organizations in Chapters 3 (All About the Arts), 5 (City Sights), and 9 (Expanding Your Mind) for groups that will welcome your volunteer participation.

ART

ART Station. Nominally priced memberships sustain the work of one of the Atlanta area's most active arts centers. Members receive the quarterly newsletter, reduced admission to events and classes, and first dibs on tickets to concerts, plays, and other events. Specially priced memberships are offered to all active performance, visual, or literary artists. 5384 Manor Dr., Stone Mountain. 469-1105.

Atlanta Artists Gallery and Club. Open to all working artists as well as those interested in art, the club fosters art and art education. Begun in 1954 by a small group of artists, the former Atlanta Watercolor Club has over 300 members and is now one of the largest and most active artists' groups in the region. The club also sponsors a gallery, which maintains, for public access, a cross-reference file of artists and artisans in every medium. Dues are substantial, but are nominal for art students. 2979 Grandview Ave., Buckhead. 237-2324; 1 Galleria Pkwy., Galleria, Northwest. 850-1310.

Atlanta International Museum of Art and Design. This innovative young museum offers the opportunity to volunteer as a docent and to serve on museum councils. The benefits of very reasonably priced memberships include invitations to workshops, lectures, and other activities. 285 Peachtree Center Ave., Marquis Two Tower, Garden Level, Downtown. 688-2467.

Callanwolde Guild. This volunteer service organization, sponsored by the Callanwolde Foundation, offers membership to persons interested in staffing the Callanwolde art shop, conducting tours of Callanwolde itself, assisting at gallery openings and catered luncheons, and working on fund-raising efforts. The guild raises funds for Callanwolde's restoration, an ongoing endeavor. One of its recent projects was the restoration of the Aeolian organ in the house. General membership is moderate, but nominal for students and seniors. 980 Briarcliff Rd., Druid Hills. 872-5338.

Fine Arts Society of Kennesaw. A young organization of about ninety members, this society provides art education and a meeting place where folks interested in art can find each other. The society uses a volunteer program, designed by the High Museum of Art, to teach art education in area elementary schools. An annual Christmas shop is set up at the society's Community House, built about 1890 and donated by the city of Kennesaw for the use of area organizations. Monthly meetings feature a speaker whose presentation focuses on art. Membership dues are nominal. 2838 Cherokee St., Community House, Kennesaw. 499-0866.

High Museum of Art Members Guild.
This is the volunteer organization of the High Museum. The guild's purpose is to extend the museum's cultural and educational activities through service and fund-raising projects. Members may belong to any of five component groups, each offering a variety of programs and events. Guild membership consists of a moderate fee added to museum membership; component group memberships cost an additional small fee. **Art Associates** devotes its energy to all kinds of art education programs, children-oriented projects, and fund-raising events. **Peachtree Arts** attracts couples and singles, mostly in their thirties and forties, to fund-raising activities for the museum, evening educational programs and special events **Suburban Art Committee** members enjoy social and educational programs both at the museum and in facilities located in the outer metro area. **Docent Volunteer Educators** train and serve as docents; they conduct museum tours and participate in a range of programs directed by the museum's Department of Education. 892-3600, Ext., 305. **Young Careers** is the High's largest support group. Ranging from college age to their thirties, members are young professionals who wish to learn more about art. Membership in the High Museum itself entitles members to free admission to the museum in addition to other special privileges. 1280 Peachtree St., Woodruff Arts Center, Midtown. 898-1152.

Michael C. Carlos Museum.
The **Museum Society Support Group** trains volunteers to work in the facility, as well as in the museum's shop, at the information desk, and on the administrative support staff. The museum's **Docent Guild** selects and trains interested members during a fall training session. Members organize tours to other galleries, private homes, and museums, both in this city and elsewhere. The group also schedules purely social activities. The moderately priced museum membership includes invitations to private previews and parties, a newsletter, and discounts on educational programs and shop purchases. 571 S. Kilgo St., Emory University, Northeast. 727-0516 (membership line).

Nexus Contemporary Art Center.
Membership in this unique arts center is moderately priced and brings with it discounts on art books, performance tickets, and workshops. Invitations to preview parties, lectures, and other members-only events are additional benefits. The quarterly newsletter, special admission to the annual **ARTPARTY**, and announcements for all Nexus events also come with membership. Volunteers assist with all manner of support activities. P.O. Box 54661, Atlanta, 30308-0661. 535 Means St., near Georgia Tech, off Ponders and Marietta Sts., Downtown. 688-1970.

Portrait Society of Atlanta. A regional organization of more than 140 portrait painters and sculptors, this society was founded in 1980 to enhance community awareness of portraiture and local arts. Membership is open to all regional portrait artists, at all levels of expertise. Members are categorized in four groups: Associate, Juried, Merit, and Excellence. Meetings convene at the North DeKalb Cultural Arts Center, 5339 Chamblee-Dunwoody Rd., Dunwoody. The membership fee is moderate, but interesting opportunities, such as workshops, are among the benefits. P.O. Box 941042, Atlanta, 31141-0042. 233-4569.

Sandy Springs Arts and Heritage Society. Formed in 1980 to support the arts and preserve the heritage of Sandy Springs, this society began its efforts by working to preserve the springs site from which Sandy Springs

took its name. From that effort arose the Sandy Springs Historical Foundation. Since then the society, with about sixty members, has directed its support toward the community's artists. Each year the society works with the local arts festivals to sponsor these artists, and its activities also support the Abernathy Arts Center. The society also interacts with the Sandy Springs Chamber Orchestra. Contact Dr. Sedgie Newsom. P.O. Box 720098, Sandy Springs, 30358. 252-1221.

Spruill Center for the Arts Guild. Membership in the Spruill Center for the Arts Guild, a fund-raising and support arm of the center, is available to center members. Guild volunteers assist teachers of Head Start classes and put on the **Artistic Affair** in the spring. This fund-raising auction, ball, and banquet is a real gala. 5339 Chamblee-Dunwoody Rd., Dunwoody. 394-3447.

DANCE

Atlanta Cajun Dance Association. The rich musical heritage of Louisiana is preserved by this association, which holds many musical workshops and

dances throughout the year. Robert D. Kwasha, contact. Mail only: 2704 Laurelwood Rd., Atlanta, 30360. 451-6611.

MUSIC

Many fine amateur performance groups, among them choruses, bands, and orchestras, flourish in Atlanta. See also the appropriate sections of Chapter 3 (All About the Arts).

Atlanta Balalaika Society. The society accepts volunteer musicians for the society orchestra, publicists, clerical workers, and ushers. It also looks for help with myriad other needs. Instruments and instructions are provided

for those who wish to participate as musicians. Contact Mike Cooper. P.O. Box 33811, Decatur, 30033. 288-9512.

Atlanta Music Club. Founded in 1915, this is the oldest chartered nonprofit music organization in Atlanta. Its mission is to provide opportunities for music education and community enrichment, and its active membership now numbers over 500 people. In 1958 the club founded the **Atlanta Community Orchestra**, and the group also works on scholarships and awards for young artists. Its **Young Performers of Atlanta** program gives young artists an opportunity to perform in professional settings. Club membership fees are substantial, but fees for Young Performers are nominal. Membership has many benefits. 975 E. Rock Springs Rd., NE. 872-9670.

Atlanta Opera. Several groups work

year-round in support of the Atlanta opera. For information: 1800 Peachtree St., Ste. 620, Midtown. 355-3311. **Atlanta Opera Guild:** For over fifty years, the Atlanta Opera Guild has promoted appreciation of opera throughout the Southeast and has worked to encourage young singers. The guild helps with the **Metropolitan Opera Southeast Region Auditions and District Auditions**. The membership fee is substantial. **Friends of the Atlanta Opera:** More than 350 members form this active group that supplies office and production assistance during the opera season. The Friends also operate the **Atlanta Opera Gift Shop**, host dinners for the cast before dress rehearsals, provide transportation for cast members, and attend to other needs that the cast might have during a performance. The group further promotes public awareness of opera through its three off-season musicales. Held in private homes, these are musical evenings with arias, lectures, and refreshments. The Friends' annual fall gala is its largest fund-raiser. Membership is

moderate. **POCO! for The Atlanta Opera:** Some 200 young professionals strive to broaden the audience and raise money for the Atlanta Opera. Taking its name from the Italian musical phrase *poco vivace*, "a little lively," POCO! hosts an annual black-tie gala and auction. Its educational course, **OPERA 101**, runs five consecutive weeks in the summer. POCO! volunteers assist in the opera's administrative offices as well as backstage, and sing in the opera chorus. Membership is moderate.

Atlanta Symphony Associates. This

volunteer support group for the Atlanta Symphony Orchestra numbers almost 1,200 members, and is divided into eight subgroups. Each unit handles specific fund-raising programs, such as the **Decorators' Show House**, the **Sleighbell Luncheon and Fashion Show**, the **Musical Marathon Ball and Auction**, and **Gifts of Note** (music-themed T-shirts and such). The associates also help with educational programs, hospitality for visiting artists, and myriad fund-raising tasks throughout the year, including the **Atlanta Symphony Ball**. To further audience development, other volunteers work with the symphony's marketing department to do subscriber surveys and conduct Symphony Hall tours. The music education programs include **Symphony Street**, presented for public elementary schools, and the **Young People's Concerts**, presented for middle school students. Music appreciation courses are taught in both the mornings and evenings, and concert previews are offered to the public. Memberships range upward from the moderate category. 1293 Peachtree St., Woodruff Arts Center, Midtown. 898-1184.

The Entertainers. Begun at the Cobb Senior Center in 1988, the group is directed by Marthe Nagy. Members produce performances at the center, as well as at hospitals, nursing homes, and churches. The 34 members sing, produce dramatic pieces, and dance. Membership is open to anyone living in Cobb who is over the age of 55—the average age of the members is around 68. Practices are held Mondays at 12:30 P.M. at the center. 1885 Roswell St., Smyrna. 801-5320.

Jubilee Cultural Alliance. An association of business leaders and citizens in Cobb County, Jubilee was founded just over a decade ago to increase cultural awareness and to ensure quality cultural events in Cobb County and the metro area. Jubilee presents a visual arts exhibition in **Gallery 300** and an annual summer concert series. All events are free and open to the public. Volunteers are welcome to assist in various concert-support activities and in the gallery. One Galleria Pkwy., Northwest. 988-9641.

Pro-Mozart Society of Atlanta. The society presents four to six annual concerts at the Atlanta History Center or at Pace Academy, both in Buckhead. Programs feature Mozart's music, but not exclusively. It also sponsors a scholarship program. Free for members, except for certain special events. The concerts are free for the public. Membership is substantial, but senior citizens enjoy a discount. P.O. Box 12217, Atlanta, 30355.

Steinway Society. Headquartered at the Piano Gallery, the society was founded in 1980 to foster fine piano music and its performance. The society gives young performers the opportunity to further their development through scholarship competition, and it presents special musical events throughout the year, including recitals, concerts, programs in members' homes, and group trips. **Keyboard Classics**, a social group within the society, sponsors two additional events each year; at least one is a black-tie affair. People from all walks of life make up the membership. Membership is moderate, and Keyboard Classics charges a substantial additional fee. 2140 Peachtree Rd., Ste. 125, Brookwood Square, Brookwood. 351-8773.

PHOTOGRAPHY

Cobb Photo Society. Founded in the mid 70s, the society promotes photography, and its members include both amateurs and professionals. About ninety active members make up the society, which meets semimonthly at the Cobb County Central Library. Competitions among the members take place once each month. An annual Christmas dinner, a photographer-of-the-year award, and various field trips throughout the year keep the society busy. Program content varies, from a lighting demonstration to how to do special-effects slides. Leo Burgess, president. P.O. Box 267, Smyrna, 30081. Home: 427-4911; Studio: 428-2955.

Southeastern Photographic Society. Founded in 1976, the society promotes photography among its members and within the community. Photographers at all levels of skill, both amateur and professional, compose the membership. Monthly meetings feature guest speakers, mini-workshops, travelogues, critiques, and competitions. The group is affiliated with both national and regional photographic societies. Membership fees are nominal. 1935 Cliff Valley Way, Ste. 210, Northeast. 633-1990.

THEATER

All the theaters listed in Chapter 3 (All About the Arts) have active volunteer groups that do everything from assisting in set construction at Theater Gael to leading community awareness programs for Theater in the Square in Marietta. These theaters *need* volunteer assistance.

Alliance Theatre. Several volunteer groups support the theatre, including: **PROS** is for professionals who cannot volunteer for daytime projects. The **Alliance Theatre Guild** and the **Alliance Children's Theatre Guild** lend support in areas too numerous to list. The **Play Support Team Project** is a special way to enjoy theater. For a nominal fee, participants attend rehearsals, symposia, dinners with cast members and directors, and receive tickets to the performances. The **Usher Corps** members enjoy seeing the productions as compensation for their services. 1280 Peachtree St., Woodruff Arts Center, Midtown. 892-2414.

Fox Theatre. Two volunteer groups work to benefit the Fox Theatre. The **Atlanta Landmarks Society** formed in the mid-1970s to save the Fox from destruction. Landmarks later established a second group called **Friends of the Fox** to develop financial resources for Fox restoration projects. Membership in this group ranges from the moderate to the extra expensive (881-2119). In addition to these groups, volunteer ushers work during performances and see the shows at no charge. Orientation courses take place about twelve times a year. 660 Peachtree St., Midtown. 249-6400.

WRITING

Atlanta Writing Resource Center. Poets and writers attend bimonthly critique groups and monthly open readings that include potluck receptions. The center, established in 1984, is a well-established organization on the Atlanta writing scene. A multi-cultural group, it produces a newsletter, conducts poetry competitions and an annual writing forum, and hosts book parties. Membership is moderate. David McCord is executive director. 750 Kalb St., Rooms 104 & 105, Grant Park. 622-4152.

First World Writers. First World formed in 1985 out of another writers collective. Its members conduct monthly critique sessions and work to promote the craft of writing. They also serve as a support group for African-American writers in the Atlanta area. First World publishes periodic anthologies. Membership is nominal. P.O. Box 92483, Atlanta, 30314. 981-3076.

Georgia Poetry Society. Composed of about 300 members from Atlanta and throughout Georgia, as well as a few from other states, the society was established in 1979 to further networking opportunities among writers. It sponsors international and national competitions, and its activities include an annual **Youth Poetry** contest for all grades. The society publishes an annual anthology, *The Reach of Song*, containing prize-winning and selective poems by society members. Membership is moderate. Contact Mr. B.I. Garland. 1302 Sunland Dr., NE, Atlanta, 30319-3133. 231-4183.

Gwinnett Writers Club. Meeting twice a month to share and encourage one another's writings, this group is more than five years old. Members include some published writers and some still striving for publication. Free. Mail only: 137 Lancelot Way, Lawrenceville, 30245.

Pinckneyville Writers Group. Twice each month, the members gather to critique their colleagues' work in progress as well as their finished pieces from every genre, including romance, nonfiction, fiction, and poetry. Writers from every background are represented, both professionals and non-professionals. Contact Kay Watkins. Free. 4300 Holcomb Bridge Rd., Norcross, 30092. 417-2215.

Poetry Atlanta. Formed in 1985 to encourage poetry in Atlanta and in Georgia, Poetry Atlanta's membership numbers about 350. Nominal dues secure members a newsletter and a resource guide, *The Poet's Phone Book*. Poetry Atlanta also publishes poetry chapbooks and hosts readings. Monthly readings take place at Oxford Too, 2395 Peachtree Rd., in front of Peachtree Battle Shopping Center. One of Poetry Atlanta's most rewarding projects is **Wordsong**, a project that tours inner-city housing projects and performs poetry readings and jazz for children. Dan Veach and Capers Limehouse are the founders. Mail only: 614 Page Ave., Atlanta, 30307. 875-1004 (Limehouse).

Village Writers Group. Established in 1979, the Village Writers Group serves about 175 members in its critique groups. Most focus on novel writing, short stories, poetry, nonfiction, and, on occasion, children's literature. Monthly meetings are held at the Decatur Public Library on the first Tuesday of the month. Mary Fowler is chairman of the board. P.O. Box 15153, Atlanta, 30333. 262-1471.

BUSINESS & PROFESSIONAL DEVELOPMENT

These groups are sources for acquiring and maintaining collateral career-enhancing skills. But they're also great for networking and brainstorming.

Atlanta Macintosh Users Group.
This organization is for owners and users of Macintosh computers, and its monthly meetings serve as forums for the exchange of information. Meetings take place in Room 208, White Hall, on the campus of Emory University. Members benefit from vendor demonstrations, receive a newsletter, enjoy access to an on-line "bulletin board" for electronic mail, and can take advantage of savings accruing from bulk purchases the group makes. Guests may attend the meetings for a very small fee. Dues are moderate. P.O. Box 15130, Atlanta, 30333. 727-2300.

Atlanta PC Users Group.
Formed in 1981 to share technical information, this group encourages and educates users in the operation of computer hardware and software, especially IBM PCs and their compatibles. The group's nearly 1,000 members receive the newsletter **LPT1: Atlanta**, a regularly published periodical that offers a free classified section. The group's extensive library and its electronic bulletin board system, called **COM1: Atlanta**, are other benefits of membership. Monthly meetings of the group and of the special interest subgroups include guest speakers, demonstrations, discussions, and door prizes. Membership is moderate. 1325 Belmore Way, Dunwoody. 393-1629.

Atlanta Songwriters Association.
This local nonprofit educational service organization for musicians and writers holds several critiques and open mike nights around the city each month. Seven newsletters and assorted competitions, including some marathon all-day Saturday critiques, are the major activities of the association. Moderate membership fee. 3121 Maple Dr., Buckhead. 266-2666.

SCORE (Service Corps of Retired Executives).
SCORE is a wing of the Small Business Administration. In Atlanta, its 75 retired executives assist people who wish to start new businesses. The members also direct a loan program in which SCORE clients may participate if qualified. SCORE volunteers conduct seminars and workshops. Volunteer candidates submit to a screening process and an interview. The volunteers enjoy semiannual luncheons. 1720 Peachtree St., Ste. 600, Brookwood. 347-2441.

CIVIC, COMMUNITY, & ENVIRONMENTAL

To participate in worthwhile—and fun!—activities, lend volunteer support to these organizations which are central to Atlanta's well-being.

The Atlanta Project. In 1991, former president Jimmy Carter realized that social ills permeated Atlanta, his home base for the Carter Center. Galvanizing civic leaders, he assembled a high-powered staff to attack the many problems of Atlanta's poor and disenfranchised. Directed by Dan Sweat, former head of Central Atlanta Progress, the Atlanta Project will also have a substantial arts component. 675 Ponce de Leon Ave., Midtown. 881-3400.

Big Trees Forest Preserve Association. In 1990, a caring group saved a magnificent ten-acre stand of red and white oaks, beech, and other hardwoods from the axe. The Southeast Land Preservation Trust now manages the land—soon to become forty acres—while the association expands. Volunteers assist in maintaining trails, keeping the forest clean, planning and building a nature center, and, of course, fund-raising. The acreage lies just south of the North Fulton Government Annex Building, on Roswell Road. The available parking (in the driver training lot of the annex) and prominently displayed brochures make it easy to find the loop trail the association has built. Contact Owen Winters for general information. Southeast Land Trust, 130 Azalea Dr., Roswell, 30075. 594-9367.

Friends of Zoo Atlanta. About 750 volunteers gave the Atlanta Zoo 52,000 hours of service in 1991. Prospective volunteers may attend one of the biannual general training sessions, completion of which qualifies them to assist in a number of areas— conducting safaris around the zoo is a favorite. Specific training sessions may last only a few hours or as long as nine days, depending on the area of service. The cost of zoo membership is moderate, and members receive the zoo's quarterly magazine, **Zoom**, free admission to more than 100 other American zoos, invitations to annual events, and discounts on programs and tours. Family memberships (substantial) also entitle members to discounts in the gift shop. The annual **Beastly Feast** is a black-tie affair that is one of the most popular events on the Atlanta social calendar. Ticket prices are very substantial, but that never deters the crowd from coming to the party. 800-A Cherokee Ave., Grant Park. 624-5600.

Georgia Canoeing Association. More than 2,000 members, including some potential Olympians as well as neophytes, comprise this group. Every skill level is offered an appropriate series of lessons (see chapter 9). The group's **Adopt-a-Stream** program encourages members to take responsibility for keeping a designated part of a river or stream clear of litter. **Stream Watch** is a program that trains members to moderate the quality of water and guard against pollutants. This friendly group is open to new members. Call to obtain a copy of the newsletter, which contains an application. P.O. Box 7023, Atlanta, 30357. 421-9729.

Habitat for Humanity in Atlanta.

Supported by former president Jimmy Carter and his wife, Rosalynn, this unique nonprofit group provides low-cost housing to families previously selected for Habitat's low-cost loans. Each family must partici-pate in the actual building of its house. Fund-rais-ing and construc-tion volunteers are always needed. Other volunteers work in family se-lection, family relations, legal affairs, property acquisition, office work, pub-lic relations, and marketing. This worth-while undertaking has enjoyed supe-rior success. 1125 Seaboard Ave., next to Inman Park's MARTA Rail Station, Reynoldstown, Northeast. 223-5180.

> *Ralph McGill, editor of* The Atlanta Constitution, *once observed*: "Atlanta was born with energy in her body. In her genes were transportation, movement, drive."

Junior Achievement of Georgia. Most

activities target the metro Atlanta area but some programs take place elsewhere in the state. Through part-nerships with the business community, the group provides economic educa-tion and business awareness programs to public, private, and parochial schools. Programs start in kindergarten and extend through high school. Founded in 1944, it numbers about 1,500 volunteers who currently serve over 25,000 students. Volunteers include col-lege students and anyone able to help students learn how to be a valu-able part of the community around them. 460 Abernathy Rd., Sandy Springs. 257-1932.

Outings in the Park. Designed to

reunite seniors with the park, Outings in the Park was founded over a decade ago. Its headquarters are in a club-house located on the grounds of Pied-mont Park, and the organization has no membership as such. Unfunded, its income depends on donations and rental of the club-house, which is available for pri-vate affairs. Volun-teers work on events, such as a monthly ballroom dance and other activities. The men-tor program puts seniors in touch with middle school students who need love and guidance. The organization also offers art classes and other learning opportunities. Anna Hirsch, founding executive director. 1085 Piedmont Rd., Piedmont Park, Midtown. 874-1452.

Project Open Hand. This is an agency

that operates as a meals-on-wheels project for AIDS patients. Founded in 1988, it needs volunteer drivers and people to pack meals and help in the kitchen. Its annual **Masquerade Ball** is a Mardi Gras–style event that benefits the project. 1080-R Euclid Ave., Little Five Points. 525-4620.

Project RACE (Reclassify All Chil-dren Equally). This community edu-

cation project was formed in 1991 to

require a multiracial designation on all forms that ask for racial data. The term "multiracial" would apply to anyone whose parents come from two different races; multiracial people, especially children, would not have to choose which parent's race they represent. This group finds that having to make such choices may lead to severe psychological stress for multiracial children. Twenty-three other states now have units of this organization. Legislation requiring the change in data collection has passed in three states, including Georgia. 1425 Market Blvd., Ste. 1320, Roswell, 30076. 640-7100.

The Sierra Club. The Georgia chapter has over 7,000 members. Local subgroups include the **Gwinnett Sierra Club**, the **Centennial Sierra Club** (Cobb and Cherokee counties), and the newest one, the **Atlanta Sierra Club**. These clubs have a total of about 5,500 members. Basic membership is moderate, and benefits include a subscription to *Sierra* (a fine national magazine dealing with environmental issues), the group newsletter, club outings, and discounts on local activities. Buckhead location: 1447 Peachtree St., Northeast. 607-1262.

CRAFTS

From decoy carving to weaving, these groups will keep your craft interests in good condition—or get you started in one of them if you're seeking a creative outlet.

Atlanta Friends of the Alphabet. The members call themselves "lovers of letters." They consist of amateur and professional calligraphers, artists who work in other media, and just folks who enjoy the art of calligraphy. The group's purpose is "to promote the interchange of ideas, techniques, and designs of letters and their application." Meetings are held five times a year at the Columbia Theological Seminary, Room 207, 701 Columbia Drive, Decatur. Dues are moderate, and members enjoy a bimonthly newsletter, workshops, a membership directory, and use of a collection of books, catalogues, and newsletters from other cities. Craft shows, exhibits, and annual special events fill the guild's calendar. Contact Carol Gray. P.O. Box 682, Decatur, 30031. 377-6806.

Atlanta Smocking Guild. Part of the Smocking Arts Guild of America founded in 1979, the local guild, established in 1982, has about fity members. Some of the group's public service projects have included smocking gowns for premature infants at Grady Hospital and Egleston. The members have also decorated trees at Festival of Trees *(see chapter 4)*. Meetings are held at Holy Innocents Church, 850 Mt. Vernon Highway, Sandy Springs. Dues are moderate. Mary Siegel, publicity chair. Mail only: P.O. Box 76769, Atlanta, 30328. 255-5949.

Atlanta Woodcarvers Club. All kinds of woodcarving—relief carving, wildlife forms, figurines (such as Santa Clauses)—interest this group of about 100 active members. They meet on the third Wednesday of each month at Stone Mountain Power Tools, 6290 Jimmy Carter Blvd., Norcross. The group publishes a quarterly newsletter, the **Chronicle**. Dues are nominal. Write or call Jim Wallace, president. 6536 River Glen Dr., Riverdale, 30296. 996-4573.

Chattahoochee Handweavers Guild.
This 150-member guild was organized in the mid-1950s to foster fiber arts and to encourage excellence in fiber art design. In addition to a biannual members show, in alternate years the guild also holds a juried show that draws artists from the entire region. The group is a member of the Handweavers Guild of America. Membership is moderate. P.O. Box 52954, Atlanta, 30355.

East Cobb Quilters' Guild.
National and award-winning quilters often address the membership on technique and history. About 200 experienced quilters compose the group, and they make, collect, and preserve quilts. Activities include workshops and the special quilt show. Meetings are held on the last Friday of the month. Parish Center, St. Ann's Catholic Church, Rte. 120 & Bishop Lake Rd., Marietta. Kathy Ingmundson, guild president. 998-2520.

Etowah Guild of Fiber Artists.
Reaching into the mountains of North Georgia for its active membership, the guild draws many members from Cherokee County, and meets at the Yarn Barn in Canton (479-5083). This group is a member of the Hand Weavers Guild of America, in existence for two decades. Membership includes mostly weavers, but spinners, knitters, basket weavers, and handmade-paper artists are among the group. The guild participates in community education projects, such as assisting in 4-H competitions and sending a traveling fiber display to area public schools. The guild's newsletter comes with a sample. Members extol the group's warm atmosphere and friendly, supportive fellowship. Contact Angela Stone. Mail only: Rte. 5, Box 5844, Dawsonville, 30534. 706-265-1375.

Georgia Association of Woodturners.
Affiliated with the American Association of Woodturners, this group is composed of people who produce turned-wood items on a lathe: bowls, candlesticks, and art pieces of all kinds. The almost 100 members meet once a month. Dues are nominal. Contact Mark Barr. 610-7775.

Woodworkers' Guild of Georgia.
Members include beginners as well as advanced woodworkers who enjoy producing furniture and other utilitarian items made of wood. Some of the guild's members are among the best in the country. The guild's 350-person membership meets once a month at DeKalb Tech. Activities include shows and seminars, which cost anywhere from nothing to $100. Dues are moderate. Mark Barr. P.O. Box 8006, Atlanta, 30306-0006. 610-7775.

CULTURAL & INTERNATIONAL

Atlanta claims to be an international city, and its many organizations of an international nature lend credence to that claim. Join one of these to become a member of the "global village."

Alliance Française d'Atlanta. Founded in 1912, the alliance fosters understanding and appreciation of French culture through events such as films, exhibitions, musical presentations, and literary programs. The organization has taught French classes for individuals and groups since 1963 *(see chapter 9)*. Membership is moderate, with discounts for French teachers. 1360 Peachtree St., Ste. 200, Midtown. 875-1211.

Amigo Friendship Program. Families offer hospitality to international students who are attending college in the metro area. Hosting meals or community events is the chief responsibility for the families. Amigo is a program of the Atlanta Ministry with International Students. First Presbyterian Church, 1328 Peachtree St., at 16th St., Midtown. 892-8461.

The Burns Club of Atlanta. A literary society, this club was founded in 1896 to honor the Scottish poet Robert Burns. Candidates for membership must demonstrate their affection for and knowledge of Burns and his poetry. The club's programs, most of which are held every month, are at the Burns Cottage, which replicates Burns' birth home. Built in 1910, the cottage is now on the National Register. The annual club bagpipe bash, the *ceilidh*, is a popular event. Mail only: 988 Alloway Pl., SE, Atlanta. 627-2941.

Círculo Hispano-Americano de Atlanta. After more than a century in Atlanta, the Circulo puts on numerous parties, social events, and theatrical programs. About 100 members bring guests, so the parties usually have 250 people in attendance. Once a year, in November, the group puts on a dance reflecting the costumes and dance of various Hispanic countries. Dues are moderate, and benefits include a quarterly newsletter. Contact Fernando Peguero. P.O. Box 13812, Atlanta, 30324. 429-2307.

English Speaking Union. Founded in Britain after WWI, the union is an educational organization with an international scope. Its headquarters are in New York City, and it has 88 branches across the country and others around the world. Recently celebrating its fiftieth anniversary, the Atlanta branch has around 450 members. To promote English language and culture, the union hosts exchange programs with Great Britain and brings in local lecturers as well as speakers from the Isles—the wife of the British ambassador is always a favorite. The union's scholarship program benefits graduate students studying in Great Britain. Membership is moderate, and there is a young professionals group. Mail only: 3285 Pine Meadow Rd., Atlanta, 30327. 261-0884.

Friends of Mexico. This member-supported organization promotes understanding of Mexican culture. Activities often include presentations of the music, visual arts (including film), dance, and authentic cuisine of Mexico in a single event. Membership is nominal. Consulate of Mexico, 3220 Peachtree Rd., Buckhead. 264-1240.

Friendship Force International. Friendship Force, through its two area chapters (Atlanta and Northeast Georgia), promotes international goodwill by bringing citizens from other countries to Atlanta and by sending Atlantans to other countries. As a result of this group's yeoman service, more than fifty foreign countries have welcomed Atlantans and hosted them in private homes. 57 Forsyth St., Downtown. 522-9490.

Georgia Council for International Visitors. Established in 1962, GCIV arranges professional and cultural exchanges among international visitors and US citizens. The internationals with whom GCIV works are in the United States at the invitation of the US Information Agency. Hosts are needed to provide daytime, evening, and extended-stay hospitality. They are sought to plan meeting programs, to work in the GCIV office, and for other activities related to making their international guests feel more at home in Atlanta. Membership is moderately priced. 999 Peachtree St., Ste. 770, Midtown. 873-6170.

Goethe-Institut Atlanta. The focus is to strengthen cultural ties between the Southeastern United States and Germany through cultural events such as film and musical presentations *(see chapter 3)*. German language classes are also taught *(see chapter 9)*. 400 Colony Sq., Midtown. 892-2388.

Hibernian Benevolent Society. One of the oldest societies of its kind in the country, the Hibernian was founded in 1858 to promote Irish culture and heritage. Meetings and monthly newsletters attract a membership from throughout the state. Many annual events, especially around St. Patrick's Day, spur the group's growth *(see chapter 4)*. Membership is moderate. Mail only: 737 Clairemont Ave., Decatur, 30030. 378-1255.

Irish Arts of Atlanta. This is the local branch of the international Irish cultural association, Comhaltas Ceoltoiri Eireann, which was founded in 1951 to preserve and promote traditional music, song, and dance and to teach Gaelic. In Atlanta, Irish Arts sponsors such activities as music sessions, dances, and Gaelic language classes *(see chapter 9)*. Membership is nominal. Mail only: 1288 Morningside Dr., Atlanta, 30306. 873-5621.

Italian Friendship Club. A social club concerned with promoting and fostering Italian culture, it meets monthly at All Saints Catholic Church, Mt. Vernon Road, Dunwoody. The annual Italian festival is a showcase of Italian food, wine, and music *(see chapter 4)*. Membership is moderate. P.O. Box 375, 3470 McClure Bridge Rd., Duluth, 30136-9998. 434-1459.

Japan America Society. Founded more than a decade ago to enhance Georgians' knowledge and understanding of Japan and Japanese culture, it presents many programs every year on business, education, and cultural affairs, as well as many purely social activities (see chapter 9). Peachtree St., Ste. 710, Downtown. 524-7399.

Louisiana Club.

Attracting about 185 members who hail from Louisiana, the club is a home for displaced Louisianans, especially Cajuns, who feel like ducks out of water in Atlanta. The annual **Mardi Gras Ball** is a function of its **Krewe of Saints**, and the annual seafood dinner is very popular. Meetings are twice a month: the second Tuesday of the month is a covered-dish social. Jane Young is president (381-6820). St. Patrick's Catholic Church, 2140 Beaver Ruin Rd., Norcross. 448-2028.

St. Andrew's Society of Atlanta.

Social events and activities revolve around the society's goal of promoting Scottish culture and heritage. Annual events include the **Stone Mountain Scottish Festival and Highland Games** (see chapter 4), which the society helps to promote. They also sponsor a **St. Andrew's Day Anniversary Banquet**, a Robert Burns's birthday celebration, and a **Hogmanay** (New Year's) event. Richard Graham, president. Mail only: 2503 River Knoll Dr., Lilburn, 30247. 979-1010.

Southern Center for International Studies.

This thirty-year-old organization serves as a foreign policy forum. SCIS brings international experts and resources to the attention of regional business, political, and academic leaders, as well as to the general public. Business, foundations, governments, and individuals support the center with memberships. Members participate in seminars and study trips abroad and attend conferences, assorted continuing education programs in international business, and customized briefings on international relations. Dinners and luncheons feature well-known international speakers and guests, such as former Chinese Vice Premier Deng Xiaoping and former French President Valéry Giscard d'Estaing.

The center produces annual conferences with former cabinet members, as well as ambassadors to the UN and other international leaders. The conferences are televised both nationally and internationally. The center also produces educational and information packets on countries, issues, and organizations. It publishes papers, educational videotapes, and teaching guides, which are made available to educational institutions around the country. Members have access to audiotapes of all center programs. Membership fees are substantial, and luncheons are separately priced, although at a lower cost for members than for nonmembers. 320 W. Paces Ferry Rd., Buckhead. 261-5763.

FOOD & WINE

Food and wine are among the "fine arts" of life. Make new friends and taste new dishes as these organizations take you around the culinary globe.

Ale Atlanta. This small, local organization formed to savor suds from around the world. Its members hold tastings on alternate Sundays at various pubs. Membership is nominal. Contact Coby Glass. 1852 Aaron Ct., Powder Springs. 943-5583.

American Institute of Wine and Food. This is a national organization founded over a decade ago by Julia Child and Robert Mondavi, among others, to foster the appreciation and study of wine and food. The Atlanta chapter has some 300 members, many of them amateurs. Members meet in each others' homes, in local restaurants, and in food- or wine-related places to learn more about the subjects in question. Several annual events *(see chapter 4)* that are open to the public have become very popular. Most events, however, are restricted to members and guests. Basic membership is substantial, and many programs require a reasonably priced additional fee. 5027 Old Branch Ct., Dunwoody. 399-9781.

American Wine Society. Begun in 1967, the society is a nonprofit, consumer organization devoted to educating people on all aspects of wine. The recently founded Atlanta chapter hosts tastings and dinners. Membership is moderate, and benefits include a quarterly journal and newsletter, discounts on admission to the society's events, and invitations to regional

meetings and a national convention. Don Reddicks is chairman. Mail only: 7055 Hunter's Branch Dr., Atlanta, 30328. 393-4584.

Brotherhood of the Knights of the Vine. The roots of this group date to thirteenth-century France; in its modern form, the group reaches back to the 1960s. The Atlanta chapter has been in existence almost twenty years and holds four dinners a year in restaurants as well as other wine- and food-tasting events in private homes. The group studies only American wine. The Atlanta chapter's sixty members come from all over the greater metro area. Membership is substantial, and inductees pay a significant onetime initiation fee. Billy Reeves, Master Commander. Mail only: 211 S. 6th St., Griffin, 30223. 227-5176.

German Wine Society. This national organization boasts some fifteen chapters; the Atlanta chapter dates from 1979 and hosts frequent wine tastings, classes, and dinners featuring German wine. Other events focus on German culture, such as a combination tasting of German wines and tour of an exhibition of German art. Membership fees are moderate and entitle members to discounts on events, the society's wine review and newsletter, and invitations to the national convention. Mail only: 7055 Hunter's Branch Dr., Atlanta, 30328. 393-4584.

GARDEN CLUBS

Atlanta's garden-like environment calls for numerous garden clubs. Members gain large measures of personal satisfaction as they beautify their own and their city's environments.

American Begonia Society. Preserving and propagating begonias keep the thirty members of the society's Greater Atlanta branch busy. The annual show and sale is held at the Atlanta Botanical Garden *(see below)* in March or April. Meetings are held on the second Sunday of alternate months at Day Hall in the Botanical Garden. The national organization is about forty years old, and the Atlanta chapter has marked a decade of growth. Dues are nominal, and members receive the bimonthly **Begonian** magazine. Mail only: 1854 Chancery Lane, Chamblee, 30341. 457-0371.

American Rhododendron Society. The Azalea Chapter's 225 members come mainly from the metro Atlanta area and the rest of the state. With the largest chapter in the region, the group's purpose is to educate the public about rhododendrons and azaleas, which are members of the same botanical family. The monthly meetings are usually held at the Atlanta History Center. The society's annual show and sale are usually one weekend apart in late April and/or early May. Dues are moderate, and members receive a fine national quarterly journal. Mail only: 132 Garden Lane, Decatur, 30030. 373-7828.

Atlanta Bonsai Society. Founded about three decades ago, the Atlanta Bonsai Society includes 175 members who meet once a month at the Atlanta Botanical Garden. The group holds two shows annually. The May show is at the garden, and the fall show is at the Botanical Garden of the University of Georgia. Dues are nominal. P.O. Box 18653, Atlanta, 30326. 434-9955.

Atlanta Botanical Garden. Established in 1977, the Atlanta Botanical Garden *(see chapter 5)* has a membership roster that numbers about 9,000 people. Membership is moderately priced, and its benefits include discounts on classes and gift shop purchases and reciprocal rights to visit other botanical gardens around the country. The garden's newsletter, **Clippings**, is an attractive publication full of news and notes on matters botanical. Volunteer docents are trained to serve as tour guides, to assist with garden maintenance by working with staff members, to work in the gift shop, and to supply clerical help. 1345 Piedmont Rd., Midtown. 876-5859.

The Garden Club of Georgia. Many Atlanta area garden clubs are affiliated with this club. To find out which clubs near you share your particular interests, drop a note containing your address, or call and leave that information on the message tape. 325 S. Lumpkin St., Athens, 30602. 706-542-3631.

Gardeners of America. Based in Des Moines, Iowa, the club has several affiliates in the Atlanta area. For information on other affiliated garden clubs in the Atlanta area, contact the Atlanta Botanical Garden, 876-5859, as many of them meet there. Nationally, this group was called the Men's Garden Clubs, and the local groups may elect to keep that word, but women may become members. Membership is moderate. Here are some of the Atlanta area clubs and their programs: **Buckhead Men's Garden Club:** About ninety active members meet monthly at Peachtree Presbyterian Church, on Roswell Road, in Buckhead. A greenhouse, a barn, and several acres of land leased from the Lovett School for demonstration purposes constitute the club's most enterprising projects. Contact William B. Long, president. 5315 Riverview Rd., Atlanta, 30327. 955-1871. **Marietta Men's Garden Club:** Established nearly fifty years ago to maintain the 88 rose bushes in the Birney Memorial Rose Garden at Marietta High School, the club participates in other fund-raising ventures as well. Contact Edward Risse. P.O. Box 37, Marietta, 30061. 428-3462. **Mt. Shadow Men's Garden Club:** Named for its proximity to the "shadow" of Stone Mountain, this ten-year-old club has about thirty members. It meets at Eastminister Presbyterian Church, 5801 Hugh Howell Rd., Stone Mountain. One of this club's members, Ralph Chewning, is the past president of the Men's Garden Club of America. Contact Ralph Chewning. 5874 Musket Lane, Stone Mountain, 30087. 938-4592.

The Greater Atlanta Rose Society.

Affiliated with the American Rose Society, the Greater Atlanta Rose Society, with a membership of about 200, holds monthly meetings at the visitor's center of the Atlanta Botanical Garden *(see below)*. The society maintains a public rose garden, which contains more than 800 bushes on the grounds of the Botanical Garden. Membership is nominal, and members receive a monthly newsletter and the quarterly *Rose Digest.* They also enjoy monthly programs, garden tours, demonstrations, and the opportunity to exhibit roses at the spring rose show. Contact Anna Davis, president. 233-7883.

The Herb Society of America.

Founded in 1933, this national organization also has units in Canada; its members foster the study and enjoyment of herbs, but unlike others, they do not attribute any medicinal properties to herbs. The society's Chattahoochee unit is the Atlanta chapter, and its 33 members meet nine times a year at the Atlanta Botanical Garden. **Herb Education Day** *(see chapter 4)*, held the first Saturday in May, is one of the unit's annual activities, and it draws hundreds of Atlantans to the garden to purchase herbs. Prospective members are asked to be presented at three meetings as guests and then to become a provisional member for a year and attend seminars before joining. Membership benefits include a quarterly newsletter, book lists, and the annual publication, *The Herbarist.* Tours and symposia with herbal themes, an annual meeting, and a library maintained at national headquarters are all available to members. Dues are substantial, except for the provisional year, which carries a nominal cost. Contact Tunkie Miller. P.O. Box 52754, Atlanta, 30355. 351-5994.

North Georgia Camellia Society. This is a support organization for the America Camellia Society, which has its national headquarters in Marshallville, in middle Georgia. Founded in 1952, the Atlanta group has a membership of about forty who meet monthly from September until March. The group stages the **Atlanta Camellia Show** during the third weekend in February at the Atlanta Botanical Garden. Proceeds benefit both the garden and the society. The Atlanta group also regularly participates in the Atlanta Flower Show *(see chapter 4)*. Mail only: 2405 Howell Mill Rd., Atlanta, 30318. 355-4478.

HISTORY & PRESERVATION

Atlanta and the surrounding towns and counties, while forward-looking and progressive, make the most of their historical roots. Check the area in which you live for other historical societies in addition to the ones included here, because this list is not exhaustive. All engage in activities similar to those listed in this selection and could use your volunteer assistance.

Atlanta Historical Society. The society is a strong, 5,000-member organization that includes some of Atlanta's most well-known citizens. Members receive free admission to the facility, the grounds *(see chapter 5)*, and all exhibitions. A monthly newsletter, the quarterly journal **Atlanta History: A Journal of Georgia and the South**, discounts on museum shop purchases and special events admission, and a free lecture series are additional benefits. Moderate membership dues. After training, volunteers may serve as costumed docents in the Tullie Smith House, while others serve as guides in the Civil War gallery. More formal classroom training is required to be a docent in the Swan House, and training continues throughout the volunteer's service. Volunteers also serve as gift shop staffers. 130 West Paces Ferry, Buckhead. 814-4000.

Atlanta Preservation Center. Volunteers representing many age groups serve as tour guides after three months of training. Training sessions begin in January and run through March. Volunteers also handle special events, help with clerical duties, and constitute a speakers bureau *(see chapter 9)*. **Circa** is a very active marketing specialty group run by the volunteers. The center's annual bash is a lighthearted, springtime affair. Membership is moderate, and members receive invitations to special events, free and unlimited access to the walking tours, and a complimentary quarterly newsletter. 156 7th St., Midtown. 876-2040.

DeKalb Historical Society. Now housed in the old Decatur courthouse, the society gathers documents and data referring to the history of DeKalb County, established in 1823. Workshops assist members with genealogy, and annual events include a dinner. Nominal dues include a quarterly newsletter. Old Courthouse on the Square, Downtown Decatur. 373-1088.

Georgia Historical Society. Founded in 1839, the society was designated a branch depository of the Georgia Department of Archives and History *(see chapter 5)* in 1965. The society's purpose is to collect, preserve, and disseminate information about the history of Georgia and America, and to maintain a library for the use of members and the public. Although based in Savannah, the society has many members in Atlanta. *The Georgia Historical Quarterly* is one of the benefits of moderate membership dues. 501 Whitaker St., Savannah, 31499. 912-651-2125.

> *Thompkins Lane near Fort McPherson was named for Sally Louise Thompkins, the only woman known to have received a commission in the Confederate Army. In Richmond, Virginia, Captain Thompkins operated one of the most successful Civil War hospitals, losing only 73 patients out of 1,300 treated during its 45 months of operation. Born in 1833 to a wealthy Virginia family, Thompkins spent her fortune caring for the ill and wounded, and died in poverty in 1916.*

Georgia Trust for Historic Preservation. The trust operates three house museums in Georgia: **Hay House** in Macon, the **McDaniel Tichenor House** in Monroe, and **Rhodes Hall** in Atlanta *(see chapter 5)*, where it is headquartered. Through education, advocacy, and direct assistance, the Georgia Trust encourages the protection of Georgia's historic resources. The staff is active in lobbying for preservation leg-

islation. Members participate in a variety of volunteer activities, such as in support of the **Salute to American Craft** show *(see chapter 4)*. Membership fees are moderate, and members receive invitations to "ram-bles" (tours to historic sites in Georgia) and a newsletter. 1516 Peach-tree St., Midtown. 881-9980.

Gwinnett Historical Society. The society is dedicated to preserving the history and heritage of Gwinnett County, named for Button Gwinnett, a signer of The Declaration of Independence. Volunteers work in the office, help with festivals and special events, conduct historic tours, write grant proposals, and work on preservation projects and other activities. Meetings convene monthly, except during the summer. Membership is nominal, and members receive quarterly issues of *The Heritage*, the society's news magazine. William Baugham, president. P.O. Box 261, Lawrenceville, 30246. 822-5174.

Historical Jonesboro / Clayton County. Through fund-raising and other volunteer activities, members support **Stately Oaks**, a plantation house maintained by volunteers *(see chapter 5)*. Members participate in the society's regular activities, such as

Indian Heritage Day, when crafts, foods, and costumes reflecting Native American culture are displayed. For the **Georgia Folklore by Moonlight** festival, members serve as storytellers and relate old tales, dressing in period–style costumes. Members serve as tour guides, assist with clerical assignments, and generally help where needed. Dues are nominal. 100 Carriage Drive, Jonesboro. 473-0197.

National Railway Historical Society.

Since 1966, the Atlanta chapter of this national organization, which dates from 1959, has maintained and directed the **Southeastern Railway Museum** *(see chapter 5)*. The Atlanta chapter is proud of its strong membership, numbering about 600, which includes both men and women. Its goal is to preserve and maintain historical railway equipment. All work on the trains is done at the museum. Special events include the **Autumn Leaf Trips** through north Georgia to watch the colors. Membership dues are moderate. Gary Singleton is director. 3966 US Hwy. 23, Duluth, 30136. 476-2013.

Newnan-Coweta Historical Society.

The society's mission is to preserve the architectural, historical, and cultural heritage of Coweta County. Established over two decades ago, it meets ten times a year and stays busy year-round with tours, educational programs, and an awards program that recognizes preservation. It also operates a historical museum (the **Male Academy Museum** *(see chapter 5)*, and holds purely social events. The society has published several volumes that examine the county's history. Membership dues are nominal, and volunteers are invited to work on pub-

lications and exhibitions, and as docents. P.O. Box 1001, Newnan, 30264. 251-0207.

Roswell Historical Society.

The society's 700 members promote the preservation of historic sites and materials that detail the history of Roswell. These materials include books, manuscripts, charts, and other documents and items. Eight meetings each year and a quarterly newsletter are among the benefits of membership. Dues are moderate. The volunteer program, begun with the society's move to the **Archibald Smith Plantation Home** in 1992, includes a course to instruct the costumed docents for tours. Other docents demonstrate hearth cooking, conduct walking tours of the historic areas, and participate in the garden guild. 935 Alpharetta St., Roswell. 992-1665.

Society for Creative Anachronism.

This is a unique historical and educational organization whose members re-create the Middle Ages and the Renaissance by dressing in period costumes and reproducing period artifacts and domestic arts. Weekend events attract hundreds. Weekly meetings convene on Wednesday evenings at 8 P.M. at the Georgia-Hill Neighborhood Facility (corner of Georgia Avenue and Hill Street, Grant Park). This international organization has its US headquarters in Berkeley, California, and boasts some 25,000 members in this country alone. The Atlanta chapter claims about 300 active members. The local *Kingdom* newsletter and a quarterly national magazine are among the benefits of membership, which is moderately priced. Christine Seelye-King, contact.

Mail only: 1039 E. Confederate Ave., Atlanta, 30316. 627-6416.

The Wren's Nest. A two-day training program, held twice annually, prepares volunteers to serve as docents who conduct the tours of the historic Joel Chandler Harris home (see *chapter 5*). Other volunteer duties include public relations, program development, clerical services, and gift shop assistance. Volunteers enjoy discounts on gift shop purchases, a volunteer newsletter, bimonthly meetings, and at least one social event per year. 1050 Ralph David Abernathy, Jr., Blvd. (formerly Gordon St.), West End. 753-7735.

HOBBIES

There's virtually no end to the hobbies a person can pursue in Atlanta. Here is a *very* small sampling of the hobby organizations you'll find. We hope our readers will alert us to other exemplary groups for future issues.

Atlanta Radio Club. Licensed amateur radio operators and anyone interested in amateur radio compose this organization, whose members come from all age groups throughout the metro area. Meetings are monthly. Members aid in handling messages and emergency communications during times of severe weather, often acting as trained weather spotters. They provide communication during such events as road races and parades, and conduct training classes to help persons prepare for the FCC licensing examination. P.O. Box 77171, Atlanta, 30357-1171. 393-1173.

Train Collectors Association. A national organization based in Strasburg, PA, TCA promotes model railroad collecting, especially of antique model trains. The association is organized into divisions that, in turn, are organized into chapters. **The Dixie Division**, founded in 1988, includes Georgia, and **Terminus** is the Georgia chapter. With about 600 members, Terminus meets four times a year at Meadowcreek High School in Gwinnett County. March and September "meets" are open to the public, but new members may join and participate in any meeting. The Dixie Division meets once a year in each chapter's region; for Terminus, that gathering takes place in January at Meadowcreek High School. A national convention is held annually. Dues are moderate. Mac McConnell, director. 3749 Wetherburne Dr., Clarkston, 30021. 292-6851.

HOSPITAL AUXILIARIES

All hospitals have basic auxiliaries for volunteer services, and they rely upon contributions of time and energy from retired persons, teens, and anyone else who can "pitch in." We've selected a few programs that have some special "twists."

Egleston Children's Hospital at Emory University. Egleston's auxiliary offers volunteers many ways to donate their services. The major fund-raising projects include the annual **Festival of Trees** and the **Egleston Children's Christmas Parade** *(see chapter 4)*. A recent Festival of Trees netted Egleston $1 million during the nine-day event. The forty or so **Twigs** groups are neighborhood units that determine and direct their own fund-raising projects. Twigs also operate city-wide fund-raising projects, which are directed by an oversight group. **The Bell South Atlanta (PGA Golf Classic)** benefits Egleston *(see chapter 4)*, and Egleston volunteers serve as tournament staffers. In the hospital, volunteers give tours of the facility, operate the hospital's express cart, and put on seasonal patient parties, including the Christmas party. Volunteers also assist the patients with their studies. And there is much, much more. Lynne Patterson is special groups coordinator. 1405 Clifton Rd., Emory University, Northeast. 325-6042.

Scottish Rite Children's Medical Center. Volunteer service at Scottish Rite consists of three basic groups. The auxiliary and **Special Children of the South (SCOTS)**—about twenty community and neighborhood fund-raising groups—are directed by the hospital. The independent **Scottish Rite Festival** sponsors various athletic events, directs a charity ball, and holds a silent auction. In-hospital service groups assist in the child and adolescent life departments, helping with play-time activities and family events. Other volunteers serve in the tutorial pools. SCOTS also directs special annual fund-raising projects and sponsors a family resource library center at the hospital. 1001 Johnson Ferry Rd., Sandy Springs. 250-2150.

Shepherd Spinal Center. This unique center specializes in helping those who have suffered spinal cord injuries or diseases. Some auxiliary volunteers, who complete a training program before beginning service, assist in the therapeutic recreation department; they help with nursing care duties, accompany patients on outings, and help them participate in outside events. Others produce accident prevention programs for local schools and church groups. Among the popular fund-raising events produced by volunteers are **Derby Day**, the **Southeastern Charity Horseshow**, the **Legendary Party** (the auxiliary's charity ball), a luncheon and fashion show at Saks Fifth Avenue, and the **Pecans on Peachtree** sale. One program allows teens fifteen or over to work with patients. 2020 Peachtree Rd., Buckhead. 350-7315.

SPORTS

In general, sports organizations are listed in Chapters 8, (Sports & Recreation) and 9 (Expanding Your Mind), according to the sport they represent. The groups listed here are primarily "booster clubs" that operate with volunteer-power in support of specific sports, both professional and amateur.

Atlanta Boardsailing Club. This group meets to improve the members' skills in windsurfing, as boardsailing is more commonly known. The group regularly holds clinics and regattas and is open to all who are interested in windsurfing. Dues are moderate. Contact Atlanta Sport Skier, also a good source for water-skiing equipment. 390 Buford Hwy., Suwanee. 271-7511.

Atlanta Fencers' Club. Established in 1977, this club has produced local and regional tournaments. Membership numbers around 100 people. Dues are substantial, but there is some reduction for members under age 22. 40 7th St., Midtown. 892-0307.

Atlanta Track Club. Founded in 1964, this nonprofit organization supports a volunteer coaching program that matches runners seeking to improve their skills with volunteer coaches. Geographic convenience and compatible abilities affect how people are matched. Membership dues are nominal. 3097 E. Shadowlawn Ave., Buckhead. 231-9064.

Atlanta Water Ski Club. Dedicated to competitive skiing and to improving members' waterskiing skills, this club is sanctioned by the American Water Ski Association. Membership is substantial. Contact Atlanta Sport Skier. 390 Buford Hwy., Suwanee. 271-7511.

The Braves 400 Club. This Atlanta Braves booster club does more than follow the home team from city to city during the season. Its more than 700 members support all levels of amateur and professional baseball. Members furnish equipment for the Boys and Girls Clubs of Atlanta, and sponsor an annual athletic scholarship to a local college or university. The monthly meetings feature Braves' players and coaches. Dues are nominal. P.O. Box 7689, Atlanta, 30309. 250-5015.

The Diamond Club. Women interested in Braves baseball volunteer to help with various duties, such as answering fan mail and decorating the team's tree at Festival of Trees. Special days at the Braves' games are among the benefits. Spouses or dates are welcome if accompanied by the woman member. Membership is nominal. P.O. Box 54552, Atlanta, 30308. 522-7630.

Lake Lanier Sailing Club. This nonprofit club—the largest sailing club on Lake Lanier—operates a first-class facility that gives members access to the clubhouse for social events, five docks for mooring their boats, small craft launching areas, and repair facilities.

A member of the US Yacht Racing Union as well as other related organizations, the club hosts regattas—club competitions as well as regional and national ones—and conducts classes of all kinds, including a sailing program for young people called the **Junior Fleet**. The summer **Reggae Regatta**, held in late June or July, is a favorite event. The membership fee is very substantial by our guidelines, but reasonable vis-à-vis other clubs of its type, and the benefits membership brings would, if secured separately, cost much more. Jim Morang is membership chair. P.O. Box 740090, Atlanta, 30374-0090; 600 Oglethorpe Ave., Athens, GA, 30606. 706-549-4748; Fax: 706-549-9822; Atlanta telephone for voice mail: 333-7311.

Trout Unlimited. Working closely with the Georgia Department of Natural Resources and the US Forest Service, Trout Unlimited works to preserve coldwater habitats and to stock them with fish. Five metro area chapters meet monthly. Membership dues are nominal. Garland Stewart is chairman of the Georgia Council of Trout Unlimited. 4453 Abingdon Dr., Stone Mountain, 30083. home: 294-0471; work: 364-2665.

The United States Coast Guard Auxiliary. This nonmilitary organization was established to assist the Coast Guard in achieving its mission "to promote efficiency in the operation of motorboats, sailboats, and yachts." The auxiliary members assist in safety patrols, regatta patrols, search and rescue, and other Coast Guard support missions. Among its activities are excellent boating courses. Training for auxiliary members includes instruction in Coast Guard and auxiliary history, as well as navigation, meteorology, and other related subjects. Membership is open to United States citizens aged seventeen and older who own at least 25% interest in a boat, aircraft, or marine radio station. Three flotillas operate in the Atlanta area. For information, check with boating supply stores, marinas, and the sports pages of local newspapers. 559 Rays Rd., Stone Mountain, 30083. 292-7093.

SUPPORT GROUPS

The number of support groups in the area has probably doubled in the last few years. We didn't list the obvious ones—such as Alcoholics Anonymous or Weight Watchers—because they are widely known and available through the telephone directory. Below is a very small sampling of the many available groups that are more difficult to find. Please let us know about any especially helpful groups for future issues. A fairly complete list of support groups is currently available in some issues of the free weekly *Creative Loafing*.

Compassionate Friends. This self-help support group aids bereaved parents, siblings, and other members of families that have lost a child. With national headquarters in Oak Brook, IL, the group is international in scope. The Atlanta group, founded in 1979, collects no dues but depends on donations for its support. The Atlanta area has four groups that meet one night each month to help grieving family members mourn appropriately and develop the coping skills that enable the survivors to move on. Contact Elaine Grier. 3096 Northbrook Dr., Atlanta, 30341. 491-7652. Associated with The Link Counseling Center, 256-9797.

SHARE. This is a support group for anyone who has miscarried or lost a stillborn or newborn child. Contact The Link Counseling Center. 348 Mt. Vernon Hwy., Sandy Springs. 256-9797; 1744 Roswell Rd., Marietta. 973-6068.

Survivors of Suicide. This group helps people cope with grief and develop survival techniques after a loved one has committed suicide. Based at The Link, a nonprofit counseling center, it accepts volunteers to handle telephone calls and assist in receiving clients. Volunteer candidates must submit to a screening interview and participate in a volunteer training program. 348 Mt. Vernon Hwy., Sandy Springs. 256-9797.

Georgia State Facts

Name: Named for King George II of England by James Edward Oglethorpe, who brought English settlers in 1733.

History: Creek Indians settled in south Georgia and Cherokee Indians in the highlands. The first Europeans in Georgia were the Spanish, who crossed the state on their way to Florida sometime around 1540.

Capital: Atlanta (since 1868). Earlier capitals: Savannah (1733–1785), Augusta (1786–1795), Louisville (1796–1806), Milledgeville (1807–1867).

Statehood: 4th State, January 2, 1788.

State flower: Cherokee Rose, a small, pinkish and sometimes white flower with a faint scent.

State tree: Live Oak, found mostly along the coast and often blown into strange shapes by sea winds.

State bird: Brown Thrasher, colored a rich chestnut on top and streaked with brown on its breast, with a long tail and curved bill. Their eggs are greenish or grayish white, thickly spotted with brown. They nest in low trees or garden shrubbery and have a very sweet song.

State song: "Georgia on my Mind," music by Lollie Belle Wylie, words by Robert Loveman. The official recording is by Ray Charles, a native Georgian.

State motto: Wisdom, Justice, and Moderation

Elevation: Sea-level along coast; 4,784 feet at Brasstown Bald mountain.

Land regions: Georgia has six land regions—the Appalachian Plateau, the Appalachian Ridge and Valley, the Blue Ridge Mountains, the Piedmont, the Atlantic Coastal Plain, and the East Gulf Coastal Plain.

Average climate:
Rainfall—48.61 inches
Snowfall—1.7 inches
Clear days—220
Days above 90—32
Days below 32—55
Rainiest month—March
Driest month—October
Coldest month—January
Hottest month—July

Special fact: Marble from Tate, Georgia, was used in building the Lincoln Memorial in the national capital and for state capitols in Rhode Island, Minnesota, Kentucky, and Arkansas. A 76-ton block, one of the largest ever quarried, is part of the Buckingham Fountain in Chicago.

Famous wildlife refuge: Okefenokee Swamp in southeastern Georgia forms a national wildlife refuge of some 700 square miles and is a haven for birds, bears, alligators, and other wildlife.

Coastline: Georgia has about 100 miles of coastline on the Atlantic Ocean.

INDEX

Numbers

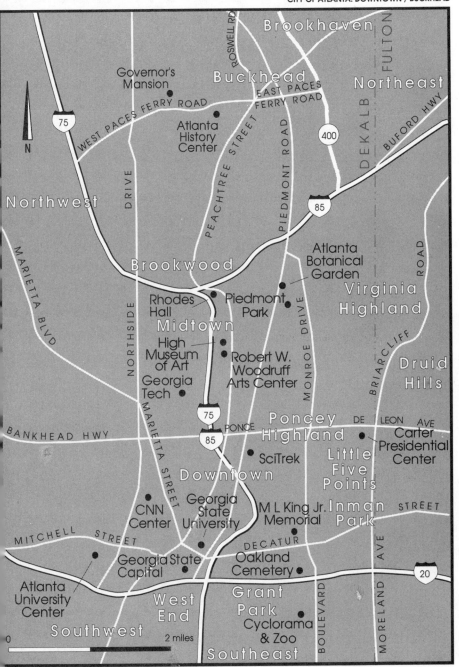

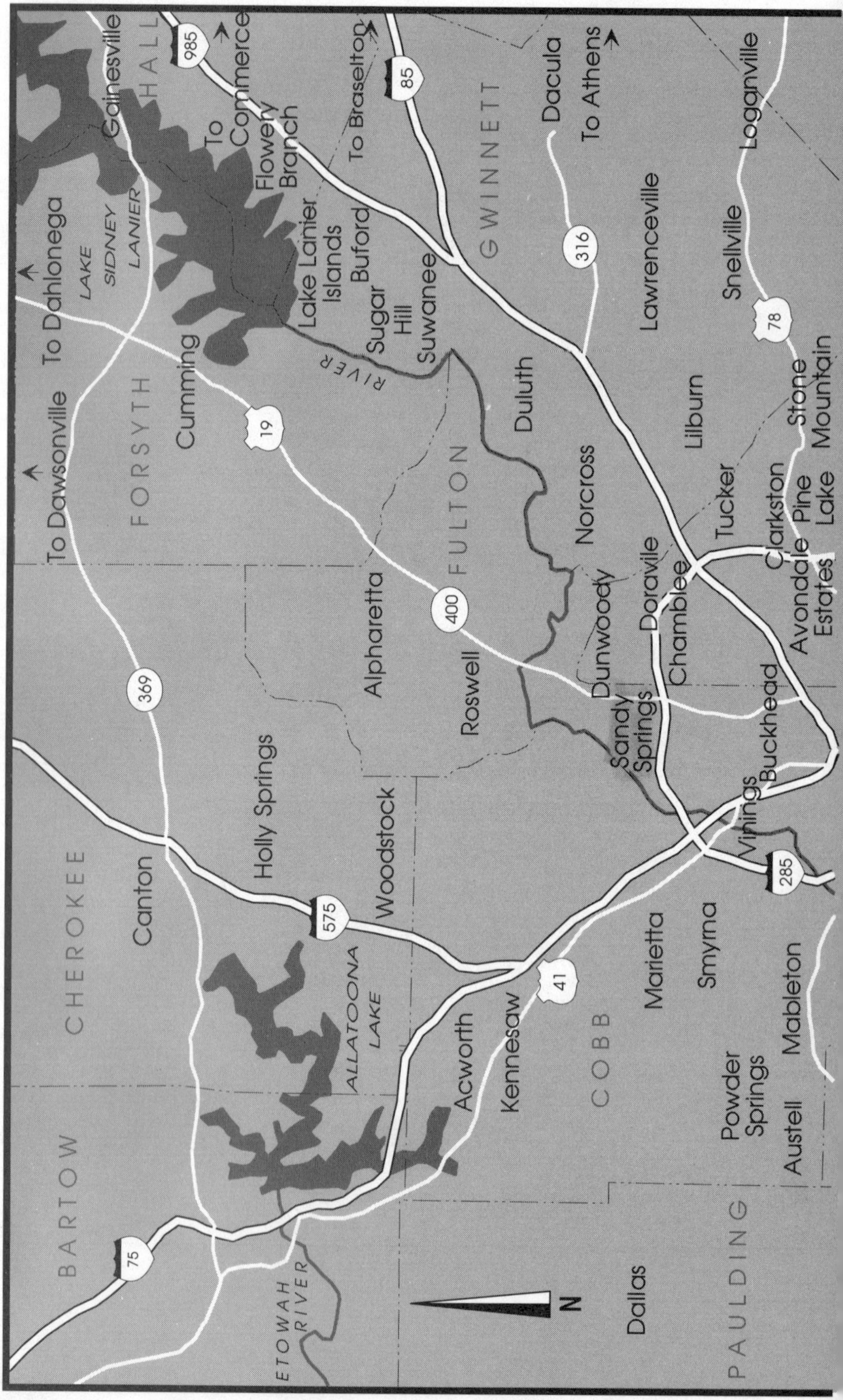
To Dawsonville
To Dahlonega
LAKE
SIDNEY
LANIER
Gainesville
HALL
985
To Commerce
Flowery Branch
To Braselton
85
GWINNETT
Dacula
To Athens
Loganville
Lake Lanier Islands
Buford
Sugar Hill
Suwanee
316
Lawrenceville
Snellville
78
Stone Mountain
FORSYTH
Cumming
19
RIVER
Duluth
Lilburn
Norcross
Tucker
Clarkston
Pine Lake
FULTON
Doravile
Chamblee
Avondale Estates
Alpharetta
400
Dunwoody
Roswell
Sandy Springs
Buckhead
369
Holly Springs
Woodstock
CHEROKEE
Canton
575
Vinings
285
Marietta
Smyrna
41
Mableton
ALLATOONA
LAKE
Acworth
Kennesaw
COBB
Powder Springs
Austell
BARTOW
75
ETOWAH
RIVER
N
Dallas
PAULDING

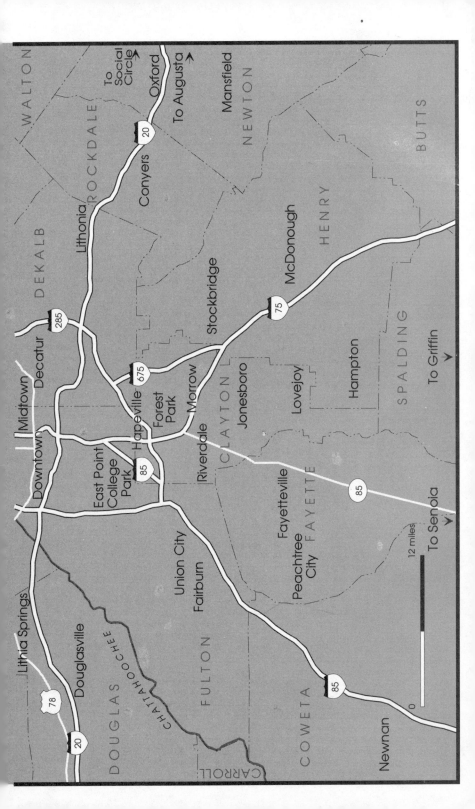

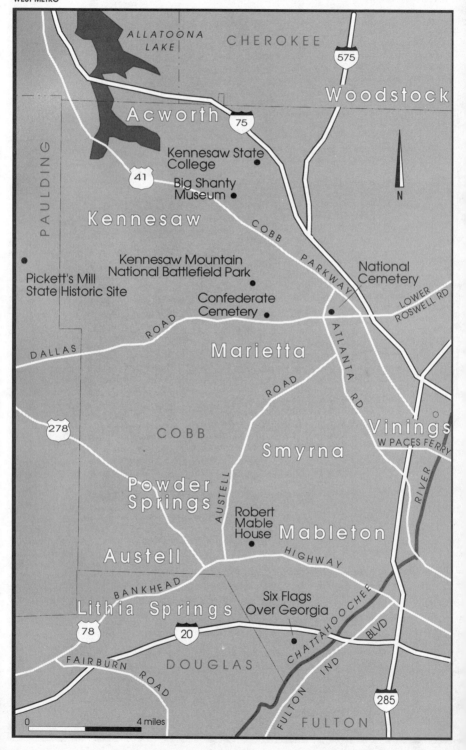

ALLATOONA LAKE

CHEROKEE

575

Woodstock

Acworth

75

PAULDING

Kennesaw State College

41

Big Shanty Museum

Kennesaw

COBB PARKWAY

National Cemetery

LOWER ROSWELL RD

Kennesaw Mountain National Battlefield Park

Pickett's Mill State Historic Site

Confederate Cemetery

ROAD

DALLAS

Marietta

ROAD

ATLANTA RD

Vinings

W PACES FERRY

278

COBB

Smyrna

RIVER

Powder Springs

AUSTELL

Robert Mable House

Mableton

Austell

HIGHWAY

CHATTAHOOCHEE

BANKHEAD

Lithia Springs

Six Flags Over Georgia

78

20

BLVD

FULTON IND

285

FAIRBURN ROAD

DOUGLAS

FULTON

0   4 miles

N

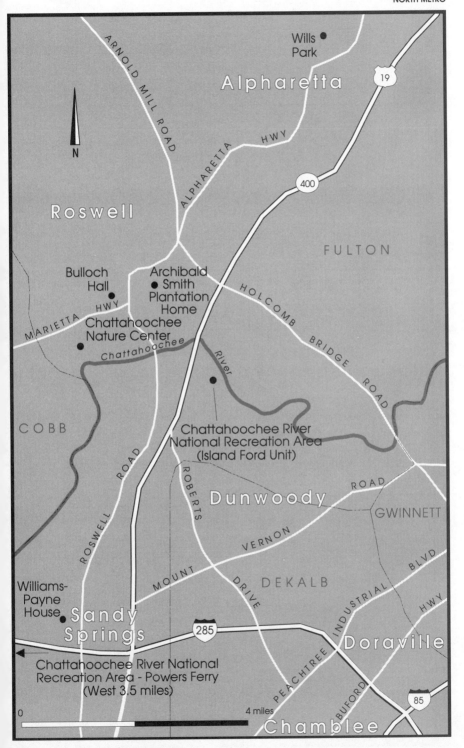

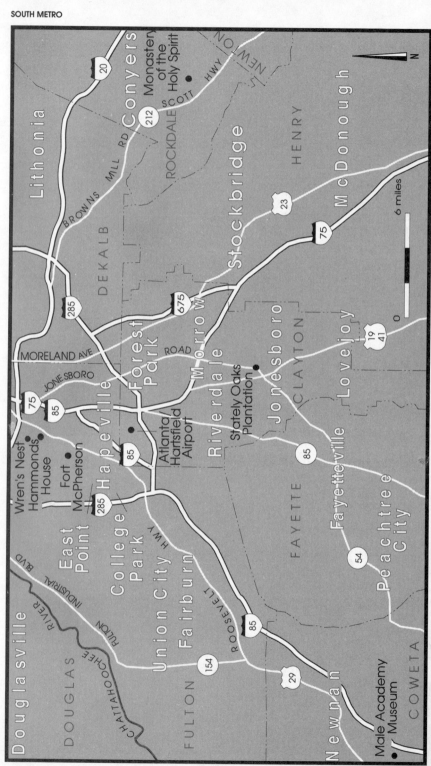

Do you have a recommendation for us? We'd love to hear about it!

Perhaps it's a plumber who always comes on time. Or your very favorite dinner spot. Or a support group that has helped you or someone you know in a special way.

Whatever it is, if you think it's an Atlanta "best," we want to know about it so we can consider it for inclusion in our next edition. Almost all our listings are based on recommendations, and we rely on readers like you to keep our information fresh and current. We're interested in hearing about possible new entries for the categories already in *Across Atlanta*, but we also want to expand our category list—maybe skydiving or Ethiopian restaurants or wine shops or... well, you get the idea— we're only limited by *your* ideas.

We're particularly interested in establishing a chapter on children, including services: clothing, toy or other stores, special educational opportunities, unusual places to have birthday parties, etc. Also, please tell us if you've had any negative experiences with anyone listed in our book—we want to know about that, too.

Thank you, and we hope to hear from you soon with your suggestions for *Across Atlanta: The Residents' Guide to the Best of the City and Suburbs!*

— —

I'd like to recommend

for the next edition of *Across Atlanta* because

Their address and phone number and a contact person (if possible)

Your name and phone number (optional)

Mail this form or your letter to the address on the reverse side, or fax to 404/875-2578. Thank you!

PLEASE FOLD HERE

_____

_____

_____

Across Atlanta
Peachtree Publishers, Ltd.
494 Armour Circle, NE
Atlanta, GA   30324-4088